Antonin Scalia and American Constitutionalism

Antonin Scalia and American Constitutionalism

The Historical Significance of a Judicial Icon

EDWARD A. PURCELL, JR.

OXFORD
UNIVERSITY PRESS

OXFORD
UNIVERSITY PRESS

Oxford University Press is a department of the University of Oxford. It furthers the University's
objective of excellence in research, scholarship, and education by publishing worldwide. Oxford is a
registered trademark of Oxford University Press in the UK and certain other countries.

Published in the United States of America by Oxford University Press
198 Madison Avenue, New York, NY 10016, United States of America.

Library of Congress Cataloging-in-Publication Data
Names: Purcell, Edward A. author.
Title: Antonin Scalia and American constitutionalism : the historical significance of a judicial icon /
 Edward A. Purcell Jr..
Description: New York, NY : Oxford University Press, 2020. | Includes index.
Identifiers: LCCN 2019057042 (print) | LCCN 2019057043 (ebook) | ISBN 9780197508763 (hardback) |
 ISBN 9780197508770 (updf) | ISBN 9780197508787 (epub) | ISBN 9780197508794 (online)
Subjects: LCSH: Scalia, Antonin—Influence. | United States. Supreme Court. |
 Constitutional law—United States.
Classification: LCC KF8745.S33 P87 2020 (print) | LCC KF8745.S33 (ebook) | DDC 347.73/2634—dc23
LC record available at https://lccn.loc.gov/2019057042
LC ebook record available at https://lccn.loc.gov/2019057043

1 3 5 7 9 8 6 4 2

Printed by Sheridan Books, Inc., United States of America

Note to Readers
This publication is designed to provide accurate and authoritative information in regard to
the subject matter covered. It is based upon sources believed to be accurate and reliable and is
intended to be current as of the time it was written. It is sold with the understanding that the
publisher is not engaged in rendering legal, accounting, or other professional services. If legal advice
or other expert assistance is required, the services of a competent professional person should be
sought. Also, to confirm that the information has not been affected or changed by
recent developments, traditional legal research techniques should be used, including checking
primary sources where appropriate.

*(Based on the Declaration of Principles jointly adopted by a Committee of the
American Bar Association and a Committee of Publishers and Associations.)*

For My Family,

Present and Departed

Contents

Acknowledgments

In completing this study, I owe debts of gratitude to many people who have supported my work in various ways and often for many years. In particular, for reading all or parts of earlier versions of this work, I owe my deepest thanks to Richard Chused, Kristin A. Collins, Stephen J. Ellmann, Doni Gewirtzman, Abner S. Greene, Lisa Grumet, Alfred S. Konefsky, Arthur S. Leonard, Jethro K. Lieberman, Carlin Meyer, Frank Munger, William E. Nelson, Stephen A. Newman, Rebecca Roiphe, Eric J. Segall, Richard Sherwin, James F. Simon, and one Oxford reviewer who remained anonymous. I also want to thank the members of the New York Law School Faculty Colloquium and the members of the New York University Law School Legal History Colloquium for their comments and suggestions on earlier drafts. Finally, I thank Alan Dershowitz for sharing with me his thoughts about his private conversations with Justice Scalia.

I owe a special debt of gratitude to Michael McCarthy for his Herculean efforts in furnishing research advice and obtaining research materials and to my assistant, Rosamond White, who has long been a source of both professional support and personal good cheer. Particular thanks are also due to Elizabeth Thomas for her support and encouragement, to Michelle Zierler, Anna Tichy, and Donald Anderson for their technical assistance, and to New York Law School students Erin P. Dyles, Kevin Hakansson, Katelyn James, Sarah Lemaster, Shukra Sabnis, and Rachel Portnoy, who provided excellent research assistance. In addition, I wish to thank New York Law School Dean Anthony Crowell and Associate Dean William P. LaPiana for their consistent support and encouragement for all of my work.

Finally, I owe a special debt to my wife, Rachel Vorspan, whose love, encouragement, and knowledge of the English common law have been constant sources of help and inspiration.

Introduction

A Google search for "originalism" in January 2018 produced a first entry that featured a photograph of Justice Antonin Scalia along with a brief definition of the term and a declaration that it "originated in the 1980s."[1] Thus, today's most widely and commonly used source of quick information identified "originalism" with Scalia and its emergence with the decade when he took his seat on the U.S. Supreme Court.

The reason for the identification was apparent. "Justice Scalia was the first prominent jurist to set forth a systematic methodology for understanding the content of legal texts by reference to their original public communicative meanings," declared Professor Gary Lawson, one of Scalia's ex–Supreme Court clerks. "That was a revolutionary development."[2] Scalia, wrote another scholar, was "orginalism's most visible and perhaps most effective proponent."[3] His resulting fame even inspired a one-act comic opera, *Scalia/Ginsburg*, about his long-running relationship with Justice Ruth Bader Ginsburg[4] and a full-length play entitled *The Originalist* that has been called "a Modern Story of a Cultural Icon."[5] By the time of his death on February 13, 2016, Scalia had become the most famous and widely visible member of the Supreme Court, its paramount advocate of originalism, and a universally acknowledged hero of the American right.

While his death understandably unleashed a flood of testimonials, its timing magnified his iconic status, placed his image at the center of American law and politics, and made his replacement on the Supreme Court a focal point of the 2016 presidential election.[6] His death left the Court evenly

[1] Google search for "originalism," *available at* https://www.google.com/search?rlz=1T4GZAZ_enUS427US428&source=hp&ei=pZBnW (last consulted Jan. 23, 2018).

[2] Gary Lawson, *Dedication: On Getting It Right: Remembering Justice Antonin Scalia*, 96 BOSTON U. L. REV. 299, 300–02 (2016).

[3] Logan E. Sawyer III, *Principle and Politics in the New History of Originalism*, 57 AM. J. LEGAL HIST. 198, 199 (2017).

[4] Derick Wang, *Scalia/Ginsburg: The Opera, available at* http://www.derrickwang.com/scalia-ginsburg/ (last consulted Aug. 26, 2019).

[5] *See* Alex Gangitano, *"The Originalist" Is a Modern Story of a Cultural Icon, available at* https://www.rollcall.com/news/hoh/originalist-modern-story-cultural-icon (last consulted Aug. 26, 2019).

[6] Neal Devins & Lawrence Baum, *Split Definitive: How Party Polarization Turned the Supreme Court into a Partisan Court*, 2016 SUP. CT. REV. 301, 302–03 (2016). For a collection of excerpts from

Antonin Scalia and American Constitutionalism. Edward A. Purcell, Jr., Oxford University Press (2020).
© Edward A. Purcell, Jr.
DOI: 10.1093/oso/9780197508763.001.0001

divided between liberals and conservatives, making the appointment of his successor a matter of decisive importance. Democratic President Barack Obama's nominee would almost certainly shift the Court from a conservative to a liberal majority, but the Republican Party controlled the Senate and could block any such nominee.

With the presidential election looming only nine months away, the Republicans were determined to do just that in a concerted effort to hold on to Scalia's seat. Mitch McConnell, the party's Senate majority leader, acted immediately. An hour after receiving confirmation of Scalia's death, he announced that "this vacancy should not be filled until we have a new president."[7] A group of influential conservative Republicans had, in fact, been working with McConnell to obstruct Obama's appointments to the federal courts, and since 2009 they "had arrived at an understanding that if a vacancy arose [on the Supreme Court] in the last year of his presidency, the Senate Republican leader would try to block it."[8] Republican Senator Charles Grassley, the Chair of the Senate Judiciary Committee, immediately backed McConnell's move, calling Scalia "an intellectual giant" whose "originalist interpretation of the Constitution set the standard for the Court."[9] Other Republican senators quickly fell in line, including presidential candidates Ted Cruz and Marco Rubio, who immediately echoed McConnell's view.[10] "Justice Scalia," Cruz declared, "was an American hero."[11] He was "one of the most influential jurists in the Court's history," added Republican Senator and ex–presidential candidate John McCain. His "principled contributions," McCain predicted, would "persist long beyond his days on the Court."[12]

testimonials, see SCALIA'S COURT: A LEGACY OF LANDMARK OPINIONS AND DISSENTS (Kevin A. Ring ed., 2016), at 541–44 [hereafter SCALIA'S COURT].

[7] Burgess Everett & Glenn Thrush, *McConnell Throws Down the Gauntlet: No Scalia Replacement Under Obama*, POLITICO, Feb. 13, 2016, *available at* https://www.politico.com/story/2016/02/mitch-mcconnell-antonin-scalia-supreme-court-nomination-219248 (last consulted Aug. 26, 2019) [hereafter Everett & Thrush, *McConnell*]. On the immediate political reaction to Scalia's death, see CARL HULSE, CONFIRMATION BIAS: INSIDE WASHINGTON'S WAR OVER THE SUPREME COURT, FROM SCALIA'S DEATH TO JUSTICE KAVANAUGH ch. 3 (2019).

[8] JOAN BISKUPIC, THE CHIEF: THE LIFE AND TURBULENT TIMES OF CHIEF JUSTICE JOHN ROBERTS 304 (2019).

[9] *Statement of Senator Charles Grassley*, L.A. TIMES, Feb. 13, 2016, *available at* http://www.latimes.com/nation/la-na-reactions-antonin-scalia-20160213-htmlstory.html#sen-charles-grassley-says-the-next-president-should-pick-the-new-supreme-court-justice (last consulted Aug. 26, 2019).

[10] Kevin Robillard, *Scalia Death Raises Stakes in Battle for Senate Control*, POLITICO, Feb. 14, 2016, *available at* https://www.politico.com/story/2016/02/scalia-2016-senate-landscape-stakes-219269 (last consulted Aug. 26, 2019).

[11] Everett & Thrush, *McConnell*.

[12] *Statement by Senator John McCain on the Passing of Supreme Court Justice Antonin Scalia*, PRESCOTT ENEWS, Feb.14, 2016, *available at* https://www.prescottenews.com/index.php/news/

Adamant, the Republican-controlled Senate achieved its goal. It refused even to hold hearings on Obama's nominee for the open seat, the well-respected and moderately liberal Judge Merrick Garland of the U.S. Court of Appeals for the District of Columbia Circuit. The Republicans simply left Garland hanging helplessly and without recourse. For eleven months, until Obama's term expired in January 2017, the seat remained vacant. Republican businessman Donald J. Trump, elected president in November 2016, would be the one who eventually filled it.

Scalia was "a conservative icon," a commentator in *Forbes* summarized,[13] and conservative legal scholars rallied behind his claim to greatness. Scalia's efforts would "secure his place among America's greatest Supreme Court justices," wrote Adam J. White, a fellow at the Hoover Institution in Washington, D.C. In the long struggle to preserve republican virtue and self-government, Scalia gave "future generations" of conservatives "an example of how victory might someday be won."[14] For thirty years on the Court, wrote Kevin A. Ring, who served as a Republican staffer in the House and Senate, "Scalia was its premier conservative, intellectual gladiator, and wordsmith."[15] Scalia "was the most powerful conservative intellect on the Court in recent years" and "the great hero of the right," wrote one law professor,[16] while another made the point in deeply personal terms. "When Justice Scalia passed away, I lost the hero of my life in the law."[17] Law professor Steven G. Calabresi, a friend and ex-clerk of Scalia's and one of the founders of the conservative Federalist Society, topped them all. "Scalia has fundamentally and forever reshaped the way Americans will think about law," he announced. He was "the most important justice in American history—greater than former Chief Justice John Marshall himself."[18]

current-news/item/27033-responses-to-tge-passing-of-justice-antonin-scalia (last consulted on Aug. 26, 2019).

[13] Ilya Shapiro, *Don't Confirm Scalia's Replacement Until After the Election*, FORBES, Feb. 14, 2016, *available at* https://www.forbes.com.sites/ilyashapiro/2016/02/14/don't-confirm-scalias-replacement-until-after-the-election/#6fe05a1e6e66 (last consulted Aug. 26, 2019).

[14] Adam J. White, *The American Constitutionalist: Antonin Scalia, 1936–2016*, 21 THE WEEKLY STANDARD (Feb. 29, 2016), 24, 29.

[15] SCALIA'S COURT ix.

[16] Stephen B. Presser, *The Principled Scalia: A Liberal Friend of Scalia's Liberal Opinions*, 18 FEDERALIST SOCIETY REVIEW (2017), *available at* https://fedsoc.org/commentary/publications/the-principled-scalia-a-liberal-friend-on-Scalia-s-liberal-opinions (last consulted Aug. 26, 2019).

[17] Richard F. Duncan, *Justice Scalia and the Rule of Law: Originalism vs. the Living Constitution*, 29 REGENT U. L. REV. 9, 10 (2016).

[18] Steven Calabresi, *Scalia Towered Over John Marshall*, USA TODAY, Feb. 14, 2016, *available at* https://www.usatoday.com/story/opinion/2016/02/13/scalia-text-legacy-clerk-steven-calabresi-column/80349810/ (last consulted Aug. 26, 2019).

The official reaction of the Federalist Society was emblematic. At its first annual convention following Scalia's death it sponsored a three-day symposium on "The Jurisprudence and Legacy of Justice Scalia." The program featured a glittering array of more than a hundred of the nation's most prominent judges, lawyers, law professors, and politicians—liberals as well as conservatives—who discussed various aspects of Scalia's jurisprudence and influence.[19] At its annual dinner, quickly renamed in Scalia's honor, the society hosted almost all of the potential Supreme Court nominees that then-president-elect Trump had identified as Scalia's possible successor. "Nearly all" of them, *USA Today* reported, "made the rounds of the judges, lawyers, politicians and professors here to sing Scalia's praises."[20] The Court's open seat, the *Washington Post* reported, "dominated the event."[21] At the society's annual dinner conservative Justice Samuel Alito advised the audience that, whenever they faced controversial constitutional issues, they should ask themselves one simple question: "What would Nino do?"[22]

After Trump took office, he selected Judge Neil Gorsuch of the U.S. Court of Appeals for the Tenth Circuit to take Scalia's seat, and the Senate confirmed the nomination. The Republicans had saved the seat for their cause, and Scalia's legacy seemed secure. Before his nomination Gorsuch had made his admiration for Scalia widely known, calling him "a lion of the law" and hailing his "great project" to "remind us of the differences between judges and legislators." Gorsuch announced that everyone should "mark me down too as a believer that the traditional account of the judicial role Justice Scalia defended will endure."[23] At the Federalist Society's annual dinner the following year, after taking his seat on the Court, Gorsuch praised Scalia and formally announced that he was taking up his jurisprudential mantle. "Originalism has regained its place at the table," he declared, and "textualism has triumphed." Neither originalism nor textualism, he promised the

---

[19] The Federalist Society, *2016 National Lawyers Convention: The Jurisprudence and Legacy of Justice Scalia* (Nov. 17–19, 2016), *available at* https://fedsoc.org/events/2016-national-lawyers-conventio, (last consulted Aug. 26, 2019).

[20] Richard Wolf, *Supreme Court Wannabes Audition in Scalia's Shadow*, USA TODAY, Nov. 20, 2016, *available at* https://www.usatoday.com/story/news/politics/2016/11/20/supreme-court-trump-judges-federalist-society/94087912 (last consulted Aug. 26, 2019) [hereafter Wolf, *Supreme Court*].

[21] Robert Barnes, *Supreme Court Vacancy Dominates Talk at National Lawyers Convention*, WASH. POST, Nov. 26, 2016, *available at* https://www.washingtonpost.com/politics/courts_law/supreme-court-vacancy-dominates-talk-at-national-lawyers-convention/2016/11/26/fd87d066-b1b3-11e6-be1c-8cec35b1ad25_story.html (last consulted Aug. 26, 2019).

[22] Wolf, *Supreme Court*.

[23] Neil Gorsuch, *2016 Sumner Canary Memorial Lecture: Of Lions and Bears, Judges and Legislators, and the Legacy of Justice Scalia*, 66 CASE WEST. RES. L. REV. 905, 906, 909 (2016).

audience, "is going anywhere on my watch."[24] Gorsuch, the *New York Times* reported, was "seen as a model" for Trump's future appointments.[25]

Although the conservative *Weekly Standard* complained that "the number of supposedly respectable liberal voices attacking Scalia is positively dispiriting,"[26] few liberals failed to acknowledge Scalia's commanding personality, the power of his intellect, the force of his slashing prose, the influence of his jurisprudential ideas, or the broad impact he had on American law. Democratic President Barack Obama led the way. On the day of Scalia's death, he hailed the justice as "a brilliant legal mind" who had "influenced a generation of judges, lawyers, and students, and profoundly shaped the legal landscape." There was "no doubt," Obama continued, that Scalia would "be remembered as one of the most consequential judges and thinkers to serve on the Supreme Court."[27] Most liberals followed suit and acknowledged, albeit often grudgingly or disapprovingly, that Scalia would go down in the Court's history as one of its most significant figures. "He was not only one of the most important justices in the nation's history, he was also among the greatest," declared liberal law professor Cass Sunstein.[28] "I may not miss his votes as a justice, but I will miss him," wrote Geoffrey Stone, Scalia's former colleague at the University of Chicago. "He added sparkle to the Court and to the lives of those who knew him."[29] Liberals agreed, moreover, on Scalia's towering status among conservatives. He was a "fiery justice," noted *Mother Jones*, "who is a hero to those within conservative legal circles."[30]

[24] Ryan Lovelace, *Neil Gorsuch: Scalia's Views on the Constitution Aren't "Going Anywhere on My Watch"*, WASH. EXAMINER, Dec. 5, 2017, *available at* http://www.washingtonexaminer.com/neil-gorsuch-scalias-views-on-the-constitution-arent-going-anywhere-on-my-watch (last consulted Aug. 26, 2019).

[25] Jeremy W. Peters, *New Litmus Test for Trump's Court Picks: Taming the Bureaucracy*, N.Y. TIMES, Mar. 28, 2018, A-1, at p. 13. For a brief comparison of Scalia and Gorsuch by the latter's sympathetic biographer, *see* JOHN GREENYA, GORSUCH: THE JUDGE WHO SPEAKS FOR HIMSELF 155–57 (2018).

[26] *Scalia and His Enemies*, 21 THE WEEKLY STANDARD (Feb. 29, 2016) 2, 3.

[27] *Remarks by the President on the Passing of the U.S. Supreme Court Justice Antonin Scalia* (Feb. 13, 2016), *available at* https://obamawhitehouse.archives.gov/the-press-office/2016/02/13/remarks-president-passing-us-supreme-court-justice-antonin-scalia (last consulted Aug 26, 2019).

[28] Jonathan H. Adler, *Sunstein on the Scalia Who Will Be "Greatly Missed,"* WASH. POST, Feb. 14, 2016, *available at* https://www.washingtonpost.com/news/volokh-conspiracy/wp/2016/02/14/sunstein-on-the-scalia-who-will-be-greatly-missed/ (last consulted Aug. 26, 2019).

[29] Geoffrey Stone, *Tough, Brilliant, and Kind: The Antonin Scalia I Knew*, DAILY BEAST, Apr. 13, 2017, *available at* https://www.thedailybeast.com/tough-brilliant-and-kind-the-antonin-scalia-i-knew (last consulted Aug. 26, 2019).

[30] Stephanie Mencimer, *Justice Scalia Goes to Conservative Legal Event, Gives Boring Speech*, MOTHER JONES (Nov. 13, 2014), *available at* http://www.motherjones.com/politics/2014/11/justice-antonin-scalia-federalist-society-sup (last consulted Aug. 26, 2019).

The political right, another liberal critic chimed in, regarded him as "their champion."[31]

There is, and honestly could be, no doubt that Scalia had an enormous impact on constitutional law, jurisprudential thinking, and the Court itself. Many years earlier, Harvard Law School Dean Elena Kagan, who subsequently became Scalia's colleague on the Court, had suggested the breadth of his impact. "His views on textualism and originalism, his views on the role of judges in our society, on the practice of judging, have really transformed the terms of legal debate in this country," she declared. "He is the justice who has had the most important impact over the years on how we think and talk about law."[32]

The fact that commentators of all varieties recognized Scalia as one of the Court's most influential justices makes it important to examine the grounds for his widely acknowledged influence and presumably enduring significance. What, in fact, is his historical legacy as a legal theorist and Supreme Court justice? More generally and fundamentally, what does his jurisprudence and judicial career have to teach us about American constitutionalism itself?

As the nation moves deeper into the twenty-first century, it seems useful to attempt an answer to those questions. Currently, and quite understandably, most assessments of Scalia's importance focus on the broad contemporary impact he had, and they range from extremes of ardent praise to fevered denunciation. Of course, as the future unfolds, many judgments about that impact will almost certainly change as new social and political developments alter current assumptions and perspectives. Fresh research and newly discovered sources will also yield new insights. When Scalia donated his papers to the Harvard Law School, for example, he directed that they remain closed until 2020 and that no materials involving specific cases be available during the lifetime of any participating judge or justice.[33] Thus, a more complete and fully grounded understanding of his actions on the Court, his influence on the justices, and his impact in individual cases necessarily lies a quarter of a century or more in the future.

---

[31] Peter Schwartz, *Wolf at the Door: Antonin Scalia and the Legal Conservative Movement*, HUFFINGTON POST, Apr. 22, 2015, *available at* https://www.huffingtonpost.com/peter-schwartz/wolf-at-the-door-antonin-_b_6723138.html (last consulted Aug. 26, 2019).

[32] JOAN BISKUPIC, AMERICAN ORIGINAL: THE LIFE AND CONSTITUTION OF SUPREME COURT JUSTICE ANTONIN SCALIA 362 (2009).

[33] *See* https://news.harvard.edu/gazette/story/2017/03/law-school-receives-scalia-papers/ (last consulted Aug. 26, 2019).

Still, though we cannot now have a fully developed understanding of either Scalia's role on the Court or the nature and extent of his enduring influence, we can begin to assess his place in the history of American constitutionalism and consider how his jurisprudence and judicial career fit into that history. Consequently, this study does not hazard predictions about the future role of his jurisprudence or its long-term influence on American law. Equally, it does not inquire into the Court's inner workings, the gestation and evolution of Court opinions, or personal relationships and interactions among the justices. Nor, finally, does it examine Scalia's personal life or his roles as devoted family man, opera lover, amusing wit, media personality, admired mentor, and beloved friend and colleague. Rather, its focus is solely on his frequently articulated jurisprudential theories, the political and social values he publicly embraced, and his work as a justice on the U.S. Supreme Court. Its concern is with the ultimate significance of Scalia's jurisprudence and career for an understanding of American constitutionalism and his place in it.

The study proceeds in three parts. Part I contains two chapters that review Scalia's general career and jurisprudence. Chapter 1 traces his rise from law school to the Supreme Court and his subsequent emergence as the iconic jurisprudential hero of the Republican Party and the political right. Chapter 2 explores the nature and qualities of the originalist jurisprudence he tirelessly promoted.

Part II considers Scalia's actual work on the Court. Chapter 3 identifies many of the different issues he addressed and emphasizes the decisive fact that in a majority of cases he either applied his jurisprudential principles inconsistently or failed to apply them at all. The following six chapters examine those inconsistencies and failures in a variety of specific areas. Chapter 4 considers Scalia's ideologically based and result-driven treatment of separation of powers and federalism; chapter 5, his inconsistencies and failures across a broad spectrum of constitutional issues; and chapter 6, his purposeful manipulation of historical and legal sources. Chapters 7 and 8 analyze his role in two of the most famous cases he heard. The first considers *District of Columbia v. Heller*, where Scalia purported to follow his jurisprudential principles but revealed them as arbitrary and result-oriented. The second considers *Bush v. Gore*, where he did not even pretend to apply those principles and contradicted virtually every one of them. The chapters show that in both cases he sought with determination to enforce his own personal and political beliefs. Finally, chapter 9 considers his views of Article III and the federal judicial power, and it shows that in seeking to limit the federal courts broadly, Scalia literally abandoned originalism altogether.

Part III considers Scalia's overall judicial career and constitutional jurisprudence and identifies their most enduring significance for an understanding of American constitutionalism. Chapter 10 argues that Scalia's career and jurisprudence constituted a pervasive methodological failure and illustrated the more general truth that there is no particular "method" of constitutional interpretation capable of producing "correct" answers to controversial questions, whether they are long-disputed or newly arising. Chapter 11 argues that his jurisprudence and career reflected the goals and values of late twentieth-century "conservatism" and the post-Reagan Republican Party and that, more generally, they exemplified in relatively unambiguous form the fusion of law and politics that drives the development of American constitutional law. Chapter 12 concludes that the most fundamental significance of Scalia's career and jurisprudence lies in the way and extent to which they illustrated the changing, dynamic, and inherently goal- and value-based nature of American constitutionalism itself, its truly "living" nature.

Thus, the paramount and enduring historical significance of Scalia's career and jurisprudence is that—against his will and intent—he exemplified three fundamental characteristics of American constitutionalism. He demonstrated its largely open and textually undetermined nature, its foundation in the political and social values of the American people and those who become its major interpreters, and its evolving and adaptive nature as an ongoing enterprise in popular and law-based self-government. Scalia thus stands as a compelling figure of irony. He was a major constitutional voice whose career unintentionally illustrated the operations of American constitutionalism while disproving the most fundamental principles of his own jurisprudence.

PART I
PUBLIC ACTOR

1

Icon

After graduating from Harvard Law School in 1960, Antonin Scalia practiced law for several years in Cleveland, taught law at the University of Virginia, and then took a position in the administration of President Richard M. Nixon. Soon he became an active participant in the fierce controversies that the Warren Court and the tumultuous decade of "the sixties" had sparked. He acknowledged, indeed proclaimed, that his constitutional views were a response to the Warren Court and the changes that those years brought.

Scalia believed that prior to the Warren Court American history had followed a relatively coherent and orderly course in significant part because the nation's constitutional thinking was guided by a general commitment to the views of the Founders and to their understanding of the Constitution's original meaning. He saw relatively little disagreement about that extended interpretive commitment before the Civil War and little dispute about it during the decades that followed.[1] In his mind the Warren Court and "the sixties" changed all that, and he was determined to reverse much of what they had accomplished. He sought to revive what he considered the original authority of the Founders and the Constitution's text and to return the operation of the three federal branches to what he regarded as their proper roles. He hoped to limit Congress, severely restrict the federal courts, and substantially expand the power and independence of the executive.

In the 1970s Scalia became a rising star in Republican and conservative circles.[2] Serving in the administrations of Nixon and his successor Gerald R. Ford, he rose through a series of positions to eventually head the prestigious Office of Legal Counsel where he became the influential legal adviser to the president. There he made a reputation as an ardent defender of the presidency and a forceful advocate for broad executive powers. When Ford lost

---

[1] *See, e.g.*, the speeches in ANTONIN SCALIA, SCALIA SPEAKS: REFLECTIONS ON LAW, FAITH, AND LIFE WELL LIVED (Christopher J. Scalia & Edward Whelan eds., 2017) [hereafter SCALIA SPEAKS].

[2] The following paragraph is drawn from two fine biographies of Scalia: JOAN BISKUPIC, AMERICAN ORIGINAL: THE LIFE AND CONSTITUTION OF SUPREME COURT JUSTICE ANTONIN SCALIA (2009) [hereafter BISKUPIC, AMERICAN ORIGINAL], and BRUCE ALLEN MURPHY, SCALIA: A COURT OF ONE (2014) [hereafter MURPHY, SCALIA].

Antonin Scalia and American Constitutionalism. Edward A. Purcell, Jr., Oxford University Press (2020).
© Edward A. Purcell, Jr.
DOI: 10.1093/oso/9780197508763.001.0001

the 1976 election to Democrat Jimmy Carter, Scalia returned to private life, working at the libertarian American Enterprise Institute, editing its journal *Regulation*, helping found the ardently conservative Federalist Society, and teaching at the University of Chicago and Stanford University. All the while he waited to return to government service in the next Republican administration, yearning in particular to become solicitor general of the United States.

Then in 1980 Republican Ronald Reagan defeated Carter and won the presidency, and American politics turned a corner. After the election Nixon told Reagan that "I very deliberately appointed conservative justices to the Court who shared my philosophy that it was the responsibility of the Court to interpret the law rather than make it." Whatever else he might do, Nixon advised the new president, "the most lasting legacy will be your impact on the Supreme Court."[3] Reagan surely needed no convincing, for he had been preaching what had become the Republican mantra in the wake of the Warren Court. "I want judges," the new president repeatedly insisted, "who will interpret the law and not legislate."[4]

To implement that goal, and also to fulfill his campaign promise to place a woman on the Court, in 1981 Reagan gave his first Court appointment to Sandra Day O'Connor. "One of the first Supreme Court vacancies in my administration," he had declared, "will be filled by the most qualified woman I can find."[5] O'Connor's "commitment to judicial restraint," he announced, "will help redefine the Court's role in our daily life." Proudly, he quoted her statement to the Senate Judiciary Committee that the "proper role of the judiciary is one of interpreting and applying the law, not making it."[6]

While calls for the Court to exercise "judicial restraint" and to "interpret not legislate" were hardly new in Republican anti–Warren Court

---

[3] BISKUPIC, AMERICAN ORIGINAL 72. Nixon had initiated the modern and concerted Republican assault on the Warren Court which, by Reagan's presidency, had become a staple of the party's rhetoric. *See, e.g.,* JAMES F. SIMON, IN HIS OWN IMAGE: THE SUPREME COURT IN RICHARD NIXON'S AMERICA (1973). Laura Kalman has suggested that, in pursuing his political agenda, "Nixon did not really care whether his nominees were qualified." LAURA KALMAN, THE LONG REACH OF THE SIXTIES: LBJ, NIXON, AND THE MAKING OF THE CONTEMPORARY SUPREME COURT 307 (2017) [hereafter KALMAN, LONG REACH].

[4] 1984-2 RONALD REAGAN, PUBLIC PAPERS OF THE PRESIDENTS OF THE UNITED STATES, 1118 (In "recent years we've had some examples of the Court actually taking the job of the Legislature and legislating rather than interpreting," *id.*) [hereafter REAGAN PUBLIC PAPERS].

[5] HENRY J. ABRAHAM, JUSTICES, PRESIDENTS, AND SENATORS: A HISTORY OF THE U.S. SUPREME COURT APPOINTMENTS FROM WASHINGTON TO CLINTON 282 (rev. ed. 1999) [hereafter ABRAHAM, JUSTICES]. O'Connor replaced Justice Potter Stewart who retired in June 1981.

[6] 1981 REAGAN PUBLIC PAPERS, 811.

rhetoric, the Reagan administration pressed its judicial goals vigorously in two well-considered ways. First, it sought more methodically than prior administrations to remake the federal bench and appoint judges who would support its policies. Reagan appointed a special Committee on Federal Judicial Selection to control the judicial nomination process, placed the committee under the direction of his chief of staff, and ordered it to screen judicial candidates rigorously and identify those who truly supported the administration's policies.[7] As a result the Justice Department "put in place the most rigorous and decidedly ideological screening process ever."[8] Reagan's team, wrote Walter F. Murphy, "wanted judges to undo much of the constitutional jurisprudence of the last half-century affecting civil rights" and to "tip the balance of the constitutional power toward the presidency rather than Congress."[9] In the process, the administration's screeners even asked potential nominees about their views on specific issues, including abortion and affirmative action.[10]

Second, dissatisfied with its progress during Reagan's first term, the administration began in 1985 to redesign its judicial rhetoric. Under the leadership of its new attorney general, Edwin Meese III, it decided to anchor its position on the idea of "original intent" and thereby give its judicial selection policy a broader and ostensibly more principled constitutional justification.[11] In July of that year, attacking the decisions of the Warren Court as "ad hoc" and "bizarre," Meese announced at the annual meeting of the American Bar Association that it "has been and will continue to be the policy of this

---

[7] Walter F. Murphy, *Reagan's Judicial Strategy, in* LOOKING BACK ON THE REAGAN PRESIDENCY 210–11, 219 (Larry Berman ed., 1990) [hereafter Murphy, *Reagan's Judicial Strategy*]. The "unifying feature" of the effort was to ensure "support for the bundle of public policies associated with Ronald Reagan." *Id.* at 220.

[8] David M. O'Brien, *The Reagan Judges: His Most Enduring Legacy?, in* THE REAGAN LEGACY: PROMISE AND PERFORMANCE 62 (Charles O. Jones ed., 1988) ("Reagan's administration had a more coherent and ambitious agenda for legal reform and judicial selection than any previous administration") [hereafter O'Brien, *Reagan Judges*]; ABRAHAM, JUSTICES, 281 ("The Reagan agenda demonstrably included an attempt to alter the contemporary jurisprudential approach of the federal judiciary" and sought to find nominees who "were in general sympathy with the philosophical thrust of the administration").

[9] Murphy, *Reagan's Judicial Strategy*, 219–20.

[10] O'Brien, *Reagan Judges*, 68.

[11] Steven M. Teles, *Transformative Bureaucracy: Reagan's Lawyers and the Dynamics of Political Investment*, 23 STUD. AM. POL. DEV. 61, 76–77 (2009) [hereafter Teles, *Transformative Bureaucracy*]. On the relation between conservatism, the Republican Party, and originalism, *see* BARRY FRIEDMAN, THE WILL OF THE PEOPLE: HOW PUBLIC OPINION HAS INFLUENCED THE SUPREME COURT AND SHAPED THE MEANING OF THE CONSTITUTION 306–13 (2009); Logan E. Sawyer III, *Principle and Politics in the New History of Originalism*, 57 AM. J. LEGAL HIST. 198, 199 (2017).

administration to press for a Jurisprudence of Original Intention."[12] Meese's speechwriter later explained that the attorney general's declaration was intended to provide "a philosophical context" for the administration's political and legal goals and to show that those goals were "rooted in something more transcendent than the disputes of the moment."[13] It spoke volumes that the administration's commitment to those political and legal goals had preceded rather than followed its announced new commitment to "original intent."

From that point on Reagan regularly employed the rhetoric of originalism[14] and frequently invoked the image of "the Founding Fathers."[15] The administration "has worked to restore a vision of government that was the Founders' own," he declared.[16] "I can count as one of the most satisfying legacies of my presidency the work my Administration has done to restore the foundations of American government through an insistence on the faithful interpretation and observance of the Constitution."[17]

To Scalia's regret, Reagan passed over him for solicitor general, but the new president soon called on him to help achieve the administration's high-priority goal of reorienting the federal judiciary. In 1982 he appointed Scalia to the U.S. Court of Appeals for the District of Columbia Circuit, often considered the second highest court in the nation and both a steppingstone and proving ground for future Court nominees. Indeed, preceding him on the court's bench by some six months sat none other than Robert Bork, the person many people regarded as Reagan's most likely nominee for the Court's next open seat.[18] Under both Nixon and Ford, Bork had held the prestigious

---

[12] Edwin Meese III, *Att'y Gen., Speech Before the American Bar Association* (July 9, 1985), *in* THE FEDERALIST SOCIETY, THE GREAT DEBATE: INTERPRETING OUR WRITTEN CONSTITUTION, 9–10 (1986).

[13] Teles, *Transformative Bureaucracy*, 77.

[14] *E.g.*, 1988-1 REAGAN PUBLIC PAPERS, 95 ("judges must faithfully interpret the text of the Constitution, as well as laws passed by the Congress, as written, in accordance with their original meaning"). *See id.* at 195, 221;1987-2 REAGAN PUBLIC PAPERS, 1079, 1178, 1260, 1295,

[15] "[O]ur Founding Fathers did not create the Supreme Court as a kind of super legislature." 1986-2 REAGAN PUBLIC PAPERS, 1200. *See, e.g., id.* at 1270–71; 1987-2 REAGAN PUBLIC PAPERS, 793, 1128; 1988-1 REAGAN PUBLIC PAPERS, 85; 1988-89-2 REAGAN PUBLIC PAPERS, 1148. *See also* 1988-1 REAGAN PUBLIC PAPERS, 94 ("the Framers"); 1987-2 REAGAN PUBLIC PAPERS, 1296 ("Our Founders").

[16] 1988-1 REAGAN PUBLIC PAPERS, 91.

[17] 1988-1 REAGAN PUBLIC PAPERS, 94. Reagan appointed to the courts conservative law professors whose "jurisprudence only permits them to interpret the [constitutional] text to implement the Framers' original intentions." James G. Wilson, *Justice Diffused: A Comparison of Edmund Burke's Conservatism with the Views of Five Conservative, Academic Judges*, 40 U. MIAMI L. REV. 913, 916 (1986).

[18] BISKUPIC, AMERICAN ORIGINAL, 78. Bork's pathbreaking originalist essay appeared in 1971. Robert Bork, *Neutral Principles and Some First Amendment Problems*, 47 Ind. L.J. 1 (1971). Indicative of the late arrival of modern originalism, only three years earlier Bork had sought to develop a radically different constitutional jurisprudence based on natural law. Robert Bork, *The Supreme Court*

position of solicitor general that Scalia desired, and over the previous decade he had established himself prominently as a vigorous critic of the Warren Court, a highly admired conservative theorist, and the leading academic advocate of "original intent." Backing up the pronouncements of Reagan and Meese, Bork insisted "that original intent is the only legitimate basis for constitutional decisionmaking."[19] An administration memo written in 1986 noted that Bork had been regarded as "the frontrunner for the next seat on the Supreme Court since the beginning of the first Reagan Administration."[20]

Scalia recognized his senior colleague as a formidable rival. Bork had long stood in the forefront of conservative legal thinkers and, as Scalia knew from his position in the Ford administration, in 1975 the president had come close to appointing Bork to the Court.[21] As a fellow conservative intellectual on the same prominent court and as a rival for appointment to the high bench, Scalia tried to distinguish himself from his older and better known colleague. Perhaps most obvious, in 1984 he criticized Bork's approach to the First Amendment by charging it with the characteristic failing that he would level against all of his future jurisprudential adversaries. Bork's approach, Scalia wrote in a partial dissent, created the "risk of judicial subjectivity," required judgments that were "quintessentially legislative," and accepted the abhorrent principle of an evolving Constitution.[22] It was "frightening to think that the existence or nonexistence of a *constitutional* rule," he declared, would result from "ongoing personal assessments" of "sociological factors."[23] Although Scalia "was not as highly credentialed as former solicitor general Bork," wrote Joan Biskupic, "his stock in the Reagan administration was rising."[24]

The next year Scalia began developing his own originalist jurisprudence more fully, and he promoted it widely in a series of public speaking engagements that extended through the fall of 1985 and into the spring of 1986. In his public appearances he elaborated his critique of the judicial use

---

Needs a New Philosophy, FORTUNE, Dec., 1968, at 138, 168. For a history of originalism, *see* JONATHAN O'NEILL, ORIGINALISM IN AMERICAN LAW AND POLITICS: A CONSTITUTIONAL HISTORY (2005).

[19] Robert H. Bork, *The Constitution, Original Intent, and Economic Rights*, 23 SAN DIEGO L. REV. 823, 823–24 (1986).
[20] KALMAN, LONG REACH, 326.
[21] BISKUPIC, AMERICAN ORIGINAL, 62.
[22] Ollman v. Evans, 750 F.2d 970, 1036, 1038 (1984) (Scalia, J., dissenting in part). For Bork's concurring opinion, *see id.* at 993. "When there is a known principle to be explicated," Bork wrote, "the evolution of doctrine is inevitable." *Id.* at 995.
[23] Ollman, 750 F.2d 1039 (Scalia, J., dissenting in part) (emphasis in original).
[24] BISKUPIC, AMERICAN ORIGINAL, 105.

of legislative history and, more cannily, implicitly criticized Bork by deni-
grating his focus on "original intent." Stressing the subjective nature of Bork's
"intent" standard, Scalia proposed instead to rely on the Constitution's "original understanding" or "original public meaning." He argued that a careful
and honest reading of the Constitution's text, illuminated where necessary
by the writings of the Founders and long-established American traditions,
would establish the true meaning that the document conveyed to those who
drafted and ratified it.[25] That meaning was unchanging, he insisted, and that
meaning was the meaning that courts should faithfully apply whenever they
construed the Constitution.

The payoff for his efforts both on and off the bench came quickly. After
Meese had invited him to address the "Attorney General's Conference
on Economic Liberties" planned for June 14, 1986, Chief Justice Warren
E. Burger announced his retirement. The day before the planned speech at
the attorney general's conference, Meese called to ask Scalia to meet with
Reagan at the White House on the following Monday. Suddenly, the sched-
uled speech took on apparently momentous significance, and Scalia was fully
prepared to seize the opportunity.[26]

Addressing Meese's conference on the subject of "Original Meaning,"
Scalia humorously claimed to have experienced a revelation and, slyly referring to Bork, criticized the theory of "original intent" and defended his own
theory of "original understanding." The former was subjective, based on identifying the "intent" of hundreds if not thousands of framers and ratifiers, and
it proposed a highly subjective and essentially unworkable standard. In contrast, he explained, "original public meaning" offered an objective standard
immune from at least many of the criticisms directed against Bork's "intent"
theory. His alternate approach rested simply on "the most plausible meaning
of the words of the Constitution to the society that adopted it—regardless of
what the Framers might secretly have intended." Although he advanced his
point deftly, seeming in one place to say that "original intent" actually implied his own more sophisticated "original understanding," Scalia concluded
by drawing a clear line. "I ought to campaign to change the label from the
Doctrine of Original Intent to the Doctrine of Original Meaning."[27]

---

[25] MURPHY, SCALIA, 109–12. For Scalia's career on the circuit court, see id., ch. 7, and BISKUPIC, AMERICAN ORIGINAL, ch. 5.

[26] For the politics of Scalia's appointment to the Court, see BISKUPIC, AMERICAN ORIGINAL, ch. 6.

[27] SCALIA SPEAKS, 183, 184, 187. See JAN CRAWFORD GREENBURG, SUPREME CONFLICT: THE INSIDE STORY OF THE STRUGGLE FOR CONTROL OF THE UNITED STATES SUPREME COURT 39–47 (2007).

Two days after the speech Scalia met with Reagan, and two days after that the president announced his plans for the Court. He nominated Associate Justice William H. Rehnquist, a stalwart conservative appointed to the Court by Nixon in 1972, to replace Burger as chief justice, and to fill Rehnquist's open associate justice seat he nominated Scalia.[28] It was "the culmination of a dream," Scalia proudly acknowledged,[29] and it meant that he had moved ahead of Bork in the president's favor.

Scalia seemed an ideal choice for Reagan. He was a decade younger than Bork, and his values and policy preferences fit perfectly with the president's.[30] Both opposed abortion, gay rights, and affirmative action, and both supported gun rights, the death penalty, school prayer, the "free enterprise" system, expansive executive powers, and what they regarded as the enduring values of religion and tradition. Centrally, both rejected what they considered the activism, liberalism, and essential illegitimacy of the Warren Court. Scalia, Reagan announced, recognized "the proper role of the courts in our democratic system."[31]

Both of Reagan's Court nominations in 1986 were successful. In the Senate Rehnquist ran into heavy opposition, not only for the conservative opinions he had issued during the fourteen years he had already served on the high bench but also for a memo he had written as a law clerk for Justice Robert Jackson in the early 1950s. Then, Rehnquist had defended the Court's 1896 decision *Plessy v. Ferguson*[32] upholding racial segregation, arguing that stare

---

[28] 1986-1 REAGAN PUBLIC PAPERS, 781.

[29] 1986-1 REAGAN PUBLIC PAPERS, 784.

[30] "Yes, we said, it's time to return to the principles of our founders, the principles of the Constitution and the principles of limited government—free enterprise and respect for family, community, and faith." 1988-89-2 REAGAN PUBLIC PAPERS, 1617. "Reagan had chosen a man for the Supreme Court whose view of the law tracked the agenda that Reagan and Meese had been pressing." BISKUPIC, AMERICAN ORIGINAL, 109. For his part, "Scalia liked Reagan's conservative agenda. It mirrored his thinking." *Id.* at 71.

[31] 1986-1 REAGAN PUBLIC PAPERS, 781. Republican Senator Mitch McConnell gave the game away in the statement he made at Scalia's Senate hearing. First, he offered legal formality. "Judicial conservatism is politically neutral," he declared, and "Judge Scalia has clearly demonstrated his adherence to this philosophy in practice." Then, he admitted political reality. "Main Street America has spoken clearly and unequivocally throughout the decade of the 1980's in articulating a new set of priorities for this Nation." Those "Main Street" votes issued a "mandate" to "rein in the extreme activism of our Federal judiciary," and President Reagan, "in nominating Judge Scalia, is carrying out that mandate." *Hearings before the Committee on the Judiciary, United States Senate, Ninety-Ninth Congress, Second Session, on the Nomination of Judge Antonin Scalia, to be Associate Justice of the Supreme Court of the United States* (Aug. 5–6, 1986), 28–29 [hereafter *Scalia Hearings*].

[32] Plessy v. Ferguson, 163 U.S. 537 (1896) (Brown, J.). Rehnquist defended himself by claiming his memo reflected Jackson's views not his own, but the evidence strongly suggested the contrary. *See, e.g.,* DAVID M. O'BRIEN, JUSTICE ROBERT H. JACKSON'S UNPUBLISHED OPINION IN BROWN V. BOARD: CONFLICT, COMPROMISE, AND CONSTITUTIONAL INTERPRETATION (2017).

decisis barred the Court from overruling it. After two months of contentious hearings and debates, the Senate approved his nomination by a vote of
65–33.[33]

Following the fight over Rehnquist's confirmation, the Senate was in no
mood for another angry partisan battle, and Scalia had a far easier and more
gratifying experience. The fact that he was the first Italian-American to be
nominated to the Court gave his appointment a special appeal, while his position as Rehnquist's replacement meant that he would not change the ideological balance on the Court. More important, his impressive professional
record, brilliant legal mind, polite and charming demeanor, and thoughtful if
cleverly vague responses to Senate questioning left Democrats with nothing
sufficiently solid on which to mount a legitimate opposition. As Republican
Senator Arlen Specter noted many years later in another confirmation
hearing, in his appearance before the Senate Judiciary Committee "Justice
Scalia answered virtually nothing."[34] Relatively quickly the Senate confirmed
Scalia's appointment by a unanimous vote in both the Judiciary Committee,
18–0, and the full Senate, 98–0.[35]

Beyond the expected praise that presidents lavished on their nominees,
Reagan used his contemporaneous appointments of Rehnquist and Scalia to
herald his ideas about the properly restrained role of the judiciary. The two
men were examples of stellar legal thinkers who shared his views. "I can assure you," he told a radio audience in 1986, "we will appoint more judges like
them to the Federal bench."[36] Thus, while Reagan used Scalia as exemplary,
he did not single him out from his other appointments or highlight either his
special professional standing or his particular jurisprudential theory.[37]

Scalia and his jurisprudence did, however, begin to take on special significance the next year with Bork's nomination and tumultuous defeat for the
Court's next open seat. When Reagan announced his nomination of Bork in
1987, the president described him as a man "who shares my views" and who
was "the most prominent and intellectually powerful advocate of judicial

---

[33] *See, e.g.,* ABRAHAM, JUSTICES, 292–93; JAMES F. SIMON, THE CENTER HOLDS: THE POWER
STRUGGLE INSIDE THE REHNQUIST COURT 34–35 (1996). For a biography, *see* JOHN A. JENKINS, THE
PARTISAN: THE LIFE OF WILLIAM REHNQUIST (2012).

[34] *Hearings before the Committee on the Judiciary, United States Senate, on the Nomination of Ruth
Bader Ginsburg to be Associate Justice of the Supreme Court of the United States, 103d Cong., 1st Sess.*
(July 20–23, 1993), 281 [hereafter *Ginsburg Hearings*].

[35] ABRAHAM, JUSTICES, 293–95.

[36] 1986-2 REAGAN PUBLIC PAPERS, 1068. *See id.* at 1055, 1200; 1987-1 REAGAN PUBLIC PAPERS, 74.

[37] 1988-89-2 REAGAN PUBLIC PAPERS, 1148 (citing O'Connor, Kennedy, and Bork along with
Rehnquist and Scalia); and 1325 (citing Scalia along with Kennedy and O'Connor).

restraint."[38] Throughout the nomination battle, Reagan stressed Bork's commitment to originalist principles, though he did not distinguish between the jurisprudential theories of Bork and Scalia. His nominee, the president declared, "believes that a judge should keep his own views from interfering with an interpretation of the laws and the Constitution according to the intentions of those who enacted them."[39]

In spite of the administration's support, Bork's nomination ran into vehement opposition in the Senate, newly controlled by Democrats after the 1986 election.[40] His performance during the confirmation hearings before the Judiciary Committee damaged his chances, as some of his explanations seemed unconvincing and his behavior appeared arrogant and occasionally obtuse. Liberal interest groups of all varieties, moreover, organized a fierce campaign against him, attacking his seemingly restrictive or negative views on almost everything they stood for. His position on abortion, civil rights, and the First Amendment stirred open hostility, while his rejection of a constitutional right to privacy seemed to alienate large numbers of people. Ultimately, the Senate rejected his nomination by a lopsided 42–58 vote. Only two Democrats voted for him, while six Republicans voted against.

Bork's defeat quickly redounded to Scalia's benefit. His own triumphant ascension to the Court and the Senate's subsequent rejection of Bork transformed Scalia's position on the political right and propelled him toward a new position of preeminence. First, while Bork had suffered a devastating 42–58 defeat, Scalia had earned confirmation by the glittering count of 98–0.[41] Second, many conservatives, like most commentators, blamed Bork for contributing to his own defeat by the tone-deaf comments he made in his confirmation testimony. They needed a new leader to look up to, and Scalia quickly emerged as the one who filled the void. Third, in the years following his defeat Bork returned to private life where he became a somewhat cranky and peripheral commentator on the evils of liberalism and the decline of

[38] 1987-1 REAGAN PUBLIC PAPERS, 736.

[39] 1987-2 REAGAN PUBLIC PAPERS, 1056. *See, e.g., id.* at 1079, 1163, 1178. Reagan also stressed Bork's commitment to judicial restraint and the independence of the judiciary, and he increasingly emphasized Bork's toughness on crime, a signature Republican issue since Nixon's early attacks on the Warren Court. *Id.* at 986, 1127, 1159, 1178, 1192, 1194, 1230.

[40] The following material in this paragraph is drawn from ETHAN BRONNER, BATTLE FOR JUSTICE: HOW THE BORK NOMINATION SHOOK AMERICA (2007).

[41] Scalia was understandably quite proud of the overwhelming vote he received. MURPHY, SCALIA 131.

America.[42] In contrast, Scalia was safely and permanently ensconced on the nation's high bench where he enjoyed immense professional prestige, unmatched legal authority, and unrivaled opportunities for gaining public attention. Indeed, on the Court itself Scalia was seizing the spotlight with his outspoken and aggressive questioning in oral arguments. In the first argument he heard, he fired his questions at the attorneys so relentlessly that Justice Lewis Powell turned to Justice Thurgood Marshall and whispered his own question: "Do you think he knows that the rest of us are here?"[43] As one of his biographers noted, Scalia "signaled to his more senior colleagues from the first moment he arrived on the Court that in his mind he was their equal, if not superior."[44]

Finally, while Bork was identified with an originalism based on "intent," Scalia became the preeminent advocate of an originalism initially termed "original understanding" and then rechristened as "original meaning" or "original public meaning." In his Senate confirmation hearing, presumably to avoid highlighting divisions among conservatives or antagonizing Bork's many admirers, Scalia had minimized the difference between "original intent" and "original public meaning."[45] Once on the bench, however, he turned his back on the idea of "original intent," dismissing it as misguided and fatally flawed. From then on, he consistently stressed the objectivity and superiority of his own theory of "original public meaning."[46]

Thus, by the end of Reagan's presidency Scalia had bested Bork politically, intellectually, and most important institutionally.[47] Those multileveled triumphs helped make him the undisputed intellectual leader of judicial

[42] Bork subsequently wrote two books that became bestsellers: THE TEMPTING OF AMERICA: THE POLITICAL SEDUCTION OF THE LAW (1989), and SLOUCHING TOWARDS GOMORRAH: MODERN LIBERALISM AND AMERICAN DECLINE (1996).

[43] JOHN C. JEFFRIES, JR., JUSTICE LEWIS F. POWELL: A BIOGRAPHY 534 (2001). Justice O'Connor had similar feelings about Scalia's behavior. EVAN THOMAS, FIRST: SANDRA DAY O'CONNOR 236–37 (2019)

[44] MURPHY, SCALIA, 138.

[45] The "difference between original meaning and original intent" was "not worth" discussing, Scalia stated, because there "is not a big difference" between them. *Scalia Hearings*, 48. "I use the term 'original meaning' rather than 'original intent,' which is maybe something of a quibble." *Id.* at 108. He amplified his answer by contrasting his "original meaning" not to "original intent" but to ideas of a "living Constitution." *Id.* at 48–49.

[46] *See, e.g.*, ANTONIN SCALIA & BRYAN A. GARNER, READING LAW: THE INTERPRETATION OF LEGAL TEXTS 391–96. On changes in originalist theories, including the general shift from "intent" to "public meaning," *see, e.g.*, ERIC J. SEGALL, ORIGINALISM AS FAITH (2018); Stephen M. Griffin, *Rebooting Originalism*, 2008 U. ILL. L. REV. 1185 (2008)

[47] "Another source of great pride was that [Scalia] had beaten out the older and initially more visible Robert Bork for the position [on the Court], the man who had enjoyed all the advantages he had not, and who had been nearly everyone's longtime odds-on choice for the nomination." MURPHY, SCALIA, 131.

conservatism and the preeminent advocate of constitutional originalism. "While Bork had long been embraced by establishment conservatives," explained one of Scalia's biographers, "Scalia was speaking to the new generation."[48] He was, concluded another, "now completely free of the intellectual shadow of Robert Bork."[49]

In the decades that followed, Scalia's name increasingly surfaced in political debates, sometimes alone and sometimes in combination with the Court's other conservative justices. In spite of the continued efforts of Republicans to place conservatives on the Court,[50] they were growing increasingly frustrated and angry because several of their appointments—Harry Blackmun (by Nixon in 1970) and John Paul Stevens (by Ford in 1975), to some extent O'Connor and Anthony Kennedy (by Reagan in 1987), and most recently and perhaps most upsetting, David Souter (by George H.W. Bush in 1990)—had proved moderate or had even moved to the left after taking their seats. Only Justice Clarence Thomas, appointed by Bush the year after Souter, had remained wholly true to their agenda.

Thomas's nomination, in fact, highlighted Scalia's growing reputation and rising heroic status among Republicans and conservatives. The hearings on Kennedy's nomination in June 1987, less than a year after Scalia went on the bench, produced few references to him or his jurisprudence.[51] The more extended hearings on Thomas four years later, however, spurred a great many. By that time Scalia had a track record on the Court, and Thomas had publicly praised him and some of his controversial decisions. Not surprisingly, Republicans generally had few problems with their highly compatible views. "Your approach would be similar to Scalia's, then?" Republican Charles Grassley asked Thomas approvingly.[52]

[48] BISKUPIC, AMERICAN ORIGINAL, 107.

[49] MURPHY, SCALIA, 150.

[50] George H.W. Bush and George W. Bush largely followed Reagan's playbook, relying on leading conservative lawyers, many from the Federalist Society, to screen judicial candidates. Neal Devins & Lawrence Baum, Split Definitive: How Party Polarization Turned the Supreme Court into a Partisan Court, 2016 SUP. CT. REV. 301, 339–41 (2016).

[51] Hearings Before the Senate Committee on the Judiciary on the Nomination of Judge Anthony Kennedy to be Associate Justice of the Supreme Court of the United States, 100th Cong., 1st Sess. (Dec. 14–16, 1987). Kennedy was subsequently confirmed by a vote of 97–0 on February 3, 1988.

[52] Hearings Before the Senate Committee on the Judiciary on the Nomination of Clarence Thomas to be Associate Justice of the Supreme Court of the United States, 102d Cong., 1st Sess. (Sept. 10–Oct. 13, 1991), Part I, 215 [hereafter Thomas Hearings]. For references to Scalia, see id., e.g., Part I, 136, 188–89, 194, 215, 224, 227–28, 232–33, 270, 271, 273, 286–87, 291–92, 361–62, 398, 399, 418, 419–20, 462, 483–84, 485–86, 487–88.

Equally unsurprising, Democrats were critical and sometimes openly hostile toward Thomas and, through him, toward Scalia. Inquiring about *Roe v. Wade*, Patrick Leahy prodded Thomas by calling his attention to the fact that "Justice Scalia has expressed opposition to *Roe*."[53] Edward Kennedy grilled the nominee because Thomas had "praised Scalia's dissent" in *Morrison v. Olson*,[54] where Scalia—disagreeing with all of his colleagues—had declared the executive-limiting Independent Counsel Act an unconstitutional invasion of presidential power.[55] Howard Metzenbaum criticized Thomas on the ground that he had "commended Justice Scalia's narrow vision of congressional power,"[56] while Joseph Biden, the committee's chair, used his position to press Thomas repeatedly on a number of Scalia-related issues. Addressing a question about fundamental constitutional rights, Biden wanted to know whether "you concur with the rationale offered by Justice Scalia."[57] Similarly, he challenged Thomas for praising Scalia's sole dissent in *Morrison*[58] and twice interjected to ask "What was Scalia doing?" and "What did Scalia do, Judge?"[59] Biden concluded sharply that Thomas "thought Scalia was right" and voted to deny confirmation.[60] Five years later he declared that the vote he cast to confirm Scalia was "the vote that I most regret of all 15,000 votes I have cast as a Senator."[61]

The Senate, delayed by a second round of hearings on unrelated charges of sexual misconduct against Thomas, finally voted to confirm him by the exceptionally close count of 52–48. Grassley and forty other Republicans combined with eleven Democrats to confirm, while Leahy, Kennedy, Metzenbaum, and Biden joined forty-two other Democrats and two Republicans voting in opposition.[62]

After the Thomas hearings, Scalia's image continued to grow in legal and political prominence. On the left, he was widely recognized as a powerful figure who championed conservative causes. When Democrat Bill Clinton

[53] *Thomas Hearings*, Part I, 224.
[54] *Thomas Hearings*, Part I, 286. The reference was to *Morrison v. Olson*, 487 U.S. 654 (1988). The vote in *Morrison* was 7–1, with Justice Anthony Kennedy not participating and Scalia dissenting alone.
[55] *Thomas Hearings*, Part I, 291–92.
[56] *Thomas Hearings*, Part I, 462.
[57] *Thomas Hearings*, Part I, 483.
[58] *Thomas Hearings*, Part I, 270.
[59] *Thomas Hearings*, Part I, 271.
[60] *Thomas Hearings*, Part I, 273; 137th CONG. REC., Part 18, 102d Cong., 1st Sess., 26354 (Oct. 15, 1991).
[61] *Ginsburg Hearings*, 115.
[62] 137th CONG. REC., Part 18, 102d Cong., 1st Sess., 26354 (Oct. 15, 1991).

won the presidency in 1992, Jeffrey Rosen wrote that in their long battle against "entitlement liberalism," conservatives were left with only the courts and "only Antonin Scalia to bear their standard."[63] Concurring in an abortion case, Justice Blackmun even identified Scalia by name, along with Rehnquist, as "world's apart" from the Court's position on a woman's "right to reproductive choice."[64]

Conversely, on the right praise for Scalia steadily mounted, and after Clinton was re-elected in 1996, Republican resentment over the Court continued to fester. It soon spurred the effort of presidential hopeful George W. Bush to generate support for his candidacy by emphasizing his special admiration for Scalia as a model of conservative jurisprudence. In 1999, the year before he received the Republican nomination, Bush told a reporter that Scalia represented the kind of justice he hoped to put on the Court. "I have great respect for Justice Scalia," Bush explained, "for the strength of his mind, the consistency of his convictions, and the judicial philosophy he defends."[65] There were, he told Tim Russert on *Meet the Press*, "a lot of reasons why I like Judge Scalia."[66] By that time Scalia had established himself as the widely recognized judicial symbol of conservative policy, and Bush hoped to energize his candidacy by seeming to make him his official model for Republican judicial appointments.

When Bush won the Republican nomination, partisans on both sides believed throughout the presidential campaign of 2000 that he had promised his supporters that he would use Scalia as his model for selecting his appointees.[67] "When Bush mentions Scalia and Thomas," noted one commentator in the *American Bar Association Journal*, "it sends an unmistakable message to grassroots conservatives that he will do the right thing" in the "culture war."[68] In opposition, Democrats sought to use Bush's supposed promise

[63] BISKUPIC, AMERICAN ORIGINAL, 146.
[64] Planned Parenthood of Southeastern Pennsylvania v. Casey, 505 U.S. 833, 922, 943 (1992) (Blackmun, J., concurring in part, concurring in the judgment in part, and dissenting in part).
[65] Fred Barnes, *Bush Scalia*, WEEKLY EXAMINER, July 5, 1999, *available at* http://www.weeklystandard.com/bush-scalia/article/11414 (last consulted Aug. 11, 2019).
[66] MURPHY, SCALIA, 255.
[67] *See, e.g.*, Jamison Foser, *Did Bush Promise to Appoint a Justice Like Scalia?*, MEDIA MATTERS FOR AMERICA, Oct. 13, 2005, *available at* https://www.mediamatters.org/cnn/did-bush-promise-appoint-justice-scalia-cnns-bash-busted-urban-myth-myth-her-own-while-fred?redirect_source=research/2005/10/13/did-bush-promise-to-appoint-a-justice-like-scal/134001 (last consulted Aug. 11, 2019). Those on both the left and right repeated the claim that Bush had made a "promise," and Bush did not deny it. Subsequently, however, doubts were raised as to whether Bush had actually made a "promise" or had merely said that he admired Scalia and regarded him as a model for future appointments. *Id.*
[68] David G. Savage, *Supreme Stumpers*, 86 AM. BAR. ASSOC. J. 26, 28 (2000).

as a scare tactic. More justices like Scalia and Thomas, wrote *New York Times* columnist Tom Wicker, would transform the Court "into a conservative bastion that could last for generations."[69] As early as January 2000 President Clinton cited Bush's statement about Scalia to warn Democrats that Bush was "sending you a signal" that he intended to transform the Court. His victory would lead to the overturning of *Roe v. Wade* and endanger "all the civil rights cases and a lot of other issues that are big, big issues."[70] Whether the right to abortion would be "preserved or scrapped depends on what happens in the Presidential race," Clinton declared on another occasion, "and to pretend otherwise is naive in the extreme."[71] In the presidential debate on October 3, 2000 Vice President Al Gore, the Democratic candidate, used the Scalia threat to attack Bush on the same grounds.[72]

At no point did Bush deny that he had made such a promise but, once elected, he downplayed the idea of a Scalia model though he sought to appoint conservative justices who were in fact similar to Scalia.[73] Bush focused his rhetoric, however, not on any specific model but on more general and established Republican themes.[74] He repeatedly emphasized his commitment to appointing judges "of the highest caliber," though adding equally that he would select "people that share my philosophy about strict constructionism

---

[69] William G. Ross, *The Role of Judicial Issues in Presidential Campaigns*, 42 SANTA CLARA L. REV. 391, 461 (2002). Similarly, the National Abortion Rights League aired television adds charging that more justices like Scalia and Thomas would "reverse the Court" on abortion. *Id.* at 463.

[70] 2000-2--1 WILLIAM J. CLINTON, PUBLIC PAPERS OF THE PRESIDENTS OF THE UNITED STATES 58 (2001) [hereafter CLINTON PUBLIC PAPERS].

[71] 2000-2--1 CLINTON PUBLIC PAPERS, 108–09 (quote appears at 108; reference to Scalia and Thomas follows at 109).

[72] "And Governor Bush has declared to the anti-choice groups," Gore emphasized, "that he will appoint justices in the mold of Scalia and Clarence Thomas, who are known for being the most vigorous opponents of a woman's right to choose." Commission on Presidential Debates, Transcript (Oct. 3, 2000). In the campaign, Richard Posner wrote, Gore "tried to frighten voters" with the idea of more justices like Scalia and Thomas on the Court. RICHARD A. POSNER, BREAKING THE DEADLOCK: THE 2000 ELECTION, THE CONSTITUTION, AND THE COURTS 6, 167 n.19 (2001).

[73] Jan Crawford Greenburg, *The Cause Bush Did Justice To*, WASH. POST, Jan. 21, 2007, *available at* https://www.washingtonpost.com/archive/opinions/2007/01/21/the-cause-bush-did-justice-to/ 8619f220-7a31-45d5-931d-3ea8eda38057/ (last consulted Aug. 11, 2019); JEFFREY TOOBIN, THE NINE: INSIDE THE SECRET WORLD OF THE SUPREME COURT 260 (2007).

[74] The Republican Party Platform for 1996, for example, stated: "The federal judiciary, including the U.S. Supreme Court, has overstepped its authority under the Constitution. It has usurped the right of citizen legislators and popularly elected executives to make law by declaring duly enacted laws to be 'unconstitutional' through the misapplication of the principle of judicial review. Any other role for the judiciary, especially when personal preferences masquerade as interpreting the law, is fundamentally at odds with our system of government in which the people and their representatives decide issues great and small." Republican Party Platforms are available at Gerhard Peters & John T. Woolley, *The American Presidency Project*, https://www.presidency.ucsb.edu/people/other/ republican-party-platforms.

on the Court."[75] By that, he explained, he meant judges who would "strictly and faithfully interpret the law" and not "use the bench from which to legis-late."[76] Bush was apparently trying to free himself from the idea of Scalia as a model in the hope of neutralizing Democratic scare tactics and avoiding unwanted constraints on his future selections.

When Bush ran for re-election in 2004, Senator John Kerry, the Democratic candidate, revived the report that Bush had said he would appoint justices like Scalia and added that the president had also praised Thomas, a second vote for Scalia in the minds of many commentators. Scalia and Thomas were Bush's "two favorite Justices," Kerry charged. Bush again refused to respond directly and avoided the issue by declaring only that "I haven't picked any-body yet." If and when he had the opportunity, he explained, "I would pick somebody who would strictly interpret the Constitution" but would other-wise impose "no litmus test."[77]

After his re-election Bush soon had the opportunity to make two new appointments to the Court. O'Connor announced her retirement at the end of the Court's term in 2005, and Bush nominated John G. Roberts, Jr. to take her seat. While the Senate was considering the nomination, Chief Justice Rehnquist died, leaving a second seat open. Bush decided to switch Roberts's nomination from replacing O'Connor as an associate justice to replacing Rehnquist as chief justice. After the Senate approved Roberts' nomination in September by a 78–22 vote, Bush nominated Samuel A. Alito, Jr. to fill O'Connor's seat, and after a somewhat more contentious process the Senate approved him in January 2006 by a closer vote of 58–42. In the Senate con-firmation hearings on both Roberts and Alito the "Scalia issue" surfaced repeatedly, but the nominees—learning the lessons of Scalia's success and Bork's failure in the confirmation process—refused to provide substantive

---

[75] 2001-1 GEORGE W. BUSH, PUBLIC PAPERS OF THE PRESIDENTS OF THE UNITED STATES 504, 368 (2003) [hereafter BUSH PUBLIC PAPERS]. While Republican presidents consistently proclaimed the need for "strict" constructionists, Scalia rejected that label. "I am not a strict constructionist, and no one ought to be," he explained. Rather, a text "should be construed reasonably, to con-tain all that it fairly means." Antonin Scalia, *Common-Law Courts in a Civil-Law System: The Role of United States Federal Courts in Interpreting the Constitution and Laws*, The Tanner Lectures on Human Values, Princeton University, March 8–9, 1995, at 98. *Accord* ANTONIN SCALIA, A MATTER OF INTERPRETATION: FEDERAL COURTS AND THE LAW 23 (1997); SCALIA SPEAKS, 207.

[76] 2004-2 BUSH PUBLIC PAPERS, 1243. *Accord id.* at 1246, 1559, 2132.

[77] 2004-3 BUSH PUBLIC PAPERS, 2416. Scalia "liked to tell audiences how amusing it was that during the 2004 election season a fundraising letter for the Democratic Party accidentally came to his house in an envelope reading 'Imagine Chief Justice Scalia.'" He drew a laugh when he would then de-clare: "Couldn't care less!" BISKUPIC, AMERICAN ORIGINAL, 317. *See* SCALIA SPEAKS, 270.

responses and relied on vague generalities and the claim that they should not comment on issues that might come before them on the Court.

During Roberts's hearing, a number of senators questioned the nominee about his views on Scalia's jurisprudential ideas. Republicans asked, for example, what the nominee thought about Scalia's positions on legislative history and deference to Congress.[78] Specter asked him directly if "you agree with Scalia" about congressional power under the Fourteenth Amendment, while Lindsey Graham wanted to know if he was "more conservative" than Scalia.[79] Democrats probed more sharply and did so on more subjects, including abortion, gay rights, and the Second Amendment. Leahy suggested unhappily that Roberts "sounds very much like Justice Scalia" in his hostility toward citizen-suit actions in environmental cases, while Biden pressed Roberts on whether he agreed with Scalia on the right to privacy and a right to die.[80] In a written question, Kennedy told the nominee that "Justice Scalia has said that he would resign if he believed that his duty as a judge required affirming the right to abortion" and asked the candidate whether "you disagree with him about that?"[81] Charles Schumer posed the Democrats' ultimate question: Would Roberts "use the Court to turn back a near century of progress and create the majority that Justices Scalia and Thomas could not achieve?"[82]

In Alito's confirmation hearings Scalia comparisons also occurred frequently, and several participants referred specifically to Bush's declaration that he would appoint justices like Scalia and Thomas.[83] "Are you in Justice O'Connor's mold," Schumer asked the nominee, "or, as the President has vowed, are you in the mold of Justices Scalia and Thomas?"[84] Hostile witnesses identified Alito with Scalia's views,[85] while defenders rejected the

[78] Committee on the Judiciary, United States Senate, *Confirmation Hearings on the Nomination of John G. Roberts to be Chief Justice of the Supreme Court of the United States*, 109th Cong., 1st Sess. (Sept. 1315, 2005) [hereafter *Roberts Hearings*], 318–20 (Charles Grassley), 301–02 (Arlen Specter).

[79] *Roberts Hearings*, 299 (Specter) and 252 (Graham).

[80] *Roberts Hearings*, 155–56 (Leahy) and 325–26 (Biden).

[81] *Roberts Hearings*, 612.

[82] *Roberts Hearings*, 442.

[83] Committee on the Judiciary, United States Senate, *Confirmation Hearing on the Nomination of Samuel A. Alito, Jr. to be an Associate Justice of the Supreme Court of the United States*, 109th Cong., 2d Sess. (Jan. 9–13, 2006) [hereafter *Alito Hearings*], 699 (statement of Prof. Michael J. Gerhardt of the University of North Carolina School of Law), 741 (statement of Kate Michelman, former president of the National Abortion and Reproductive Rights Action League, Pro-Choice America), 764 (statement of Representative Charles A. Gonzales from Texas).

[84] *Alito Hearings*, 37.

[85] *Alito Hearings*, 726 (separate statements of Prof. Erwin Chemerinsky of the Duke University School of Law; Beth Nolan, partner in law firm of Crowell & Moring; and Prof. Laurence Tribe of the Harvard Law School).

charge.[86] Republican Senator John Cornyn led the protective counterattack. Bemoaning "the abuse that you suffer during the confirmation process," he told Alito that the evidence before the committee showed that "you are a clone of no one."[87] Cornyn did not help his case, however, when he mistakenly called the nominee by his pejorative nickname, "Judge Scalito," a gaff for which he later apologized profusely.[88]

In 2008 and 2012 the Republican presidential candidates, Senator John McCain and Governor Mitt Romney, respectively, put less emphasis on Scalia and more on the Court's reliable conservatives as a bloc.[89] McCain, for example, said he would "look for people in the cast of John Roberts, Samuel Alito, and my friend the late William Rehnquist" who were "jurists of the highest caliber."[90] Scalia, however, was "so beloved by the political right," one reporter found, that he alone was the justice who "some conservatives dream of" as John McCain's running mate."[91] For his part, Romney hailed Scalia as a model but did not single him out from the Court's three other reliable conservatives, Roberts, Thomas, and Alito.[92] Republican notables followed suit, though many continued to hail Scalia as preeminent. Former Speaker of the House Newt Gingrich called him "probably the most intellectual of the four," while Congresswoman Michelle Bachman declared that she would

---

[86] *Alito Hearings*, 726 (statement of Prof. Charles Fried of Harvard University).

[87] *Alito Hearings*, 559.

[88] *Alito Hearings*, 448, 559–60. For the prior use of the nickname, *see* JOAN BISKUPIC, THE CHIEF: THE LIFE AND TURBULENT TIMES OF CHIEF JUSTICE JOHN ROBERTS 142 (2019).

[89] In the campaigns of 2008 and 2012 the importance of the Court, and the image of Scalia, seemed to decline in popular political salience. William G. Ross, *The Supreme Court Should Be a Key Election Issue*, JURIST—Forum, Oct. 31, 2012, *available at* http://jurist.org/forum/2012/10/william-ross-scotus-election.php (last consulted Aug. 11, 2019).

[90] Andrew Koppelman, *On Not Getting Over It*, BALKANIZATION (May 7, 2008), *available at* https://balkin.blogspot.com/2008/05/on-not-getting-over-it.html?m=0&version=meter+at+null (last consulted Aug. 11, 2019).

[91] Nina Totenberg, *Justice Scalia, the Great Dissenter, Opens Up*, NPR, Morning Edition (Apr. 28, 2008), *available at* http://www.npr.org/templates/story/story.php?storyId=89986017 (last consulted Aug. 11, 2019). Discussing the rumor, Scalia scorned the possibility and suggested McCain would never choose him because he had held that McCain's "signal achievement," the McCain-Feingold Campaign Finance Law, was unconstitutional. "When someone . . . disparages what you think is your life's principal achievement, you're not likely to want him to be on your presidential ticket." *Id.*

[92] "On his website, Romney says he would nominate federal judges in the mold of Scalia, Chief Justice John Roberts, and Justices Clarence Thomas and Samuel Alito. Romney says his judicial appointees 'will exhibit a genuine appreciation for the text, structure, and history of our Constitution and interpret the Constitution and the laws as they are written. And his nominees will possess a demonstrated record of adherence to these core principles.'" *Who Would Romney Appoint to Supreme Court?*, U.S.A. TODAY, Oct. 1, 2012, *available at* https://www.usatoday.com/story/onpolitics/2012/10/01/obama-romney-supreme-court-vacancy/1606025/ (last consulted Aug. 11, 2019).

"put Antonin Scalia at the top of the list."[93] Scalia was "the great hero of the right," declared one conservative scholar, and he was the justice "after whom Republican candidates for President have modeled their ideal Supreme Court justices since 2000."[94]

While the Republicans transformed Scalia into a symbol of constitutional rectitude, the Democrats continued to make him a symbol of virtually everything they opposed. "Tying his views of the Constitution to the views of Scalia and Thomas," wrote two optimistic Democratic critics in 2012, should positively harm Romney's chances of election.[95] The Democratic support group People for the American Way noted that "Romney has said that he wants to nominate more Supreme Court Justices like Clarence Thomas, Samuel Alito, and Antonin Scalia," and it published a detailed analysis of issues facing the Court and warned that "America can't afford this kind of extremism."[96] More delicately, Obama also weighed in. Arguments based on "original intent," he commented vaguely but nonetheless pointedly, often "end up giving judges an awful lot of power, in fact, sometimes more power than duly elected representatives."[97]

Four years later, in the 2016 presidential campaign, the "Scalia issue" again surfaced, this time even more prominently. Donald Trump, the Republican candidate, told Fox News that he "thought Scalia was terrific" and promised explicitly to use him "as the model" in making appointments to the Court. He assured his followers that he would select "someone as close to Scalia as I could find."[98] Trump repeated that assertion often, and in the second presidential debate he told a national audience that Scalia was a "great judge" and "I am looking to appoint judges very much in the mold of Justice Scalia."[99]

[93] Eric Ostermeier, *What Does Mitt Romney Think About Chief Justice John Roberts?*, available at http://editions.lib.umn.edu/smartpolitics/2012/06/28/what-does-mitt-romney-think-ab/ (last consulted Aug. 11, 2019).

[94] Stephen B. Presser, *The Principled Scalia: A Liberal Friend on Scalia's Liberal Opinions*, 18 FEDERALIST SOCIETY REV., available at https://fedsoc.org/commentary/publications/the-principled-scalia-a-liberal-friend-on-scalia-s-liberal-opinions (last consulted Aug. 11, 2019).

[95] Calvin Sloan, *Mitt Romney's Scalia-filled Supreme Court Visits Columbus, Ohio* (Sept. 19, 2012), available at http://www.pfaw.org/blog-posts/mitt-romney's-scalia-filled-supreme-court-visits-columbus-ohio/ (last consulted Aug. 11, 2019).

[96] People for the American Way, *The Importance of the Supreme Court in the 2012 Presidential Election* (Nov. 2012), available at http://www.pfaw.org/report/the-importance-of-the-supreme-court-in-the-2012-presidential-election/ (last consulted Aug. 11, 2019).

[97] 2010-2 BARACK OBAMA, PUBLIC PAPERS OF THE PRESIDENTS OF THE UNITED STATES 573 (2013).

[98] *Trump: My Supreme Court Pick "Closest to Scalia I Can Find,"* NEWSMAX, Mar. 16, 2016, available at https://www.newsmax.com/newsfront/trump-scotus-pick-close/2016/03/16/id/719332/ (last consulted Aug. 11, 2019).

[99] *Transcript of the Second Debate*, N.Y. TIMES, Oct. 10, 2016, available at https://www.nytimes.com/2016/10/10/us/politics/transcript-second-debate.html (last consulted Aug. 11, 2019).

Indeed, Trump repeatedly used Scalia's death and the opening on the Court that resulted as a basis for appealing to voters who might otherwise regard him unfavorably. "Even if they don't like me," he crowed to supporters, they will "have to vote for me because I am going to pick great Supreme Court justices."[100]

Thus, over the course of some three decades Scalia came to serve as a paramount political and judicial symbol for both major political parties. It was no surprise, then, that when Justice Kennedy announced his retirement from the Court in June 2018, Republican Vice President Mike Pence immediately sounded the clarion. "POTUS Trump," he announced on Twitter, "will nominate a strong conservative, in the tradition of the late Justice Scalia."[101]

---

[100] Steven Ertelt, *Donald Trump: "I Will Pick Great Supreme Court Justices" Like Antonin Scalia* (Aug. 2, 2016), *available at* http://www.lifenews.com/2016/08/02/donald-trump-i-will-pick-great-supreme-court-justices-like-antonin-scalia (last consulted Aug. 11, 2019). *See* Benjamin Pomerance, *Justice Denied: The Peculiar History of Rejected United States Supreme Court Nominees*, 80 ALBANY L. REV. 627, 627–629 (2017).

[101] Mike Pence (June 27, 2018), *available at* https://twitter.com/VP/status/1012077857563119617 (last consulted Aug. 11, 2019).

2

Theorist

Scalia's jurisprudential theory, frequently and forcefully articulated, was relatively clear and straightforward.[1] He placed the foundation of his originalism not on "intent" but on what he called "original public meaning," basing it not on the intentions of the Founders but on the reasonable and generally accepted meaning that the constitutional text had for those who drafted and ratified it.[2] "Intent" was a subjective and unworkable standard, he maintained, while "public meaning" was objective and knowable. "The conclusive argument in favor of [public meaning] originalism is a simple one," he declared. "It is the only objective standard of interpretation even competing for acceptance."[3] He stood foursquare on that fundamental claim. "Originalists have nothing to trade!" he insisted. "We can't do horse-trading" because the originalist conclusion "is what it is" and should necessarily prevail.[4]

While Scalia anchored his originalism on the text of written documents, he recognized that the Constitution did not invariably provide clear or explicit answers to controverted questions. When the text itself was not dispositive, he explained, its meaning was properly determined by consulting the history of the founding, evidence of what the founding generation understood the words to mean, the agreed-on practices of the Founders and their immediate successors, and the values and practices that were embedded in long-established and prevailing national traditions.[5] It was what he sanctioned as

---

[1] Scalia explained his originalist theories on many occasions. *See, e.g.,* ANTONIN SCALIA, A MATTER OF INTERPRETATION: FEDERAL COURTS AND THE LAW 3–47, 129–49 (1997) [hereafter SCALIA, MATTER]; ANTONIN SCALIA, SCALIA SPEAKS: REFLECTIONS ON LAW, FAITH, AND LIFE WELL LIVED 155–303 (Christopher J. Scalia & Edward Whelan eds., 2017) [hereafter SCALIA SPEAKS]; ANTONIN SCALIA & BRYAN GARNER, READING LAW: THE INTERPRETATION OF LEGAL TEXTS 78–92, 399–414, and *passim* (2012) [hereafter SCALIA, READING]; Antonin Scalia, *Originalism: The Lesser Evil,* 57 U. CINCINNATI L. REV. 849, 856 (1989) [hereafter Scalia, *Originalism*].

[2] Originalism "should mean not 'original intent of the Framers' but 'original intent of the Constitution.' What was the most plausible meaning of the words of the Constitution to the society that adopted it—regardless of what the Framers might secretly have intended." SCALIA SPEAKS, 183. *See id.* at 183–84.

[3] SCALIA, READING, 89.

[4] JEFFREY TOOBIN, THE NINE: INSIDE THE SECRET WORLD OF THE SUPREME COURT 55–56 (2007).

[5] When "there is no constitutional text speaking to this precise question," Scalia explained, constitutional answers "must be sought in historical understanding and practice, in the structure of the

Antonin Scalia and American Constitutionalism. Edward A. Purcell, Jr., Oxford University Press (2020).
© Edward A. Purcell, Jr.
DOI: 10.1093/oso/9780197508763.001.0001

"tradition," an element in his theory that he often underplayed compared to the emphasis he put on originalism and textualism as methodologies, that undergirded his jurisprudence and often ensured its conservative results. "[I]n the nature of things," he maintained, "the Court cannot stand against a departure from our traditional attitudes" that were "deep and sustained."[6]

In construing texts, Scalia distinguished between the Constitution and statutes. For the Constitution, he emphasized the importance of consulting history and tradition because they could aid in understanding the "original public meaning." The "expressions of the Framers" were a "strong indication of what the most knowledgeable people of the time understood the words to mean."[7] In contrast, in construing statutes he rejected the use of analogous "legislative history" materials such as congressional speeches and reports surrounding a measure's enactment. He maintained that those materials were illegitimate for several reasons, most prominently because they were subjective, unreliable, and often partisan. Commonly and increasingly, he maintained, legislative history materials were merely calculated, lobbyist-created devices for special pleading that had no necessary relation to the statutory text. Such materials, he insisted, "should be consulted *not at all*."[8]

There was, of course, a certain inconsistency in his theory given the different ways he treated constitutional and statutory interpretation.[9] He

---

Constitution, and in the jurisprudence of this Court." Printz v. United States, 521 U.S. 898, 905 (1997) (Scalia, J.).

[6] SCALIA SPEAKS, 167. "I believe that history and not judicially analyzed policy governs this matter." Richardson v. McKnight, 521 U.S. 399, 414, 418 (1997) (Scalia, J., dissenting). In *Town of Castle Rock v. Gonzales*, 545 U.S. 748 (2005) (Scalia, J.), for example, Scalia construed a state statute narrowly and denied relief to a plaintiff on the basis of a "well established tradition of police discretion," *id.* at 760, and further denied that any "right" under a state court order came within the Due Process Clause because "such a right would not, of course, resemble any traditional conception of property." *Id.* at 766. *Accord, e.g.*, Burson v. Freeman, 504 U.S. 191, 214 (1992) (Scalia, J., concurring in the judgment) (relying on "longstanding tradition," at 216, in construing First Amendment).

[7] SCALIA SPEAKS, 183.

[8] SCALIA SPEAKS, 234–42 (quote at 234) (emphasis in original). *Accord* National Endowment for the Arts v. Finley 524 U.S. 569, 590, 594 (Scalia, J., concurring in the judgment) ("More fundamentally, of course, all this legislative history has no valid claim upon our attention at all"). For his general attack on legislative history, *see* SCALIA, READING, 369–90, and for a critique of Scalia's position *see, e.g.*, Paul E. McGreal, *A Constitutional Defense of Legislative History*, 13 WM. & MARY BILL RTS. J. 1267 (2005).

[9] In discussing administrative law, Scalia also seemed to contradict himself about the reliability of legislative history. SCALIA SPEAKS, 240–41. Some of his defenders denied that there was a tension between his two positions. *See, e.g., Hearings before the Committee on the Judiciary, United States Senate, on the Nomination of Stephen G. Breyer to be Associate Justice of the Supreme Court of the United States*, 103d Cong., 2d Sess. (July 12–15, 1994), 283–84 (Senator Orin Hatch). Without discussing constitutional interpretation as such, Scalia declared that using legislative history "to establish what the legislature 'intended' is quite different from using it for other purposes." SCALIA, READING, 388.

overstated substantially the problems involved in using legislative history and, equally, overlooked the fact that the speeches and writings of the Founders were themselves often as partisan, calculated, and misleading as any piece of legislative history. The Founders took positions that were often shrewdly designed to exaggerate the importance of some matters or to finesse, obscure, or avoid others in an effort to advance their goals more persuasively in the different contexts they faced.[10] For all their brilliance, the essays of Hamilton and Madison in the *Federalist* were not without their cunning, deceptive, and expedient qualities.[11] Indeed, one of the most important originalist sources, Madison's extensive notes on the Constitutional Convention, had been repeatedly altered over the years by Madison himself to reflect his own changing views and politics.[12]

On the claimed ground that originalism promised an objective standard to determine constitutional meaning, Scalia maintained that it had many corollary virtues. Most centrally, it limited the discretion of judges. Originalism was "the only real, verifiable criterion that can prevent judges from making the Constitution say whatever they think it should say."[13] It "prevents judges, conservatives and liberals alike, from judging according to their desires."[14] Further, and as a result, originalism was also a reliable guarantor of individual rights. Any theory that rejected originalism, he warned, was "a two-way street that handles traffic both to and from individual rights."[15]

Equally important, he maintained that originalism was fully consistent with—indeed required by—the principles of democracy. Anything that the Constitution did not mandate originally was beyond the power of judges to enforce and was thus properly subject to the will of the people through their legislatures.[16] Issues not covered by the constitutional text or settled

[10] "[D]uring the ratification debates, the Federalists disingenuously offered justifications for the Constitution's most aristocratic features that differed from the arguments they had made in Philadelphia for including those provisions in the Constitution in the first place." MICHAEL J. KLARMAN, THE FRAMERS' COUP: THE MAKING OF THE UNITED STATES CONSTITUTION 609 (2016) [hereafter KLARMAN, FRAMERS' COUP].

[11] *See, e.g.*, NOAH FELDMAN, THE THREE LIVES OF JAMES MADISON 180–83, 198–211, 213–16 (2017) [hereafter FELDMAN, THREE LIVES]; EDWARD A. PURCELL, JR., ORIGINALISM, FEDERALISM, AND THE AMERICAN CONSTITUTIONAL ENTERPRISE: A HISTORICAL INQUIRY 50–51 (2007) [hereafter PURCELL, ORIGINALISM].

[12] MARY SARAH BILDER, MADISON'S HAND: REVISING THE CONSTITUTIONAL CONVENTION (2015) [hereafter BILDER, MADISON'S HAND].

[13] SCALIA SPEAKS, 211.

[14] SCALIA SPEAKS, 207.

[15] "Scalia, *Originalism*," 856. *Accord, e.g.*, SCALIA SPEAKS, 194.

[16] SCALIA SPEAKS, 260–70, "The legislative branch is the core of democracy." *Id.* at 213. *See, e.g.*, Obergefell v. Hodges, 135 S. Ct. 2584, 2626, 2629 (2015) (Scalia, J., dissenting) (Court's decision upholding gay marriage was a "threat to American democracy" and a "judicial putsch").

historical practices were "to be decided through the democratic processes of a free people, and not by the decrees of this Court."[17] Originalism thus ensured the power of the people to govern according to the rules they themselves chose to adopt. It was, Scalia concluded, "more compatible with the nature and purpose of a Constitution in a democratic system."[18]

Finally, by providing an objective standard that identified the true meaning of the Constitution, originalism also provided the only legitimate justification for judicial review. Originalism, Scalia explained, was "the very principle that legitimizes judicial review of constitutionality."[19] In passing on the actions of other governmental levels and branches, originalist judges were not imposing their own views but the mandate of the Founders and the Constitution itself.

Although Scalia never faltered in asserting the legitimacy and superiority of his originalism, he sometimes—especially in his earlier years on the Court—acknowledged candidly its imperfections and limitations. In an essay in 1989 he made significant concessions. There was "plenty of room for disagreement as to what original meaning was," he admitted, "and even more as to how that original meaning applies to the situation before the Court."[20] Moreover, he also recognized that in "new fields" of law "the Court must follow the trajectory of developing law," a task that was "not entirely cut-and-dried but requires the exercise of judgment."[21] Further, he conceded that "almost every originalist would adulterate [the original meaning] with the doctrine of *stare decisis*."[22] Perhaps most striking, he acknowledged the sheer complexity involved in trying to ascertain original meanings.

[17] Booth v. Maryland, 482 U.S. 496, 519, 520 (1987) (Scalia, J., dissenting).

[18] Scalia, *Originalism*, 862. *Accord* SCALIA, READING, 82. This is a common claim among originalists. *E.g.*, ROBERT H. BORK, THE TEMPTING OF AMERICA 143 (1991) (only originalism has "democratic legitimacy" and "is consonant with the design of the American Republic").

[19] Scalia, *Originalism*, 854.

[20] SCALIA, MATTER, 45. *Accord, e.g.*, SCALIA SPEAKS, 195–96, 210.

[21] SCALIA, MATTER, 45. At varying times Scalia acknowledged that the law had to face changing challenges, and in his Senate confirmation hearing he even admitted that it might have some evolutionary content. "I think," he stated, "that there are some provisions of the Constitution that may have a certain amount of evolutionary content within them." *Hearings before the Committee on the Judiciary, United States Senate, on the Nomination of Judge Antonin Scalia to be Associate Justice of the Supreme Court of the United States*, 99th Cong., 2d Sess. (Aug. 5–6, 1986), 49 [hereafter *Scalia Hearings*].

[22] Scalia, *Originalism*, 861. "Any espousal of originalism as a practical theory of exegesis," he explained, "must somehow come to terms with that [stare decisis] reality." *Id.* at 861. *Accord* SCALIA, READING, 87. Sometimes Scalia suggested that stare decisis should be the general rule and that his textualist and originalist "prescriptions are for the future." SCALIA, READING, 87.

And further still, [originalist analysis] requires immersing oneself in the political and intellectual atmosphere of the time—somehow placing out of mind knowledge that we have which an earlier age did not, and putting on beliefs, attitudes, philosophies, prejudices and loyalties that are not those of our day. It is, in short, a task sometimes better suited to the historian than the lawyer.[23]

An originalist analysis, he concluded, should be at least compatible with what "a serious historian would consider minimally adequate." Thus, the "greatest defect" of originalism was "the difficulty of applying it correctly."[24]

Notwithstanding those seemingly serious if not devastating admissions, Scalia clung to his foundational contention and adamantly insisted that originalism was the only valid standard for interpreting the Constitution. More important, as the years passed he increasingly minimized the weaknesses of originalism and on most occasions downplayed or dismissed the significance of the problems he had earlier acknowledged.[25] In his 1989 essay, for example, he had described himself as a "faint-hearted originalist" who believed that some extreme actions that an originalist interpretation would justify—he mentioned "public flogging and hand branding"—would not likely be upheld by the courts.[26] Later in his career, however, he repudiated the "faint-hearted" label and declared that a statute requiring flogging would be constitutional.[27] With growing fervor over the years he insisted on originalism's general power, workability, and reliability. Seemingly forgetting the damaging admissions he had previously made, he increasingly proclaimed that originalism was usually "easy to discern and simple to apply" and that it would "not very often" lead to "disagreement regarding the original meaning."[28] For originalists, he declared with great confidence in 1994,

---

[23] Scalia, *Originalism*, 856–57.

[24] Scalia, *Originalism*, 860, 856. Scalia subsequently and unconvincingly sought to minimize the problems involved in serious historical analysis. Instead, he simply claimed that historical scholarship was adequate and that consequently originalism commonly provided "clear" answers to constitutional questions. SCALIA, READING, 399–402 (quote at 401).

[25] E.g., "Statutes often—and constitutions always—employ general terms such as *due process, equal protection, cruel and unusual punishments.* What these generalities meant as applied to many phenomena that existed at the time of their adoption was well understood and accepted." SCALIA, READING, 85 (emphasis in original).

[26] Scalia, *Originalism*, 862, 864, 861.

[27] Jennifer Senior, *In Conversation: Antonin Scalia*, NEW YORK MAGAZINE, Oct. 6, 2013, *available at* https://nymag.com/news/features/antonin-scalia-2013-10 (last consulted Aug. 12, 2019). *See* MARCIA COYLE, THE ROBERTS COURT: THE STRUGGLE FOR THE CONSTITUTION 165 (2013).

[28] SCALIA, MATTER, 45.

"most constitutional questions pose no difficulty at all." By 2012 he was prepared to assert that in "the vast majority of cases—and especially the most
controversial ones—the historical inquiry will be easy." Two years later he
repeated the claim, declaring sweepingly that in most cases "the originalist
answer is entirely clear."[29]

To drive home the superiority of originalism, Scalia emphasized what he
saw as the fundamental flaws that inhered in any and all "nonoriginalist"
theories of constitutional interpretation. Lumping all such theories together under the label of "living" constitutionalism, he charged that they
were the false and dangerous offspring of the wayward Warren Court.[30] He
condemned ideas of a "living" Constitution on normative grounds as illegitimate, on methodological grounds as subjective and unworkable, and
on political grounds as dangerous and destructive. A "living Constitution,"
he warned, "can evolve toward less freedom as well as toward more."[31] He
scorned nonoriginalist ideas as the cynical instrument of liberal activists who
cared little for the Founders and who sought only to use the courts to impose their own subjective, elitist, and antidemocratic values on the country.
Although advocates of a "living" Constitution "once pretended to reflect at
least the current society's revised beliefs (always as perceived by judges, to be
sure)," Scalia declared,

> in recent years that pretense has been abandoned, and it has been explicitly
> acknowledged that the Living Constitution means what reform-minded
> judges think it should mean. So abortion and homosexual sodomy, which
> society so much disapproved that they were criminal under the laws of most
> states and had been for centuries, are now constitutionally protected—and
> off limits to the democratic process.[32]

Further, Scalia maintained that ideas of "living" constitutionalism did not
resolve any of the fundamental problems that beset constitutional interpretation. On theoretical grounds, he pointed out that even if "the Constitution
was originally *meant* to expound evolving rather than permanent values,"
there was "no basis for believing that supervision of the evolution would

[29] SCALIA, READING, 196, 210–11, 401.
[30] SCALIA SPEAKS, 189–92; SCALIA, READING, 405.
[31] *E.g.*, SCALIA SPEAKS, 194. *See id.* at 194–200, 211–12, 220–22, 228–30, 232–33, 253–57, 266,
268–69; SCALIA, READING, 403–10.
[32] SCALIA, READING, 411. *See, e.g., id.* at 208.

have been committed to the courts" rather than to the people and their legislatures.[33] Thus, he argued, "living" constitutional ideas could not justify a special and activist role for the judiciary but merely highlighted the primacy of the legislature.

On practical grounds, he made two additional arguments against nonoriginalist theories. One was "the impossibility of achieving any consensus on what, precisely, is to replace original meaning, once that is abandoned." That was "the central practical defect of nonoriginalism," and it was "fundamental and irreparable." His other practical objection to "living" constitutionalism was that it exacerbated the great danger inherent in constitutional interpretation, "that the judges will mistake their own predilections for the law." Nonoriginalism "plays precisely to this weakness," he explained, while originalism checked the danger because "it establishes a historical criterion that is conceptually quite separate from the preferences of the judge."[34] Whatever its imperfections, originalism was the safest and most reliable method of constitutional interpretation.

Scalia's opposition to all ideas of a "living" Constitution was implacable and unrelenting. "My Constitution is not living, it is dead," he declared.[35] Emphasizing the point on another occasion, he insisted that the Constitution was not "living" but "dead, dead, dead."[36] "I urge you," he pleaded with an audience at Wesleyan University in 2012, "not to yield to that seductive and extremely undemocratic falsehood."[37]

As a jurisprudential matter, Scalia's originalism was important and deeply thought-provoking because it highlighted and sought to resolve the central interpretive problem of American constitutionalism. If the Constitution was supreme, and if it guaranteed the nation's legitimate and established rule of law, how were Americans to understand and apply its many different, commonly interrelated, often abstract and general, and sometimes practically conflicting provisions? How were they to ensure that the Constitution itself

---

[33] Scalia, *Originalism*, 862 (emphasis in original).

[34] Scalia, *Originalism*, 862–63, 864. In his early 1989 article he noted that the practical defects of originalism, "while genuine enough, seem to me less severe." Scalia, *Originalism*, 863.

[35] Nina Totenberg, *Justice Scalia, the Great Dissenter, Opens Up*, NATIONAL PUBLIC RADIO, Apr. 28, 2008, *available at* http://www.npr.org/templates/story/story.php?storyId=89986017 (last consulted Aug. 12, 2019). *Accord* Terry Eastland, *The "Good Judge," available at* https://www.weeklystandard.com/the-good-judge/article/2001069 (last consulted Aug. 12, 2019) ("I defend a dead Constitution").

[36] Katie Glueck, *Scalia: The Constitution Is Dead*, POLITICO, Jan. 29, 2013, *available at* http://www.politico.com/story/2013/01/scalia-the-constitution-is-dead-086853 (last consulted Aug. 12, 2019) (quoting statement made in talk at Southern Methodist University).

[37] SCALIA SPEAKS, 212.

controlled the nation's government and protected the individual rights it enshrined? How were they to construe its meaning under new conditions and challenges? To his great credit, Scalia confronted those questions and advanced answers that were plausible, forcefully argued, and broadly appealing.

In spite of those admirable qualities, however, Scalia's originalism remained deeply flawed and the methods he proposed wholly inadequate. He did not actually resolve that fundamental jurisprudential problem so much as skate over it wearing ideologically colored lenses. His originalism may have satisfied an understandable human yearning for a coherent theory to underwrite an admirable ideal of democratic constitutionalism, but—if it satisfied those deep yearnings emotionally and psychologically—it did not satisfy them historically, analytically, or methodologically. It identified neither a truly objective general theory of constitutional interpretation nor truly objective methods capable in most cases of directing lawyers and judges to "correct" constitutional decisions.[38]

Indeed, Scalia's fundamental claim about the centrality of democracy, majority rule, and legislative primacy itself represented anything but an originalist view. One of the most well-documented facts about the Constitution was that its Framers were deeply skeptical of legislatures, did not believe in democracy, and established governmental institutions designed to cabin quite tightly the powers of their newly proclaimed sovereign people.[39] "Our chief danger arises from the democratic parts of our constitutions," Edmund Randolph declared, while Elbridge Gerry believed that the "evils we experience flow from the excess of democracy." The people "should have as little to do as may be about the Government," Roger Sherman declared at the Constitutional Convention. "They want information and are constantly liable to be misled."[40] Hamilton hoped that the Constitution would prevent "the depredations which the democratic spirit is apt to make on property,"[41] while

---

[38] Contemporary advocates continue the understandable if similarly ill-fated quest to develop objective and specifically directive theories of "originalist" constitutional interpretation. *See, e.g.*, Randy E. Barnett & Evan D. Bernick, *The Letter and the Spirit: A Unified Theory of Originalism*, 107 GEO. L.J. 1 (2018); John O. McGinnis & Michael B. Rappaport, *Original Methods Originalism: A New Theory of Interpretation and the Case Against Construction*, 103 Nw. U. L. REV. 751 (2009).

[39] *See* GORDON S. WOOD, THE CREATION OF THE AMERICAN REPUBLIC, 1776–1787 (1998 ed.) [hereafter WOOD, CREATION]; JACK N. RAKOVE, ORIGINAL MEANINGS: POLITICS AND IDEAS IN THE MAKING OF THE CONSTITUTION (1996) [hereafter RAKOVE, ORIGINAL MEANINGS]; KLARMAN, FRAMERS' COUP.

[40] 1 THE RECORDS OF THE FEDERAL CONVENTION OF 1787 26, 48 (Max Farrand ed., 1911) [hereafter, FARRAND, RECORDS].

[41] Alexander Hamilton to George Washington, circa Sept., 1787, in THE ESSENTIAL HAMILTON: LETTERS & OTHER WRITINGS 107 (Joanne B. Freeman ed., 2017).

in the *Federalist* both he and Madison warned, in the latter's words, that the legislative branch was "everywhere extending the sphere of its activity, and drawing all power into its impetuous vortex." Consequently, they designed the Constitution to check the "danger from legislative usurpations."[42]

In fact, originalist theories of constitutional interpretation in all their various forms were subject to the gravest criticisms.[43] While originalism and textualism were standard English and American judicial methods, they had long been recognized as merely two sometimes useful techniques in a much broader and well-tested Anglo-American judicial methodology that employed other techniques as well.[44] Later generations continued to agree on the utility and desirability of that more comprehensive, context-sensitive, and fully developed methodology. Textualism sometimes forced analysts to "talk evasively" about issues and "contains within itself no guarantee that it

---

[42] THE FEDERALIST PAPERS No. 48, at 306 (Madison) (Clinton Rossiter ed., originally published in 1961, with Introduction and Notes by Charles R. Kessler, 2003) [hereafter FEDERALIST PAPERS]; *id.* No. 71, at 432. The Constitution, for example, structured both the Senate and the Electoral College to severely limit democracy. "But though Hamilton's dream died, it did not follow, even with their complete victory in the short term, that the dream of Jefferson and Madison lived. Their vision was no less elitist than Hamilton's." ANDREW SHANKMAN, ORIGINAL INTENTS: HAMILTON, JEFFERSON, MADISON, AND THE AMERICAN FOUNDING 143 (2018).

[43] The critical literature is vast and constantly expanding. For a brief and relatively arbitrary sampling, *see, e.g.*, JONATHAN GIENAPP, THE SECOND CREATION: FIXING THE AMERICAN CONSTITUTION IN THE FOUNDING ERA (2018) [hereafter GIENAPP, SECOND CREATION]; ERIC J. SEGALL, ORIGINALISM AS FAITH (2018) [hereafter SEGALL, ORIGINALISM]; DENNIS J. GOLDFORD, THE AMERICAN CONSTITUTION AND THE DEBATE OVER ORIGINALISM (2005); RICHARD H. FALLON, JR., THE DYNAMIC CONSTITUTION: AN INTRODUCTION TO AMERICAN CONSTITUTIONAL LAW (2004); DANIEL A. FARBER & SUZANNA SHERRY, DESPERATELY SEEKING CERTAINTY: THE MISGUIDED QUEST FOR CONSTITUTIONAL FOUNDATIONS (2002); H. JEFFERSON POWELL, A COMMUNITY BUILT ON WORDS: THE CONSTITUTION IN HISTORY AND POLITICS (2002); Thomas B. Colby, *The Sacrifice of the New Originalism*, 99 GEO. L.J. 713 (2011) [hereafter Colby, *Sacrifice*]; Mitchell N. Berman, *Originalism Is Bunk*, 84 N.Y.U. L. REV. 1 (2009); Jamal Greene, *On the Origins of Originalism*, 88 TEX. L. REV. 1 (2009); Stephen M. Griffin, *Rebooting Originalism*, 2008 U. ILL. L. REV. 1185 (2008); Henry Paul Monaghan, *Doing Originalism*, 104 COLUM. L. REV. 32 (2004); Mark A. Graber, *Clarence Thomas and the Perils of Amateur History*, *in* REHNQUIST JUSTICE: UNDERSTANDING THE COURT DYNAMIC (Earl M. Maltz ed., 2003); Laurence H. Tribe & Michael C. Dorf, *Levels of Generality in the Definition of Rights*, 57 U. CHI. L. REV. 1057 (1990); Erwin Chemerinsky, *Foreword: The Vanishing Constitution*, 103 HARV. L. REV. 43 (1989); Paul Brest, *The Misconceived Quest for the Original Understanding*, 60 BOSTON U. L. REV. 204 (1980).

[44] *See, e.g.*, MORTON J. HORWITZ, THE TRANSFORMATION OF AMERICAN LAW, 1780–1860 2 (1977); LAWRENCE M. FRIEDMAN, A HISTORY OF AMERICAN LAW 79 (3d ed., 2005). *See generally* WILLIAM E. NELSON, AMERICANIZATION OF THE COMMON LAW: THE IMPACT OF LEGAL CHANGE ON MASSACHUSETTS SOCIETY, 1760–1830 (1975); BARRY FRIEDMAN, THE WILL OF THE PEOPLE: HOW PUBLIC OPINION HAS INFLUENCED THE SUPREME COURT AND SHAPED THE MEANING OF THE CONSTITUTION (2009) [hereafter FRIEDMAN, WILL OF THE PEOPLE]; G. EDWARD WHITE, THE MARSHALL COURT AND CULTURAL CHANGE, 1815–1835 (1988) [hereafter WHITE, MARSHALL COURT].

will make sense," Charles Black noted.[45] Originalism, Judge Learned Hand declared, was simply "fatuous."[46]

By itself, the inherent complexity of the task that the Constitution's drafters had faced severely undermined originalism's basic plausibility. In spite of their agreements on certain basic principles and goals, they were divided by innumerable disagreements and conflicting interests, held views that were uncertain and vague, and frequently shifted their positions on many issues.[47] The fleeting four months they had available to do their work meant that they could not possibly have reached a shared understanding about the meaning of many of the provisions they adopted. Even more, it also meant that they could not possibly have reached a shared understanding on the innumerable issues that they failed to address or could scarcely even imagine. A consideration of the conceptual, linguistic, and political problems the Framers faced, James Madison acknowledged, "shows that the convention must have been compelled to sacrifice theoretical propriety to the force of extraneous considerations."[48] Originalism, wrote Mary Sarah Bilder after completing her intensive study of Madison's notes of the Constitutional Convention, "requires that the Constitution be a type of document literally beyond the capacity and purpose of the framers."[49] On a multitude of issues—even many of those clearly recognized at the time—there simply was no specific and shared "original public meaning."

Consequently, a compelling range of problems limited and often disabled originalism and textualism as generally adequate guides in construing the Constitution. One was that the text of the Constitution too often contained vague, abstract, or general terms that simply failed to provide clear answers to most questions about their proper meaning and application. Although some provisions were clear and explicit, many others—those that raised

---

[45] Charles L. Black, Jr., Structure and Relationship in Constitutional Law 13, 22 (1969).

[46] Learned Hand, The Bill of Rights 34 (1958). "If I had been sitting on the Supreme Court when Learned Hand was still alive," Scalia wrote about statutory interpretation, "it would similarly have been, as a practical matter, desirable for me to accept his views in all of his cases under review, on the basis that he is a lot wiser than I, and more likely to get it right." Antonin Scalia, *Judicial Deference to Administrative Determinations of Law*, 1989 Duke L.J. 511, 514 (1989).

[47] *See, e.g.,* Klarman, Framers' Coup; Wood, Creation; Rakove, Original Meanings.

[48] Federalist Papers No. 37, at 226 (Madison). *See generally, e.g.,* Purcell, Originalism, 24–37.

[49] Mary Sarah Bilder, *The Constitution Doesn't Mean What You Think It Means*, The Boston Globe, Apr. 2, 2017, *available at* https://www.bostonglobe.com/ideas/2017/04/01/the-constitution-doesn-mean-what-you-think-means/2fvpqWcbd7BP1CPLCBHIZP/story.html (last consulted Aug. 13, 2019). *See* Bilder, Madison's Hand (showing that Madison revised his notes over the years to take into account new developments).

the live controversial questions that judges and lawyers actually struggled with—were not. Second, the Constitution itself provided no interpretative instructions and certainly identified no rule for determining the proper level of generality at which its abstract terms were to be construed. A third problem was that originalism's methods were themselves elastic, imprecise, and contested. They welcomed selection bias and invited conscious and unconscious manipulation to serve partisan purposes.[50]

Another more practical problem also plagued originalism. It constituted an inherently dubious guide because it subjected decisions on novel questions to ostensible but commonly disputed and often imaginary views of Founders whose thinking was based on radically different conditions, assumptions, and challenges. As a result of the discordance between inconclusive originalist sources and pressing new constitutional questions, those employing originalist reasoning could use their pervasive discretion to adopt expedient qualifications, debatable inferences, cherry-picked evidence, suspect inferential leaps, and ideologically fired conclusions.

The Supreme Court's jurisprudence over the years fully revealed those and other inadequacies. The justices had seldom found originalism a consistent or sure guide in construing the Constitution, and they usually disagreed on issues that were socially and politically controversial. The historical arguments they employed were often based on little more than unsound and partisan-fabricated "law office history."[51]

An even broader failing was that originalism was unrealistic in its central analytical premise. It assumed that generation after generation could look back at the Constitution's text and, notwithstanding their altered concerns and perspectives, agree that it carried some single and "true" meaning. That assumption flew in the face of everything known about the nation's actual constitutional history as well as the pervasive impact of presentism on human thinking—the conscious or unconscious tendency to understand the meaning of old documents through the filter of later-day views, values, and word usage. Although Scalia recognized the danger of presentism in the

---

[50] *See, e.g.,* Richard Kay, *Adherence to the Original Intentions in Constitutional Adjudication: Three Objectives and Responses,* 82 Nw. U. L. Rev. 226 (1988) (most constitutional law "only tenuously connected" to the language of the text, at 227); Colby, *Sacrifice* ("new" originalism allows "massive discretion" to judges, at 715).

[51] Classic accounts include Arthur Selwyn Miller, The Supreme Court: Myth and Reality (1978) [hereafter Miller, Supreme Court]; Alfred H. Kelly, *Clio and the Court: An Illicit Love Affair,* 1965 Sup. Ct. Rev. 119; William M. Wiecek, *Clio as Hostage: The United States Supreme Court and the Uses of History,* 24 Cal. W. L. Rev. 227 (1988).

abstract,[52] he was unwilling to acknowledge its influence on his own jurisprudential thinking and certainly unwilling to acknowledge it in his judicial
opinions.

Scalia, in fact, seemed unaware of one of the most distinctive characteristics of historical analysis, the fact that over time scholars revised all manner
of interpretations, understandings, and conclusions. New source materials,
research techniques, and interpretative theories combined with altered social conditions, assumptions, and challenges to periodically qualify, reorient,
or reject previously accepted understandings of the past.[53] "Every present
has a past of its own," R. G. Collingwood explained in his classic work on
historical analysis, "and any imaginative reconstruction of the past aims at
reconstructing the past of this present, the present in which the act of imagination is going on, as here and now perceived."[54] Ultimately, there was a pervasive naiveté in Scalia's idea of originalism and his assumptions about the
nature and uses of historical knowledge and understanding.[55]

Perhaps most telling, the history that Scalia invoked to undergird his
jurisprudence demonstrated quite clearly why the Constitution's text

---

[52] Scalia, *Originalism*, 856–57.

[53] There are oceans of examples of historical revisionism. On the origins of the Constitution, *com-
pare* CHARLES A. BEARD, AN ECONOMIC INTERPRETATION OF THE CONSTITUTION OF THE UNITED
STATES (1913); ROBERT E. BROWN, CHARLES BEARD AND THE CONSTITUTION: A CRITICAL ANALYSIS
OF "AN ECONOMIC INTERPRETATION OF THE CONSTITUTION" (1954). On slavery, *compare* ULRICH
B. PHILLIPS, LIFE AND LABOR IN THE OLD SOUTH (1929); KENNETH M. STAMPP, THE PECULIAR
INSTITUTION: SLAVERY IN THE ANTE-BELLUM SOUTH (1956); NEW STUDIES IN THE HISTORY
OF AMERICAN SLAVERY (Edward E. Baptist & Stephanie M.H. Camp eds., 2006). On the Civil
War, *see* THOMAS J. PRESSLY, AMERICANS INTERPRET THEIR CIVIL WAR (1954); PAUL D. ESCOTT,
RETHINKING THE CIVIL WAR ERA: DIRECTIONS FOR RESEARCH (2018). On Reconstruction, *see*
WILLIAM A. DUNNING, RECONSTRUCTION, POLITICAL AND ECONOMIC, 1865–1877 (1907); ERIC
FONER, RECONSTRUCTION: AMERICA'S UNFINISHED REVOLUTION, 1863–1877 (1988); C. VANN
WOODWARD, THE FUTURE OF THE PAST (1989). On the Cold War, *see* JOHN LEWIS GADDIS, WE NOW
KNOW: RETHINKING COLD WAR HISTORY (1997). For examples of changes in research techniques,
see, e.g., Kellen Funk & Lincoln A. Mullen, *The Spine of American Law: Digital Text Analysis and
U.S. Legal Practice*, 123 AM. HIST. REV. 132 (2018) (explanation of digital analysis technique and
application to debtor-creditor relations during Reconstruction); Nathan Kozuskanich, *Originalism
in a Digital Age*, 29 J. EARLY REPUB. 585 (2009) (examination of meaning of phrase "bear arms"
as used during the period 1750 to 1800 by searching three vast digitalized data bases of different
materials published in the United States). On changes in historiography generally, *see, e.g.*, JOHN
HIGHAM, HISTORY: PROFESSIONAL SCHOLARSHIP IN AMERICA (1989); PETER NOVICK, THAT NOBLE
DREAM: THE "OBJECTIVITY QUESTION" AND THE AMERICAN HISTORICAL PROFESSION (1988).

[54] R.G. COLLINGWOOD, THE IDEA OF HISTORY 247 (1956). Similarly, Peter Gay, who argued that
historical method was science as well as art and that it sought an "objective" understanding of the
past, nonetheless acknowledged that "a conclusive interpretation—the map that will never need
revision—is unrealizable in principle. . . . The meaning of an event for its posterities, as distinct from
its contemporary meaning or its causes, is perpetually open to revision. . . . History, in a word, is unfinished in the sense that the future always uses its past in new ways." PETER GAY, STYLE IN HISTORY
202 (1974).

[55] *E.g.*, SCALIA, READING, 399–402.

contained vague, general, and abstract terms and why it failed to provide clear definitions, sharp lines, and operational specifics on so many issues.[56] The history of the founding revealed that, beyond agreeing on a few specific provisions, establishing a general institutional structure, and embracing certain underlying republican values and assumptions, the Founders shared little in the way of consensus on many issues involving the Constitution's meaning and application.[57] The document was the product of shrewd compromise and pragmatic avoidance.[58] It purposely employed vague provisions with undefined terms, adopted principles guaranteed to conflict with one another, established an institutional structure designed to operate through built-in tensions, and created an overall governmental system that was novel, untried, and intrinsically dynamic and adaptive. The Constitution was rooted partly in past experience, partly in innovative theories, partly in buoyant if somewhat unrealistic hopes, partly in compelling practical interests, partly in sometimes faulty estimates about the future, and often in a willingness simply to leave critical issues unresolved.[59] The subsequent ratification process exposed many of those profound disagreements and misunderstandings, and it spurred the incorporation of further generalities, compromises, and finesses. The Tenth Amendment, for example, was added

[56] The following paragraph is based on a vast historical literature that explores the changing nature of American constitutional thought in the late eighteenth century. *See, e.g.*, PAULINE MAIER, RATIFICATION: THE PEOPLE DEBATE THE CONSTITUTION, 1787–1788 (2010); WOOD, CREATION; GORDON S. WOOD, THE EMPIRE OF LIBERTY: A HISTORY OF THE EARLY REPUBLIC, 1789–1815 (2009) [hereafter WOOD, EMPIRE]; RAKOVE, ORIGINAL MEANINGS.

[57] *E.g.*, "The historical record, which contains both narrow legalistic cases and broad, controversial political ones, is simply too ambiguous to establish what kind of judicial review, narrowly legal or broadly policy-oriented, the Constitution's framers had in mind when they adopted judicial review by giving the Supreme Court jurisdiction to review state-court judgments." WILLIAM E. NELSON, *MARBURY V. MADISON*: THE ORIGINS AND LEGACY OF JUDICIAL REVIEW 151 (2d ed., rev. & expanded 2018).

[58] *See, e.g.*, KLARMAN, FRAMERS' COUP; FELDMAN, THREE LIVES, ch. 5 (2017); WOOD, CREATION; RAKOVE, ORIGINAL MEANINGS.

[59] For uncertainty and disagreement about the meaning of various clauses and concepts, *see, e.g.*, WILLIAM M. WIECEK, THE GUARANTEE CLAUSE OF THE U.S. CONSTITUTION 72 (1972) (Guarantee Clause); RICHARD H. KOHN, EAGLE AND SWORD: THE FEDERALISTS AND THE CREATION OF THE MILITARY ESTABLISHMENT IN AMERICA, 1783–1802 (1975) (military provisions); RAKOVE, ORIGINAL MEANINGS, 179–80 ("indirect taxes"); JENNIFER NEDELSKY, PRIVATE PROPERTY AND THE LIMITS OF AMERICAN CONSTITUTIONALISM: THE MADISONIAN FRAMEWORK AND ITS LEGACY (1990) (property); PURCELL, ORIGINALISM (federalism); Steven R. Boyd, *The Contract Clause and the Evolution of American Federalism, 1789–1815*, 3d ser. 44 WM. & MARY Q. 529 (1987) (Contract Clause); William E. Nelson, *The American Revolution and the Emergence of Modern Doctrines of Federalism and Conflict of Laws*, 62 PUBLICATIONS OF THE COLONIAL SOCIETY OF MASSACHUSETTS: LAW IN COLONIAL MASSACHUSETTS 419, 453 (judicial provisions); Michael G. Collins, *Article III Cases, State Court Duties, and the Madisonian Compromise*, 1995 WISC. L. REV. 39 (art. III); Nicole Stelle Garnett, *Justice Scalia's Rule of Law and Law of Taking*, VT. L. REV. 717, 729 (2017) (Takings Clause).

in 1791 to assuage state anxieties over federal power, but it did little but preserve the ambiguities inherent in the original Constitution.[60] Moreover,
almost immediately after ratification many of the Founders shifted their
positions on the nature and meaning of the Constitution when they suddenly
confronted new issues in a new political context. Those shifts highlighted the
fact that their understandings of many issues had been and continued to be
uncertain, changing, and diverse.[61]

Moreover, the decade immediately following ratification demonstrated
quite clearly the fact that the Founders shared only a limited agreement
about the Constitution's true meaning and proper operation. The 1790s, in
fact, was a decade of intense, bitter, and sometimes violent party warfare.[62]
The Founders feared and condemned the threat of "factions" and "parties,"
but within a few years of ratification they began organizing rival national
parties, a development that immediately forced them to rethink, among
other things, their basic ideas about the operation of the Constitution's structure of separated and checking governmental powers.[63] One of the principal
purposes in founding national political parties, after all, was precisely to
overcome that separation and negate those checks. Although the Founders
often based their opposed contentions on appeals to the Constitution's original meaning, when critical new issues divided them, they could not agree on
what that original meaning was.[64]

[60] Charles A. Lofgren, *The Origins of the Tenth Amendment: History, Sovereignty, and the Problems
of Constitutional Intention, in* CONSTITUTIONAL GOVERNMENT IN AMERICA 331 (Ronald K.L. Collins
ed., 1980); Walter Berns, *The Meaning of the Tenth Amendment, in* A NATION OF STATES: ESSAYS ON
THE AMERICAN FEDERAL SYSTEM 139 (Robert A. Goldwin & Morton Grodzins eds., 1974).

[61] *E.g.*, SHANKMAN, ORIGINAL INTENTS 5 ("Almost immediately, then, after uniting to support
the Constitution in 1787, Jefferson and Madison found themselves in complete disagreement with
Hamilton about what the constitution meant and what the government it created could and should
do"). *See* PURCELL, ORIGINALISM, 32–35.

[62] *See, e.g.*, R. KENT NEWMYER, JOHN MARSHALL AND THE HEROIC AGE OF THE SUPREME COURT
70 (2001). *See* JAMES ROGER SHARP, AMERICAN POLITICS IN THE EARLY REPUBLIC: THE NEW NATION
IN CRISIS (1993); John R. Howe, Jr., *Republican Thought and Political Violence of the 1790s*, 19 AM. Q.
147 (1967); Marshall Smelser, *The Federalist Period as an Age of Passion*, 10 AM. Q. 391 (1958). On
the tumultuous social and political transformations that remade American politics in the period, *see*
WOOD, EMPIRE.

[63] *See, e.g.*, STANLEY ELKINS & ERIC MCKITRICK, THE AGE OF FEDERALISM: THE EARLY AMERICAN
REPUBLIC, 1788–1800, esp. ch. 7 (1993); RICHARD HOFSTADTER, THE IDEA OF A PARTY SYSTEM: THE
RISE OF LEGITIMATE OPPOSITION IN THE UNITED STATES, 1780–1840, esp. ch. 2 (1970); JOSEPH
CHARLES, THE ORIGINS OF THE AMERICAN PARTY SYSTEM (1984).

[64] "[D]espite disagreement about what the Constitution meant or required and the variety of
sources invoked, few at the time thought interpretation was anything other than the ascertainment
and application of original intent." JONATHAN O'NEILL, ORIGINALISM IN AMERICAN LAW AND
POLITICS: A CONSTITUTIONAL HISTORY 17 (2005) [hereafter O'NEILL, ORIGINALISM]. *See generally* SEGALL, ORIGINALISM. Historians disagree as to when originalism became a central concern
of American constitutionalism. One identifies the battles of the 1790s as critical, GIENAPP, SECOND
CREATION, while another argues that "Americans constructed an authoritative Founding between

The early nineteenth century confirmed the absence of any shared original understanding on controverted issues as well as the fact that the Constitution's interpretation was consequently subject to change in various ways, at various times, on various issues, and for various reasons.[65] Quite early on it became clear that the text was ambiguous and that it invited the infusion of new meanings. The Marshall Court gave "a universalistic meaning" to many of the document's key words and, once those words were "packed with nontextual meanings," they were "made applicable to a situation not explicitly contemplated by the Framers."[66] In spite of frequent appeals to originalism, interpretations of the Constitution continued to shift in rough accord with the evolving values, goals, and interests of those who constructed the alleged original meanings to which they appealed. The text was always open to those who would shape originalist arguments to advance their goals, just as it was always open to their adversaries to develop counter originalist contentions supporting their own opposed goals. John Marshall's "nationalist inclinations shaped American constitutional law from the unformed condition in which he found it," explained Jonathan O'Neill, a sympathetic historian of originalism, and Marshall's decision "in turn generated criticism based on competing conceptions of original intent."[67]

Those early disagreements that divided the Founders were particularly revealing, too, because the members of the founding generation shared for the most part the same general historical conditions, experiences, assumptions, and challenges. Even with those shared commonalities and, for many of them, close personal associations from the Revolution through the drafting and ratification of the Constitution, they still disagreed about the document's meaning when they confronted divisive new issues. Given the Founders' diverse and often opposed goals, values, and interests, the

---

1819 and 1835." Aaron R. Hall, *"Plant Yourselves on Its Primal Granite": Slavery, History and the Antebellum Roots of Originalism*, 37 L. & HIST. REV.743, 748 (2019). Historical originalism, however, is quite different from modern and highly political post-Reagan originalism.

[65] *See, e.g.,* Michael G. Collins, *The Federal Courts, the First Congress, and the Non-Settlement of 1789*, 91 VA. L. REV. 1515 (2005) (congressional power and federal judiciary); Jack N. Rakove, *Taking the Prerogative Out of the Presidency: An Originalist Perspective*, 37 PRESIDENTIAL STUD. Q. 85 (2007) (presidential power); Laura S. Underkuffler, *On Property: An Essay*, 100 YALE L.J. 127 (1990) (ideas about property).

[66] WHITE, MARSHALL COURT, 8. "A word is not a crystal, transparent and unchanged," Justice Oliver Wendell Holmes, Jr. wisely noted, "it is the skin of a living thought and may vary greatly in color and content according to the circumstances and the time in which it is used." Towne v. Eisner, 245 U.S. 418, 425 (1918) (Holmes, J.).

[67] O'NEILL, ORIGINALISM, 18.

Constitution's frequently inconclusive text welcomed and even encouraged their disagreements.

In the final analysis, then, Scalia's defense of originalism caricatured the idea of a "living" Constitution. That idea, he declared, led to "the creation of a Constitution that is an instrument of change rather than of stability."[68] His claim was misleading and essentially off the point for three quite different reasons.

First, as a textual matter, the Constitution was a document designed not only for stability but equally for practical flexibility, growth, and adaptation. It not only relied on innumerable general and abstract terms, but it also incorporated specific provisions designed to ensure that the structure of American government itself could and would evolve over time. Some of those provisions mandated change, others authorized it, and yet others invited it.[69] Further, it incorporated other provisions that required pragmatic adaptation to meet changing times and conditions.[70] "In framing a system which we wish to last for ages," Madison declared at the Constitutional Convention, "we shd. not lose sight of the changes which ages will produce."[71] In fact, the Constitution was an instrument that anticipated and enabled change as much as one that preserved stability.

Second, as a historical matter, Americans had repeatedly interpreted the Constitution—even when they appealed to some alleged original meaning— as a flexible document that could be shaped to serve their needs and meet the perceived demands of new conditions and possibilities. In spite of their frequent paeans to its unchanging nature, they nonetheless repeatedly found ways to make it serve their new purposes. In the 1790s, for example, Thomas Jefferson and James Madison had both maintained that the power of the federal government to acquire new territory "did not exist within the Constitution."[72] A few years later and then in power, however, they agreed that the United States had the constitutional authority to buy the Louisiana

---

[68] SCALIA SPEAKS, 230.

[69] *E.g.*, The Constitution mandated regular elections, U.S. CONST. art. I, sec. 2, cl. 3 (House); art. I, sec. 3, cl. 1 (Senate); art. II, sec. 1, cl. 1 (presidential electors); changes in representation through a decennial census, art. I, sec. 2, cl. 3 (House) and art. II, sec. 1, cl. 2 (presidential electors); authorized Congress to structure both the executive and judicial branches, art. II, sec. 2, cl. 2 (executive); art. III, sec. 1 & sec. 2, cl. 2 (judicial); the admission of new states, art. IV, sec. 3, cls. 1 & 2; and its own amendment, art. V.

[70] PURCELL, ORIGINALISM, esp. chs. 5–8.

[71] FARRAND, RECORDS, 422.

[72] RALPH KETCHAM, JAMES MADISON: A BIOGRAPHY 421 (1990) [hereafter KETCHAM, JAMES MADISON].

Territory from France. Jefferson simply suppressed his narrow constitutional principles, while Madison changed his mind and argued that the power was inherent in the federal government.[73] Even more boldly, Jefferson stretched executive power broadly when he sent the U.S. Navy to war against the Barbary pirates without seeking the approval of Congress.[74] Subsequently, under the aegis of the Constitution Americans moved rapidly westward across the continent, aggressively expanded their actions on the hemispheric and global stages, and continually reshaped their government and its operations to meet their changing goals and challenges. They conducted a long-term constitutional enterprise in their continuous, collaborative, and often discordant efforts to preserve an enduring, if imperfect and periodically readjusting, system of popular self-government under law and the Constitution.

Third, as a factual matter, few proponents of a "living" Constitution rejected the importance of the document but, instead, embraced it as a genuine source of understanding, guidance, and inspiration. They recognized that the Constitution established both the nation's fundamental political values and goals and its complex institutional structure—the element that Scalia repeatedly hailed as the Constitution's most important element.[75] Justice Louis Brandeis, for example, declared that the Constitution must have a "capacity of adaptation to a changing world,"[76] but he surely sought to honor both the Constitution's values and goals as well as the institutional structure it ordained. So, too, did Chief Justice Charles Evans Hughes when he responded to the crisis of the Great Depression. If one maintained "that the great clauses of the Constitution must be confined to the interpretation which the framers, with the conditions and outlook of their time, would have placed upon them," he explained, "the statement carries its own refutation."[77] Such proponents of a "living" Constitution agreed that whatever issues an explicit textual provision clearly settled should be accepted, but they also recognized the fact that such issues had generally been settled long ago for the obvious reason that the text of the Constitution did actually settle them. They also recognized that whatever issues those original meanings did not settle

---

[73] RICHARD B. BERNSTEIN, THOMAS JEFFERSON 141–43 (2003) [hereafter BERNSTEIN, THOMAS JEFFERSON]; KETCHAM, JAMES MADISON, 418–22.

[74] BERNSTEIN, THOMAS JEFFERSON, 145–46.

[75] E.g., Scalia Hearings, at 32; SCALIA SPEAKS, 163. See, e.g., PURCELL, ORIGINALISM, 196–200.

[76] Olmstead v. United States, 277 U.S. 438, 471, 472 (1928) (Brandeis, J., dissenting).

[77] Home Building & Loan Association v. Blaisdell, 290 U.S. 398, 442–43 (1934) (Hughes, C.J.).

remained—as far as authentically originalist sources could determine—still unsettled and thus open to debate, reconsideration, and wise adaptation.

It was revealing, too, that Scalia's ultimate justification for the superiority of originalism did not justify anything but merely begged the question. Unlike advocates of the "living" constitution, he declared, "the originalist at least knows what he is looking for: The original meaning of the text."[78] Although that proposition seemed commonsensical, it resolved none of the difficulties that plagued the proposed concept of a generally knowable and specifically directive "original public meaning." Hunters could know with certainty that they were seeking centaurs or gryphons, but their quest would not make those imaginary creatures real.

[78] SCALIA, MATTER, 45.

PART II

SUPREME COURT JUSTICE

3

An Angle of Vision

A judicial philosophy is not something that springs full-blown, Athena-like, from a person's head, nor something that the text of the Constitution and the *Federalist Papers* magically imprint on a tabula rasa. Rather, it is something that individuals develop over time, both consciously and unconsciously, and something that takes shape under the influence of their backgrounds, educations, and experiences and in at least rough accord with their most fundamental values, desires, goals, and interests. Thus, on disputed constitutional issues an individual's "personal" views and his or her "formal" legal views do not exist in insulated mental chambers. In varying ways and to varying degrees, they interact and mold one another.

Scalia essentially denied that proposition. Sometimes he even seemed to suggest the tabula rasa principle. "Why listen to me?" he once asked an audience. "Read the *Federalist Papers*."[1]

To a Catholic gathering in 1992 he made a claim of pure judicial objectivity even more strongly. There was "no Catholic way to interpret a text, analyze a historical tradition, or discern the meaning and legitimacy of prior judicial decisions," he declared, "—except, of course, to do those things *honestly* and *perfectly*." Judging meant following nothing but "the law" itself, and doing that, he insisted, was exactly what he did on the bench. The "ideal" judge, he explained on another occasion, "sets to the side his personal preferences in favor of the law."[2]

Naturally, in his confirmation hearing Scalia assured the Senate Judiciary Committee that he would and could do just that.

There are doubtless laws on the books apart from abortion that I might not agree with, that I might think are misguided, perhaps some that I might even think in the largest sense are immoral in the results that they produce.

---

[1] ANTONIN SCALIA, SCALIA SPEAKS: REFLECTIONS ON LAW, FAITH, AND LIFE WELL LIVED 222 (Christopher J. Scalia & Edward Whelan eds., 2017) [hereafter SCALIA SPEAKS].

[2] SCALIA SPEAKS, 152 (emphasis in original), 171. "It is necessary to judge according to the written law—period." *Id.* at 245.

Antonin Scalia and American Constitutionalism. Edward A. Purcell, Jr., Oxford University Press (2020).
© Edward A. Purcell, Jr.
DOI: 10.1093/oso/9780197508763.001.0001

In no way would I let that influence my determination of how they apply. And if indeed I felt that I could not separate my repugnance for the law from my impartial judgment of what the Constitution permits the society to do, I would recuse myself from the case.[3]

Those guarantees, without doubt pledged honestly and sincerely, were the standard and absolutely necessary guarantees required of every judicial candidate, and properly so. They are essential to the judicial role and should inspire the efforts of every decent and honest judge to be as fair, open-minded, even-handed, fact-based, and legally dutiful as is humanly possible. Still, those guarantees are not, and never could be, the whole story of American constitutional judging, certainly not at the level of the U.S. Supreme Court.

Interpretations of the Constitution, especially where the text fails to provide clearly applicable and express terms or where it uses abstract or general language, are unavoidably influenced by a judge's background, experiences, and personal views of law, life, morality, social welfare, and judicial methodology.[4] Justice George Sutherland, for example, the Court's leading conservative in an earlier day, acknowledged that basic human truth. He agreed wholeheartedly with Scalia that the Constitution's meaning was fixed when it was adopted and, absent amendment, was to remain unchanged and unchanging thereafter. The judge's duty was simply to interpret that preexisting law, Sutherland explained, and the only "check upon the judge is that imposed by his oath of office, by the Constitution and by his own conscientious and

---

[3] *Hearings before the Committee on the Judiciary, United States Senate, on the Nomination of Judge Antonin Scalia to be Associate Justice of the Supreme Court of the United States*, 99th Cong., 2d Sess. (Aug. 5–6, 1986), 43 [hereafter *Scalia Hearings*].

[4] Addressing nonjudicial actors, the Court, speaking through the conservative Justice Lewis F. Powell, Jr., acknowledged that basic human truth. "In contrast with the thought processes accompanying 'ministerial' tasks, the judgments surrounding discretionary action almost inevitably are influenced by the decisionmaker's experiences, values, and emotions." Harlow v. Fitzgerald, 457 U.S. 800, 816 (1982) (Powell, J.). Scholars have demonstrated conclusively that Supreme Court justices are often influenced by their political and social views, as well as by other personal, contextual, tactical, and strategic considerations. The more the relevant constitutional text contains general and abstract terms and the more the issues presented are controversial and divisive, the greater the influence of those factors. The vast literature supporting the point includes, *e.g.*, NEAL DEVINS & LAWRENCE BAUM, THE COMPANY THEY KEEP: HOW PARTISAN DIVISIONS CAME TO THE SUPREME COURT (2019); LAWRENCE BAUM, IDEOLOGY IN THE SUPREME COURT (2017); LEE EPSTEIN, WILLIAM M. LANDES, & RICHARD A. POSNER, THE BEHAVIOR OF FEDERAL JUDGES: A THEORETICAL AND EMPIRICAL STUDY OF RATIONAL CHOICE (2013); JEFFREY SEGAL & HAROLD SPAETH, THE SUPREME COURT AND THE ATTITUDINAL MODEL REVISITED (2002); Geoffrey R. Stone, *The Behavior of Supreme Court Justices When Their Behavior Counts the Most: An Informal Study*, 97 JUDICATURE 82 (2013); Stefanie A. Lindquist & Rorie Spill Solberg, *Activism, Ideology, and Federalism: Judicial Behavior in Constitutional Challenges Before the Rehnquist Court, 1986–2000*, 3 J. EMPIRICAL LEGAL STUD. 237 (2006).

informed convictions."[5] Sutherland recognized, in other words, that all constitutional judges, striving to act honestly according to the law, necessarily relied to some extent, consciously or not, on their own personal "conscientious and informed convictions," that is, on their own individually formed understandings of the Constitution's proper meaning and application.

Scalia inevitably harbored his own "conscientious and informed convictions," and the convictions that guided his "impartial judgment" seemed in good measure to be shaped by three broad influences.[6] First, Scalia's family background and upbringing apparently influenced his views profoundly. His beloved father, a first-generation Italian immigrant who became a professor of romance languages, impressed his son deeply with his "strict code of integrity" and taught him to appreciate "cast-iron rules akin to those found in Dante's orderly universe of sin and suffering."[7] Scalia later described his father as "a man of unbending principle,"[8] the kind of strict, rule-following judge his son sought to become.

Second, Scalia was raised as a devout Catholic, and his religion played a vital and pervasive role in his life.[9] Catholic dogma was authoritative for all the faithful, he insisted, and it was essential for all true believers to adhere to Church doctrine.[10] Although he regularly declared that his religion had nothing to do with his constitutional views,[11] that was a claim open to question. The rigidly rule-oriented nature of his Catholicism seemed to shape his

---

[5] West Coast Hotel Co. v. Parrish, 300 U.S. 379, 400, 402 (Sutherland, J., dissenting). *See id.* at 402–04 for Sutherland's general views about the unchanging nature of the Constitution.

[6] On the Court Scalia stated that "it is virtually impossible to find a judge who does not have preconceptions about the law," but he couched his language in a way that suggested that such "preconceptions" involved only judges' views of strictly "legal issues" and did not implicate their personal values and beliefs. Republican Party of Minnesota v. White, 536 U.S. 765, 768, 777–78 (2002) (Scalia, J.).

[7] JOAN BISKUPIC, AMERICAN ORIGINAL: THE LIFE AND CONSTITUTION OF SUPREME COURT JUSTICE ANTONIN SCALIA 17 (2009) [hereafter BISKUPIC, AMERICAN ORIGINAL]. *See* SCALIA SPEAKS, 105–54.

[8] ALAN DERSHOWITZ, TAKING THE STAND: MY LIFE IN THE LAW 271 (2013).

[9] *See, e.g.*, ANTONIN SCALIA, ON FAITH: LESSONS FROM AN AMERICAN BELIEVER (Christopher J. Scalia & Edward Whelan eds., 2019) [hereafter SCALIA, ON FAITH]. Scalia was "a vocal defender of traditional Catholic morality" and was "fiercely protective of religion's role in the public square." Michael O'Loughlin, *Scalia was a champion of traditional Catholicism*, CRUX, Feb. 14, 2016, *available at* https://cruxnow.com/faith/2016/02/14/scalia-was-a-champion-of-traditional-catholicism/ (last consulted June 14, 2018). *Accord* Maureen Fiedler, *Justice Antonin Scalia: A Very Traditional Catholic*, NATIONAL CATHOLIC REPORTER, Feb. 15, 2016, *available at* https://www.ncronline.org/blogs/ncr-today/justice-antonin-scalia-very-traditional-catholic (last consulted June 14, 2018). *See* George Kannar, *The Constitutional Catechism of Antonin Scalia*, 99 YALE L.J. 1297 (1990).

[10] *See, e.g.*, Jennifer Senior, *In Conversation: Antonin Scalia*, NEW YORK MAGAZINE, Oct. 6, 2013, *available at* http://nymag.com/nymag/features/antonin-scalia-2013-10/index2.html; *id.*, index3 (last consulted June 14, 2019) [hereafter Senior, *In Conversation*].

[11] *E.g.*, SCALIA, ON FAITH, 80–83.

commitment to the idea of law as a set of clear and predetermined rules,[12] and the substance of the Church's moral teachings powerfully confirmed the rightness, if they did not actually shape, many of his formal legal views. "A religious person cannot divide his view of man," Scalia acknowledged on one occasion. "He can't separate religion from his own natural inclinations."[13] Legal views, he acknowledged on another occasion, were "inevitably affected by moral and theological perceptions."[14]

Third, as a political matter, Scalia was an instinctively conservative person who deeply respected and drew sustenance from what he honored as the traditional values, attitudes, and practices that he absorbed in his youth. Although his parents were Roosevelt Democrats, he was drawn early on to the ideas and values of the opposition Republican Party.[15] Growing to professional maturity with the rise of the post–World War II conservative intellectual movement,[16] he found its underlying assumptions and values compelling. Harboring a sense of unease and discomfort with ideas of historical change, social egalitarianism, institutional evolution, and grand visions of human progress, he showed an intense dislike for contemporary political liberalism, a contempt for the ideas and movements that exploded in the 1960s, and a visceral hostility to many of the innovative rulings of the Warren Court. "Willful judges who bend a text to their wishes have always been with us," he declared, but the Warren Court had changed all that. Under its influence "it no longer matters what the Constitution meant."[17]

---

[12] Antonin Scalia, *The Rule of Law as a Law of Rules*, 56 U. CHI. L. REV. 1175, 1180 (1989).

[13] BRUCE ALLEN MURPHY, SCALIA: A COURT OF ONE 42 (2014) [hereafter MURPHY, SCALIA]. "Without playing Dr. Freud, I wonder whether Justice Scalia's attraction to this conception of a static form of originalism may be reinforced by the fact that, like me, he was brought up immersed in pre–Vatican II Roman Catholicism. The idea of doctrine evolving (at least after the doctrinal consolidation worked by the great ecumenical councils in the fourth and fifth centuries) is not naturally congenial to many in my generation. And the doctrine is in the details. The Pope does not alter 'originalist' doctrine because he believes he cannot do so; no place exists for overruling original understanding based on the argument that it is now arguably socially undesirable." Henry Paul Monaghan, *Symposium: Doing Originalism*, 104 COLUM. L. REV. 32, 34 (2004).

[14] Robert Barnes, *Supreme Court Justice Antonin Scalia Dies at 79*, WASH. POST, Feb. 13, 2016, *available at* https://www.washingtonpost.com/politics/supreme-court-justice-antonin-scalia-dies-at-79/2016/02/13/effe8184-a62f-17e3-asfa-55f0c77bf39c_story.html?utm_term=.282e62e618731? (last consulted June 14, 2018).

[15] MURPHY, SCALIA, 12; BISKUPIC, AMERICAN ORIGINAL, 22–23.

[16] *See, e.g.*, GEORGE H. NASH, THE CONSERVATIVE INTELLECTUAL MOVEMENT IN AMERICA SINCE 1945 (1976); PETER STEINFELS, THE NEO-CONSERVATIVES: THE MEN WHO ARE CHANGING AMERICA'S POLITICS (1979); STEVEN M. TELES, THE RISE OF THE CONSERVATIVE LEGAL MOVEMENT: THE BATTLE FOR CONTROL OF THE LAW (2008); JASON STAHL, RIGHT MOVES: THE CONSERVATIVE THINK TANK IN AMERICAN POLITICAL CULTURE SINCE 1945 (2016); and the symposium on the historiography of the modern conservative movement in 98 J. AM. HIST. 723 (2011).

[17] SCALIA SPEAKS, 189, 190. *Accord id.* at 197, 203, 228–29, 266, 269. *See* RICHARD A. BRISBIN, JR., JUSTICE ANTONIN SCALIA AND THE CONSERVATIVE REVIVAL 6 (1997). For other evaluations, *see, e.g.*,

Scalia approached the law as he approached life, on the basis of an all-encompassing world view. That world view was rooted in a set of culturally homogeneous values, attitudes, and behavioral assumptions that he absorbed in the 1940s and 1950s, a world view that supported the era's prevailing embrace of the social and political status quo and that was underwritten by the strict teachings of pre–Vatican Council American Catholicism. It was a world view, Scalia believed, that instantiated the norms that undergirded America's social order and made it stable, cohesive, and morally proper.

Whatever the animating sources of his personal "conscientious and informed convictions," however, one thing about Scalia was certain. Those convictions helped make him a man of passionate beliefs, fierce commitments, and deep resentments who profoundly believed in certain substantive moral, social, and political values. "He was," wrote his close friend and co-author Bryan A. Garner, "a passionate man who, because he thrived on argument, imbued almost every situation with some degree of drama and tension."[18] Few could write with his anger, scorn, and contempt without such driving passions and without an embedded core conviction of his own rightness and righteousness.[19] Most fundamentally, Scalia believed wholeheartedly in the death penalty, market economics, limited government, the centrality of religion, the right to possess firearms, and a broad set of values he considered "traditional." He was adamantly opposed to abortion, gay rights, affirmative action, and a right to assisted suicide.[20] In his mind

DAVID A. SCHULTZ & CHRISTOPHER E. SMITH, THE JURISPRUDENTIAL VISION OF JUSTICE ANTONIN SCALIA (1996); and JAMES B. STAAB, THE POLITICAL THOUGHT OF JUSTICE ANTONIN SCALIA: A HAMILTONIAN ON THE SUPREME COURT (2006).

[18] BRYAN A. GARNER, NINO AND ME: MY UNUSUAL FRIENDSHIP WITH JUSTICE ANTONIN SCALIA 342 (2018).

[19] In both his public statements and judicial opinions "Scalia displayed an unparallelled level of nastiness and sarcasm." RICHARD L. HASEN, THE JUSTICE OF CONTRADICTIONS: ANTONIN SCALIA AND THE POLITICS OF DISRUPTION 67 (2018) [hereafter HASEN, JUSTICE OF CONTRADICTIONS]. See id. at 70 (up to the 2013 term Scalia's sarcastic opinions were more numerous than the combined sarcastic opinions of all of the other justices on the Court with whom he served). For examples of his biting opinions, see Brown v. Plata, 563 U.S. 493, 550 (2011) (Scalia, J., dissenting); Boumedienne v. Bush, 553 U.S. 723, 826 (2008) (Scalia, J., dissenting); Board of Education of Kiryas Joel Village School District v. Grumet, 512 U.S. 687, 732 (1994) (Scalia, J., dissenting)

[20] On abortion, he recognized that "at some point the moral imperatives are so overwhelming that there is no room for prudential compromise" and that his view was "in essence the Church's position regarding laws permitting abortion." SCALIA SPEAKS, at 151. See, e.g., Callins v. Collins, 510 U.S. 1141 (1994) (Scalia, J., concurring in denial of writ of certiorari and rejecting attacks on death penalty); Kansas v. Marsh, 548 U.S. 163, 182 (2006) (Scalia, J., concurring, defending the death penalty); Webster v. Reproductive Health Services 492 U.S. 490, 532 (1989) (Scalia, J., concurring in part and concurring in the judgment and declaring that Roe v. Wade should be overruled); Lawrence v. Texas, 539 U.S. 558, 586 (2003) (Scalia, J., dissenting and attacking decision ruling unconstitutional the criminalization of homosexual conduct); Washington v. Glucksburg, 521 U.S. 702 (1997) (Rehnquist,

two truths were beyond question: His position on each of those issues was morally right, and on each of those issues the Constitution was either fully consistent with his moral position or, at a minimum, failed absolutely to support those who disagreed with him.[21]

In nearly thirty years on the Supreme Court Scalia wrote hundreds of majority opinions and hundreds of separate concurrences and dissents, often speaking only for himself and freely advancing his own distinctive ideas. Those opinions, like his general jurisprudence, were well developed, carefully articulated, and usually forcefully—and often colorfully and bitingly—argued. To consider his body of judicial work opens up virtually the entire corpus of American constitutional law.

Those decisions and opinions came in many varieties. Some addressed issues that were relatively noncontroversial and required only the Court's definitive word, producing unanimous or nearly unanimous decisions.[22] Some dealt with complex questions that divided the Court in unusual or unexpected ways, often because the issues forced the justices to make subtle technical judgments or choose between their own internally conflicting views and values.[23]

Some, too, came to surprisingly "liberal" conclusions that seemed to contradict his image as a "conservative" justice.[24] The great majority, however,

---

C.J., joined by Scalia, J., upholding constitutionality of state statute banning physician-assisted suicide); Grutter v. Bollinger, 539 U.S. 306, 346 (2003) (Scalia, J., concurring in part and dissenting in part and rejecting all forms of affirmative action as unconstitutional racial discrimination).

[21] Scalia insisted, for example, that he did not impose his personal views regarding abortion and homosexual conduct on the Constitution. He maintained only that the Constitution did not protect either and that their legal status was beyond the Constitution's purview and consequently subject to legislative judgment. He was, however, a devout Catholic who subscribed faithfully to Catholic doctrine, and that doctrine held that abortion, suicide, and homosexual conduct were mortally sinful. Although he stated that he was "not a hater of homosexuals," Senior, *In Conversation*, index 3, he also declared that "Catholic teaching" held homosexual conduct "wrong." *Id.* index 4. On church-state relations, moreover, he was willing to ignore the history of Catholic doctrine in order to equate the Church's teaching with American constitutional law. The Catholic "faith's message on the subject," he declared, "is essentially the same as that of the Constitution." SCALIA SPEAKS, 136.

[22] In 2014–2015, for example, the Court decided seventy-six cases on full opinions, and in twenty-eight of them Scalia wrote or joined unanimous opinions. Jon O. Newman, *The Supreme Court— Then and Now*, 19 J. APP. PRAC. & PROCESS 1, 17 (2018).

[23] E.g., Shady Grove Orthopedic Associates v. Allstate Insurance Co., 559 U.S. 393 (2010) (Scalia writing partly for the Court and partly for a plurality composed of Rehnquist, Thomas, and Sotomayor, and partly only for Rehnquist and Thomas; Stevens concurring in part only for himself; and Ginsburg dissenting, joined by Kennedy, Breyer, and Alito); Empire Healthchoice Assurance, Inc. v. McVeigh, 547 U.S. 677 (2006) (Ginsburg writing for Rehnquist, Stevens, Scalia, and Thomas; Breyer dissenting, joined by Kennedy, Souter, and Alito); Pittston Coal Group v. Sebben, 488 U.S. 105 (1988) (Scalia writing for Brennan, Marshall, Blackmun, and Kennedy; Stevens dissenting, joined by Rehnquist, White, and O'Connor).

[24] See generally DAVID M. DORSEN, THE UNEXPECTED SCALIA: A CONSERVATIVE JUSTICE'S LIBERAL OPINIONS (2017) [hereafter DORSEN, UNEXPECTED].

did not.[25] One sympathetic critic of Scalia's jurisprudence, using what seemed an overly broad characterization of "liberal" principles, classified 135 of his some nine hundred opinions as liberal, barely 15 percent of the total.[26]

Scalia's "liberal" opinions surely deserve recognition, especially because in some of them he relied on originalist or textualist arguments. Perhaps most prominent were a handful of Sixth Amendment cases where he wrote opinions that defended an individual right that, in stereotypical political terms, was "pro-criminal" and thus "liberal."[27] One of the judge's "most significant roles, in our system," he declared, was to "protect the individual criminal defendant against the occasional excesses of popular will."[28] To that end, he construed the Confrontation Clause of the Sixth Amendment with what he regarded as originalist and textualist rigor, insisting that "confrontation" meant an actual, unscreened, face-to-face meeting at trial unless witnesses were unavailable and the defendant had previously had the opportunity to cross-examine them.[29] On some issues, too, he construed the Fourth Amendment in a way that provided important protections for criminal defendants. He did so, for example, to limit some government searches and to require probable cause hearings within twenty-four hours of arrest.[30]

---

[25] *E.g.*, Padilla v. Kentucky, 559 U.S. 356. 388 (2010) (Scalia, J., dissenting) (no violation of Sixth Amendment right to counsel if lawyer does not inform client that guilty plea subjected him to automatic deportation); Dickerson v. United States, 530 U.S. 428, 444 (2000) (Scalia, J., dissenting) (rejecting *Miranda* rule and Court's declaration that *Miranda* is a "constitutional" decision); Mitchell v. United States, 526 U.S. 314, 331 (1999) (Scalia, J., dissenting) (denying that Constitution bars jury from drawing unfavorable inference from defendant's refusal to testify); Kansas v. Ventris, 556 U.S. 586 (2009) (Scalia, J.) (narrowing scope of Sixth Amendment to allow use of defendant's statement to jailhouse informer for impeachment purposes).

[26] DORSEN, UNEXPECTED, 25. The author included among twenty-one typical "liberal" positions "respect for and the primacy of the individual," a "broad right to free speech," and "the rule of law and an independent judiciary." *Id.* at 2.

[27] *See. e.g.*, Kyllo v. United States, 533 U.S. 27 (2001) (Scalia, J.) (Fourth Amendment search); Johnson v. United States, 135 S. Ct. 2551 (2015) (Scalia, J.) (Fifth Amendment Due Process Clause); Michigan v. Bryant, 562 U.S. 344, 379 (2011) (Scalia, J., dissenting) (Sixth Amendment Confrontation Clause).

[28] Antonin Scalia, *The Rule of Law as a Law of Rules*, 56 U. CHI. L. REV. 1175, 1180 (1989).

[29] *See, e.g.*, Crawford v. Washington, 541 U.S. 36 (2004) (Scalia, J.) (government cannot use testimony if witness did not testify at trial unless unavailable and defendant had prior opportunity to cross-examine); Maryland v. Craig, 497 U.S. 836, 860 (1990) (Scalia, J., dissenting) (government cannot protect child witnesses by allowing them to testify by closed-circuit television); Coy v. Iowa, 487 U.S. 1012 (1988) (Scalia, J.) (government cannot protect young girls testifying about sexual assault by allowing them to testify behind a screen). There is reason to believe, however, that Scalia's originalist analysis was badly flawed. *See* Bernadette Meyler, *Common Law Confrontation*, 37 L. & HIST. REV. 763 (2019).

[30] *E.g.*, Hicks v. Arizona, 480 U.S. 321 (1987) (Scalia, J.) (holding search invalid because officer, without probable cause, moved stereo equipment slightly in order to locate its serial number); County of Riverside v. McLaughlin, 500 U.S. 44, 59, 66 (1991) (Scalia, J., dissenting) (Fourth Amendment imposes strict limits on government discretion and, absent special circumstances, requires probable cause hearing after arrest within twenty-four hours). Similarly, *e.g.*, in *Maryland v. King*, 569 U.S. 439, 466 (2013), he dissented with Justices Ginsburg, Sotomayor, and Kagan and argued that without

Similarly, Scalia used the Due Process Clause to protect the right of criminal defendants to a jury trial by insisting that all considerations going to
"enhanced" sentencing be found by the jury, not the judge.[31] In addition,
beyond the area of criminal law, he also invoked the Due Process Clause
in cases challenging the constitutionality of "excessive" punitive damages,
thereby adopting what was considered a "liberal" and pro-plaintiff position, one that corporate interests and many Republicans had long assailed.
The "Due Process Clause," he insisted, "provides no substantive protections
against 'excessive' or 'unreasonable' awards of punitive damages."[32]

Although the criminal cases reflected Scalia's suspicion of government
power and the punitive damages cases reflected his rejection of substantive
due process, in both sets of cases he employed originalist reasoning. Those
cases showed that on some occasions Scalia followed his jurisprudential theories to their conclusion even though he likely regretted their consequences.[33]

The cases where Scalia reached "conservative" results, however, were many
times more numerous, and the conclusions he reached in them wholly unsurprising in political and social terms.[34] This category included numerous cases
involving corporate rights, which he favored, and plaintiffs' rights, which he
did not; but most notably it included highly controversial cases involving
abortion, gay rights, gun rights, religion, assisted suicide, and the death penalty. On those issues he used his originalism, textualism, and traditionalism
to readily and directly reach conclusions he believed unalterably right.

Those results were particularly easy to achieve, moreover, with the aid of
the subsidiary interpretive rules he added to his jurisprudence and sometimes invoked: construing traditional rights at their most particularized level

---

probable cause the Fourth Amendment did not allow states to take DNA samples from those in cus-
tody. *Accord* United States v. Jones, 565 U.S. 400 (2012) (Scalia, J.); Florida v. Jardines, 569 U.S. 1
(2013) (Scalia, J.).

[31] Apprendi v. New Jersey, 530 U.S. 466, 498 (2000) (Scalia, J., concurring); Blakely v. Washington,
542 U.S. 296 (2004) (Scalia, J.); Almendarez-Torres, 523 U.S. 224, 248 (1998) (Scalia, J., dissenting).

[32] State Farm Mutual Automobile Insurance Co. v. Campbell, 538 U.S. 408, 429 (2003) (Scalia,
J., dissenting). *Accord* BMW of North America, Inc. v. Gore, 517 U.S. 559, 598 (1996) (Scalia, J.,
dissenting); Philip Morris, U.S.A. v. Williams, 549 U.S. 346, 362 (2009) (Ginsburg, J., dissenting,
joined by Scalia, J.).

[33] A thoughtful analysis of Scalia's jurisprudence and his "liberal" opinions concluded that his originalism and textualism were principled approaches to the Constitution and ones that he generally,
though not always, sought to follow. DORSEN, UNEXPECTED. For a similarly sympathetic, though
somewhat more critical account, *see* RALPH A. ROSSUM, ANTONIN SCALIA'S JURISPRUDENCE: TEXT
AND TRADITION (2006).

[34] As a general matter, Scalia "was a reliable conservative vote on core criminal-law issues." HASEN,
JUSTICE OF CONTRADICTIONS, 156.

of meaning[35] and employing a powerful "rule of silence" whereby subjects not specifically identified in the constitutional text were necessarily beyond judicial authority.[36] Thus, on one track, the First and Second Amendments explicitly mentioned "religion" and "Arms," respectively, while the Fifth Amendment referred to "capital" crimes. Those provisions provided ready textual anchors for the positions he favored on religion, gun rights, and the death penalty.[37] On the other track, the Constitution made no mention of assisted suicide, abortion, or homosexuality. That absence together with his principles of traditionalism, most particularized meaning, and the rule of silence combined to demonstrate to his satisfaction that the Court's decisions protecting rights on those subjects were unfounded and illegitimate.[38]

Those cases showed that on certain issues Scalia seemed to follow the jurisprudential principles he proclaimed and that they led him to predominantly "conservative" results. More to the point, they also showed that on the issues he cared about most intensely his principles allowed him to move invariably and directly to the results he deeply believed right.[39] Indeed, as he framed his originalist jurisprudence, it seemed to guarantee those intensely desired results. Openly, in fact, he identified the "questions that are the easiest for the originalist" as those involving "abortion, assisted suicide, sodomy, the death penalty."[40] His jurisprudential principles, in other words, yielded for him an

[35] Michael H. v. Gerald D., 491 U.S. 110, 127 n.6 (Scalia, J.) (requiring that the Court adopt "the most specific level at which a relevant tradition protecting, or denying protection to, the asserted right can be identified" and claiming that it was necessary "if arbitrary decisionmaking is to be avoided, to adopt the most specific tradition as the point of reference").

[36] E.g., "Since the Constitution of the United States says nothing about this subject [homosexuality], it is left to be resolved by normal democratic means, including the democratic adoption of provisions in state constitutions. This Court has no business imposing upon all Americans the resolution favored by the elite class from which the Members of this institution are selected, pronouncing that 'animosity' toward homosexuality, ante, at 634, is evil." Romer v. Evans, 517 U.S. 620, 636 (1996) (Scalia, J., dissenting). Accord Stenberg v. Carhart, 530 U.S. 914, 953, 956 (2000) (Scalia, J., dissenting) (abortion).

[37] U.S. CONST. amends. 1, 2, 5. For Scalia's views on religion, see, e.g., Lee v. Weisman, 505 U.S. 577, 631 (1992) (Scalia, J., dissenting); Locke v. Davey, 540 U.S. 712, 726 (2004) (Scalia, J., dissenting); Lamb's Chapel v. Center Moriches Union Free School District, 508 U.S. 384, 397 (1993) (Scalia, J., concurring in the judgment). On firearms, see District of Columbia v. Heller, 554 U.S. 570 (2008) (Scalia, J.). On the death penalty, see, e.g., Atkins v. Virginia, 536 U.S. 304, 337 (2002) (Scalia, J., dissenting); Roper v. Simmons, 543 U.S. 551, 607 (2005) (Scalia, J., dissenting); Callins v. Collins, 510 U.S. 1141 (1994) (Scalia, J., concurring).

[38] For Scalia's opinions on abortion, see, e.g., Webster v. Reproductive Health Services, 492 U.S. 490, 532 (1989) (Scalia, J., concurring in part and concurring in the judgment); Stenberg, 530 U.S. at 953 (Scalia, J., dissenting). On assisted suicide, see, e.g., Cruzan v. Missouri Department of Health, 497 U.S. 261, 292 (1990) (Scalia, J., dissenting). On homosexuality, see, e.g., Lawrence, 539 U.S. at 586 (Scalia, J., dissenting); Obergefell v. Hodges, 135 S. Ct. 2584, 2626 (2015) (Scalia, J., dissenting).

[39] See, e.g., SCALIA SPEAKS, at 262.

[40] ANTONIN SCALIA & BRYAN A. GARNER, READING LAW: THE INTERPRETATION OF LEGAL TEXTS 402 (2012). Accord id. at 401 ("the originalist answer is entirely clear" in that the Constitution does

essentially automatic constitutional blessing for his most intensely held personal beliefs.[41] Those cases, then, raise the possibility that those results, and perhaps other constitutional conclusions as well, may have been purposely built in to Scalia's originalism from, as it were, its own Scalian origins.

That possibility means that the examination of another, final category of cases promises to provide a particularly penetrating angle of insight that can yield a far more soundly based and illuminating understanding of both his jurisprudence and his judicial career. That category includes the cases where Scalia applied his originalism dubiously or inconsistently, where he failed to apply it at all, and where he explicitly rejected it. That category, in fact, contains the majority of cases he participated in and, more important, a majority of the opinions he wrote. To fully and fairly evaluate Scalia's jurisprudence, then, it is essential to move beyond the fact that he enthusiastically promoted originalism, claimed to follow it faithfully, and actually applied it in some cases. What is of far greater significance, and far more likely to reveal the true nature of his jurisprudence and judicial career, is his behavior in this last category of cases—a large and broadly inclusive class that encompasses most of the constitutional issues he addressed—cases where he misapplied, manipulated, ignored, rejected, or abandoned the jurisprudential principles he proclaimed.

The hundreds of cases that fell within this last category covered a wide spectrum of legal issues, and Scalia's departures from his jurisprudential principles were frequent, varied, and often extreme. Some involved originalist or textualist reasoning that was strained, unfounded, or simply arbitrary. Some involved reasoning that ignored originalism and textualism altogether. Some treated "tradition" in different ways, sometimes dubiously or misleadingly. Some ignored tradition completely. Many relied on stare decisis, while many others dismissed its significance, seldom attempting to explain in any consistent manner exactly why it was sometimes controlling and sometimes not. In sum, Scalia's application of his jurisprudential principles in these cases was inconsistent and contradictory. Above all, and considered across the board, his conclusions were far more consistent in the social and political results

not guarantee "a right to abortion, or to sodomy, or to assisted suicide"). For Scalia's passionate opposition to the Court's abortion jurisprudence, *see, e.g.*, Hill v. Colorado, 530 U.S. 703, 741, 750 (2000) (Scalia, J., dissenting) (condemning "this Court's relentlessly proabortion jurisprudence").

[41] *E.g.*, United States v. Windsor, 570 U.S. 744, 778 (2013) (Scalia, J., dissenting); Hein v. Freedom from Religion Foundation, Inc., 551 U.S. 587, 618 (2007) (Scalia, J., concurring in the judgment).

they brought than in their underlying methodological practices and juris-prudential reasoning. There was, then, a substantial disjuncture between Scalia's vaunted jurisprudential claims and his actual judicial performance.

Analysis of the cases in this last category promises a broadly based answer to a fundamental question: Was Scalia's originalism a neutral and preformed jurisprudence that just happened to justify the results he favored on the is-sues that he cared about most intensely? Or, conversely, were the issues he cared about most intensely actually the driving force that inspired him to shape a constitutional jurisprudence that would guarantee the results he was determined to reach on those issues? Were his legal conclusions on those is-sues logical deductions from an objective jurisprudence, in other words, or was his jurisprudence a subjectively constructed framework designed to jus-tify those very conclusions?

Scalia's originalism purported to be objective, comprehensive, and au-thoritative. Far more than any of his contemporaries, and probably far more than any other Supreme Court justice in American history, he repeatedly proclaimed his own judicial objectivity and neutrality. "You have to be princi-pled," he insisted, "and I try to be."[42] Persistently and passionately, he assured everyone that his particular jurisprudence of "public meaning" originalism could produce correct answers to constitutional questions and ensure judi-cial fidelity to the Constitution's true meaning. Persistently and passionately, he assured his audiences that he followed and applied that jurisprudence fairly and consistently. "I try to be an honest originalist!" he boasted. "I will take the bitter with the sweet."[43] An examination of this last, extensive cate-gory of cases, the majority of cases he heard, provides a particularly illumi-nating vantage point from which to test his claims.

---

[42] Marcia Coyle, The Roberts Court: The Struggle for the Constitution 165 (2013).
[43] Senior, *In Conversation*, index 1.

4

A Subjective Jurisprudence:
The Structural Constitution

The Constitution of the United States has two structural axes, separation of powers and federalism. The former divides the power of the national government among three distinct branches, while the latter divides power between the national government and the several states. In theory, both structural divisions are designed to protect individual liberties and republican government by ensuring that any abuse of power by one government unit could be checked by another government unit. Scalia grounded his constitutional jurisprudence on his interpretation of those fundamental structural divisions, especially separation of powers, and he claimed that his firmly held views about their nature and application were based on the Founders' original understanding of the Constitution's meaning. They were not. Rather, they were based on his own personal values and goals, and his opinions on the structural Constitution illuminated the subjective and instrumentalist nature of his originalism and textualism.

Separation of Powers

Scalia regarded separation of powers, which he termed somewhat misleadingly "a distinctively American political doctrine,"[1] as the most fundamental principle of American constitutionalism. It was an authentically "originalist" principle that was central to the thinking of the Founders and inscribed in both the text and structure of the Constitution. Long before going on the Court and consistently after joining it he reiterated that conviction. "The principle of separation of powers is expressed in our Constitution in the first

---

[1] Plaut v. Spendthrift Farm, Inc. 514 U.S. 211, 240 (1995) (Scalia, J.). The doctrine has a pedigree that scholars trace back to Aristotle and Polybius. *See,* e.g., SCOTT DOUGLAS GERBER, A DISTINCT JUDICIAL POWER: THE ORIGINS OF AN INDEPENDENT JUDICIARY, 1606–1787, ch. 1 (2011).

Antonin Scalia and American Constitutionalism. Edward A. Purcell, Jr., Oxford University Press (2020).
© Edward A. Purcell, Jr.
DOI: 10.1093/oso/9780197508763.001.0001

section of each of the first three Articles," he explained.[2] It was the "fundamental principle" that served as "the cornerstone of our Constitution and the
North Star of our founding fathers' constellation."[3]

In his Senate confirmation hearing he maintained that the secret of the
Constitution's enduring success was "the structure of government that the
original Constitution established." That meant, he stressed pointedly, "checks
and balances among the three [federal] branches, in particular." The guarantees in the Bill of Rights "by themselves, do not do anything," but the separation of powers prevented each branch from running "roughshod" over
those rights and consequently was essential in preserving "the liberties of
the people."[4] On that general point, he never wavered. "The Framers of the
Federal Constitution" considered "the principle of separation of powers as
the absolutely central guarantee of a just Government," he subsequently
declared from the high bench. "Without a secure structure of separated
powers, our Bill of Rights would be worthless, as are the bills of rights of
many nations of the world that have adopted, or even improved upon, the
mere words of ours."[5]

In addressing separation-of-powers questions Scalia insisted on the necessity of following the original understanding. "If the division of federal
powers central to the constitutional scheme is to succeed in its objective,"
he maintained, "it seems to me that the fundamental nature of those powers
must be preserved as that nature was understood when the Constitution was
enacted."[6] Consistently, he claimed to rely on that original understanding in
addressing a variety of structural issues.

[2] Morrison v. Olson, 487 U.S. 654, 697 (1988) (Scalia, J., dissenting).

[3] Antonin Scalia, comments in Calvin J. Collier, moderator, *Oversight and Review of Agency Decisionmaking: Part II, Morning Session*, 28 ADMIN. L. REV. 661, 684, 693 (1976) [hereafter Collier, *Oversight*].

[4] *Hearings before the Committee on the Judiciary, United States Senate on the Nomination of Judge Antonin Scalia, to be Associate Justice of the Supreme Court of the United States*, 99th Cong., 2d Sess. (Aug. 5–6, 1986), 32 [hereafter *Scalia Hearings*]. *Accord* ANTONIN SCALIA, SCALIA SPEAKS: REFLECTIONS ON LAW, FAITH, AND LIFE WELL LIVED (Christopher J. Scalia & Edward Whelan eds., 2017), 163 [hereafter SCALIA SPEAKS]. Scalia's point paralleled the argument Hamilton made in the ratification debate when he argued that a Bill of Rights was unnecessary and that the liberties of the people were protected by the structure of the original Constitution. THE FEDERALIST PAPERS No. 84, at 514 (Hamilton) (Clinton Rossiter ed., originally published in 1961, with Introduction and Notes by Charles R. Kessler, 2003) [hereafter FEDERALIST PAPERS].

[5] Morrison, 487 U.S. at 697 (Scalia, J., dissenting). "The principle of separation of powers is central to the American system of government," and it "was the single most important guarantee of
freedom." SCALIA SPEAKS, 223. The check against tyranny, he believed, following Madison, lies in
"precisely that jealousy between the branches fostered by the separation of powers." *Id.* at 214.

[6] James B. Beam Distilling Co. v. Georgia, 501 U.S. 529, 548, 549 (Scalia, J., concurring in the
judgment).

There were, however, four fundamental and interrelated problems with Scalia's originalist claims about separation-of-powers issues. First, they required him to read far more into the constitutional text and structure than was actually there and to misconstrue the historical sources relevant to understanding the Constitution's separated national powers. The fact was that the document provided no comprehensive definition of legislative, executive, and judicial powers. Worse, it intermingled those powers in its express provisions and left undetermined most issues involving the proper relationships among the three branches and the borders between their respective powers. Those textual inadequacies were largely the result of the fact that the Founders themselves had only vague, undeveloped, and conflicting ideas about the separation of powers. Beyond the general principle that there were properly three branches of government and the idea that their separation would protect liberty and republican government, they shared no specific understanding of the scope of the three powers, the extent of their separation, or their proper relationships in practice.[7] "Experience has instructed us," Madison wrote in the *Federalist*, "that no skill in the science of government has yet been able to discriminate and define, with sufficient certainty, its three great provinces—the legislative, executive, and judiciary; or even the privileges and powers of the different legislative branches." Then, he confessed the inescapable truth: "Questions daily occur in the course of practice, which prove the obscurity which reigns in these subjects, and which puzzle the greatest adepts in political science."[8]

The Founders themselves repeatedly illustrated the truth of Madison's statement. Alexander Hamilton, the great defender of the federal judiciary, summarized his understanding of the "judicial branch," for example, by claiming that courts had both "judicial and ministerial" duties and that the latter were "performed out of Court and often without reference to it."[9] Hamilton's understanding was totally at odds with what came to be accepted constitutional law as well as with Scalia's own view of the judicial branch.

---

[7] EDWARD A. PURCELL, JR., ORIGINALISM, FEDERALISM, AND THE AMERICAN CONSTITUTIONAL ENTERPRISE: A HISTORICAL INQUIRY 38–47 (2007) [hereafter PURCELL, ORIGINALISM]; William B. Gwyn, *Symposium: Separation of Powers and the Executive Branch; The Reagan Era in Retrospect: The Indeterminacy of the Separation of Powers and the Federal Courts*, 57 GEO. WASH. L. REV. 474, 477–81, 503 (1989); Martin S. Flaherty, *The Most Dangerous Branch*, 105 YALE L.J. 1725, 1755 (1996); Gerhard Casper, *An Essay in Separation of Powers: Some Early Versions and Practices*, 30 WM. & MARY L. REV. 211, 261 (1989) [hereafter Flaherty, *Most Dangerous*].

[8] FEDERALIST PAPERS NO. 37, at 224 (Madison).

[9] GORDON S. WOOD, EMPIRE OF LIBERTY: A HISTORY OF THE EARLY REPUBLIC, 1789–1815, at 413 (2009) [hereafter WOOD, EMPIRE].

Confirming that blurred concept of the judicial power, John Jay served simultaneously as both the nation's first chief justice and its secretary of state, while both he and Oliver Ellsworth, who became chief justice in 1796, conducted diplomatic missions while sitting on the Court.[10] For its part, Congress assigned federal judges nonjudicial—and, in modern thinking, executive or legislative—functions, including responsibility for conducting the census and working to reduce the public debt. "In nearly all cases," Gordon S. Wood pointed out, "the judges willingly accepted these administrative responsibilities."[11] President George Washington's Neutrality Proclamation after the outbreak of war between England and France in 1793 and the subsequent battle over Jay's Treaty in 1795 immediately prompted bitter new disputes over the proper relationship among the federal branches and the practical application of the Constitution's separation of powers.[12] With no specific agreement on either the nature of the three branches or the proper operation of the separation of powers, the Founders had no specifically directive original understanding to incorporate into the Constitution's text or to pass on to later generations.

Second, and consequently, Scalia's readings of the Constitution's separation-of-powers provisions were often overblown and unpersuasive. He maintained that those provisions created a "prescribed structure" that was "carefully designed,"[13] defined a correct institutional "equilibrium,"[14] and mandated an "assigned balance of responsibility and power among the three branches."[15] Understanding the meaning of separation of powers, he maintained, did not depend on amorphous theories or collections of "factors" but simply on "the text of the Constitution and the division of power that it established."[16] In considering the extent to which governmental functions could be intermixed, he insisted that "the Framers *themselves* considered how much commingling was, in the generality of things, acceptable, and set forth their conclusions in the document."[17] Thus, contradicting Madison's recognition of "the obscurity which reigns in these subjects,"

---

[10] GORDON S. WOOD, THE RADICALISM OF THE AMERICAN REVOLUTION 324 (1991).

[11] WOOD, EMPIRE, 413.

[12] PURCELL, ORIGINALISM, 41–43.

[13] Mistretta v. United States, 488 U.S. 361, 413, 426 (1989) (Scalia, J., dissenting).

[14] "The allocation of power among Congress, the President, and the courts [was made] in such a fashion as to preserve the equilibrium the Constitution sought to establish." Morrison v. Olson, 487 U.S. at 699 (Scalia, J., dissenting).

[15] *James B. Beam*, 501 U.S. at 549 (Scalia, J., concurring in the judgment).

[16] *Morrison*, 487 U.S. at 719 (Scalia, J., dissenting).

[17] *Mistretta*, 488 U.S. at 426 (Scalia, J., dissenting) (emphasis in original).

Scalia proclaimed that the bare terms "legislative," "executive," and "judicial" carried an immense amount of detailed constitutional meaning that was far in excess of the limited and contestable meanings that originalist and textualist analysis could fairly support. Indeed, his explicit acknowledgment that the Founders' provisions regarding "commingling" reached only "the generality of things" admitted implicitly the vagueness of the Constitution's terms and their failure to provide specific direction on disputed issues.

Contrary to his opinion in *Morrison v. Olson*, for example, the "executive" power did not include the exclusive authority to "prosecute" crimes because—contrary to his separate opinion in *Young v. United States ex rel. Vuitton*[18]—the "judicial power" included that power with respect to both direct and indirect contempts.[19] Further, in *Mistretta* Scalia himself claimed that the executive actually possessed some power to make law, acknowledging that the lines between the three branches—in that case between the executive and the legislature—were blurred and incomplete.[20] Even more arresting, addressing a complex issue of governmental structure, he conceded that "adjudication" was "no more an 'inherently' judicial function than the promulgation of rules governing primary conduct is an 'inherently' legislative one."[21] Thus, by his own admission the textual provisions he relied on were commonly imprecise and failed to provide the clear lines that his general rhetoric proclaimed.

Third, insofar as Scalia invoked and purported to draw conclusions from the principles of separation of powers, those principles were unexceptionable generalities that did not require the conclusions he favored.[22] They were so abstract that they commanded the general assent of virtually everyone, but they provided little or no specific direction in resolving most of the particular problems the Court confronted. The inconclusive nature of those general principles was apparent, for example, when the Court addressed the divisive issue of the availability of habeas corpus to detainees caught up in the

[18] Young v. United States ex rel. Vuitton, 481 U.S. 787, 815 (1987) (Scalia, J., concurring in the judgment).

[19] *See, e.g.,* Daniel N. Reisman, *Deconstructing Justice Scalia's Separation of Powers Jurisprudence: The Preeminent Executive,* 53 ALBANY L. REV. 49, 55–58, 81–88 (1988) [hereafter Reisman, *Deconstructing*].

[20] *Mistretta*, 488 U.S. at 415 (Scalia, J., dissenting).

[21] Freytag v. Commissioner, 501 U.S. 868, 892, 910 (1991) (Scalia, J., concurring in part and concurring in the judgment).

[22] In his confirmation hearing, Democratic Senator Howell Heflin commented that "I ended the day with a sense and feeling that [Scalia] had been elusive, evasive, and had perhaps overly hidden behind some concepts of separation of powers." *Scalia Hearings,* 121.

"war on terror." In one case Scalia thought issuance of the writ proper. There, he maintained that "[t]he very core of liberty secured by our Anglo-Saxon system of separated powers has been freedom from indefinite imprisonment at the will of the Executive."[23] In another case, however, he thought that issuance of the writ was improper. There, it was the majority he opposed that invoked the "freedom from arbitrary and unlawful restraint and the personal liberty that is secured by adherence to the separation of powers."[24] To that use of separation of powers, Scalia exploded in anger. The majority's analysis, he charged, "distorts the nature of the separation of powers and its role in the constitutional structure."[25] There was, in truth, no "distortion" whatever on either side, only honest disagreement about the significance of inconclusive generalities.

In those two "war-on-terror" cases it was apparent that separation-of-powers principles settled none of the issues raised. The challenges the cases presented were novel, intensely divisive, and of immense practical import, and only the most careful and astute legal, institutional, and practical judgments could hope to resolve them wisely. Indeed, though Scalia defended his position in the latter case by invoking originalist grounds, he began his opinion by stressing the severe dangers that the "war on terror" threatened and highlighted the "disastrous consequences" that would follow the Court's decision. It would, he berated the majority, "almost certainly cause more Americans to be killed."[26] Scalia understood, if he would not admit, that the "principles" of separation of powers resolved nothing in the cases and that the issues raised had of necessity to be settled on relatively specific, practical, and institutional grounds.

[23] Hamdi v. Rumsfeld, 542 U.S. 507, 554, 554–55 (2004) (Scalia, J., dissenting).
[24] Boumediene v. Bush, 553 U.S. 723, 797 (2008) (Kennedy, J.). "[T]he writ of habeas corpus is itself an indispensable mechanism for monitoring the separation of powers." Id. at 765. "It is from these principles that the judicial authority to consider petitions for habeas corpus relief derives." Id. at 797.
[25] Boumediene, 553 U.S. at 833 (2008) (Scalia, J., dissenting). Scalia sought to defend his interpretation of separation of powers by relying on what he proposed unconvincingly as a more faithful method of textual analysis. "The 'fundamental separation-of-powers principles' that the Constitution embodies are to be derived not from some judicially imagined matrix, but from the sum total of the individual separation-of-powers provisions that the Constitution sets forth. Only by considering them one-by-one does the full shape of the Constitution's separation-of-powers principles emerge. It is nonsensical to interpret those provisions themselves in light of some general 'separation-of-powers principles' dreamed up by the Court. Rather, they must be interpreted to mean what they were understood to mean when the people ratified them." Id. at 833 (Scalia, J., dissenting) (emphasis in original).
[26] Boumediene, 553 U.S. at 833, 828 (Scalia, J., dissenting). Unsurprisingly, Scalia attacked the majority justices on the ground that "an inflated notion of judicial supremacy" was "[w]hat drives today's decision." Id. at 842.

In both of those "war-on-terror" cases the justices divided sharply. They were unable to agree on a majority opinion in the first and split 5–4 in the second. It was not any disagreement on the generalities of separation-of-powers principles that divided them, however, but the vexing problem of dealing with distressing new challenges in the light of a vague and nondirective text that could be interpreted to support a variety of conclusions. In truth, the constitutional principles of separation of powers did little more than identify a problem of institutional conflict and suggest the need for a deeply thoughtful resolution compatible with the requirements of practical governmental operations, the maintenance of a critical if sometimes shifting degree of interbranch balance, and the effective protection of the rights and liberties of the people.

Fourth, in separation-of-powers cases Scalia sought to apply a formalistic method that was, consequently, wholly ill suited to the actual judicial task at hand. In *Morrison v. Olson*, where he dissented alone from the Court's decision upholding the Independent Counsel Act, he wrote what was perhaps his most elaborate opinion on separation-of-powers issues.[27] There, he posed the question of the act's constitutionality by reducing a complex issue of intergovernmental relations and the pressing problems involved in checking executive branch abuses to two purportedly simple questions:

> (1) Is the conduct of a criminal prosecution (and of an investigation to decide whether to prosecute) the exercise of purely executive power? (2) Does the statute deprive the President of the United States of exclusive control over the exercise of that power?[28]

Although his purportedly decisive questions presented the issue as one of a clear definition and a dispositive text, the constitutional definition was not clear—much less actually specified—and the statutory text was not dispositive.

Indeed, at times Scalia admitted as much about separation-of-powers issues. In *Morrison*, for example, he conceded that there was "no provision in the Constitution stating who may remove executive officers, except

---

[27] Scalia regarded *Morrison* as his "most impressive opinion" and thought it "devastating— devastating of the majority." Jennifer Senior, *In Conversation: Antonin Scalia*, NEW YORK MAGAZINE, Oct. 6, 2013, *available at* http://nymag.com/nymag/features/antonin-scalia-2013-10/index7.html [hereafter Senior, *In Conversation*].

[28] *Morrison*, 487 U.S. at 705 (Scalia, J., dissenting).

the unhelpful and inadequate provisions for removal by impeachment." On that point he largely abandoned originalism and relied on the Court's precedents.[29] Similarly, in a later case he misstated the scope of the executive power and ignored the fact that it had evolved far beyond the constitutional text. The executive "has no power to bind private conduct in areas not specifically committed to his control by Constitution or statute."[30] Contrary to that statement, the law had long moved beyond the strict text of Article II and held that the president did have the power to bind private conduct through an implied power to make executive agreements with foreign countries without the approval of either the Senate or the Congress as a whole.[31] That power was clearly not "specifically committed" to the executive by the text of the Constitution. More pointedly, as a textual matter it appeared inconsistent with both the Treaty Clause and the Supremacy Clause.[32] Scalia simply glossed over such textual inadequacies and ignored the institutional compromises that marked the changing historical operations of the three branches.[33]

Revealingly, in an effort to make his views in *Morrison* persuasive, Scalia backed up his formalistic reasoning, as he would do again in the later "war-on-terror" cases, with substantive and thought-provoking arguments based on history, precedent, and practical considerations. An "independent" prosecutor, he argued forcefully, could become a ruthless partisan tool, intimidate ordinary executive appointees, deprive the presidency of expert advice, erode public confidence in the administration, unleash an unpredictable prosecutorial discretion, create a force free from responsible political

[29] *Morrison*, 487 U.S. at 723–24 (Scalia, J., dissenting) (quote at 723).

[30] *James B. Beam*, 501 U.S. at 549 (Scalia, J., concurring in the judgment).

[31] United States v. Belmont, 301 U.S. 324 (1937) (Sutherland, J.); United States v. Pink, 315 U.S. 203 (1942) (Douglas, J.) (1942); Dames & Moore v. Regan, 453 U.S. 654 (1981) (Rehnquist, J.). *See, e.g.,* LOUIS HENKIN, FOREIGN AFFAIRS AND THE U.S. CONSTITUTION 215, 219–24 (2d ed. 1996) [hereafter HENKIN, FOREIGN AFFAIRS].

[32] U.S. CONST. art. II, sec. 2, para. 2 (Treaty Clause); art. VI, para. 2 (Supremacy Clause).

[33] Scalia maintained that the Constitution gave the president "complete control" over the executive branch. It "is not for us to determine, and we have never presumed to determine, how much of the purely executive powers of government must be within the full control of the President. The Constitution prescribes that they all are," he declared. Thus, the Court's decision "effects a revolution in our constitutional jurisprudence." *Morrison*, 487 U.S. at 708–09 (Scalia, J., dissenting). As a textual matter, the Constitution did not use the word "complete," mention either investigations or prosecutions, or define the scope of the "executive Power." Further, Scalia often compared the executive to the other two branches, but in so doing he ignored two institutional facts that undermined his assertions. The "delegation" doctrine allowed legislative power out of the hands of Congress, and Article I tribunals and Article III "adjuncts" took considerable practical power from the Article III judiciary. *Id.* at 709–10. Scalia's opinion in *Morrison* "had once again demonstrated the ease with which he could structure his originalism to reach the result he was certain was correct." BRUCE ALLEN MURPHY, SCALIA: A COURT OF ONE 254 (2014) [hereafter MURPHY, SCALIA].

oversight, and disrupt the entire governmental system.[34] Those were weighty
dangers that merited the Court's serious consideration, but they arose from
neither originalist nor textualist sources but from entirely practical and con-
sequentialist concerns.[35]

Similarly, Scalia again grounded his general separation-of-powers analysis
in practical concerns in *Plaut v. Spendthrift Farm, Inc.* There, he defended
his formalistic, bright-line approach on the basis of a realistic institutional
consideration. Denying the power of Congress to reopen "final" judgments
of the federal courts in actions at law, he argued that "the doctrine of separation of powers is a *structural safeguard*" that established "high walls and clear
distinctions because low walls and vague distinctions will not be judicially
defensible in the heat of interbranch conflict."[36] Bright separation-of-powers
lines were essential, in other words, because the formulation and assertion of
such rules served a paramount and highly practical institutional interest of
the judiciary.

Scalia's separation-of-powers opinions were forcefully argued and sometimes compelling for the simple reason that they did not actually rest on his
formalist and originalist claims. Instead, insofar as they were persuasive, they
rested on other more substantial historical, precedential, and practical considerations.[37] Thus, while separation of powers required the drawing of lines,
it was necessary to draw those lines on the basis of quite practical and institutionally effective reasons, not because the Constitution itself had actually
specified them and identified their locations.[38]

[34] *Morrison*, 487 U.S. at 712–15, 727–34 (Scalia, J., dissenting).
[35] Scalia's "eloquent oral statement" in dissent, Justice Stevens later opined, "may have helped to convince some members of Congress that even if the [independent counsel] statute was consti-tutional, it would be unwise to reenact it." JOHN PAUL STEVENS, FIVE CHIEFS: A SUPREME COURT MEMOIR 182 (2011).
[36] *Plaut*, 514 U.S. at 239 (Scalia, J.) (emphasis in original). In *Plaut*, he successfully identified a clear line limiting the power of Congress to reopen judicial judgments. He similarly sought to protect the power of the Article III judiciary in *Stern v. Marshall*, 564 U.S. 462, 503, 504–05 (2011) (Scalia, J., con-curring). *See also Morrison*, 487 U.S. at 710 (Scalia, J., dissenting).
[37] Sometimes his opinions advanced fresh and provocative arguments. In *Mistretta*, he made the nice checks-and-balances argument against the delegation of legislative power to a commission that was not part of either of the other two branches of government. Such a delegation created a special danger of congressional overreaching that the Court should not allow, he argued. As long as legis-lative delegations went to either the executive or the judiciary, Congress would likely employ such delegations more reluctantly and carefully because the other branches were its competitors for fed-eral power. *Mistretta*, 488 U.S. at 421–22 (Scalia, J., dissenting).
[38] The Court has recognized the fact that separation of powers and the idea of checks and bal-ances gave the federal government an intrinsically dynamic quality. "The Constitution sought to di-vide the delegated powers of the new Federal Government into three defined categories, Legislative, Executive, and Judicial, to assure, as nearly as possible, that each branch of government would con-fine itself to its assigned responsibility. The hydraulic pressure inherent within each of the separate

Ultimately, the vagueness of separation-of-powers principles forced Scalia to acknowledge that clear lines between the branches often did not exist. There were, he admitted in a dissent, issues at the "margins, where the outline of the framework itself is not clear."[39] Although the Constitution created legislative, executive, and judicial branches, he conceded in another opinion, "it does not attempt to define those terms." Instead, he retreated to the vague proposition that the "central mechanism of separation of powers depends largely upon common understanding of what activities are appropriate to legislatures, to executives, and to courts."[40] In novel or controverted cases, a standard based on such a "common understanding" was as plausible as it was nondeterminative, nontextualist, and nonoriginalist.

Understandably, then, issues involving the doctrine of delegation of powers proved particularly troublesome for Scalia. Although he could state the formal doctrine readily,[41] he nonetheless recognized the difficulty of applying it with any degree of strictness. It was "very difficult for the courts to say how much delegation is too much," he told the Senate Judiciary Committee in his confirmation hearing. He concluded "that, in most cases, the courts are just going to have to leave that constitutional issue to be resolved by the Congress."[42]

In *Mistretta v. United States*, a case challenging the sentencing guidelines promulgated by the U.S. Sentencing Commission on the ground that

---

Branches to exceed the outer limits of its power, even to accomplish desirable objectives, must be resisted." Immigration and Naturalization Service v. Chadha, 462 U.S. 919, 951 (1982) (Burger, C.J.).

[39] *Mistretta*, 488 U.S. at 426 (Scalia, J., dissenting). *Accord Vuitton*, 481 U.S. at 821 (Scalia, J., concurring in the judgment) (the "implicit powers" of the branches "may take a form that appears to be nonlegislative, nonexecutive, or nonjudicial respectively"); Printz v. United States, 521 U.S. 898, 927–28 (1997) (Scalia, J.) ("Executive action that has utterly no policymaking component is rare, particularly at an executive level as high as a jurisdiction's chief law enforcement officer," and therefore "we would have to fall back upon a line of 'not too much policymaking.' How much is too much is not likely to be answered precisely").

[40] Lujan v. Defenders of Wildlife, 504 U.S. 555, 559–60 (1992) (Scalia, J.). He again relied on the same vague standard when he tried to draw a line between executive and judicial power. "The Constitution's line of demarcation between the Executive power and the judicial power," he wrote, "presupposes a common understanding of the type of interest needed to sustain a 'case or controversy' against the Executive in the courts." Federal Election Commission v. Akins, 524 U.S. 11, 29, 36 (Scalia, J., dissenting).

[41] "But the Constitution guarantees not merely that no branch will be forced by one of the other branches to let someone else exercise its assigned powers—but that none of the branches will *itself* alienate its assigned powers. Otherwise, the doctrine of unconstitutional delegation of legislative power (which delegation cannot plausibly be compelled by one of the other branches) is a dead letter." Peretz v. United States, 501 U.S. 923, 952, 955–56 (1991) (Scalia, J., dissenting) (emphasis in original).

[42] *Scalia Hearings*, 40.

Congress had unconstitutionally delegated lawmaking power to the com-mission, he made an even more revealing admission.

> Once it is conceded, as it must be, that no statute can be entirely precise,
> and that some judgments, even some judgments involving policy consider-
> ations, must be left to the officers executing the law and to judges applying
> it, the debate over unconstitutional delegation becomes a debate not over a
> point of principle but over a question of degree.[43]

A "certain degree of discretion, and thus of lawmaking, *inheres* in most exec-utive or judicial action," he continued, "and it is up to Congress, by the rela-tive specificity or generality of its statutory commands, to determine—up to a point—how small or how large that degree shall be."[44] Article I "legislative Powers" could not be exercised by any branch but Congress, in other words, except that they could also be exercised—and regularly had to be exercised—by both the executive and judiciary. The two other branches, however, could only exercise those legislative powers "up to a point," an imprecise limit sim-ilar to the equally imprecise "generality of things" limit he offered in the same opinion. Those theoretical "limits" were vague and unhelpful, and neither the constitutional text nor the original understandings of the Founders clar-ified them further.[45]

In truth, the questions that the Constitution and originalist sources did actually resolve had long been settled, either because the Founders had adopted explicit language in some constitutional provisions or because they had agreed on specific practices that became embedded in the nation's polit-ical and constitutional culture. Given the express terms of Article I, no one disputed the executive's power to veto congressional legislation, for example, just as no one disputed the power of Congress to override the executive's

---

[43] *Mistretta*, 488 U.S. at 415 (Scalia, J., dissenting). Consequently, "it is small wonder that we have almost never felt qualified to second-guess Congress regarding the permissible degree of policy judg-ment that can be left to those executing or applying the law." *Id.* at 416. *Accord* Clinton v. New York, 524 U.S. 417, 458, 465 (1998) (Scalia, J., dissenting) (the delegation/separation-of-powers issue was "whether the authorizations *went too far* by transferring to the Executive a *degree* of political, law-making power that our traditions demand be retained by the Legislative Branch" (emphasis added)).

[44] *Mistretta*, 488 U.S. at 417 (Scalia, J., dissenting) (emphasis in original).

[45] Even making such admissions, Scalia still tried to rescue his bright-line separation-of-powers ideas. "Strictly speaking, there is *no* acceptable delegation of legislative power," he declared, quoting John Locke as a respectable originalist source. *Mistretta*, 488 U.S. at 419 (Scalia, J., dissenting) (em-phasis in original). There was an absolute category of prohibited delegation, the "pure delegation of legislative power" that was a delegation "completely divorced from any responsibility for execution of the law or adjudication of private rights under the law." *Id.* at 420.

veto by a two-thirds vote of both Houses.[46] In contrast, the questions that originalist and textual sources did not settle were the live and controversial questions that the Founders themselves disputed or that subsequently arose as times, issues, conditions, challenges, and institutions changed. All of those questions required for their resolution not simple scrutiny of the constitutional text or a survey of eighteenth-century notions but sagacious judgments about contemporary conditions and governmental operations.

Scalia, in fact, understood that ultimate truth. Despite his theoretical claims about originalism and textualism, he did not develop his separation-of-powers jurisprudence by simply reading the words of the Founders and the text of the Constitution. Rather, he did so by construing the Constitution in light of his own personal values and political goals. Personally, he was suspicious of Congress, deeply distrustful of the federal judiciary, and above all fiercely loyal to the idea of a powerful and independent executive power.[47] His determination to shape the law to reflect those attitudes and serve his institutional goals drove his separation-of-powers jurisprudence.

Scalia's wholehearted devotion to the executive branch likely had roots in the strict and hierarchical nature of his family and religious upbringing, but his wholehearted commitment to the Nixon and Ford administrations intensified and hardened that devotion. Confronting the politics of Watergate, the threat of presidential impeachment, judicial limitation on the power of the executive, and extensive congressional efforts to rein in executive power, he deeply resented what he saw as the humiliations that the Democrats and the other two branches of government were inflicting on the presidency and the Republican Party.[48] "It was a terrible time" for the executive branch, he later recalled. "It was such a wounded and enfeebled presidency, and Congress

[46] U.S. Const. art. I, sec. 7, para. 2.

[47] Scalia was willing, for example, to ignore a separation-of-powers problem when the result was to constrain federal judicial power to order prison reforms. Miller v. French, 530 U.S. 327 (2000) (O'Connor, J., joined by Scalia). See id. at 350–51 (Souter, J., concurring in part and dissenting in part). Scalia had no sympathy for judicial efforts to supervise prison conditions and sought to limit them sharply. See, e.g., Wilson v. Seiter, 501 U.S. 294 (1991) (Scalia, J.); Lewis v. Casey, 518 U.S. 343 (1996) (Scalia, J.).

[48] Murphy, Scalia, 73–78. Congressional rejection of Scalia's efforts to protect Nixon's ownership of the Watergate tapes was one of the episodes "that caused Scalia to jealously guard executive power and, in an atmosphere of distrust and suspicion, to consider Congress an adversary." Joan Biskupic, American Original: The Life and Constitution of Supreme Court Justice Antonin Scalia 44 (2009) [hereafter Biskupic, American Original]. The expansion of the Freedom of Information Act over President Gerald Ford's veto was another similar episode. It was "a formative moment for Scalia and Cheney. It was part of the genesis of their respective concerns over a wearing down of executive power." Id. at 47. On the efforts of Congress to rebalance federal power after Watergate, see James L. Sundquist, The Decline and Resurgence of Congress (1981). On the Court's limitation of executive power at the time, see United States v. Nixon, 418 U.S. 683 (1974).

was eating us alive."[49] From his position as head of the Office of Legal Counsel Scalia vigorously defended the administration's use of electronic surveillance and covert actions by the Central Intelligence Agency,[50] and before congressional committees he repeatedly defended it on a variety of issues, especially its assertions of executive privilege. By the end of his service in the executive branch in 1977 Scalia had become an inveterate, battle-tested, and passionately devoted advocate of executive power.

His vigorously stated claims about executive privilege revealed not only his commitment to the executive branch but, once again, the indeterminate nature of separation-of-powers principles. "Executive privilege," he insisted, "is indispensable to the functioning of our system of checks and balances and separation of powers."[51] However plausible that claim, it was like so many of the other claims he made about separation of powers. It had no support in the Constitution's text, which made no mention of such a privilege, and no clear support from originalist sources, which revealed nothing but uncertainty and disagreement. Indeed, in spite of a long history of disputes and compromises between Congress and the presidency, the Court itself did not even attempt to address the issue until almost two hundred years after the Founding.[52] Once he was on the Court, Scalia was forced to admit that executive privilege was "a protection of somewhat uncertain scope." Consequently, he added ruefully, presidents who invoked it risked suffering "political damage."[53]

Scalia's subsequent identification with the Reagan administration and its goals confirmed and strengthened his commitment to executive power. When the administration found that the Independent Counsel Act was

[49] Senior, *In Conversation*, Index 1.

[50] MURPHY, SCALIA, 68–73. "It was in the area of foreign policy that Scalia learned the most about the power of the presidency, and demonstrated the lengths to which he would go to protect that power." *Id.* at 70. On Scalia's work in the Nixon and Ford administrations, *see id.*, ch. 5.

[51] MURPHY, SCALIA, 74. Scalia "had an authoritarian instinct and a natural inclination to jealously guard presidential papers and prerogatives. He was suspicious of members of Congress." BISKUPIC, AMERICAN ORIGINAL, 51. On the relationship between executive branch service and pro-executive and conservative political leanings, *see, e.g.,* Michael C. Dorf, *Does Federal Executive Branch Experience Explain Why Some Republican Supreme Court Justices "Evolve" and Others Don't?,* 1 HARV. L. & POL'Y REV. 457 (2007); Rob Robinson, *Executive Branch Socialization and Deference on the U.S. Supreme Court,* 46 L. & SOC. REV. 889 (2012).

[52] One of the first battles over executive privilege occurred between the Washington administration and the House of Representatives over the Jay Treaty. *See, e.g.,* DAVID P. CURRIE, THE CONSTITUTION IN CONGRESS: THE FEDERALIST PERIOD, 1789–1801, at 20–32, 36–42 (1997). The Court's first effort to define "executive privilege" did not come until *United States v. Nixon,* 418 U.S. 683 (1974), and its opinion made the application of the privilege dependent on careful judgments based on specific issues, contexts, and consequences.

[53] Webster v. Doe, 486 U.S. 592, 606, 621 (1988) (Scalia, J., dissenting).

causing it serious problems, it "waged a long and bitter campaign" against it.[54] Just as Scalia had been committed to the stalwart defense of the Nixon and Ford administrations, he was equally committed to a vigorous defense of the Reagan administration. In *Morrison* he dissented alone and at length, carefully molding the amorphous principles of separation of powers to support the administration and condemn as unconstitutional the statute it opposed.[55]

Scalia developed his separation-of-powers jurisprudence, then, not by plumbing originalist and textualist sources to identify the Constitution's "true" meaning but by purposely shaping jurisprudential sources to serve his own intense personal commitment to protect and enhance executive power. *Morrison, Mistretta*, and his other separation-of-powers opinions sought in varying ways to do exactly that, just as his opinions in many other doctrinal areas were designed to accomplish the same result. His opinions involving standing and the Administrative Procedure Act served to insulate executive power,[56] while his defense of the *Chevron* doctrine,[57] which required the courts to defer to reasonable agency interpretations of the statutes they administered, similarly expanded the authority and flexibility of executive agencies.[58]

Most broadly, his theory of the "unitary" executive served that purpose in a variety of areas. It claimed that all "executive power" was under the sole authority of the president and in large part beyond the control of the other two branches.[59] That theory would give the president total control of the executive

---

[54] Walter F. Murphy, *Reagan's Judicial Strategy, in* LOOKING BACK ON THE REAGAN PRESIDENCY (Larry Berman ed., 1990), 226.

[55] "The Reagan administration's very open and public embrace of the theory of the unitary executive in the 1980s led to several high-profile judicial decisions in addition to the decisions in *Morrison v. Olson* and *INS v. Chadha.*" STEVEN G. CALABRESI & CHRISTOPHER S. YOO, THE UNITARY EXECUTIVE: PRESIDENTIAL POWER FROM WASHINGTON TO BUSH 13 (2008) [hereafter CALABRESI & YOO, UNITARY EXECUTIVE].

[56] Reisman, *Deconstructing*, 49, 50.

[57] Chevron, U.S.A., Inc. v. National Resources Defense Council, 467 U.S. 837 (1984) (Stevens, J.).

[58] "Some additional power will go to the executive" under *Chevron*, Scalia acknowledged. SCALIA SPEAKS, 240. *See, e.g.*, United States v. Mead Corp., 533 U.S. 218, 237, 257 (2001) (Scalia, J., dissenting) (supporting *Chevron* because it "sets forth an across-the-board presumption, which operates as a background rule of law against which Congress legislates"). Setting aside originalist concerns, Scalia defended *Chevron* on the ground that it was necessary in light of the broad changes in the way government operated in the twentieth century. "Broad delegation to the Executive," he wrote, "is the hallmark of the modem administrative state." Antonin Scalia, *Judicial Deference to Administrative Interpretations of Law*, 1989 DUKE L.J. 511, 516 (1989). Surprisingly, he defended *Chevron* on that practical ground rather than on separation-of-powers principles, a proposed justification for *Chevron* that he specifically rejected as too rigid and judicially limiting. *Id.* at 515–16.

[59] *See generally Morrison*, 487 U.S. at 697 (Scalia, J., dissenting) (president holds all executive power and must control all federal prosecutorial officials); *Vuitton*, 481 U.S. at 815 (Scalia, J., concurring in the judgment) (power to appoint prosecutor for contempt proceeding not a judicial power but solely

branch, insulate high federal officials from independent prosecutors, severely limit the ability of both Congress and the courts to check executive abuses, and broadly expand both the power and independence of the president and the whole executive branch.[60] In *Mistretta*, for example, he declared that notwithstanding the fact that Congress was the legislative branch, the president held basic policymaking and even lawmaking authority "in a few areas constitutionally committed to the Executive Branch."[61] As one scholar concluded, "Justice Scalia's vision of a powerful and largely unchecked executive power—and not a neutral, textually based theory of separation of powers—is the transcendent guiding principle of his jurisprudence."[62]

Although Scalia claimed an originalist pedigree for his separation-of-powers jurisprudence, originalist sources were wholly inadequate to carry the weight he assigned them. The ultimate problems with his separation-of-powers jurisprudence, then, were twofold. It hypothesized bright lines where few such lines existed, and it was driven not by originalism and textualism but by his own personal values, primarily his determination to protect and expand executive power while limiting both Congress and the Court.[63]

an executive power and a power that is discretionary). For specific statements, *see, e.g.*, Franklin v. Massachusetts, 505 U.S. 788, 823, 826 (1992) (Scalia, J., concurring in part and concurring in the judgment) ("no court has authority to direct the President to take an official act"); *Boumediene*, 553 U.S. at 843 (Scalia, J., dissenting) (limits on habeas corpus "entrust the President with the crucial wartime determinations about [the] status and continued confinement" of enemy aliens); Clinton v. New York, 524 U.S. 417, 458, 465 (1998) (Scalia, J., dissenting on separation of powers grounds to protect the power of the executive to cancel, under congressional authorization, individual budgetary spending items); Rasul v. Bush, 542 U.S. 466, 488, 499, 501 (2004) (Scalia, J., dissenting) (condemning Court for requiring "courts to oversee one aspect of the Executive's conduct of a foreign war" and citing precedent that the president is "exclusively responsible" for the "conduct of diplomatic and foreign affairs"); Chaney v. Heckler, 718 F. 2d 1174, 1192, 1198 (2d Cir. 1983) (Scalia, J., dissenting) (allowing judicial review of agency constituted the "shattering of well established barriers separating the proper business of the executive and judicial branches"). On the unitary executive idea historically, *see* CALABRESI & YOO, UNITARY EXECUTIVE.

[60] *See, e.g.*, Philip J. Weiser, *Towards a Constitutional Architecture for Cooperative Federalism*, 79 N. C. L. REV. 663 (2001); Lawrence Lessig & Cass R. Sunstein, *The President and the Administration*, 94 COLUM. L. REV. 1 (1994); Flaherty, *Most Dangerous*.

[61] *Mistretta*, 488 U.S. at 415 (Scalia, J., dissenting). *See, e.g., Webster*, 486 U.S. at 614 (Scalia, J., dissenting) ("Indeed, it seems to me that if one is in a mood to worry about serious constitutional questions the one to worry about is not whether Congress can . . . give the President . . . unreviewable discretion in firing the agents that he employs to gather military and foreign affairs intelligence, but rather whether Congress could constitutionally permit the courts to review all such decisions if it wanted to.").

[62] Reisman, *Deconstructing*, 50. For an insightful examination of the underdetermined, dynamic, and intrinsically political nature of separation of powers, *see, e.g.*, JOSH CHAFETZ, CONGRESS'S CONSTITUTION: LEGISLATIVE AUTHORITY AND THE SEPARATION OF POWERS (2017).

[63] Scalia wanted bright lines wherever possible, and he claimed to find them in many areas. *See, e.g.*, Thompson v. Thompson, 484 U.S. 174, 188, 191 (1988) (Scalia, J., concurring in the judgment) (no right of action should ever be implied); *Plaut*, 514 U.S. 211 (Congress can never reopen a federal judgment at law for damages); *Stern*, 564 U.S. at 504–05 (Scalia, J., concurring) (clear lines regarding

Federalism

Scalia's commitment to federalism did not match his far more fervent commitment to separation of powers. That marked divergence in his views was both curious and revealing.[64] It was curious because separation of powers and federalism enjoyed equal status as the Constitution's two underlying structural axes. It was revealing because Scalia's different regard for the two highlighted the distinctive nature of his own views and illustrated both the inadequacies of his originalism and the extent to which his personal values and goals shaped his thinking about the structural Constitution.

There has never been a dispute over the fact that the Founders incorporated the principles of both separation of powers and federalism in the Constitution or that both principles were fundamental to its original design. Mountains of eighteenth-century sources and a variety of explicit constitutional provisions testified to the foundational nature of both. Few passages were more famous or regarded as more authoritative than Madison's description of the Constitution's architectural design in *Federalist No. 51*:

> In the compound republic of America, the power surrendered by the people is first divided between two distinct governments, and then the portion allotted to each subdivided among distinct and separate departments. Hence a double security arises to the rights of the people. The different governments will control each other, at the same time that each will be controlled by itself.[65]

requirement of Article III judges for federal adjudication); Shady Grove Orthopedic Associates v. Allstate Insurance Co., 559 U.S. 393 (2010) (Scalia, J.) (bright line construction of F.R.C.P. Rule 23 preferable to honoring federalism values); Burnham v. Superior Court of California, 495 U.S. 604, 607, 623 (1990) (Scalia, J.) (rejecting proposed test for personal jurisdiction as requiring "subjective assessment of what is fair and just"). Scalia rejected a "proportionality" principle in Eighth Amendment cases precisely because it was "an invitation to imposition of subjective values." Harmelin v. Michigan, 501 U.S. 957, 1986 (1991) (Scalia, J., announcing judgment of Court and partial opinion for the Court). Absent a clear statement by Congress mandating a "totality of the circumstances" test, "courts properly assume that "categorical decisions may be appropriate and individual circumstances disregarded when a case fits into a genus in which the balance characteristically tips in one direction." Antonin Scalia, *The Rule of Law as a Law of Rules*, 56 U. CHI. L. REV. 1175, 1183 (1989) (quoting United States Department of Justice v. Reporters Committee, 109 S Ct 1468, 1483 (1989) (Stevens, J., joined by Scalia, J.)..

[64] Scholars noted Scalia's different attitude toward the two structural principles early in his judicial career. *See* M. David Gelfand & Keith Werhan, *Federalism and Separation of Powers on a "Conservative" Court: Currents and Cross-Currents from Justices O'Connor and Scalia*, 64 TULSA L. REV. 1443, 1456–57, 1460 (1990) [hereafter Gelfand & Werhan, *Federalism*].

[65] FEDERALIST PAPERS No. 51, at 320 (Madison). Scalia quoted this passage, for example, in his opinion for the Court in *Printz v. United States*, 521 U.S. at 922.

Separation of powers and federalism were twin structural components designed to secure, in combination, the people's liberties and their right of self government.

Yet Scalia distinguished sharply between the two. He honored and sought to implement separation-of-powers principles far more rigorously and creatively than he did federalism principles. It was the former, not the latter, that captured his imagination and that he sought most assiduously to bend to his own particular and calculated purposes.

Scalia's different attitude toward the two structural axes was most strikingly apparent during his confirmation hearings. While he assured the Senate Judiciary Committee that he was committed to showing deference to Congress, he stressed that he would be especially deferential on federalism issues. A federalism dispute, he testified, most commonly presented "a question of prudence," and that meant that "it is most often a question for this body to decide, when it wishes to displace State law, and when not." Asked specifically about his "general philosophy of the role of the judiciary relative to federalism," he responded that "the primary defender of the constitutional balance" on federalism issues and "the primary institution to strike the right balance is the Congress." For emphasis, he reiterated his point, insisting that the maintenance of the proper federalism balance "is essentially the function of the Congress."[66]

Indeed, going even further, he assured the committee that the courts had been wise to abandon the job of policing the federal-state boundary. That deferential conclusion, he continued, was the result of sound judicial reasoning.

> I think what the Supreme Court decisions on the subject show is that it is very hard to find a distinct justiciable line between those matters that are appropriate for the states and those that are appropriate for the Federal Government, that finding that line is much easier for a legislator than for a court.[67]

His embrace of judicial deference on federalism issues seemed to accept the Court's reasoning the previous year in *Garcia v. San Antonio Metropolitan Transit Authority*, where it had ruled that Congress, not the federal judiciary,

---

[66] *Scalia Hearings*, 33, 81 (question by Senator Howell Heflin).
[67] *Scalia Hearings*, 82. Federalism issues, he had previously argued, required essentially pragmatic judgments of policy. Antonin Scalia, *The Two Faces of Federalism*, 6 HARV. J.L. & PUB. POL'Y 19, 20 (1982) [hereafter Scalia, *Two Faces*].

was the proper constitutional guardian of the states.[68] "The court's struggles to prescribe what is the proper role of the Federal Government vis-a-vis the State," Scalia acknowledged, "have essentially been abandoned for quite a while."[69]

Although he told the Senate Judiciary Committee that he regarded the enforcement of federalism principles as "essentially the function of the Congress," he refused to do the same with separation-of-powers principles. Judicial deference was not appropriate in applying the axial principle that was "the North Star of our founding fathers' constellation."[70] Indeed, in *Morrison* he insisted that the deference ordinarily due to congressional statutes—even those that impinged severely on state powers and raised federalism questions—did not apply in separation-of-powers cases.

> Where a private citizen challenges action of the Government on grounds unrelated to separation of powers, harmonious functioning of the system demands that we ordinarily give some deference, or a presumption of validity, to the actions of the political branches in what is agreed, between themselves at least, to be within their respective spheres. But where the issue pertains to separation of powers, and the political branches are (as here) in disagreement, neither can be presumed correct.[71]

Accordingly, he argued, the federal courts had broad authority to decide separation-of-powers issues in spite of the far more limited role they properly played in federalism disputes.

Exemplifying his jurisprudential inconsistency as well as his driving ideological goals, however, once safely seated on the high bench Scalia was quite ready to cast aside the deferential principles he had claimed before the Senate Judiciary Committee and enforce more stringent federalism limits on

---

[68] In an opinion that had broken with prior law, the conservative justices had maintained that the Court had a special duty to protect the rights and interests of the states. National League of Cities v. Usury, 426 U.S. 833 (1976) (Rehnquist, J.). Only the year before Scalia's testimony, however, over a strong dissent by Rehnquist, *National League*'s author, the Court's liberals had succeeded in getting a majority to overrule *National League*. Garcia v. San Antonio Metropolitan Transit Authority, 469 U.S. 528, 532 (1985) (Blackmun, J.). The liberal majority maintained that the constitutional structure enabled the states to protect themselves through their power in the national government and, consequently, that the judiciary's proper role lay not in protecting the states but in enforcing national law. *Id.* at 550–54.

[69] Scalia, *Hearings*, 82. "I think what I am saying is that on the basis of the court's past decisions, at any rate, the main protection for [the states] in the policymaking area, is in the Congress." *Id.*

[70] Scalia, *Hearings*, at 32; Collier, *Oversight*, 693.

[71] *Morrison*, 487 U.S. at 704–05 (Scalia, J., dissenting).

both Congress and the federal courts. Less than two years after his confirmation hearing, he began reversing position. In *South Carolina v. Baker* he questioned the Court's deferential reasoning in *Garcia* and seemed to suggest that the Tenth Amendment imposed its own independent limits on the federal government.[72] Subsequently, he declared that there were, after all, bright constitutional lines that limited federal power over the states and that the courts properly enforced. "It is the very *principle* of separate state sovereignty that such a law offends," he ruled in voiding a federal statute in 1997, "and no comparative assessment of the various interests can overcome that fundamental defect."[73] As a textual matter, of course, the Constitution did not mention any "principle of separate state sovereignty" nor ever even use the constitutionally ambiguous word "sovereignty" itself.

Notwithstanding his contrary assurances to the Senate Judiciary Committee, then, in the early 1990s Scalia joined the Court's other four conservatives in pressing what came to be called a "federalism revolution" that was designed to reduce the power of both Congress and the federal judiciary over the states. In a series of 5–4 decisions he joined the new conservative majority in limiting federal judicial power by enhancing state immunity from suit in the federal courts under the Eleventh Amendment and by restricting congressional power on three related fronts. The five conservatives narrowed the general scope of Congress's power under the Commerce Clause, completely denied its power to subject states to liability under the Commerce Clause, and severely restricted its power to impose liability on the states under Section 5 of the Fourteenth Amendment. In little more than a decade the five made significant changes in the law of federalism, all restricting the power of Congress and the federal courts and strengthening the independence of the states.[74]

In those major "federalism revolution" cases Scalia took a less prominent role and wrote less commonly for the conservative majority than he did in

---

[72] South Carolina v. Baker, 485 U.S. 505, 528 (1988) (Scalia, J., concurring in part and concurring in the judgment) (limiting *Garcia* and seemingly agreeing with Rehnquist's opinion concurring in the judgment that defended a substantive Tenth Amendment).

[73] *Printz*, 521 U.S. at 935 (Scalia, J.) (emphasis in original). Conversely, Scalia privileged the text of a congressional statute over general "federalism" concerns in *City of Columbus v. Ours Garage and Wrecker Service*, 536 U.S. 424, 442, 447–50 (2002) (Scalia, J., dissenting).

[74] *See generally* THOMAS M. KECK, THE MOST ACTIVIST SUPREME COURT IN HISTORY: THE ROAD TO MODERN JUDICIAL CONSERVATISM 236–43 (2004); Symposium, *Federalism after Alden, 31 Rutgers L. Rev. 631 (2000)*; Symposium, *Shifting the Balance of Power? The Supreme Court, Federalism, and State Sovereign Immunity*, 53 STAN. L. REV. 1115 (2001). In 2011, late in his career, Scalia condemned Congress for making "extravagant" inroads on the powers of both the other federal branches and the states. SCALIA SPEAKS, 216.

separation-of-powers cases.[75] Instead, he generally joined the opinions of others, most prominently those of Chief Justice Rehnquist.[76] In 1989, however, before the conservatives had gained a solid fifth vote with the appointment of Justice Clarence Thomas in 1991, he wrote a dissenting opinion for Rehnquist and Justices O'Connor and Kennedy rejecting the power of Congress to impose liability on states under the Commerce Clause. There, in *Pennsylvania v. Union Gas Co.*, he vigorously defended the states' "sovereign prerogative of immunity" and characterized the Eleventh Amendment as authoritatively "enunciating a fundamental principle of federalism."[77]

Once the conservative majority had formed and began its "federalism revolution," Scalia did write for it on occasion.[78] He likely enjoyed especially the opportunity he had in 1999 to both overturn a decision of the Warren Court and to confirm that his own earlier dissent in *Union Gas* had become the law. There, in the *College Savings Bank* case he charged that the Warren Court's decision, written by its liberal pillar, Justice William Brennan, "stands as an anomaly in the jurisprudence of sovereign immunity, and indeed in the jurisprudence of constitutional law." It was "ill-conceived" and "broke sharply with prior cases," and there was "no merit in attempting to salvage any remnant of it." "Whatever may remain" of it, he declared emphatically, "is expressly overruled."[79]

Though Scalia turned his back on the deferential federalism principles he had announced in his confirmation hearing and consistently supported the

---

[75] On occasion Scalia refused to push federalism doctrines as far as Rehnquist and Kennedy wished. *Compare, e.g.*, Idaho v. Coeur d'Alene Tribe of Idaho, 521 U.S. 261 (1997) (Kennedy, J., joined by Rehnquist, C.J.), *with id.* at 288 (O'Connor, J., joined by Scalia, J., concurring in part and concurring in the judgment); Quackenbush v. Allstate Insurance Co., 517 U.S. 706, 731 (Scalia, J., concurring), *with id.* at 733 (Kennedy, J., concurring); New Orleans Public Service, Inc. v. Council of the City of New Orleans, 491 U.S. 350 (1989) (Scalia, J., *with id.* at 373 (Rehnquist, C.J., concurring in only two parts of Scalia's opinion and concurring in the judgment).

[76] *E.g.*, United States v. Lopez, 514 U.S. 549 (1995) (Rehnquist, C.J.); Seminole Tribe of Florida v. Florida, 517 U.S. 44 (1996) (Rehnquist, C.J.); Florida Prepaid Postsecondary Education Expense Fund v. College Savings Bank, 527 U.S. 627 (1999) (Rehnquist, C.J.); United States v. Morrison, 529 U.S. 598 (2000) (Rehnquist, C.J.). For Scalia's agreement with similar federalism opinions written by the other conservative justices, *see, e.g.*, New York v. United States, 505 U.S. 144 (1992) (O'Connor, J.); Alden v. Maine, 527 U.S. 706 (1999) (Kennedy, J.); Kimel v. Florida Board of Regents, 528 U.S. 62 (2000) (O'Connor, J.); Federal Maritime Commission v. South Carolina State Ports Authority, 535 U.S. 743 (2002) (Thomas, J.); Coleman v. Court of Appeals of Maryland, 566 U.S. 30 (2012) (Kennedy, J., joined by Rehnquist, C.J. and Thomas and Alito, JJ.; Scalia, J., concurring in the judgment).

[77] Pennsylvania v. Union Gas Co., 491 U.S. 1, 29, 37 (1989) (Scalia, J., dissenting, joined by Rehnquist, C.J. and O'Connor and Kennedy, JJ.).

[78] *See, e.g.*, Armstrong v. Exceptional Child Center, 135 S. Ct. 1378 (2015) (Scalia, J.).

[79] College Savings Bank v. Florida Prepaid Postsecondary Education Expense Board, 527 U.S. 666, 680 (1999) (Scalia, J.). The case Scalia overruled was *Parden v. Terminal Railway Co.*, 377 U.S. 184 (1964) (Brennan, J.).

conservatives' "federalism revolution,"[80] he remained true to his long and firmly held position on the primary importance of separation of powers. Over the years he deployed its principles broadly, purposefully, and creatively. His stronger commitment to separation of powers was apparent, for example, in his standing jurisprudence. Repeatedly he insisted that separation of powers shaped standing doctrine to protect the executive, but he refused to recognize that federalism principles might do the same to protect the states.[81] In *Massachusetts v. Environmental Protection Agency* the Court upheld the right of a state to protect its endangered coastline by challenging the failure of a federal agency to enforce federal environment laws. "We stress" the "special position and interest" of Massachusetts, the Court announced. "It is of considerable relevance that the party seeking review here is a sovereign State" and not a "private individual."[82] Scalia, however, would not abide federalism principles used for such a purpose. He joined Chief Justice Roberts's dissent rejecting the state's standing claim. "Relaxing Article III standing requirements because asserted injuries are pressed by a State" had "no basis in our jurisprudence," Roberts wrote, and applicable law "affords States no special rights or status."[83] While principles of separation of powers were fundamental for standing purposes, principles of federalism and state sovereignty were irrelevant.

The intriguing question was why Scalia viewed the two axial principles so differently.

One possible explanation was that he saw a greater need for a judicial referee in separation-of-powers disputes than in federalism disputes. However much that claim might seem reasonable to later generations, on originalist grounds it lacked any plausible support. History, after all, demonstrated two indisputable facts. The first was that at the founding and through the nation's

---

[80] In dissent, Scalia also joined one or more of the conservatives in advocating stricter federalism limits on congressional power. *See, e.g.*, National Federation of Independent Business v. Sibelius, 567 U.S. 519, 646 (2012) (Scalia, Kennedy, Thomas, and Alito, JJ., dissenting); United States v. Comstock, 560 U.S. 126, 158 (2010) (Thomas, J., dissenting, joined by Scalia, J.); United States v. Kebodeaux, 570 U.S. 387, 407 (Scalia, J., dissenting), 408 (Thomas, J., dissenting, joined in part by Scalia, J.).

[81] Scalia joined four other justices in rejecting the authority of the California Supreme Court to authorize the sponsors of an initiative proposal to represent the state in defending the constitutionality of legislation they had successfully enacted by referendum. The state, the five justices maintained, did not have the power to create "standing" or bypass federal standing law. Hollingsworth v. Perry, 570 U.S. 693 (2013) (Roberts, C.J., joined by Scalia, J.). Four dissenting justices argued that the state had the right to identify the parties properly entitled to represent the state. "The Court's opinion," they declared, "disrespects and disparages both the political process in California and the well-stated opinion of the California Supreme Court in this case." *Id.* at 726–27 (Kennedy, J., dissenting).

[82] Massachusetts v. Environmental Protection Agency, 549 U.S. 497, 518 (2007) (Stevens, J.).

[83] Massachusetts v. E.P.A., 549 U.S. at 536, 537 (Roberts, C.J., dissenting, joined by Scalia, J.).

earliest days federalism disputes were frequent, central, divisive, and pivotal, while separation-of-powers disputes were far less common, disruptive, or dangerous. As H. Jefferson Powell noted, federalism, not separation of powers, raised "The Oldest Question of Constitutional Law."[84] Indeed, Scalia agreed that the Court was necessary to resolve federalism issues. Sounding a very different note than the one he had voiced before the Senate Judiciary Committee, he announced from the high bench that there was an "inherent necessity of a tribunal for peaceful resolution of disputes between the Union and the individual States."[85] The second historical fact was that the federal courts had decided federalism cases virtually from the nation's founding and had decided literally hundreds of them ever since, ruling on all manner of federalism issues under any number of constitutional provisions. In contrast, they had decided comparatively few separation-of-powers cases, not only when the Founders were still active but long afterward as well.

Thus, as an originalist matter, the history of American constitutionalism and the traditions of the nation's government and politics showed that a judicial referee had been far more necessary and far more commonly utilized in federalism disputes than in separation-of-powers disputes. Indeed, that conclusion accorded precisely with Madison's thinking. In the *Federalist* he never asserted the supremacy of the Supreme Court in separation-of-powers disputes, but he explicitly did so on federalism questions.[86]

Another possible explanation for Scalia's different treatment of federalism and separation of powers was that the textual provisions underlying separation of powers were clearer and more specific than those underlying federalism. Certainly in his confirmation testimony he had justified his deferential attitude on federalism issues by arguing that it was "very hard to find a distinct justiciable line" between state and federal realms.[87] But it was hardly obvious that separation of powers principles presented any clearer "distinct and justiciable line." Such a contention, in fact, was obviously ill-founded.

Although Scalia claimed that separation-of-powers principles provided bright lines in the Constitution's first three articles, the text no more spelled out the exact meaning and scope of the legislative, executive, and judicial powers—or of the overlapping, intermixed, and supposedly checking nature of their respective powers—than it spelled out the complex

[84] H. Jefferson Powell, *The Oldest Question of Constitutional Law*, 79 VA. L. REV. 633 (1993).

[85] *Union Gas*, 491 U.S. at 33 (Scalia, J., concurring in part and dissenting in part).

[86] FEDERALIST PAPERS NO. 39, at 242 (Madison).

[87] *Scalia Hearings*, 82.

relationships between the federal and state governments. More specifically, the Constitution contained far more federalism provisions than separation-of-powers provisions. Scalia even seemed to acknowledge that fact in *Printz v. United States* where, claiming "to mention only a few examples," he identified seven separate constitutional provisions—not including the Eleventh Amendment—that recognized the sovereignty of the states.[88] Thus, if one believed that the Constitution created any bright lines, one would have to believe that the Founders at least made a much more concerted effort to draw such lines to deal with federalism issues than to deal with separation-of-powers issues. In any event, Scalia offered no reason why separation-of-powers principles might possibly be thought to contain more or brighter bright lines than federalism principles.

The Primacy of Separation of Powers

In fact, there was no originalist, textualist, or traditionalist basis for privileging the principles of separation of powers over those of federalism. On any reasonably disputed issue, bright lines in either area appeared mainly in the eyes of the beholder. Consequently, Scalia's stress on separation of powers must be explained on other grounds. Three seemed most probable, none of which was originalist, textualist, or traditionalist.

First, Scalia's personal focus and concerns were national, not local. He had grown up and lived in the nation's capital as well as in seven different states from New York to California and from Massachusetts to Virginia. His career experiences in a variety of positions—lawyer, scholar, editor, teacher, administrative law specialist, and federal executive official—gave him a national orientation. He accepted as given—however much he disliked—the basic centralizing results of the post–New Deal Constitution and the reality of a large-scale national government with its bureaucracy and administrative agencies. He understood the benefits of American political, cultural, economic, and military power, and he believed in the necessity of a strong foreign policy and the importance of American leadership in the world. He also believed strongly in Chicago-style market economics and the benevolent power of a national "free market."[89] Thus, separation-of-powers ideas, with

---

[88] *Printz*, 521 U.S. at 918–19 (Scalia, J.).
[89] A conflict between Scalia's free-market convictions and his textualism surfaced in the doctrine of the "negative" or "dormant" Commerce Clause. The doctrine was an instrument for the

their inherent focus on the operations of the national government and the relations between its three branches, compelled his attention and inspired his imagination far more than did the localist and fragmenting thrust of federalism principles.[90]

Second, separation-of-powers principles offered him a far greater opportunity to place his own distinctive imprint on the Constitution. The law of federalism was stiffly encrusted with precedents that went back to the founding era, and its principles were heavily freighted with divisive connotations and implications grounded in the historical conflicts that had often bitterly divided the nation. In contrast, the law of separation of powers was marked by fewer precedents and a far thinner history of controversy, especially on issues related to the scope of executive, as opposed to legislative and judicial, power. Thus, its principles regarding executive power were relatively free of deeply embedded and fiercely contested connotations and implications, and they offered him a relatively more unformed and promising set of principles to shape and deploy in the ways he wished.

Third, and most likely decisive, separation of powers provided Scalia with a more focused jurisprudential instrument for reshaping the law of the national government along two tracks that were dearest to his heart. First, its principles would allow him to impose ever tighter limits on the power of the federal judiciary, the institution that he resented as the bastion of liberal judicial activism and the institution that he was determined to bring to heel. Second, those same principles would enable him to strengthen the executive branch and ensure its vigor and independence against what he regarded as an intrusive Congress on one side and an overreaching judiciary on the other. Indeed, in *Massachusetts v. E.P.A.* he made those goals clear. He not only joined Roberts's dissent on the standing issue but also wrote a separate dissent to emphasize the need to protect executive authority. Federalism principles and the constitutional importance of state sovereignty—however pivotal when parties sought to limit Congress or the federal courts—had no bearing when a state sought to protect itself from environmental dangers by

---

judicial protection of an open national market, but it also was unjustified under a strict reading of the constitutional text. On that conflict, textualism won, and Scalia rejected the doctrine. *See* RALPH A. ROSSUM, ANTONIN SCALIA'S JURISPRUDENCE: TEXT AND TRADITION 91–98 (2006) [hereafter ROSSUM, ANTONIN SCALIA'S JURISPRUDENCE].

[90] Scalia differed in this regard, for example, from the more moderately conservative O'Connor. *See* Gelfand & Werhan, *Federalism*.

challenging executive authority. The controlling statute, he stressed, gave "broad discretion, not to us but to an executive agency."[91]

Long before he went on the bench Scalia had come to understand that he could generate maximum constitutional leverage by giving new pre-eminence and meaning to the indeterminate principles of separation of power. By stressing the centrality of those principles and proclaiming a sharp division between the powers of the three federal branches he could advance both of his paramount goals. He could define the judicial power with a new narrowness and severely limit what he saw as liberal judicial activism, and he could define the executive power with a new breadth, expanding its authority and largely freeing it from legislative and judicial oversight. While he could generally use federalism principles only in matters involving the rights and powers of the states, he could invoke separation-of-powers principles in a far wider range of areas and use them to fashion a more flexible and widely applicable constitutional tool to serve his purposes.

As for his desire to limit the federal judiciary, Scalia repeatedly announced his scorn for the Warren Court and what he condemned as continuing illegitimate decision-making by activist liberal judges. He attacked them for what he saw as their arrogant and self-important elitism that trampled on traditional values and majoritarian sentiments. More particularly, he attacked them for the rulings they made on the issues he cared about most passionately—abortion, gay rights, assisted suicide, affirmative action, the death penalty, and church-state relations. Separation-of-powers principles suggested potentially sweeping constitutional arguments capable of undermining and overturning their decisions on those focal issues.

Most basically, separation-of-powers principles allowed him to stress the textual fact that the Constitution granted "legislative Powers" only to Congress, not to the federal judiciary.[92] Hence, he could portray any "lawmaking" the courts might do as prima facie illegitimate and impugn as illicit "judicial activism" any decision that went beyond the express text of a constitutional provision or federal statute. That ever-available condemnation

---

[91] Massachusetts v. E.P.A., 549 U.S. at 549, 560 (Scalia, J., dissenting).

[92] Scalia of course knew that courts did, and necessarily had to, make law in a variety of contexts. "I am not so naive (nor do I think our forebears were) as to be unaware that judges in a real sense 'make' law. But they make it as judges make it, which is to say as though they were 'finding' it." *James B. Beam*, 501 U.S. at 549 (Scalia, J., concurring in the judgment).

tracked perfectly the incessant Republican condemnation of the federal courts for illegitimately "legislating."[93]

More specifically, Scalia realized that he could also use separation of powers to limit the federal courts in a variety of doctrinal areas. In a series of cases he chastised the Court for implying private rights of action from the Constitution and federal statutes, charging that such actions were beyond the federal judicial power.[94] Similarly, he rejected the idea that the Court could oust state court jurisdiction over issues of federal law on its own authority and without an express statutory command.[95] Again, he rejected outright the so-called "negative" or "dormant" Commerce Clause by which the Court had acted for well over a century to prevent the states from imposing burdens and discriminations on interstate commerce.[96] "I believe that this [Commerce Clause] jurisprudence takes us, self-consciously and avowedly, beyond the judicial role itself," he declared. "The text from which we take our authority to act in this field" was "nothing more than a grant of power to Congress, not the courts."[97]

Most prominently, he seized on separation-of-powers principles to anchor a more demanding doctrine of standing and directly indict the Warren Court. Judicial liberals, he believed, had radically changed the law to allow the federal courts to decide suits that they never should have heard and that enabled them to intrude improperly on both the legislative and executive branches.[98] With particular intensity he attacked the Warren Court's decision in *Flast v. Cohen*[99] that allowed standing to individuals who invoked the Establishment Clause to challenge the distribution of federal resources for the benefit of religious organizations or purposes. While Scalia joined the conservative justices in severely narrowing the *Flast* rule and thereby

---

[93] *E.g.*, in "recent years we've had some examples of the Court actually taking the job of the Legislature and legislating rather than interpreting," Ronald Reagan had declared. "I want judges who will interpret the law and not legislate." 1984-2 Ronald Reagan, Public Papers of the Presidents of the United States 1118 [hereafter Reagan Papers].

[94] *E.g., Thompson*, 484 U.S. at 191 (Scalia, J., concurring in the judgment).

[95] Tafflin v. Levitt, 493 U.S. 455, 469, 472 (1990) (Scalia, J., concurring).

[96] In *Tyler Pipe Industries v. Washington State Department of Revenue*, 483 U.S. 232, 254, 260 (1987) (Scalia, J., concurring in part and dissenting in part), he traced the doctrine's origin back to the Marshall Court's decision in *Gibbons v. Ogden*, 22 U.S. (9 Wheat.) 1, 209, 226-29, 235-39 (1824) (Johnson, J., concurring in judgment), and its formal adoption to *State Freight Tax*, 82 U.S. (15 Wall.) 232 (1873) (Strong, J.).

[97] American Trucking Associations, Inc. v. Smith, 496 U.S. 167, 200, 202 (1990) (Scalia, J., concurring in the judgment). "[O]ur exercise of the 'negative' Commerce Clause function has ultimately cast us in the essentially legislative role of weighing the imponderable." *Id.* at 203.

[98] Antonin Scalia, *The Doctrine of Standing as an Essential Element of the Separation of Powers*, 17 Suffolk U. L. Rev. 881 (1982).

[99] Flast v. Cohen, 392 U.S. 83 (1968) (Warren, C.J.).

protecting a variety of programs designed to funnel government benefits to religious groups,[100] he was not satisfied with merely narrowing the Warren Court precedent. "*Flast*," he charged, "is wholly irreconcilable with the Article III restrictions on federal-court jurisdiction."[101] The Court should flatly overrule it, and no plaintiff should have standing to challenge any such program. "*Flast* is an anomaly in our jurisprudence, irreconcilable with the Article III restrictions on federal judicial power that our opinions have established," he insisted. "I would repudiate that misguided decision and enforce the Constitution."[102]

For Scalia, standing as a doctrine built on separation of powers ensured a sharply restricted judiciary. "[T]he law of Art. III standing is built on a single basic idea—the idea of separation of powers," he insisted. "It keeps us minding our own business."[103]

In *Lujan v. Defenders of Wildlife* Scalia was able to write his restrictive views on standing into an opinion of the Court, emphasizing that the requirements for standing were exacting and that Congress itself had only limited power to grant standing to would-be litigants.[104] His opinion was a perfect example of the ironies that marked his jurisprudence. His opinion enhanced the power of the judiciary in the name of restricting it and then used that power boldly to limit Congress, protect the executive, and bar from the federal courts much of the "liberal" and "public-interest" litigation that he disdained.[105]

The utility of linking separation of powers to standing was apparent in his opinion. Plaintiffs in *Defenders* sought to enforce the Endangered Species Act by invoking its "citizen-suit" provision that allowed "any person" to bring

---

[100] Hein v. Freedom From Religion Foundation, Inc., 551 US. 587 (2007) (Alito, J.) (denying standing under *Flast* to challenge federal executive program intended to assist religious groups); Arizona Christian School Tuition Organization v. Winn, 563 U.S. 125 (2011) (Kennedy, J.) (denying standing under *Flast* to challenge state program giving tax credits to parents who contributed money to intermediary institution that provided scholarships to students who attended religious school); Valley Forge Christian College v. Americans United for Separation of Church and State, Inc., 454 U.S. 464 (1982) (Rehnquist, J.) (denying standing to plaintiff challenging action of federal agency transferring federal property to religious college). On a parallel path, the Court also upheld a program that allowed tuition aid to parents enrolling children in religious school. Zelmon v. Simmons-Harris, 536 U.S. 639 (2002) (Rehnquist, C.J.).

[101] *Hein*, 551 US. at 618 (Scalia, J., concurring in the judgment).

[102] *Winn*, 563 U.S. at 146–47 (Scalia, J., concurring).

[103] Arizona State Legislature v. Arizona Independent Redistricting Commission, 135 S. Ct. 2652, 2695 (2015) (Scalia, J., dissenting).

[104] *Defenders*, 504 U.S. at 576 (Scalia, J.). He criticized the idea that standing and other "justiciability" doctrines had a "prudential" component and suggested that all justiciability limits were constitutionally mandated. *See* Honig v. Doe, 484 U.S. 305, 332, 339 (1988) (Scalia, J., dissenting); Lexmark International, Inc. v. Static Control Components, Inc., 572 U.S. 118, 127 & n.3 (2014) (Scalia, J.).

[105] Dissenting, Blackmun termed Scalia's opinion "a slash-and-burn expedition through the law of environmental standing." *Defenders*, 504 U.S. at 606 (Blackmun, J., dissenting).

an action to vindicate a "procedural injury" suffered as a result of improper agency enforcement. The plaintiffs alleged that the secretary of the interior had failed to follow statutory procedures in adopting regulations that applied the statute with insufficient geographical breadth. Writing for the Court in a 6–3 decision, Scalia rejected their claim on two distinct constitutional grounds, both of which were rooted in separation-of-powers principles.

He based the first ground on Article III and the principle that Congress lacked power to confer standing on individuals who had not suffered sufficiently "concrete, de facto injuries."[106] Plaintiffs' claims to be enforcing the law or protecting the general public interest were wholly insufficient to meet that requirement. The Court, not Congress, held final authority to determine whether plaintiffs had standing because the standing requirement was part of a constitutional "core" established by Article III.[107] Regardless of congressional mandates, then, only those injuries the Court itself found to be "concrete, de facto injuries" were constitutionally sufficient. There was "absolutely no basis for making the Article III inquiry turn on the source of the asserted right," Scalia announced.[108] If the courts acted merely "on the invitation of Congress" and ignored constitutional standing requirements, "they would be discarding a principle fundamental to the separate and distinct constitutional role of the Third Branch."[109]

Scalia's contention was inconsistent with the long history of citizen-suit actions and failed to support its conclusions on "originalist" grounds. First, until the twentieth century, the Court simply did not link the doctrine of standing to Article III.[110] Second, no historical evidence supported the claim that "the Constitution limited Congress' power to confer a cause of action" and thereby allow citizens to bring suits in the public interest.[111] Finally, at the founding and long afterward American law allowed various congressionally sanctioned actions enabling individuals to sue to protect the public interest.[112] The "public action," that is, "an action brought by a private

---

[106] *Defenders*, 504 U.S. at 578 (1992) (Scalia, J.).

[107] *Defenders*, 504 U.S. at 560 (Scalia, J.) ("the core component of standing is an essential and unchanging part of the case-or-controversy requirement of Article III").

[108] *Defenders*, 504 U.S. at 576 (Scalia, J.). Scalia quoted this statement from *Defenders* in *Federal Election Commission v. Akins*, 524 U.S. at 33 (Scalia, J., dissenting).

[109] *Defenders*, 504 U.S. at 576 (Scalia, J.).

[110] Evan Tsen Lee, Judicial Restraint in America: How the Ageless Wisdom of the Federal Courts was Invented, chs. 1–3 (2011).

[111] Cass R. Sunstein, *What's Standing After Lujon? Of Citizen Suits, "Injuries," and Article III*, 91 Mich. L. Rev. 163, 170 (1992) [hereafter Sunstein, *What's Standing*].

[112] Sunstein, *What's Standing*, 173–79. Accord Randy Beck, *Qui Tam Litigation Against Government Officials: Constitutional Implications of a Neglected History*, 93 Notre Dame L. Rev. 1235 (2018). Similarly, Congress and the federal courts long allowed suits brought in the absence of

person primarily to vindicate the public interest in the enforcement of public obligations," explained Louis L. Jaffe, had "long been a feature of our English and American law."[113]

Scalia's opinion in *Defenders* was equally inconsistent with more recent Supreme Court law. Prior to *Defenders*, the Court had declared that plaintiffs with statutory rights of action "may invoke the general public interest in support of their claim" and thereby overcome "prudential" limitations on standing.[114] More important, it had also declared that standing "often turns on the nature and source of the claim asserted" and that the "actual or threatened injury required by Art. III may exist solely by virtue of 'statutes creating legal rights, the invasion of which creates standing.' "[115] Thus, Scalia's opinion rejected prior case law, limited established principles, and tightened the constitutional limits that Article III imposed on the powers of Congress.[116]

Scalia based his second constitutional ground in *Defenders* on Article II. Allowing Congress to confer standing on its own authority, he argued, would violate the executive's constitutional powers and responsibilities. "To permit Congress to convert the undifferentiated public interest in executive officers' compliance with the law into an 'individual right' vindicable in the courts," he declared, "is to permit Congress to transfer from the President to the courts the chief executive's most important constitutional duty, to 'take Care that the Laws be faithfully executed.' "[117] The power of the president was broad and unitary, and neither Congress nor the Court could impinge on it.

a "concrete injury," and that practice undermined the claim that the Constitution always required an "injury-in-fact." James E. Pfander, *Standing, Litigable Interests, and Article III's Case-or-Controversy Requirement*, 65 U.C.L.A. L. REV. 170 (2018).

[113] Louis L. Jaffe, *Standing to Secure Judicial Review: Private Actions*, 75 HARV. L. REV. 255, 302 (1961).

[114] Warth v. Selden, 422 U.S. 490, 501 (1975) (Powell, J.) (citing, *e.g.*, Sierra Club v. Morton, 405 U.S. 727, 737 (1972), and Federal Communications Commission v. Sanders Radio Station, 309 U.S. 470, 477 (1940)).

[115] *Warth*, 422 U.S. at 500 (Powell, J.) (citing Linda R.S. v. Richard D., 410 U.S. 614, 617 n.3 (1973), and Sierra Club v. Morton, 405 U.S. 727, 732 (1972)). Concerning the judicial review of agency action, which was at issue in *Defenders*, one scholar noted that courts "read the 'zone of interest' test as recognizing that it is within congressional discretion, as a matter of policy, to decide who may obtain review of agency actions." Michael A. Perino, *Justice Scalia: Standing, Environmental Law, and the Supreme Court*, 15 B.C. ENVTL. AFF. L. REV. 135, 142 (1987).

[116] Although Scalia construed *Trafficante v. Metropolitan Life Insurance Co.*, 409 U.S. 205 (1972), as consistent with his opinion in *Defenders*, 504 U.S. at 578, the interpretation of standing and the power of Congress in *Trafficante* were both quite different than Scalia's interpretation in *Defenders*. Not only did *Trafficante* treat standing more broadly and flexibly, but it also recognized an injury (the loss to third parties of "important benefits from interracial associations," *Trafficante*, 409 U.S. at 210) that was both new and manifestly the product of massive social change and responsive congressional lawmaking.

[117] *Defenders*, 504 U.S. at 577 (Scalia, J.).

Thus, with a single opinion Scalia advanced all three of his pivotal structural goals. He elaborated doctrines that limited the power of Congress, restricted the jurisdiction of the federal courts, and privileged the executive over Congress in matters involving the enforcement of federal law. All on constitutional grounds; all using separation-of-powers reasoning.

Dissenting in *Defenders*, Justice Harry Blackmun illustrated the extent to which separation-of-powers principles were easily manipulable and could be construed to support a variety of conclusions. The "principal effect" of the majority's ruling, Blackmun argued, was "to transfer power into the hands of the Executive at the expense—not of the courts—but of Congress, from which that power originates and emanates." In many regulatory areas "Congress often legislates, as it were, in procedural shades of gray," Blackmun explained. "That is, it sets forth substantive policy goals and provides for their attainment by requiring Executive Branch officials to follow certain procedures, for example, in the form of reporting, consultation, and certification requirements."[118] Nothing in the text of the Constitution or the understandings of the Founders about separation of powers established whether Scalia or Blackmun was "correct," much less whether there was any such "correct" original view on the issue at all.[119]

Typical of Scalia's result-oriented decision-making, moreover, in an entirely different doctrinal area—one where he sought not to protect executive power but rather to limit the federal courts and bar private civil rights suits—he readily accepted Blackmun's interpretation of separation of powers and the authority of Congress. In *Alexander v. Sandoval* Scalia accepted the principle that Congress had the right to impose limitations and procedures on the enforcement powers of federal agencies. The controlling statute in that case provided that the agency could take no enforcement action until it had "advised the appropriate person or persons of the failure to comply" with its regulations and had, in addition, "determined that compliance cannot be secured by voluntary means." Further, if the agency sought to enforce the

---

[118] *Defenders*, 504 U.S. at 602 (Blackmun, J., dissenting).

[119] For examples of the ease with which separation-of-powers principles can easily be shaped to reach contrary results, *compare* the majority opinion in *United States v. Windsor*, 570 U.S. 744, 762 (2013) (Kennedy, J.), *with* the dissents, *id.* at 770, 779, 788 (Scalia, J.) and *id.* at 802, 813 (Alito, J.); the majority opinion in *Gonzaga University v. Doe*, 536 U.S. 273, 286 (2002) (Rehnquist, C.J., joined by Scalia), *with* the dissent, *id.* at 293, 300 (Stevens, J.); and the plurality opinion in *Northern Pipeline Construction Co. v. Marathon Pipe Line Co.*, 458 U.S. 50, 63–64 & n.15 (1982) (Brennan, J.), *with* the dissent, *id.* at 98, 115 (White, J.). The plurality opinion and a separate concurrence in the case, Justice White wrote in *Northern Pipeline*, "turn the separation-of-powers doctrine, upon which the majority relies, on its head." *Id.* at 98.

law by using its authority to terminate funding, Scalia continued, "still more restrictions apply." Then, the agency had to comply with the statute's mandate that it "file with the committees of the House and Senate having legislative jurisdiction over the program or activity involved a full written report of the circumstances and the grounds for such action." Moreover, he added, the statute also provided that the agency could not actually terminate funding "until thirty days have elapsed after the filing of such report." Those limitations, Scalia explained, "tend to contradict a congressional intent to create privately enforceable rights" because an "express provision of one method of enforcing a substantive rule suggests that Congress intended to preclude others."[120]

Thus, in *Sandoval* Scalia agreed with Blackmun's point in *Defenders* that separation of powers allowed Congress to limit executive authority by specifying the procedures executive officials were required to use in enforcing federal law. In *Sandoval*, to limit the federal courts and defeat a civil rights action, he readily embraced that idea. In *Defenders*, however, determined to defeat a suit seeking to enforce environmental regulations that he disdained, he rejected that idea and construed separation-of-powers principles to free executive power and discretion from such congressional restrictions. The two cases showed once again both the plasticity of separation-of-powers principles as well as Scalia's willingness to exploit that plasticity in ways that served his own ideological goals.

While *Defenders* illustrated Scalia's determination to use separation of powers to protect and expand executive power, *Printz v. United States* revealed that determination even more clearly. There, the question was whether a federal gun-control statute imposing enforcement duties on state officers was constitutional, and a recent Court decision offered strong federalism grounds for the five conservative justices to invalidate the measure. Only five years earlier they had held in *New York v. United States*[121] that state legislatures were not subject to the direction of Congress, and the case was taken to stand for the general proposition that the inherent sovereignty of the states, as mandated by the Constitution and the Tenth Amendment,[122]

---

[120] *Alexander v. Sandoval*, 532 U.S. 275, 289–90 (2001), citing 42 U.S.C. § 2000d-1 (2001) (Scalia, J.).

[121] New York v. United States, 505 U.S. 144 (1992) (O'Connor, J., joined by Scalia, J.). Justice Souter joined the five conservatives, while Justices White, Blackmun, and Stevens concurred in part and dissented in part.

[122] "Whether one views the [federal statute requiring state action] as lying outside Congress' enumerated powers, or as infringing upon the core of state sovereignty reserved by the Tenth

barred Congress from "commandeering" the institutions of state government.[123]

Rather than relying solely on *New York* and its federalism principles, however, Scalia used his opportunity to write for the conservative majority in *Printz* to highlight separation-of-powers principles and further expand the realm of executive authority. More was involved in the case than federalism issues, he explained, for the statute under review "would also have an effect upon the second [axial] element: the separation and equilibrium of powers between the three branches of the Federal Government itself."[124] His opinion echoed the argument he had made in *Defenders*. The Constitution gave the president the duty to "take Care that the Laws be faithfully executed,"[125] and the statute "effectively transfers this responsibility" to state officials who "are left to implement the program without meaningful Presidential control." Emphasizing the "insistence of the Framers upon unity in the Federal Executive," he held that the statute violated the Constitution not only on federalism grounds but also on separation-of-powers grounds. The Founders' concept of a unitary executive, he announced, "would be shattered, and the power of the President would be subject to reduction, if Congress could act as effectively without the President as with him, by simply requiring state officers to execute its laws."[126]

Scalia's invocation of the "take Care" Clause in *Printz* was expansive, and the conclusion he drew from it was hardly required by the constitutional text. As a strictly textual matter, the clause did not provide that the president's duty was exclusive, nor did it provide that Congress could not mandate special enforcement procedures or require the cooperation of state officials. In fact, the

---

Amendment, the provision is inconsistent with the federal structure of our Government established by the Constitution." New York v. United States, 505 U.S. at 177 (O'Connor, J., joined by Scalia, J.).

[123] The Court declared that "the Act commandeers the legislative processes of the States by directly compelling them to enact and enforce a federal regulatory program" and that such an action was "an outcome that has never been understood to lie within the authority conferred upon Congress by the Constitution." New York v. United States, 505 U.S. at 176 (O'Connor, J., joined by Scalia, J.) (quoting Hodel v. Virginia Surface Mining & Reclamation Association, Inc., 452 U.S. 264, 288 (1981) (Marshall, J.)). Scalia similarly defended executive power in *Akins*, 524 U.S. at 29 (Scalia, J., dissenting).

[124] *Printz*, 521 U.S. at 922 (Scalia, J.).

[125] U.S. CONST. art. II, sec. 3.

[126] *Printz*, 521 U.S. at 922, 923 (Scalia, J.). He admitted that there was "no constitutional text speaking to [the] precise question" at issue and explained that an answer "must be sought in historical understanding and practice, in the structure of the Constitution, and in the jurisprudence of this Court." *Id.* at 905. His argument was essentially the same as the one he made in both *Morrison* and *Defenders*.

Constitution gave Congress substantial power over the executive by virtue of its general lawmaking authority as well as its specific powers to establish and organize the structure of the executive branch, determine what executive officials the president could appoint, and control the size and organization of the civil and military resources the president commanded, including the power to commandeer state militias for the purpose of enforcing federal law.[127] Indeed, as the dissenters in *Printz* made clear, there was substantial evidence in the *Federalist* that both Hamilton and Madison had assumed that Congress could utilize state officials in arranging for the enforcement of federal laws.[128] To provide greater independence and authority for the executive, Scalia sought to limit the significance of those powers and negate the import of those textual and originalist authorities.

Given the 5–4 lineup of the justices, Scalia had little choice in *Printz* but to accept the federalism rationale that the conservatives had relied on in *New York*,[129] but he nonetheless went out of his way to use the opportunity to put his own personal stamp on the law by protecting and expanding the power of the executive. He used *Printz* to follow up his dissent in *Morrison* and his majority opinion in *Defenders* to further cement his separation-of-powers and unitary executive ideas in the Court's jurisprudence. Indeed, he shaped *Printz* to shift the basis of the "anti-commandeering" doctrine from federalism to separation-of-powers grounds and thus to serve his primary goal in reshaping the structural Constitution along his favored lines.[130]

Further, beyond providing what he regarded as a far sounder constitutional basis for the anti-commandeering doctrine, he also advanced a separation-of-powers rationale that suggested an additional provocative instrumentalist idea for conservatives. If the Constitution required complete control by the federal executive over all efforts to enforce federal law, then they could use that principle to restrict or invalidate federal welfare and

---

[127] U.S. Const. art. II, sec. 1, cl. 7 (presidential removal, inability to serve, and succession); art. II, sec. 2, para. 2 (executive departments and appointments); art. I, sec. 8, cls. 12 through 14 (federal armed forces); art. I, sec. 8, cls. 15 & 16 (state militias).

[128] *Printz*, 521 U.S. at 945–48 (Stevens, J., dissenting) and 970, 971–76 (Souter, J., dissenting) (1997) (together citing *Federalist Nos. 27 and 36* (Hamilton) and *Nos. 44 and 45* (Madison). Scalia rejected the significance of the historical evidence. *Id.* at 910–15.

[129] O'Connor wrote the Court's opinion in *New York*, and Souter joined the other four conservative justices in signing on to her opinion, while the remaining three justices concurred in part and dissented in part. In *Printz*, however, the vote was 5–4, and the other four conservatives—including O'Connor—were necessary for Scalia's majority.

[130] On Scalia's commitment to his executive-oriented separation-of-powers analysis in *Defenders* and *Printz* over the federalism analysis in *New York v. United States, see* ROSSUM, ANTONIN SCALIA'S JURISPRUDENCE, 105–06.

regulatory programs that relied on state and local officials for their admin-istration.[131] Thus, his separation-of-powers reasoning in *Printz* floated the possibility of a new legal tactic that could further expand federal executive power, limit federal legislative power, and strike directly at the operations of the modern American welfare state.

Scalia developed and shaped principles of separation of powers as he did because his primary concerns were national and his broadest structural goal was to reconfigure the powers allocated to the branches of the federal gov-ernment. He was more than happy to enforce federalism limits by checking Congress and the federal courts when opportunities presented themselves and federalism grounds served his purposes. He concentrated his own most creative architectural efforts, however, on shaping separation-of-powers principles to limit generally the power of the judiciary and to expand broadly the power of the executive. Whatever the merits of his opinions in *Defenders, Printz*, and his other federalism and separation-of-powers opinions, his rea-soning and textual interpretations stemmed from his own goals and values, not from the compulsion of textual or originalist sources.

The deeply personal and ultimately political nature of his separation-of-powers jurisprudence was strikingly apparent in *Clinton v. Jones*.[132] There, in spite of the fact that he was an inveterate defender of the executive, he refused—only one month after handing down his opinion in *Printz*—to de-fend its powers and privileges. In that politically explosive case—a public re-lations bonanza for Republicans—the Court held that a highly embarrassing private lawsuit charging sexual misconduct against Democratic President Bill Clinton could go forward while Clinton was still in office and that he had no immunity against claims that arose from conduct occurring before he became president.[133] Scalia, who was "all but openly hostile to Clinton and his agenda," publicly mocked the president's claim that he was too busy to submit to such a suit and that doing so would be burdensome and disrup-tive to the presidency. "We see presidents riding horseback, chopping fire-wood, fishing for stick fish, playing golf and so forth and so on," he told an

[131] *See, e.g.*, Evan Caminker, Printz, *State Sovereignty, and the Limits of Formalism*, 1997 Sup. Ct. Rev. 199.

[132] Clinton v. Jones, 520 U.S. 681 (1997) (Stevens, J., with Scalia, J. joining an eight-justice ma-jority). In a similar display of political partisanship, Scalia again ignored his commitment to execu-tive power when he criticized President Barack Obama and supported state efforts to target suspected illegal immigrants. Arizona v. United States, 567 U.S. 387, 416, 423–24, 428 (2012) (Scalia, J., concur-ring in part and dissenting in part).

[133] The Court had previously held that the president had an absolute immunity to suits based on actions taken while in office. Nixon v. Fitzgerald, 457 U.S. 731 (1982) (Powell, J.).

audience, provoking its laughter.[134] It was wholly implausible, he suggested, that Clinton would find the suit truly burdensome on his presidency. Scalia joined the majority opinion that subjected the president to the continued and nearly fatal legal and political pressures the suit helped generate. In both *Morrison* and *Mistretta* he had been willing to dissent vigorously and all alone to defend executive power and independence, but in *Clinton* he did not write separately nor did he defend that power and independence. Instead, he silently joined the majority opinion and helped intensify the political pressures that Republicans were forcing on the sitting Democratic president.

Even more revealing was something else that Scalia did not do. He refused to join Justice Stephen Breyer's separate opinion concurring in the judgment but advancing a somewhat more executive-protective position than the majority adopted. Breyer invoked Scalia's cherished favorites—Article II, separation of powers, and the constitutional nature of executive authority—to argue that the president should enjoy more leeway to stop or delay such private lawsuits. If the president showed a conflict between his "public duties" and the demands of "an ordinary civil damages action," Breyer maintained, a judge should consider scheduling a trial "only within the constraints of a constitutional principle—a principle that forbids a federal judge in such a case to interfere with the President's discharge of his public duties."[135]

Breyer's proposed principle was one that fit perfectly with the executive-protective jurisprudence that Scalia so emphatically proclaimed. It advanced a principle that he could not possibly have failed to approve. But in a politically damaging suit against Bill Clinton that was cheered on rabidly by Republicans intent on impeaching a Democrat president, refuse to approve it he did.

Branch Affinities and Structural Instrumentalism

Scalia's jurisprudential efforts to realign the structural Constitution exemplified two fundamental characteristics of American constitutionalism. The first was that personal factors necessarily molded views of the vague principles of the structural Constitution. Scalia's preference for separation of

---

[134] JEFFREY TOOBIN, THE NINE: INSIDE THE SECRET WORLD OF THE SUPREME COURT 116, 117 (2007).

[135] Clinton v. Jones, 520 U.S. at 710 (Breyer, J., concurring in the judgment).

powers over federalism was rooted not in constitutional text, structure, or tradition but rather in his own political and institutional goals. Separation-of-powers principles allowed him most effectively to achieve the critical practical results he sought. He was a classic structural opposite of those ante-bellum constitutional theorists, such as John C. Calhoun and John Taylor of Caroline, who did the reverse, subordinating separation of powers to feder-alism not because they failed to recognized the former but because the latter gave them the constitutional leverage they thought essential to achieve their goals.[136]

The second characteristic was the process whereby the diverging po-litical and ideological drives of succeeding generations altered branch and level affinities and inspired changing views of the structural Constitution. In the nation's earliest political battles Federalists favored the judiciary, while Republicans hailed the legislatures. In the pivotal battles of antebellum con-stitutional politics Northerners sided with national power, while Southerners magnified the importance of states' rights. Progressives praised the capacities of the legislature, while their conservative adversaries sanctified the judiciary. When the Warren Court induced the descendants of Progressivism to ac-cept an innovating judiciary, their conservative opponents quickly turned to embrace the legislative branch they had previously belittled. Throughout the nation's history Americans shaped their views of the structural Constitution according to their expectations about which levels and branches would most likely accommodate or frustrate their dominant values and interests.[137]

Scalia's jurisprudence exemplified both of those classic characteristics, and his efforts made him a paradigmatic figure in the history of the juris-prudence of the structural Constitution. Indeed, a powerful undercurrent of political pragmatism drove his thinking about the structure and operation of American government, and the election of Ronald Reagan in 1980 drew that undercurrent to the surface. Constitutional federalism did not prescribe general opposition to federal power, he explained in 1982, for federalism had a "duality of meaning." It was "a form of government midway between two extremes," one involving the "conflict of independent states" and the other the "monotony of one centralized government." Federalism was a balancing

---

[136] See, e.g., JOHN C. CALHOUN, UNION AND LIBERTY: THE POLITICAL PHILOSOPHY OF JOHN C. CALHOUN (Ross M. Lence ed., 1992); JOHN TAYLOR, TYRANNY UNMASKED (E. Thornton Miller ed., 1992).

[137] Edward A. Purcell, Jr., The Courts, Federalism, and the Federal Constitution, 1920–2000, in 3 THE CAMBRIDGE HISTORY OF LAW IN AMERICA: THE TWENTIETH CENTURY AND AFTER (1920–), esp. 127–28 (Michael Grossberg & Christopher Tomlins eds., 2008).

device designed to avoid those two undesirable extremes, "a stick that can be used to beat either dog."[138]

The fact that liberals had long exercised federal power was "an understandable tactical reason for opposition to the exercise of federal power," he explained, but conservatives had taken "a tactic employed for half a century" forged to oppose Democratic policies and mistakenly transformed it into a philosophy that rejected federal power generally and on principle. Such a philosophy, Scalia advised, "seems to me simply wrong." With the Reagan administration in power, conservatives should revise their views and begin to use federal power boldly to implement their own policy goals. To illustrate his point, he called for extensive assertions of federal legislative power to enforce market principles in the national economy, terminate rent controls in American cities, establish "a federal policy excluding state regulation" in many areas, eliminate "new tort theories" affecting interstate businesses, and restrict state laws that involved antitrust issues or imposed other burdens on corporations. The national government "is not bad but good," Scalia argued, and federal power was "a legitimate and useful instrument of policy." It all depended on who controlled that power and what they sought to do with it. "The trick," he instructed, "is to use it wisely."[139]

He delivered that same institutionally instrumentalist message when he addressed administrative law reform, his area of special legal expertise. On that issue, too, he criticized conservatives because they were "not only less eager than their political opponents to grasp the levers of government power but are also inclined to view all impediments to the exercise of that power as a victory for their cause." That belief, like their pro-federalism philosophy that opposed national power generally, was dead wrong. Conservatives who were "[d]istrustful of government in general and executive government in particular" failed to understand the dynamics of regulatory reform and the great opportunity the Reagan administration offered. Conservatives mistakenly continued to push legislative proposals to restrict executive and agency discretion at the very time when the new Reagan administration planned to use that power and exercise that discretion to substantially reduce the regulatory state. "[E]very curtailment of desirable agency discretion obstructs (principally) departure from a Democrat-produced, pro-regulatory status quo," and

---

[138] Scalia, *Two Faces*, 19.
[139] Scalia, *Two Faces*, 20, 21–22, 22.

such curtailments will "do major harm to the drive for genuine regulatory reform."[140]

Conservatives must realize, Scalia urged, "that the election has altered the game." They should abandon their "understandable but nonetheless disastrous aversion" to the "vigorous use of the legitimate machinery of government to achieve their goals." Policy results were what counted, not a "philosophy of government" that was rigidly committed to "executive-enfeebling measures."[141]

Scalia's political advice to conservatives and Republicans in the early 1980s demonstrated his acute recognition that the institutions of government were flexible and that activists could use them for many different purposes. The key to successful action lay not in embracing a rigid political philosophy but in adopting shrewd political tactics. He fully understood that he could use both federalism and separation of powers to reshape the contours of American government and, especially, that he could use the latter to realign the relationships of the three federal branches. Believing that the only "trick" was to do so "wisely," he sought self consciously to do just that. His own personal values and policy goals defined what was wise.

Scalia's jurisprudence addressing the structural Constitution demonstrated not what he thought it did but quite the opposite, not the existence of original bright lines but rather the unexceptionable practice of partisan constitutional interpretation. In establishing its twin axes of federalism and separation of powers, the Constitution created a fluid, elastic, and underdetermined system of government that Americans had throughout their history struggled to bend to the service of their diverse interests and ideologies.[142] Seeking to achieve his own personal and ideological goals, Scalia simply fell in line with that standard practice and methodically tried to do the same. His jurisprudence addressing the structural Constitution was originalist and textualist only in its rhetorical dressing, not in the animating goals and values that shaped it or the political results it was designed to achieve.

---

[140] Antonin Scalia, *Regulatory Reform—The Game Has Changed*, REGULATION (Jan./Feb. 1981), 13 [hereafter Scalia, *Regulatory Reform*].

[141] Scalia, *Regulatory Reform*, 15. Scalia echoed the same expedient approach in 1991 when he attacked the use of legislative history. "The principle change that will occur under a regime that rejects legislative history as binding upon the courts is that agencies will be enabled to accommodate (within the bounds of the statutory text) the desires of their *future* oversight committees (as well as their own evolving desires) instead of being ruled, in most minute detail, by the dead hand of the committee that happened to be in office when the statute was passed." SCALIA SPEAKS, 240–41.

[142] *See, e.g.*, PURCELL, ORIGINALISM.

5

An Inconsistent Jurisprudence: The Doctrinal Spectrum

Both on and off the bench Scalia proclaimed his commitment to originalism and textualism, but he applied those approaches differently in different areas and frequently failed to apply them at all.[1] He readily cited Blackstone as a classic originalist authority when the Englishman's views were in accord with his own, for example, but he dismissed them when not.[2] While the reasoning in his opinions varied greatly, it varied in ways that commonly served his political and ideological goals.

On First Amendment speech issues, to begin, Scalia essentially abandoned originalism[3] and adopted a strong version of the muscular free-speech law that developed only in the twentieth century.[4] In a highly controversial 5–4

---

[1] Commentators left and right have repeatedly demonstrated Scalia's inconsistencies. *See, e.g.,* Randy E. Barnett, *Scalia's Infidelity: A Critique of "Faint-Hearted" Originalism,* 75 U. CINCINNATI L. REV. 7 (2006); Richard A. Posner, *The Spirit Killeth, but the Letter Giveth Life,* NEW REPUBLIC, Sept. 13, 2012, at 18, 23; James B. Staab, *The Tenth Amendment and Justice Scalia's "Split Personality,"* 16 J.L. & POL'Y. 231; Erwin Chemerinsky, *The Jurisprudence of Justice Scalia: A Critical Appraisal,* 22 U. HAW. L. REV. 385 (2000) [hereafter Chemerinsky, *Jurisprudence of Justice Scalia*]; BRUCE ALLEN MURPHY, SCALIA: A COURT OF ONE 396, 405–06, 412–14, 561 n.1 (2014) [hereafter MURPHY, SCALIA]; Craig S. Lerner, *Justice Scalia's Eighth Amendment Jurisprudence: The Failure of Sake-of-the-Argument Originalism,* 42 HARV. J.L. & PUB. POL'Y 91 (2009)); Gene R. Nichol, *Justice Scalia and the Printz Case: The Trials of an Occasional Originalist,* 70 U. COLO. L. REV. 953, 969–71 (1999); Jeffrey Rosen, *Originalist Sin,* THE NEW REPUBLIC, May 5, 1997, *available at* https://newrepublic.com/article/74152/originalist-sin. For an effort to defend the contrary view, *see, e.g.,* SCALIA'S COURT: A LEGACY OF LANDMARK OPINIONS AND DISSENTS, at 6–19 (Kevin A. Ring ed., 2016).

[2] *Compare* ANTONIN SCALIA, SCALIA SPEAKS: REFLECTIONS ON LAW, FAITH, AND LIFE WELL LIVED (Christopher J. Scalia & Edward Whelan eds., 2017), 209 (citing Blackstone in support of private right to bear arms) [hereafter SCALIA SPEAKS], *with* Antonin Scalia, *Common Law Courts in a Civil Law System: The Role of United States Federal Courts in Interpreting the Constitution and Laws,* The Tanner Lectures on Human Values, Princeton University, March 8–9, 1995, at 91 (rejecting Blackstone on the "intent of the legislature" as an interpretative standard) [hereafter Scalia, *Common-Law Courts*].

[3] The Supreme Court justices in the 1790s generally approved prosecutions under the Alien and Sedition Acts on circuit, and they favored a strong state over the right of dissenters. WENDELL BIRD, PRESS AND SPEECH UNDER ASSAULT: THE EARLY SUPREME COURT JUSTICES, THE SEDITION ACT OF 1798, AND THE CAMPAIGN AGAINST DISSENT (2016).

[4] Scalia, for example, accepted the expansive idea that "expressive conduct" may be protected. "Where the government prohibits conduct *precisely because of its communicative attributes,* we hold the regulation unconstitutional." Barnes v. Glen Theatre, Inc., 501 U.S. 560, 572, 577 (1991) (Scalia, J., concurring in the judgment) (emphasis in original). For Scalia's defense of a strong, if nonoriginalist,

Antonin Scalia and American Constitutionalism. Edward A. Purcell, Jr., Oxford University Press (2020).
© Edward A. Purcell, Jr.
DOI: 10.1093/oso/9780197508763.001.0001

decision, for example, he voted with the majority to defend the right to burn the American flag as an act of "symbolic speech."[5] By protecting an action that he personally found offensive,[6] he demonstrated his genuinely strong commitment to free speech but demonstrated equally his willingness to disregard originalism when it suited his purposes. Acknowledging that "the freedom of speech" required adaptation to modern conditions, he justified his departure from originalism with a glaring dash of living constitutionalism, stating that "the Court must follow the trajectory of the First Amendment."[7]

More striking, Scalia also went far beyond any strict textualism by declaring that the terms "speech" and "press" in the First Amendment "stand as a sort of synecdoche" for the "full range of communicative expression."[8] That was certainly an understandable approach, but it also represented an exceptionally elastic form of textualism. Obviously it violated on its face his "most specific meaning" principle. More telling, it was not the textualism he applied when he dealt with concepts that he sought to limit sharply, such as "liberty," "due process," "equal protection," and "cruel and unusual punishments."[9] Surely those concepts could equally be seen as "synecdoches" standing for a "full range" of related rights. Indeed, if such relatively specific

First Amendment, *see, e.g.,* Hill v. Colorado, 530 U.S.703, 741 (2000) (Scalia, J., dissenting); R.A.V. v. St. Paul, 505 U.S. 377 (1992) (Scalia, J.). He relied heavily on political "tradition" in Burson v. Freeman, 504 U.S. 191, 214 (1992) (Scalia, J., concurring in the judgment). Sometimes, in rhetorical flourishes, he would make a weak stab at invoking the "Founders" in support of his modern First Amendment views. *See, e.g.,* Austin v. Michigan State Chamber of Commerce, 494 U.S. 652, 679, 693–94 (1990) (Scalia, J., dissenting) (relying on the ideas of Holmes and Brandeis and declaring that "for the first time since Justice Holmes left the bench" the Court was holding that "the mere *potential* for producing social harm" allowed a restriction on speech, at 689, and then adding later in his opinion that "I doubt that those who framed and adopted the First Amendment would agree" with the majority opinion, at 693).

[5] Texas v. Johnson, 491 U.S. 397 (1989) (Brennan, J., joined by Scalia, J.). *See generally* ROBERT JUSTIN GOLDSTEIN, FLAG BURNING & FREE SPEECH: THE CASE OF *TEXAS V. JOHNSON* (2000). When Scalia came to breakfast the morning after the decision was announced, he found his wife marching around the kitchen table singing "It's a Grand Old Flag." *Id.* at 112.

[6] "Don't get me wrong," he assured audiences. "I don't like scruffy, bearded, sandal-wearing people who go around burning the United States flag." JOAN BISKUPIC, AMERICAN ORIGINAL: THE LIFE AND CONSTITUTION OF SUPREME COURT JUSTICE ANTONIN SCALIA 232 (2009) [hereafter BISKUPIC, AMERICAN ORIGINAL].

[7] Scalia, *Common Law Courts,* 118–19. The interpretative "enterprise is not entirely cut-and-dried, but requires the exercise of judgment." *Id.* at 119.

[8] Scalia, *Common Law Courts,* 112.

[9] Scalia, for example, did not see "equal protection" as a synecdoche for a more comprehensive concept of equality when he dissented from the Court's ruling that the Equal Protection Clause prohibited gender discrimination. Instead, he condemned a "self-righteous Supreme Court, acting on its Members' personal view of what would make a 'more perfect Union,'" and that sought to "impose its own favored social and economic dispositions nationwide" even in the face of "dispositions that are centuries old." United States v. Virginia, 518 U.S. 515, 566, 601 (1996) (Scalia, J., dissenting).

terms as "speech" and "press" were synecdoches for a broader range of expressive rights, those other more general and capacious terms seemed even
more clearly designed to serve as synecdoches for even broader ranges of
equally protected rights.

Brown v. Entertainment Merchants Association exemplified the elasticity of
Scalia's First Amendment textualism. There, writing for the Court, he voided
a state statute that restricted the availability of violent video games to minors.
His opinion gave the First Amendment a seemingly all-encompassing sweep
that lacked any convincing originalist justification and seemed an exceptionally
expansive, if not virtually boundless, use of his "synecdoche" method."[10] Justice
Thomas, a more consistent originalist than Scalia, indicted his colleague's approach. "The Court's decision today does not comport with the original
public understanding of the First Amendment," Thomas wrote in dissent, and
the amendment did not have the expansive meaning that Scalia gave it. "The
practices and beliefs of the founding generation establish that 'the freedom of
speech,' as originally understood, does not include a right to speak to minors (or
a right of minors to access speech) without going through the minors' parents
or guardians."[11]

More obvious, Scalia played fast and loose with both history and tradition in his embarrassingly strained effort to square his originalism with the
Court's interpretation of the Equal Protection Clause in the pathbreaking civil
rights case *Brown v. Board of Education*.[12] He simply insisted that the original
understanding of the clause prohibited racial discrimination.[13] In doing so
he ignored the actual genesis and meaning of the clause in the Thirty-Ninth
Congress that enacted it and—contrary to his theoretical claims—ignored
as well the "original" racial assumptions of those who drafted, debated, and
voted for it.[14] More pointedly, he ignored the fact that the same Thirty-Ninth
Congress had also voted to segregate the public schools in the District of
Columbia.[15] As Michael Klarman concluded, the "original understanding of

[10] Brown v. Entertainment Merchants Association, 564 U.S. 786 (2011) (Scalia, J.).

[11] Brown v. Entertainment Merchants Association, 564 U.S. at 821 (Thomas, J., dissenting).

[12] Brown v. Board of Education of Topeka, 347 U.S. 483 (1954) (Warren, C.J.).

[13] Rutan v. Republican Party of Illinois, 497 U.S. 62, 92, 95–96 & n.1 (1990) (Scalia, J., dissenting).
Abandoning originalism and tradition, he subsequently turned to a severely watered down textu-
alism to furnish a justification for *Brown*. ANTONIN SCALIA & BRYAN A. GARNER, READING LAW: THE
INTERPRETATION OF LEGAL TEXTS 88 (2014) [hereafter SCALIA, READING].

[14] ANDREW KULL, THE COLORBLIND CONSTITUTION, chs. 4–5 (1992). The "preference" that was
"shared by the Thirty-Ninth Congress and by most of our government authorities" at the time "was to
retain the discretion to discriminate by race as appropriate." *Id.* at 82.

[15] Chemerinsky, *Jurisprudence of Justice Scalia*, 398. There was a broad consensus that the original
understanding of the Fourteenth Amendment did not require an end to racial segregation. *See, e.g.*,

the Fourteenth Amendment plainly permitted school segregation."[16] Finally, Scalia dismissed the interpretive significance of the obvious and painful racist tradition of the subsequent three-quarters of a century as well as the fact that over those same decades the Court had refused to invalidate laws that enforced racial segregation, discrimination, and disenfranchisement.

To avoid the glaring contradiction between his acceptance of *Brown* and his strong jurisprudential claims about "tradition," Scalia substituted a different standard than the one he usually used when he invoked its normative authority. The tradition of racial segregation and disenfranchisement commanded no authority, he explained, because it was not "unchallenged."[17] In fact, few traditional patterns of human behavior in America or elsewhere in the modern world have ever existed without some challenge or variation, but when Scalia invoked tradition as a controlling norm in other areas he treated the "traditions" he approved as authoritative, unproblematic, and seemingly universally honored.[18] For those traditions he did not inquire into the extent of agreement they commanded or consider who or what, if anything, challenged their authority. For example, he declared that the "religious tradition" of the United States "has consistently affirmed a national belief in God," but in recognizing that tradition he gave no heed to the millions of Americans who questioned or rejected that belief or even to the many atheists who not only challenged it but did so formally in the courts.[19] Similarly, he defended his interpretation of the Second Amendment on grounds of a "tradition" of gun possession while dismissing the contrary

Michael W. McConnell, *Originalism and the Desegregation Decisions*, 81 VA. L. REV. 947 (1995) (identifying numerous scholars who took that view, at 951–52, but contradicting that consensus).

[16] MICHAEL J. KLARMAN, FROM JIM CROW TO CIVIL RIGHTS: THE SUPREME COURT AND THE STRUGGLE FOR RACIAL EQUALITY 26 (2004).

[17] *Rutan*, 497 U.S. at 95 n.1 (Scalia, J., dissenting).

[18] *See, e.g.*, J.E.B. v. Alabama ex rel. T. B., 511 U.S. 127, 156, 163 (1994) (Scalia, J., dissenting); United States v. Virginia, 518 U.S. at 568 (Scalia, J. dissenting); Obergefell v. Hodges, 135 S. Ct. 2584, 2626, 2628 (2015) (Scalia, J., dissenting). *See* BISKUPIC, AMERICAN ORIGINAL, 269–70; RICHARD A. BRISBIN, JUSTICE ANTONIN SCALIA AND THE CONSERVATIVE REVIVAL 221–22, 327 (1997); LAURENCE H. TRIBE & MICHAEL C. DORF, ON READING THE CONSTITUTION 97–109 (1991). On "invented traditions," *see* Eric Hobsbawm, *Introduction: Inventing Traditions*, *in* THE INVENTION OF TRADITION 1–14 (Eric Hobsbawm & Terence Ranger eds. 1983).

[19] SCALIA SPEAKS, 320. In *Elk Grove Unified School District v. Newdow*, 542 U.S 1 (2004) (Stevens, J.), an atheist challenged the phrase "under God" in the Pledge of Allegiance, and Scalia had to recuse himself because of his prior public statements supporting religion. BISKUPIC, AMERICAN ORIGINAL, 267–68. For other similar challenges by atheists, *see, e.g.*, Torasco v. Watkins, 367 U.S. 488 (1961) (ruling unanimously that states cannot bar an atheist from holding local office because he refuses to take oath asserting a belief in God); Laurie Goodstein, *In 7 States, Atheists Fight for Removal of Belief Rule*, N.Y. TIMES, Dec. 7, 2014, p. A23.

"tradition" of widespread regulation and restriction on the possession of firearms.[20] Thus, to defend *Brown*, Scalia made an exception to his standard concept of the normative authority of tradition and reshaped it to conform to the dominant contemporary—and entirely nonoriginalist—social judgment about race that he had come to accept in the late twentieth century.

Three years later, moreover, he had no qualm about denouncing the Warren Court for doing exactly what he had done in justifying *Brown*. In *Minnesota v. Dickerson*, a Fourth Amendment case, he indicted his judicial bête noir on the ground that in 1968 it had "made no serious attempt to determine compliance with traditional standards" but had merely relied on "current estimations" of reasonableness.[21] Given that he had done exactly the same thing in justifying his acceptance of *Brown*, his condemnation of the Warren Court in *Dickerson* illustrated the inconsistency, if not sheer expedience, of the accusations he made and the arguments he deployed.

When necessary, Scalia's view of the role of tradition could also change in other ways as well.[22] In *Michael H. v. Gerald D.*, writing for the Court, he declared that tradition gave meaning to the Due Process Clause and that "our traditions have protected the marital family." Consequently, he upheld a state statute that created an irrebuttable presumption against a child's biological father who was not married to the child's mother. He ruled that the child of a married woman living with her husband was a child of that marriage. "Our decisions establish that the Constitution protects the sanctity of the family," he explained, "precisely because the institution of the family is deeply rooted in this Nation's history and tradition."[23]

A decade later, however, in *Troxel v. Granville* he ignored those same traditions and rejected a mother's appeal to the "traditional" protections that the Due Process Clause gave to the "marital family." There, as applied to a petition filed by a child's grandparents and opposed by the mother, the Court voided a state statute that gave "any person" the right to petition for visitation rights over the objection of the child's parents. Scalia dissented.

---

[20] *E.g.*, McDonald v. City of Chicago, 561 U.S. 742, 791, 792 (2010) (Scalia, J., concurring). *See* chapter 7.

[21] Minnesota v. Dickerson, 508 U.S. 366, 379, 380 (1993) (Scalia, J., concurring).

[22] Scalia was willing to massively distort Church history and its "traditional" doctrines when he told a Catholic audience that "our faith's message" on the separation of church and state was "essentially the same as that of the Constitution: church and state are separate." ANTONIN SCALIA, ON FAITH: LESSONS FROM AN AMERICAN BELIEVER 102–03 (Christopher J. Scalia & Edward Whelan eds., 2019).

[23] Michael H. v. Gerald D., 491 U.S. 110, 123–24 (1989) (Scalia, J.). Scalia's opinion stressed the defining power of traditions to create "fundamental rights." *Id.* at 122–24.

The traditions protecting the "marital family" that had been so compelling a decade earlier in *Michael H.* suddenly had no force. "Judicial vindication of 'parental rights' under a Constitution that does not even mention them" was wholly improper, he declared, suddenly and inconsistently invoking his "rule of silence" to negate the relevance of "tradition." Thus, enforcing the mother's right "will be ushering in a new regime of judicially prescribed, and federally prescribed, family law."[24] His counterpoised principles of "tradition" and constitutional "silence" proved handy alternatives, and he could deploy one or the other depending on the particular result he sought.[25]

Scalia played equally fast and loose with the Fourth Amendment. He defended the Court's 1928 decision in *Olmstead v. United States*, which held that wiretapping was not covered by the amendment.[26] "Easy case," he explained, for in *Olmstead* "the real Fourth Amendment governed," and a "conversation is not a person, house, paper, or effect"—the specific and limited categories of things that the amendment explicitly protected.[27] Fair enough, one might suppose as a matter of strict textualism, but once again Scalia was unwilling to adhere to any strict textualism. If "speech" and "press" were synecdoches for a broader range of communicative activities, then "person, house, paper, or effect" could be seen equally as synecdoches for a broader range of protected items, areas, or interests. Without explicitly explaining his departure from the text, he nonetheless applied his elastic synecdoche method in some Fourth Amendment cases. In *United States v. Jones*, for example, he held that the amendment voided the search of an automobile, surely not a "person, house, paper, or effect."[28] Thus, in spite of his heralded claims about textualism and originalism, he was prepared to extend the Fourth Amendment's protection to new types of cases that lacked historical or precedential foundations, and he rejected both when he wished to stretch the amendment's reach to meet modern conditions.[29] In those cases, he was

---

[24] Troxel v. Granville, 530 U.S. 57, 91, 92–93 (2000) (Scalia, J., dissenting).

[25] Noticeably, in *Adoptive Couple v. Baby Girl*, 570 U.S. 637, 667 (2013) (Scalia, J., dissenting), which did not involve a substantive due process claim, Scalia treated tradition differently than he did in *Troxel* and *Michael H.* There, unlike his opinion in *Troxel*, he found tradition relevant, *Adoptive Couple* at 668, but, unlike his opinion in *Michael H.*, he found it supporting rather than opposing the claim of an unmarried biological father.

[26] Olmstead v. United States, 277 U.S. 438 (1928) (Taft, C.J.).

[27] SCALIA SPEAKS, 247.

[28] United States v. Jones, 565 U.S 400 (2012) (Scalia, J.).

[29] DAVID M. DORSEN, THE UNEXPECTED SCALIA: A CONSERVATIVE JUSTICE'S LIBERAL OPINIONS 61–63, 65, 181–82 (2017) (citing, inter alia, Arizona v. Hicks, 480 U.S. 321 (1987) (Scalia, J.) [hereafter DORSEN, UNEXPECTED].

ready to abandon the text of "the real Fourth Amendment" and embrace a more flexible, expanding, and thus "living" approach.[30]

Scalia tried to limit such "living" interpretations of the Fourth Amendment by rooting its protection in a property-based theory.[31] In *Jones* he emphasized that the government had "physically occupied private property" by attaching a GPS device to defendant's automobile and that "such a physical intrusion would have been considered a 'search' within the meaning of the Fourth Amendment when it was adopted."[32] The following year in *Florida v. Jardines* he fit his property-based approach to a case involving the police use of a drug-sniffing dog on defendant's front porch. There, he held the police action an unconstitutional search because it intruded into another "constitutionally protected" property right—control over "the curtilege of the house"—that was not "explicitly or implicitly permitted by the homeowner."[33]

He was not consistent, however, in applying that limiting theory. As six justices in *Jones* and *Jardines* agreed, such a property-based limitation was ill-adapted to meet the challenges posed by modern technological developments,[34] and Scalia had in effect already surrendered his property-based theory to that obvious new reality. In *Kyllo v. United States* he invalidated the search of a house based on police use of a thermal imagining device located on a public street.[35] There, the police action was arguably "unreasonable," but it involved neither an intrusion into any traditional property right nor any kind of "search" that the Founders could possibly have recognized.[36] On the basis of the amendment's term "unreasonable," however, Scalia ruled the police action an unlawful search and in effect accepted the idea that the Fourth Amendment, like the First, had some kind of practically

---

[30] SCALIA SPEAKS, 247.

[31] Scalia's goal was to limit or overrule the Warren Court's decision in *Katz v. United States*, 389 U.S. 347 (1967), which came to stand for the proposition that government violated the Fourth Amendment when its conduct violated "reasonable expectation of privacy." The quoted phrase appeared in the concurring opinion of Justice John Marshall Harlan, *id.* at 360 and 362. LAURENCE TRIBE & JOSHUA MATZ, UNCERTAIN JUSTICE: THE ROBERTS COURT AND THE CONSTITUTION 233–35 (2014) [hereafter TRIBE & MATZ, UNCERTAIN JUSTICE].

[32] *Jones*, 565 U.S. at 404–05 (Scalia, J.).

[33] Florida v. Jardines, 569 U.S. 1, 6, 7 (2013) (Scalia, J.).

[34] *Jones*, 565 U.S. at 413 (Sotomayor, J., concurring) and *id.* at 418 (Alito, J., concurring in the judgment, joined by Ginsburg, Breyer, and Kagan, JJ.); *Jardines*, 569 U.S. at 12 (Kagan, J., concurring, joined by Ginsburg and Sotomayor, JJ.) and *id.* at 16 (Alito, J., dissenting, joined by Kennedy and Breyer, JJ.).

[35] Kyllo v. United States, 533 U.S. 27 (2001) (Scalia, J.).

[36] In contrast, Scalia upheld another search that the Founders would similarly have been unable to imagine, the police use of a helicopter hovering 400 feet over a person's greenhouse looking for marijuana. Florida v. Riley, 488 U.S. 445 (1989) (White, J., joined by Scalia, J.).

adaptive and readily expansive quality—precisely what he condemned in *Dickerson* and elsewhere as "living constitutionalism."

In originalist terms, in fact, Scalia's Fourth Amendment jurisprudence was remarkably inconsistent. In one case, for example, he argued that the original purpose of the Fourth Amendment was to bar general warrants issued without an individualized basis of suspicion and hence that it barred the random drug-testing of customs workers.[37] In a subsequent case, however, he contradicted that view by setting aside what he had described as the amendment's original purpose and approving the random drug-testing of high school athletes on practical grounds.[38] Similarly, in his historical argument in *Jones* was dubious, while his originalist analysis in *Dickerson* seemed "unsustainable on historical grounds."[39]

Scalia's opinion in *Dickerson*, moreover, illustrated the amorphous nature of his originalism in Fourth Amendment cases. "The purpose" of the amendment, he explained, was "to preserve that degree of respect for the privacy of persons and the inviolability of their property that existed when the provision was adopted."[40] On that ground, he took another opportunity to castigate the Warren Court, this time for its nonoriginalist decision in *Terry v. Ohio* which purportedly controlled in *Dickerson*.[41] *Terry* held that the police could "stop" a person if they had a "reasonable" suspicion of wrongdoing and that, in the process, they could conduct a pat down "frisk" to ensure that the person was not armed. Speculating that "the 'stop' portion of the *Terry* 'stop-and-frisk' holding accords with the common law," Scalia expressed skepticism about the originalist legitimacy of its "frisk" ruling. "I frankly doubt," he speculated with nothing but filio-pietistic reverence to back him up, that "the fiercely proud men who adopted our Fourth Amendment would have allowed themselves to be subjected, on mere *suspicion* of being armed and dangerous, to such indignity." Claiming to "adhere to original meaning," however, he nonetheless accepted both parts of *Terry*. "And though I do not favor the mode of analysis in Terry," he admitted, "I cannot say that its result was wrong."[42] His opinion in *Dickerson* exemplified both his casual, offhanded, and sometimes

---

[37] National Treasury Employees Union v. Von Raab, 489 U.S. 656, 680 (1989) (Scalia, J., dissenting).
[38] Vernonia School District v. Acton, 515 U.S. 646 (1995) (Scalia, J.).
[39] DORSEN, UNEXPECTED, 181.
[40] *Dickerson*, 508 U.S. at 380 (Scalia, J., concurring).
[41] Terry v. Ohio, 392 U.S. 1 (1968) (Warren, C.J.).
[42] *Dickerson*, 508 U.S. at 380–82 (Scalia, J., concurring) (emphasis in original).

wholly speculative use of history as well as the subjective and ad hoc nature of the originalist methodology he claimed to apply.[43]

Indeed, judged by his own originalist standard, Scalia's opinion in *Dickerson* was inconsistent with his ruling in *Kyllo*. If the purpose of the Fourth Amendment was "to preserve that degree of respect" for privacy "that existed when the provision was adopted," as he declared in *Dickerson*, then it was clear in *Kyllo* that the amendment could not possibly protect against the use of a thermal imaging device placed on a public street. Such a "degree of respect" for privacy did not, and could not, have existed—or even been imagined—"when the provision was adopted."

Scalia's opinion in *Kyllo* highlighted the gulf that often existed between his actual legal reasoning and his proclaimed originalist theory. "Words in the Constitution," he claimed, "were not to be interpreted in the abstract, but rather according to the understandings that existed when they were adopted."[44] The Constitution's "general terms" could be readily applied, he explained similarly on another occasion, because "[w]hat these generalities meant as applied to many phenomena that existed at the time of their adoption was well understood and accepted."[45] Thermal imagining devices, of course, were included in neither "understandings that existed" nor "phenomena that existed" when the Constitution was adopted.[46]

Beyond those inconsistent applications of originalism tower two more comprehensive inconsistencies in Fourth Amendment cases. First, in accepting the Court's broad "reasonableness" standard in search cases, Scalia abandoned the amendment's narrow original meaning that limited its prohibition only to the government's use of "general warrants."[47] Second, and

---

[43] Scalia, for example, tossed in an entirely speculative and unfounded historical contention when he dissented from the Court's decision to uphold the taking of a DNA swab as a "minimal" intrusion. "But I doubt that the proud men who wrote the charter of our liberties would have been so eager to open their mouths for royal inspection." Maryland v. King, 569 U.S. 435, 466, 482 (2013) (Scalia, J., dissenting). *Accord Austin*, 494 U.S. at 693 (Scalia, J., dissenting) (giving formal and hypothetical nod to the Founders by speculating on what they might have believed).

[44] SCALIA SPEAKS, 198.

[45] SCALIA, READING, 85. "I take it to be a fundamental principle of constitutional adjudication that the terms in the Constitution must be given the meaning ascribed to them at the time of their ratification." *Dickerson*, 508 U.S. at 379 (Scalia, J., concurring).

[46] Scalia similarly violated those statements of his originalist theory to achieve the result he sought in the Second Amendment. The word "Arms" there, he declared, "extends, prima facie, to all instruments that constitute bearable arms even those that were not in existence at the time of the founding." District of Columbia v. Heller, 554 U.S. 570, 582 (20008) (Scalia, J.).

[47] Thomas Y. Davies, *Recovering the Original Fourth Amendment*, 98 MICH. L. REV. 547, 553, 591 and *passim* (1999). For Scalia's acceptance of the reasonableness standard in the absence of clear common-law precedents, *see, e.g.*, Wyoming v. Houghton, 526 U.S. 295, 299–300 (1999) (Scalia, J.).

even more arresting, for the most part he simply abandoned originalism altogether in Fourth Amendment cases. He invoked originalist reasoning in only 18.63 percent of the Fourth Amendment cases he heard.[48]

Scalia was similarly inconsistent in addressing the Fifth Amendment's Takings Clause. There, he sought to expand protections for private property by bringing certain "regulatory" takings within the amendment's coverage, and his controversial opinion in *Lucas v. South Carolina Coastal Council* was triply revealing.[49] First, it demonstrated how he was willing to squeeze inferences from the thinnest of historical materials when he had little else to support his political and ideological goal. In *Lucas* he tried to justify his broadened interpretation of the Takings Clause by citing the fact that the First Congress deleted the part of Madison's original draft of the amendment that seemed to restrict the clause to only "physical deprivations."[50] With no historical support, Scalia opined that the First Congress could have changed Madison's language because it wished to broaden the clause so it would extend to "regulatory takings." As in *Dickerson*, his reasoning was once again entirely speculative.

Second, his opinion also revealed other inconsistencies. "It is always perilous," he chided Justice Stevens in a later case, "to derive the meaning of an adopted provision from another provision deleted in the drafting process."[51] That was, of course, exactly what he himself had done with Madison's draft in *Lucas*. More notably, his use of Madison's draft also contradicted his rule that one should never use "legislative history."[52] The original draft of the clause was precisely one tiny fragment of legislative history. Scalia's transgression was particularly acute, moreover, because the draft was the barest possible kind of "legislative history," a single brief fragment from the past, wholly lacking in the kind of depth and detail that sometimes made modern

[48] Lawrence Rosenthal, *An Empirical Inquiry into the Use of Originalism: Fourth Amendment Jurisprudence During the Career of Justice Scalia*, 70 HASTINGS L.J. 75 (2018). Justice Thomas did slightly worse, relying on originalism only 15.71 percent of the time, and the Court itself invoked originalism in less than 14 percent of the cases it decided.

[49] Lucas v. South Carolina Coastal Council, 505 U.S. 1003, 1028 n.15 (1992) (Scalia, J.). On Scalia's inconsistent originalism in Takings Clause cases, *see* Nicole Stelle Garnett, *Justice Scalia's Rule of Law and Law of Takings*, 41 VERMONT L. REV. 717 (2017).

[50] Scalia argued that "the text of the Clause can be read to encompass regulatory as well as physical deprivations (in contrast to the text originally proposed by Madison)." Madison's original draft provided that "No person shall be . . . obliged to relinquish his property, where it may be necessary for public use, without a just compensation". *Lucas*, 505 U.S. at 1028 n.15 (Scalia, J.). For a historical analysis showing that regulatory takings were not part of the original understanding, *see* William Michael Treanor, *The Original Understanding of the Takings Clause*, 95 COLUM. L. REV. 782 (1995).

[51] *Heller*, 554 U.S. at 590 (Scalia, J.).

[52] SCALIA SPEAKS, 234; SCALIA, READING, 388.

"legislative history" a highly informative and relatively reliable source. In spite of that, Scalia was still willing to use that tiny scrap of legislative history when it served his purpose.

Third, and most fundamental, Scalia's opinion in *Lucas* showed that, when historical sources furnished him little or no support, he was more than ready to abandon originalism altogether and take recourse in other more immediately serviceable rationales. Conceding that the dissenters were "correct that early constitutional theorists did not believe the Takings Clause embraced regulations of property at all," he simply dismissed that "original" understanding as "entirely irrelevant."[53] Instead, he invoked and relied on a principle that the Court first accepted only in 1922 in *Pennsylvania Coal. Co. v. Mahon.*[54] Indeed, he even admitted that prior to *Mahon* "it was generally thought that the Takings Clause reached only a 'direct appropriation' of property."[55] Underlying his decision was neither originalism nor textualism but his own antiregulatory and antidistributionist political views.[56]

The fact that Scalia's own antiregulatory political views shaped his interpretation of the Takings Clause and inspired his efforts to expand private property rights had been even more apparent five years earlier in *Nollan v. California Coastal Commission.* There, Scalia wrote for a five-justice majority that overturned a state court ruling requiring the owners of a beachfront residence to allow a narrow, ten-foot-wide public easement across their property along the beachfront. The easement would make a minimal intrusion on the property while allowing the public to walk between two public beaches that were located approximately a half-mile apart on either side of the owners' property. Equally important, it would allow the owners their continued and full access to the beach and ocean, and its public use would not intrude in any way on the bulk of their property which was rigidly blocked off from the easement pathway by an eight-foot-high concrete seawall.[57] Thus,

[53] In a footnote rejecting the historical understanding, Scalia accepted the criticism that "our description of the 'understanding' of land ownership that informs the Takings Clause is not supported by early American experience. That is largely true, but entirely irrelevant." It was irrelevant because Scalia declared that, on his own present-day reading, the text meant something different from what earlier judges had thought it meant. *Lucas*, 505 U.S. at 1028 n.15 (Scalia, J.).

[54] Pennsylvania Coal Co. v. Mahon, 260 U.S. 393 (1922) (Holmes, J.). Scalia referred to *Mahon* six times in his opinion. *Lucas*, 505 U.S. at 1014, 1015, 1018, 1026, 1027, 1028 (Scalia, J.).

[55] *Lucas*, 505 U.S. at 1014 (Scalia, J.).

[56] *See* Pennell v. San Jose, 485 U.S. 1, 15, 21–24 (1988) (Scalia, J., concurring in part and dissenting in part); Stop the Beach Renourishment, Inc. v. Florida Department of Environmental Protection, 560 U.S. 702 (2010) (Scalia, J., announcing the judgment of the Court and writing for a plurality in Parts II and III of an opinion, joined by Rehnquist, C.J. and Thomas and Alito, JJ.).

[57] Nollan v. California Coastal Commission, 483 U.S. 825, 827 (1987) (Scalia, J.). I am indebted to my colleague Richard Chused for his insights on Scalia's reasoning in *Nollan.*

the easement served a genuine public interest in providing access between two public areas while, at the same time, preserving both the owners' access to the beach and the ocean as well as their exclusive use and control of most of their property, including the largest part of it that was located inside the seawall where their residence stood.[58]

To invalidate the state ruling, Scalia reshaped the law. First, he seemed to raise the showing required to overcome a Takings Clause claim by imposing a higher burden on government regulatory actions than the Due Process and Equal Protection Clauses imposed. To justify a land-use regulation, he maintained, more was required than a mere showing of "rationality." Although the Court's precedents had not determined the nature of the relevant standard under the Takings Clause, as he acknowledged,[59] he nonetheless declared that the clause required the government to show that a regulation would "substantially advance" a "legitimate state interest" and serve "a substantial government purpose."[60] He did not explain those standards further because he found that there was no "essential nexus" between the state's regulation and its claimed justifications.[61] His rejection of due process and equal protection standards together with his invocation of the "substantially advance" and "substantial" purpose standards, however, suggested a new and more restrictive approach to the Takings Clause.[62]

Second, and far more fundamental, Scalia asserted a constitutional premise that was sweeping, false, textually without support, and entirely nonoriginalist. "Had California simply required the Nollans to make an easement across their beachfront available to the public on a permanent basis in order to increase public access to the beach," he declared, it would have left

---

[58] "As this Court made clear in PruneYard Shopping Center v. Robins, 447 U.S. 74, 83 (1980), physical access to private property in itself creates no takings problem if it does not 'unreasonably impair the value or use of [the] property.' Appellants can make no tenable claim that either their enjoyment of their property or its value is diminished by the public's ability merely to pass and repass a few feet closer to the seawall beyond which appellants' house is located." Nollan, 483 U.S. at 854–55 (Brennan, J., dissenting).

[59] "Our cases have not elaborated on the standards for determining what constitutes a 'legitimate state interest' or what type of connection between the regulation and the state interest satisfies the requirement that the former 'substantially advance' the latter." Nollan, 483 U.S. at 834 (Scalia, J.).

[60] Nollan, 483 U.S. at 834 & n.3 (Scalia, J.). Scalia drew the phrase "substantial government purpose" from Penn Central Transportation Co. v. New York City, 438 U.S. 104 (1978). Id. at 834.

[61] Nollan, 483 U.S. at 837 (Scalia, J.).

[62] Scalia essentially acknowledged the reasonableness of the state's action but held that such reasonableness was not enough to justify the easement. Nollan, 483 U.S. at 841–42 (Scalia, J.). In another 5-4 decision, the Court subsequently expanded on Nollan and imposed a relatively restrictive limit on a city's effort to take private property as part of its land-use plan. Dolan v. City of Tigard, 512 U.S. 374 (1994) (Rehnquist, C.J., joined by Scalia, J.).

"no doubt there would have been a taking."[63] The right of owners to exclude others, he continued, was an essential element of private property.[64] The problem with that underlying premise was that neither traditional property law nor established constitutional law supported it. From the time of the Founders to the present the law had commonly required property owners to grant entirely analogous easements across private property for public streets and sidewalks.[65] Further, the law had also upheld a wide range of zoning limitations on both the uses of property and the kind of structures their owners could build, including restrictions on size, height, and proximity to the property of others.[66] All of those regulations were "takings" of property, and the law had long approved them on grounds of their reasonableness for general public convenience. Thus, the easement at issue in *Nollan* was easily proper under established law. Scalia, however, asserted an essentially absolute principle that promised to expand constitutional protections for property and limit government regulatory efforts significantly. In supporting his goal, he made no mention of the Founders and cited no originalist sources.

Scalia ignored history once again and misleadingly cited originalist sources when he advanced one of his most characteristic claims, that "standing" doctrine had a constitutional basis in the principle of separation of powers. "My thesis," he wrote in an early law review article, "is that the judicial doctrine of standing is a crucial and inseparable element" of separation of powers.[67] For originalist support he advanced only abstract and general quotations from *Federalist No. 48* and *Marbury v. Madison*, none of which stated or even clearly implied his "thesis."[68] In fact, it was not until the early twentieth century when the Court first suggested—and then

---

[63] *Nollan*, 483 U.S. at 831 (Scalia, J.). The case turned on whether the Coastal Commission could require the Nollans to agree to the easement in exchange for permission to build a new house on the property. The Court's negative answer to that question was ultimately controlled by Scalia's preemptive assertion that the easement was an unconstitutional "taking." *Id.* at 836–39, 842–42 (Scalia, J.).

[64] *Nollan*, 483 U.S. at 831 (Scalia, J.). Requiring "uncompensated conveyance of the easement outright would violate the Fourteenth Amendment." *Id.* at 834.

[65] *Nollan*, 483 U.S. at 854 (Brennan, J., dissenting).

[66] *See, e.g., Penn Central*, 438 U.S. 104; Minnesota v. Clover Leaf Creamery Co., 449 U.S. 456 (1981) (Brennan, J.); Euclid v. Ambler Realty Co., 272 U.S. 365 (1926).

[67] Antonin Scalia, *The Doctrine of Standing as an Essential Element of the Separation of Powers*, 17 SUFFOLK U. L. REV. 881 (1982) [hereafter Scalia, *Doctrine of Standing*].

[68] The quote from the *Federalist Papers* referred only generally to the comparative reach of the three branches, and the quote from *Marbury* noted only that the judiciary had no general jurisdiction to inquire into the discretionary acts of the executive. In addition, Scalia played loose with history by including a purportedly supporting footnote reference to *Hayburn's Case*, 2 U.S. (2 Dall.) 409 (1792), and suggesting that its requirement of "adverse parties with personal interest in the matter" were required for Article III standing. Scalia, *Doctrine of Standing*, 882–83. *Hayburn's Case* did not, in fact, place its requirement of standing on Article III.

somewhat obliquely—that standing and separation of powers were directly connected.[69] Scalia's standing thesis, moreover, was entirely presentist and political in its target. He used it to attack Chief Justice Earl Warren's 1968 opinion in *Flast v. Cohen* that linked separation of powers with the Article III concepts of "cases" and "controversies" but partitioned standing doctrine off from that constitutional basis.[70] When Scalia was able to write his "thesis" into the nation's law a decade later in *Lujan v. Defenders of Wildlife*, he did no better in providing it with an originalist foundation. There, he simply asserted brashly—and wrongly—that the Court had "always" linked the concrete injury requirement of standing to a constitutional foundation in the doctrine of separation of powers.[71]

Similarly, Scalia abandoned both originalism and textualism when he considered the law of treaty enforcement. Like a majority of the modern Court, he rejected the original doctrine that treaties were supreme federal law and consequently enforceable in the courts under the explicit terms of the Supremacy Clause.[72] In its place he accepted the later interpretation that treaties were supreme federal law only if they were "self-executing," a requirement that the Court had developed on its own and held that most treaties failed to satisfy. That interpretation meant that, absent special congressional action, most treaties were not enforceable in the courts. The doctrinal change that he embraced was another instance of the "living" constitutionalism that he purportedly scorned but frequently accepted and used.

Equally telling, the change in the Court's interpretation of treaties had been driven by the rise of the United States to a dominant international position over the course of the nineteenth and early twentieth centuries and

[69] EVAN TSEN LEE, JUDICIAL RESTRAINT IN AMERICA: HOW THE AGELESS WISDOM OF THE FEDERAL COURTS WAS INVENTED 39 (2011) (citing Massachusetts v. Mellon, 262 U.S. 447, 488–89 (1923) (Sutherland, J.)) [hereafter LEE, JUDICIAL RESTRAINT]. *See id.* at 68, 132–35. *Accord* Cass R. Sunstein, *What's Standing after Lujan? Of Citizen Suits, "Injuries," and Article III*, 163, 169, 171, 173–77 (1992).

[70] Flast v. Cohen 392 U.S. 83 (1968) (Warren, C.J.). Scalia finessed his lack of originalist sources by attacking *Flast* on the ground that "never before had the doctrine of standing been severed from the principles of separation of powers." Scalia, *Doctrine of Standing*, 891. His claim was true only because the two doctrines had not been explicitly linked until the twentieth century, and it was only after the linkage had been recognized that *Flast* attempted to separate them in distinguishing among the various "justiciability" doctrines. *See* LEE, JUDICIAL RESTRAINT, 132–35.

[71] "If the concrete injury requirement has the separation-of-powers significance we have always said, the answer [to the question at issue] must be obvious." Lujan v. Defenders of Wildlife, 504 U.S. 555, 577 (1992) (Scalia, J.). For originalist authority, he quoted only from the same two inadequate sources he used in his 1982 article, *Federalist No. 48, id.* at 560, and *Marbury v. Madison, id.* at 576.

[72] *See* DAVID L. SLOSS, THE DEATH OF TREATY SUPREMACY: AN INVISIBLE CONSTITUTIONAL CHANGE 65 and *passim* (2016) (treaties of their own force preempt state law and create enforceable federal law under original meaning of Supremacy Clause) [hereafter SLOSS, DEATH OF TREATY].

then by the subsequent efforts of conservatives after World War II to prevent international human rights treaties from having domestic effect, especially as they could be used to challenge racial discrimination in the United States.[73] The result of the changed doctrine was twofold: it limited judicial power, and it deprived minority groups of the protection offered by international human rights agreements. Scalia readily accepted both the Court's nonoriginalist and nontextualist interpretation of the treaty power as well as the appealingly "conservative" social and political results it brought.[74]

Scalia also accepted the Fourteenth Amendment incorporation doctrine on modern and nonoriginalist grounds. The doctrine was highly dubious on originalist grounds, facially unsupported on textual grounds, and inconsistently and variously applied on logical grounds.[75] "The incorporation doctrine," explained one scholar who studied Scalia's jurisprudence, "is supported neither by the constitutional text nor by the traditional understanding of it."[76] Scalia nonetheless accepted the doctrine on the ground that it was "long established and narrowly limited."[77] Its "long established" status did not rest on any clear originalist or textualist determination but

[73] See SLOSS, DEATH OF TREATY, Part III.

[74] For Scalia's rejection of the original treaty supremacy doctrine, see Sanchez-Llamas v. Oregon, 548 U.S. 331, 346 (2006) (Roberts, C.J., joined by Scalia, J.) ("non-self-executing" treaties do not preempt state law unless Congress legislates to the contrary); Medillin v. Texas, 552 U.S. 491, 504–05 (2008) (Roberts, C.J., joined by Scalia, J.) (same).

[75] McDonald, 561 U.S. at 765 n.13 (Alito, J., joined by Scalia, J.), noted that the Court has not incorporated the Third Amendment's protections against quartering of soldiers and imposing excessive fines, the Fifth Amendment's grand jury indictment requirement, the Sixth Amendment right to a unanimous jury verdict, the Seventh Amendment right to a jury trial in civil cases, and the Eighth Amendment's prohibition on excessive fines. The opinion acknowledged, moreover, the changing nature of incorporation law and noted in particular that "[o]ur governing decisions regarding the Grand Jury Clause of the Fifth Amendment and the Seventh Amendment's civil jury requirement long predate the era of selective incorporation." Id. at 765 n.13. In addition to creating such gaps in the incorporation doctrine, the Court added important elements to some of the rights in the amendments. To the First Amendment it added a right of "expressive association," Roberts v. United States Jaycees, 468 U.S. 609, 622 (1984) (Brennan, J.); to the Fourth Amendment it added the prophylactic "exclusionary rule," Mapp v. Ohio, 367 U.S. 643 (1961) (Clark, J.); and to the Fifth Amendment's privilege against self-incrimination it added certain specified protective warnings, Miranda v. Arizona, 384 U.S. 436 (1966) (Warren, C.J.), and declared that the warnings were of constitutional stature in Dickerson v. United States, 530 U.S. 428 (2000) (Rehnquist, C.J.).

[76] RALPH A. ROSSUM, ANTONIN SCALIA'S JURISPRUDENCE: TEXT AND TRADITION 169 (2006) (citing Charles Fairman, Does the Fourteenth Amendment Incorporate the Bill of Rights? The Original Understanding, 2 STAN. L. REV. 5 (1949)) [hereafter ROSSUM, ANTONIN SCALIA'S JURISPRUDENCE]; RAOUL BERGER, THE FOURTEENTH AMENDMENT AND THE BILL OF RIGHTS (1989).

[77] "Except insofar as our decisions have included within the Fourteenth Amendment certain explicit substantive protections of the Bill of Rights—an extension I accept because it is both long established and narrowly limited—I reject the proposition that the Due Process Clause guarantees certain (unspecified) liberties, rather than merely guarantees certain procedures as a prerequisite to deprivation of liberty." Albright v. Oliver, 510 U.S. 266, 275–76 (1994) (Scalia, J., concurring). See McDonald, 561 U.S. at 791 (Scalia concurring).

began only in 1897 when, for the first time, the Court repudiated its earlier "originalist" precedents and used the Fourteenth Amendment to make a provision of the Bill of Rights, the Fifth Amendment's Takings Clause, applicable to the states.[78]

Although he surely did fight to keep incorporation "narrowly limited" when it was used to advance the kinds of rights that he opposed,[79] he nonetheless wielded it boldly and enthusiastically when he could use it to serve his own dominant personal values. Specifically, he used it readily and vigorously when it enabled him to protect guns and religion. To accomplish the former, he joined the other four conservatives in holding that incorporation made the Second Amendment applicable against the states.[80] He did so even though on originalist grounds it was clear that the Founders had adopted the Second Amendment to placate the states, protect their authority, and guarantee their right to maintain their militias free from federal interference.[81] Thus, as an originalist matter, incorporating the Second Amendment and thereby restricting the states and limiting their ability to regulate the ownership and possession of firearms simply made no sense.

To accomplish the latter, protecting religion, Scalia also cast originalism aside. The Founders had adopted the Establishment Clause, he acknowledged, to prevent the federal government from either establishing a national church or interfering with religious establishments in the states.[82] Given that

[78] In 1833 the Court rejected the idea that the Bill of Rights applied to the states in *Barron v. Baltimore*, 32 U.S. 243 (1833), and after adoption of the Fourteenth Amendment confirmed that proposition in *United States v. Cruikshank*, 92 U.S. 542 (1876). The first incorporation came only in 1897 in *Chicago, Burlington & Quincy Railroad v. Chicago*, 166 U.S. 226 (1897) (Harlan, J.).

[79] "I am willing to accept the proposition that the Due Process Clause of the Fourteenth Amendment, despite its textual limitation to procedure, incorporates certain substantive guarantees specified in the Bill of Rights; but I do not accept the proposition that it is the secret repository of all sorts of other, unenumerated, substantive rights." TXO Production Corp. v. Alliance Resources Corp, 509 U.S. 443, 470–71 (1993) (Scalia, J., concurring in the judgment).

[80] *McDonald*, 561 U.S. 742 (2010) (Alito, J., joined by Scalia) (incorporating the Second Amendment into the Fourteenth and thereby making it mandatory on the states). Scalia also wrote a concurring opinion responding to Stevens's dissent and defending judicial reliance on "the traditions of our people." *Id.* at 791, 792.

[81] *See* chapter 7.

[82] "The Establishment Clause was adopted to prohibit such an establishment of religion at the federal level (and to protect state establishments of religion from federal interference)." Lee v. Weisman, 505 U.S. 577, 631, 641 (1992) (Scalia, J., dissenting). The Court had affirmed that principle in *Permoli v. First Municipality of New Orleans*, 44 U.S. 589, 609 (1845) (Catron, J.). *See, e.g.*, Philip B. Kurland, *The Origins of the Religion Clauses of the Constitution*, 27 WM. & MARY L. REV. 839, 843 (1986). For a study arguing that the clause was not intended as a positive effort to support state establishments, *see* STEVEN K. GREEN, THE SECOND ESTABLISHMENT: CHURCH AND STATE IN NINETEENTH-CENTURY AMERICA, ch. 2, esp. 67–68 (2010) [hereafter GREEN, SECOND ESTABLISHMENT], and for a study arguing that the prohibition of a national religion was the sole point that the Founders agreed on in adopting the Establishment Clause, *see* DONALD L. DRAKEMAN, CHURCH, STATE, AND ORIGINAL INTENT, viii–ix, 260–62 (2010) [hereafter DRAKEMAN, CHURCH].

original understanding, the incorporation of the Establishment Clause—
like the incorporation of the Second Amendment—made no sense. It also
transformed two state-protective guarantees into state-limiting restrictions,
a result that was the precise opposite of the clause's original understanding
and purpose.[83]

Equally striking and more revealing about his jurisprudence and career,
Scalia not only accepted that nonoriginalist result, but he also proceeded to
use it to interpret the Establishment Clause in ways that advanced his own
personal beliefs. While still on the court of appeals, he had declared that the
jurisprudence of the clause was "in a state of utter chaos,"[84] and he was determined to reorder it to serve his own purposes. Rejecting interpretations and
doctrines that required strict separation of church and state, he maintained
that the clause meant that government could not favor a particular religion
over any other particular religion but that it could favor religion in general
over nonreligion.[85] Further, he sought to restrict the meaning of the word
"religion" to privilege what he accepted as "traditional" monotheistic faiths.

As a strictly textual matter, the Establishment Clause supported neither
of those goals. It simply stated that Congress "shall make no law respecting
an establishment of religion."[86] That text, John Witte, Jr. and Joel A. Nichols
concluded in their study of the Constitution's religion clauses, "has no plain
meaning."[87] On its face, however, the text seemed inconsistent with Scalia's
claim that the clause allowed governments to provide positive support for
religion. The text did not prohibit laws establishing some particular sect or
denomination but rather laws establishing "religion" in general. More particularly, it did not prohibit establishing "a religion" but simply "religion," using

---

[83] The Court did not incorporate the First Amendment's religion clauses until 1940. Cantwell
v. Connecticut, 310 U.S. 296, 303 (1940) (Roberts, J.). Scalia took the essentially arbitrary and
unfounded position that incorporation was fully consistent with the original meaning of the
Establishment Clause. McCreary County v. American Civil Liberties Union of Kentucky, 545 U.S.
844, 885, 898 (2005) (Scalia, J., dissenting). He has, however, "never written an opinion that asks
the unanswerable question of how it is that the Establishment Clause, intended by the words used
by the Framers in the First Congress to prevent the federal government from tampering with state
establishments of religion, can possibly be construed to mandate precisely such tampering." ROSSUM,
ANTONIN SCALIA'S JURISPRUDENCE 129.

[84] DEREK DAVIS, ORIGINAL INTENT: CHIEF JUSTICE REHNQUIST AND THE COURSE OF AMERICAN
CHURCH/STATE RELATIONS 157 (1991) [hereafter DAVIS, ORIGINAL INTENT].

[85] Lamb's Chapel v. Center Moriches Union Free School District, 508 U.S. 384, 397, 401 (1993)
(Scalia, J., concurring in the judgment); Board of Education of Kiryas Joel v. Grumet, 512 U.S. 687,
732, 748 (1994) (Scalia, J., dissenting).

[86] U.S. CONST. amend. 1.

[87] JOHN WITTE, JR. & JOEL A. NICHOLS, RELIGION AND THE AMERICAN CONSTITUTIONAL
EXPERIMENT 81 (4th ed. 2016) [hereafter WITTE & NICHOLS, RELIGION]; DAVIS, ORIGINAL INTENT,
chs. 3–4.

the term in the most comprehensive sense possible. Indeed, neither the constitutional text nor the history of the clause's origin gave the slightest guidance as to "where to draw the line between religion and nonreligion."[88] Thus,
contrary to Scalia's contention, the text itself strongly pointed to the conclusion that the clause prohibited government from officially recognizing and
giving practical aid to "religion" in general.[89]

As an originalist matter, Scalia's claim rested on somewhat stronger
though still dubious grounds. While extensive historical scholarship produced conflicting findings, the one general conclusion it warranted most
clearly was that the Founders thought religion was very important but disagreed on the truly critical issue of its proper relationship to government.[90]
The Founders, Derek H. Davis concluded from his study of the historical
origins of the Establishment Clause, "were on the whole themselves unclear
and in some disagreement about the role that religion should play in national
life."[91] Beyond general agreement that the clause was designed to prohibit
Congress from establishing a national religion, Donald L. Drakeman confirmed in his similar study, "there is no body of evidence that supports any
more detailed sense of what the language meant to the people who voted for
[the Establishment Clause] or to the American public who received it."[92]

Seeking to support his claim that the clause positively favored religion,
Scalia turned to the Free Exercise Clause and his ever-serviceable backup
concept of tradition. He maintained that the former, which barred Congress

[88] WITTE & NICHOLS, RELIGION, 95. On the Court's subsequent struggle to determine what is "religion," see, e.g., MICHAEL W. McCONNELL, JOHN H. GARVEY, & THOMAS C. BERG, RELIGION AND THE
CONSTITUTION 712–41 (2006).

[89] "All of the evidence then, when examined in historical context, supports separationism as that
paradigm of church-state thought that best captures the progressively evolving intentions of the
founding fathers." DAVIS, RELIGION, 227. Scalia rejected, for example, the Court's earlier declaration that the Establishment Clause meant that no government, state or federal, "can pass laws which
aid one religion, aid all religions, or prefer one religion over another" and that "religious beliefs or
disbeliefs" were both equally protected. Everson v. Board of Education, 330 U.S. 1, 15-16 (1947)
(Black, J.).

[90] See, e.g., LEONARD W. LEVY, THE ESTABLISHMENT CLAUSE: RELIGION AND THE FIRST
AMENDMENT (1994) (finding that the Establishment Clause requires strict separation between
church and state); PHILIP HAMBURGER, SEPARATION OF CHURCH AND STATE (2004) (rejecting the
idea that the Establishment Clause requires a "wall of separation" between church and state).

[91] DEREK H. DAVIS, RELIGION AND THE CONTINENTAL CONGRESS, 1774–1789, at 212 (2000) [here-
after DAVIS, RELIGION]. Accord VINCENT PHILLIP MUNOZ, GOD AND THE FOUNDERS: MADISON,
WASHINGTON, AND JEFFERSON 207 (2009) (the "Founders' disagreement means that there is no single
church-state position that can claim the exclusive authority of America's founding history") [here-
after MUNOZ, GOD AND THE FOUNDERS].

[92] DRAKEMAN, CHURCH, 260. "The congressional record holds no Rosetta Stone for easy interpretation, and no 'smoking gun' that puts all evidentiary disputes to rest." WITTE & NICHOLS, RELIGION,
81–82; DAVIS, ORIGINAL INTENT, chs. 3–4.

from "prohibiting the free exercise" of religion, mandated "preferential treatment" for "religion in general"[93] and that the latter demonstrated that Americans and their government officials had from the nation's beginning invoked God in a variety of ways.[94] The problem with both of those arguments was apparent. As a strictly textual matter, the Free Exercise Clause did not necessarily imply government favoritism or positive support for religion as opposed to merely protecting all religions by requiring government to take a neutral and hands-off attitude toward all of them.[95] Similarly, the fact that Americans and their government officials thought religion highly important and often invoked God, the Deity, or Divine Providence did not mean that such ceremonial practices authorized positive governmental actions of an entirely different nature, actions that conferred on religious groups and institutions official recognition, approval, or support.[96]

Even more clearly, neither textual nor originalist sources provided support for Scalia's further effort to distinguish among religions by favoring traditional monotheistic ones. "One cannot say the word 'God,' or 'the Almighty,'

---

[93] *Lamb's Chapel*, 508 U. S. at 400 (Scalia, J., concurring in the judgment).

[94] In *Lee v. Weisman*, for example, Scalia dissented from the Court's ruling that the Establishment Clause prohibited religious invocations and benediction prayers at public school graduation ceremonies. There, the majority reasoned that public schools had no business incorporating religious elements into their ceremonies and that such religious rites exerted a degree of psychological coercion on the school's students. That decision, Scalia charged, "lays waste a tradition that is as old as public-school graduation ceremonies themselves, and that is a component of an even more longstanding American tradition of nonsectarian prayer to God at public celebrations generally." Lee v. Weisman, 505 U.S. at 631, 632 (Scalia, J., dissenting). Concurring with the Court's judgment, Justice David Souter rejected Scalia's reading of both the text and the "extratextual evidence of original meaning" that he presented. The latter stood "so unequivocally at odds with the textual premise inherent in existing precedent," Souter wrote, that it offered no significant basis for reconsidering the Court's precedents. *Id.* 505 U.S. at 609, 618 (Souter, J., concurring).

[95] The Court and some scholars have regarded the Free Exercise Clause and the Establishment Clause as in tension with one another, the former requiring the kind of special accommodations to religion that the latter prohibits. *See, e.g.*, Thomas v. Review Board of the Indiana Employment Security Division, 450 U.S. 707 (1981) (Burger, C.J.). Others have argued that the Establishment Clause was informed by the Free Exercise Clause and consequently permitted the government to support religion in general. *See, e.g.*, Noah Feldman, *The Intellectual Origins of the Establishment Clause*, 77 N.Y.U. L. REV. 346 (2002); Robert G. Natelson, *The Original Meaning of the Establishment Clause*, 14 WM. & MARY BILL RTS. J. 73 (2005). A neutral, hands-off interpretation of both clauses resolves those purported interpretative difficulties by eliminating the need to hold either that the two clauses are inconsistent or that one controls the other.

[96] Several justices referred to such public expressions about God and Divine Providence as "ceremonial deism." Lynch v. Donnelly 465 U.S. 668, 694, 716 (1984) (Brennan, J., dissenting); County of Allegheny v. American Civil Liberties Union, 492 U.S. 573, 623, 630 (1989) (O'Connor, concurring in part and concurring in the judgment). Scalia criticized the justices who disagreed with him by claiming that "indifference to 'religion in general' is *not* what our cases, both old and recent, demand." *Lamb's Chapel*, 508 U.S. at 400 (Scalia, J., concurring in the judgment) (emphasis in original). Justices who rejected Scalia's position emphasized that neutrality did not mean "indifference" to religion but rather full and equal respect for all religions in a pluralistic society. *E.g.*, County of Allegheny, 492 U.S. at 610 (Blackmun, J.); Lee v. Weisman, 505 U.S. at 589–90, 597–98 (1992) (Kennedy, J.).

one cannot offer public supplication or thanksgiving," he complained sorely, "without contradicting the beliefs of some people that there are many gods, or that God or the gods pay no attention to human affairs." Such religions he arbitrarily excluded from the Establishment Clause's coverage. Historical practices, he asserted, showed "that the Establishment Clause permits this disregard of polytheists and believers in unconcerned deities, just as it permits the disregard of devout atheists."[97]

In reaching that exclusionary conclusion Scalia again ignored both textual and originalist sources. As for textualism, he ignored the fact that the Constitution did not even mention the word "God," much less refer to any single or specific kind of "god." Not surprisingly, he refused to apply his "rule of silence" to declare the issue beyond judicial authority. Further, he ignored the fact that, contrary to the Constitution's treatment of so many key words that had specific substantive meanings, the clause did not capitalize the word "religion."[98] That fact suggested once again that the Constitution used the term, as it used the other rights-related terms in the First Amendment, in the broadest possible generic sense. In fact, the Court had previously accepted that principle before Scalia joined it. There was no need for a judicial judgment about any "particular belief or practice," it explained in 1981, because "religious beliefs need not be acceptable, logical, consistent, or comprehensible to others in order to merit First Amendment protection."[99]

As for originalism, Scalia ignored the indisputable and decisive fact that many of the Founders were themselves either deists who saw God as aloof from human affairs or rationalistic theists who embraced ideas of "natural" religion rather than strict versions of Christianity.[100] "A majority of the delegates" to the Constitutional Convention," Steven K. Green wrote in his

---

[97] *McCreary*, 545 U.S. at 893 (Scalia, J., dissenting). For a critique of Scalia's generalized monotheism, *see* ANDREW KOPPELMAN, DEFENDING AMERICAN RELIGIOUS NEUTRALITY 40–41 (2013); Thomas Colby, *A Constitutional Hierarchy of Religions? Justice Scalia, the Ten Commandments, and the Future of the Establishment Clause*, 100 Nw. L. REV. 1097 (2006); Andrew M. Koppelman, *Phony Originalism and the Establishment Clause* (2011), Faculty Working Papers, Paper 3, at 7–14, *available at* http://scholarlycommons.law.northwestern.edu/facultyworkingpapers/3 (last consulted Aug. 26, 2019) [hereafter Koppelman, *Phony Originalism*].

[98] Contrast the uncapitalized form of "religion" with references, *e.g.*, to the "States" (passim), the "Power" of the federal branches (arts. I, II, and III), Electors (art. II), "Full Faith and Credit" and "Privileges and Immunities of Citizens" (art. IV), "Debts and Engagements" (art. VI), and "Ratification," "Conventions of nine States" and "Establishment of this Constitution" (art. VII). The Bill of Rights similarly capitalized many words with specific meanings, *e.g.*, "Government," "Militia," "Arms," "Soldier," "Owner," "Warrants," "Oaths," "Affirmation," etc.

[99] *Thomas*, 450 U.S. at 714 (Burger, C.J.).

[100] GREGG L. FRAZER, THE RELIGIOUS BELIEFS OF AMERICA'S FOUNDERS: REASON, RATIONALISM, AND REVOLUTION 173–74, 185 (2012); DAVID L. HOLMES, THE FAITHS OF THE FOUNDING FATHERS 49–51 (2006).

examination of the Establishment Clause, "held deistic or heterodox beliefs and drew their understanding of rights and governance from Enlightenment and Whig writers." A "majority of the founding documents were all but bereft of religious language," he continued, and they generally "took on secular or, at best, deistic overtones."[101] Further, Scalia also ignored the variety of opinions that the Founders had expressed about what religions were properly included under the Establishment Clause. "Some set the legal line at Protestantism, others at Christianity in general (thereby including Catholics and Eastern Orthodox)," Witte and Nichols explained, "and still others at theism (thereby including Jews, Muslims, and Deists)." Indeed, Scalia ignored the fact that some quite prominent Founders—Madison and Jefferson, for example—argued "for the equality of religious and nonreligious individuals before the law," urging inclusion of those who held any kind of religious belief, theist or not. "Most founders," Witte and Nichols concluded, "extended the principle of equality before the law to all peaceable theistic religions, including not only Christianity, but also Judaism, Islam, and Hinduism."[102] Thus, on originalist grounds, the amendment seemed designed to include all religions that somehow recognized a god or gods.[103]

In excluding deists and polytheists Scalia not only contradicted the originalist record but contradicted his own interpretive methodology as well. Without explanation, in construing the meaning of the word "religion" he failed to apply the synecdoche method that he used to justify his expansive interpretation of other key words in the First Amendment. If the Founders placed "speech," "press," and "religion" in the very same amendment, and if the first two were synecdoches standing for a wide range of communicative acts, why was the generic word "religion" not equally a synecdoche standing for a wide range of religious beliefs? Considered as a synecdoche, it should surely have included both deists and polytheists. Scalia, however, was not pursuing interpretive consistency but his own narrower religious goals.

Scalia's exclusion of deists and polytheists also contradicted the broad pronouncement he made when he sought to protect a different religion that met

---

[101] GREEN, SECOND DISESTABLISHMENT, 56, 31.

[102] WITTE & NICHOLS, RELIGION, 95, 51. "The founders' principal concern was directed to equality among theistic religions before the law." WITTE & NICHOLS, RELIGION, 51. The Establishment Clause was "designed to protect all theists, but only theists." Natelson, *Original Meaning*, 112. *See id.* at 97, 107, 109–12, 138–39.

[103] None of the Founders "argued seriously about extending constitutional protection" to "non-Western religious traditions practiced by, for example, African slaves or Native American tribes—let alone nontheistic traditions like Buddhism." WITTE & NICHOLS, RELIGION, 95.

his approval. "I have always believed," he announced in *Board of Education of Kiryas Joel v. Grumet* in 1994, a case involving a small Jewish community, that "the Establishment Clause prohibits the favoring of one religion over others."[104] But in dismissing deists and polytheists from consideration under the Establishment Clause, he did just that.

Specifically, Scalia insisted that the Establishment Clause was intended to refer only to religions that taught the existence of "a benevolent, omnipotent Creator and Ruler of the world."[105] He defended the "ceremonial" use of the Ten Commandments by two counties in Kentucky, for example, on the ground that the commandments were "not so closely associated with a single religious belief" but were "recognized by Judaism, Christianity, and Islam alike as divinely given."[106] Neither the constitutional text nor the original understanding singled out those three monotheistic religions as jointly circumscribing the meaning of the Establishment Clause, however, just as neither called for the exclusion of deists and polytheists. Thus, as a matter of original understanding, Scalia's interpretation arbitrarily narrowed the category of theistic religions that many or most of the Founders understood as falling within its coverage.

Originalist sources underscored other flaws as well in his appeal to those monotheistic religions. One was that at the founding Americans tended to be quite hostile toward Islam and its theology, and they were not moved to attribute any authority to it merely because it was a monotheistic religion. Rather, they were deeply suspicious of Islam because they believed that "Muslims submitted to religious despotism and were taught to accept political despotism."[107] Another flaw was that, insofar as the Founders did generally agree on more particular religious matters, they agreed not on generalized

---

[104] *Kiryas Joel*, 512 U.S. at 748 (Scalia, J., dissenting). Ironically, and seemingly consistent with Scalia's statement, the majority in *Kiryas Joel* found the state statute that created a school district for members of the Satmar Hasidic community an unconstitutional religious preference violating the Establishment Clause. Thus, contrary to the ostensible import of Scalia's statement quoted in the text, he did not oppose but rather supported that special arrangement. The statute at issue, he explained, was "facially neutral" because it "does not mention religion" and because, in any event, it provided merely a reasonable "accommodation" of religion. *Id.* at 752.

[105] Lee v. Weisman, 505 U.S. at 641 (Scalia, J., dissenting).

[106] *McCreary*, 545 U.S. at 909 (Scalia, J., dissenting). *Accord, e.g., id.* at 894; Transcript of oral argument in *Salazar v. Buono*, No. 08-472 (Oct. 7, 2009), at 39, 51 [hereafter Oral Argument in *Salazar*] (remarks of Scalia, J.).

[107] ROBERT J. ALLISON, THE CRESCENT OBSCURED: THE UNITED STATES AND THE MUSLIM WORLD, 1776–1815, at 59 (1995). *See* Thomas S. Kidd, *"Is It Worse to Follow Mahomet than the Devil?": Early American Uses of Islam*, 72 CHURCH HIST. 766 (2003). During the ratification debates, critics occasionally attacked Article VI's no-religious-test provision as an invitation to "Mahometans," WITTE & NICHOLS, RELIGION, 72, but many of the Founders viewed Islam as a theistic religion and would, in theory at least, have believed that it should receive equal protection. *Id.* at 51.

monotheism but on the virtues of specifically Protestant Christianity.[108] All but two states disqualified Jews, Unitarians, and agnostics from office, while some states refused even to allow them to vote. Rhode Island even barred Jews from citizenship and maintained that bar until 1842.[109] Moreover, in most states only Protestants could hold public office, thus extending the founding generation's religious discrimination to Catholics who, as Madison noted, constituted "a small & even unpopular sect in the U.S."[110]

Scalia's Establishment Clause jurisprudence, then, was the result of neither originalist nor textualist requirements but the product of his own determination to find a way to ensure a vibrant role in American life and politics for religion, especially what he regarded as traditional monotheistic religion.[111] "If religion in the public forum had to be entirely nondenominational," he declared, "there could be no religion in the public forum at all."[112] Scalia would not tolerate that result, so he simply construed the bare text of the Establishment Clause to mean what he wanted it to mean. He attributed his interpretation to the Founders, but it was not the Founders but his own personal convictions that shaped his constitutional views. He was determined not only to foster religion in the "public forum" but also to expand the ability of government to provide resources and funding for religious groups and organizations. Consistently he upheld programs and policies that provided such support[113] and repeatedly denied standing to those who sought

---

[108] See, e.g., WITTE & NICHOLS, RELIGION, 95; MORTON BORDEN, JEWS, TURKS, AND INFIDELS 8–20 (1984) [hereafter BORDEN, JEWS].

[109] Michael W. McConnell, The Origins and Historical Understanding of the Free Exercise of Religion, 103 HARV. L. REV. 1409, 1425 (1990) [hereafter McConnell, Origins and Historical Understanding]; BORDEN, JEWS, 13. "The constitution of New York (1777), was the only [state constitution] without restrictions on holding office for Jews," id. at 13.

[110] Koppelman, Phony Originalism, 9; James Madison to Edward Livingston, July 10, 1822, in 9 THE WRITINGS OF JAMES MADISON 101 (Gaillard Hunt ed., 1910). During the ratification debates critics sometimes attacked Article VI's no-religious-test provision as "an invitation to Papists." WITTE & NICHOLS, RELIGION, 72. The Revolution and Constitution, wrote Federalist legal scholar James Kent in 1794, effected a break from "papal tyranny." KUNAL M. PARKER, COMMON LAW, HISTORY, AND DEMOCRACY IN AMERICA, 1790–1900: LEGAL THOUGHT BEFORE MODERNISM 69 (2011).

[111] "[T]hose who adopted our Constitution," he declared, certainly "believed that the public virtues inculcated by religion are a public good." Lamb's Chapel, 508 U.S. at 400 (Scalia, J., concurring in the judgment). For Scalia' efforts to protect religion under the Free Exercise Clause, see, e.g., Locke v. Davey, 540 U.S. at 726 (Scalia, J., dissenting).

[112] McCreary, 545 U.S. at 893 (Scalia, J., dissenting).

[113] See, e.g., Zelman v. Simmons-Harris, 536 U.S. 639 (2002) (Rehnquist, C.J., joined by Scalia, J.); Mitchell v. Helms, 530 U.S. 793 (2000) (Thomas, J., joined by Scalia, J., announcing judgment of Court); Bowen v. Kendrick, 487 U.S. 589 (1988) (Rehnquist, C.J., joined by Scalia, J.); Agostini v. Felton, 521 U.S. 203 (1997) (O'Connor, J., joined by Scalia, J.).

to use the Establishment Clause to challenge them.[114] Indeed, he was even willing to defend a state statute that required the teaching of the religiously inspired and motivated theory of "creation science" as if the issue was one truly involving academic freedom and the theory one truly involving scientific inquiry.[115]

While Scalia at least nodded toward originalism in construing the Establishment Clause, in construing the Free Exercise Clause he essentially abandoned it in his important decision in *Employment Division v. Smith*.[116] Relying on grounds of precedent and expedience, he ruled that the Free Exercise Clause did not protect Native Americans from the application of "general" antidrug laws when they used peyote as part of their religious practices.[117] He based his decision on the fact that the United States had changed drastically since the founding and that constitutional law had to adapt to the vastly expanded religious diversity that marked modern America. Otherwise, he warned, such diversity would threaten "anarchy." That "danger increases in direct proportion to the society's diversity of religious beliefs," he explained, and the United States had become "a cosmopolitan nation made up of people of almost every conceivable religious preference."[118] That extreme religious diversity was constitutionally determinative. "[P]recisely because we value and protect that religious divergence," he declared, "we cannot afford the luxury" of giving the Free Exercise Clause a more protective meaning.[119] For that facially practical and adaptive reason—another

[114] *See, e.g.,* Hein v. Freedom From Religion Foundation, Inc., 551 U.S. 587, 618 (2007) (Scalia, J., concurring in the judgment); Arizona Christian School Tuition Organization v. Winn, 563 U.S. 125, 146 (2011) (Scalia, J., concurring).

[115] Edwards v. Aguillard, 482 U.S. 578, 610, 626 (1987) (Scalia, J., dissenting). Scalia's opinion exemplified his determination to use the law to advance religious ideas over "secular" ones. His opinion "confuses science with religion," and in "confusing science teaching with religious catechism, and referring to the teaching of evolution as 'indoctrination,' Scalia apes (so to speak) the advocacy that his favored parties, the anti-evolutionists, have employed to undermine science and mislabel evolution as some sort of improperly imposed religious belief." Stephan A. Newman, *Evolution and the Holy Ghost of Scopes: Can Science Lose the Next Round?*, 8 RUTGERS J.L. & RELIGION 11, 37 (2007).

[116] *Smith*, 494 U.S. 872 (1992) (Scalia, J.). "In rewriting free-exercise jurisprudence in *Employment Division of Oregon v. Smith*, 494 U.S. 872 (1990), for example, Scalia eschewed textual and historical approaches in favor of seizing upon a weak precedential base as the foundation for persuasively mischaracterizing existing doctrines." DAVID A. SCHULTZ & CHRISTOPHER E. SMITH, THE JURISPRUDENTIAL VISION OF JUSTICE ANTONIN SCALIA 209 (1996). Scalia tried to defend his originalism in *Smith* in *City of Boerne v. Flores*, 521 U.S. 507, 537 (Scalia, J., concurring in part).

[117] *Smith*, 494 U.S. at 885 (Scalia, J.).

[118] Scalia quoted the latter phrase from *Braunfeld v. Brown*, 366 U.S. 599, 606 (1961). *Smith*, 494 U.S. at 888 (Scalia, J.). If Americans "strictly observed original intent, much of what constitutes religion in the twenty-first century would be excluded from First Amendment protection." WITTE & NICHOLS, RELIGION, 95.

[119] *Smith*, 494 U.S. at 888 (Scalia, J.). A broader interpretation "would open the prospect of constitutionally required religious exemptions from civic obligations of almost every conceivable kind."

example of his now-and-then "living" constitutionalism—he concluded that the Court had to restrict the protection that the clause provided. Thus, as he excluded deists and polytheists from the protection of the Establishment Clause, he excluded Native Americans whose religious practices incorporated peyote from the protection of the Free Exercise Clause.

Scalia's "living" constitutionalism in *Smith* served his more particular purposes well, for subjecting all religions to "neutral" laws of "general" applicability substantially advantaged the traditional monotheistic religions he favored. Those religions commanded widespread public acceptance and consequently would be able to protect their own particular interests and practices in the political process. "It may fairly be said," he acknowledged candidly, "that leaving accommodation to the political process will place at a relative disadvantage those religious practices that are not widely engaged in."[120] Thus, for religions he adopted a reverse *Carolene Products* approach,[121] subjecting "discrete and insular minorities" to the political power of large and well-connected ones. In particular, his "living" constitutionalism placed his beloved Catholicism in a strong position. In the eighteenth century it had been but a "small and even unpopular sect" whose members were generally barred from holding public office, but by Scalia's day it had become a religion that was "widely engaged in," politically powerful, and highly effective in defending its interests in the political arena.[122]

On occasion, too, as in *Smith*, Scalia's parochial views on religion could be rawly apparent.[123] In an Establishment Clause case involving a single large Latin cross that marked a national war memorial cemetery, he insisted in open court that the cross had a universal significance as a symbol of respect for the war dead. "The cross," he declared in oral argument in *Salazar v. Buono* in 2009, "is the most common symbol" in war memorial cemeteries

---

Id. at 888. For a critique of Scalia's position in *Smith, see, e.g.,* McConnell, *Origins and Historical Understanding.*

[120] *Smith,* 494 U.S. at 890 (Scalia, J.).

[121] United States v. Carolene Products Co., 304 U.S. 144, 152 n.4 (1938) (Stone, J.) (suggesting the need for special judicial protection of "discrete and insular minorities" unable to protect themselves in the ordinary political process).

[122] The political power of the Catholic Church, as well as that of other mainline religions, had been apparent when Congress enacted national prohibition in the Volstead Act in 1919 but excepted sacramental wine from its ban. Michael D. Newsom, *Some Kind of Religious Freedom: National Prohibition and the Volstead Act's Exemption for the Religious Use of Wine,* 70 BROOK. L. REV. 739, 744 (2005).

[123] In *Smith* Scalia showed little understanding or sympathy for the peyote-using religious practices of Native Americans. *See* GARRETT EPPS, TO AN UNKNOWN GOD: RELIGIOUS FREEDOM ON TRIAL (2001).

to signal "the resting place of the dead." The lawyer arguing the case objected immediately. "The cross is the most common symbol of the resting place of Christians," he replied. "I have been in Jewish cemeteries," and there was "never a cross on a tombstone of a Jew." Recognizing the incongruity of Scalia's presumption, the audience broke into laughter. The cross, the lawyer then repeated, "is the most common symbol to honor Christians." While the audience had immediately caught on, Scalia did not. Instead, he scornfully repeated his earlier assertion. "I don't think you can leap from that to the conclusion that the only war dead that that cross honors are the Christian war dead." Then, fiercely obstinate or invincibly clueless, he doubled down. "I think that's an outrageous conclusion."[124]

While Scalia's interpretation of the Constitution's religion clauses showed his willingness to distort or abandon both originalism and textualism, his interpretation of two other key constitutional provisions revealed similar inconsistencies and contradictions. In construing the Commerce Clause he relied strictly on the constitutional text to challenge the "negative" or "dormant" commerce power, the doctrine that the Court could use the clause to invalidate state laws that impinged improperly on interstate commerce even in the absence of congressional legislation.[125] That doctrine, he insisted, had "no foundation in the text of the Constitution."[126] In construing the Eleventh Amendment, however, he abandoned the constitutional text entirely and expanded the amendment's reach far beyond its explicit terms[127] and contrary to the Court's early decisions interpreting it.[128] To justify that antitextual result he was even willing to join an opinion by Chief Justice Rehnquist for

---

[124] Oral Argument in *Salazar* at 38–39. Subsequently Scalia wrote a separate opinion in the case maintaining that the plaintiff who challenged the use of the cross lacked standing. Salazar v. Buono, 559 U.S. 700, 729 (2010) (Scalia, J., concurring in the judgment).

[125] *E.g.*, Tyler Pipe Industries Inc. v. Washington State Department of Revenue, 483 U.S. 232, 254 (1987) (Scalia, J., concurring in part and dissenting in part). "From his first term on the Court, Scalia has consistently opposed what he calls the Court's 'negative' Commerce Clause jurisprudence." ROSSUM, ANTONIN SCALIA'S JURISPRUDENCE, 91. For Scalia's treatment of the dormant Commerce Clause, *see id.* at 91–98.

[126] Pharmaceutical Research & Manufacturers Association of America v. Walsh, 538 U.S. 644, 674 (2003) (Scalia, J., concurring in the judgment). *Accord West Lynn Creamery*, 512 U.S. 186, 207, 209–10 (1994) (Scalia, J., concurring in the judgment).

[127] *E.g.*, Blatchford v. Native Village of Noatak, 501 U.S. 775, 779 (1991) (Scalia, J.) (applying Eleventh Amendment to bar suit by Native American tribe, a category clearly not covered by the amendment's text). *See also* Alden v. Maine, 527 U.S. 706, 728–29 (1999) (Kennedy, J., joined by Scalia) (because the "Eleventh Amendment confirmed rather than established sovereign immunity as a constitutional principle, it follows that the scope of the States' immunity from suit is demarcated not by the text of the Eleventh Amendment alone, but by fundamental postulates implicit in the constitutional design"). *Accord* Federal Maritime Commission v. South Carolina State Ports Authority, 535 U.S. 743 (2002) (Thomas, J., joined by Scalia).

[128] *E.g.*, Cohens v. Virginia, 19 U.S. (6 Wheat.) 264, 405–12 (1821) (Marshall, C.J.).

a 5–4 majority that explicitly rejected textualism. That opinion scorned "blind reliance upon the text of the Eleventh Amendment" and declared that an argument based on a "lengthy analysis of the text of the Eleventh Amendment is directed at a straw man."[129] While precedents supported Scalia's nontextualist interpretation of the Eleventh Amendment, a longer line of precedents supported the Court's nontextualist interpretation of the dormant Commerce Clause. Thus, a commitment to stare decisis could not explain the divergent positions he took in the two areas.[130] Inconsistent on both textual and precedential grounds, his opinions in these two areas were consistent in only one respect. They both served one of his primary ideological goals, to limit federal judicial power.

Addressing the Commerce Clause, moreover, Scalia was capable of a stunning aberration. While he had joined the conservative majority's "federalism revolution" in confining congressional power under the clause,[131] at a critical moment he switched sides. Choosing to write a separate—and therefore wholly unnecessary—concurrence in *Gonzales v. Raich*, he advanced an exceptionally broad view of the commerce power that stretched it well beyond the limits that he and the other conservatives had previously upheld.[132] There, he voted with the Court's liberals to set aside a state statute and uphold federal authority to prohibit the use of marijuana for medical purposes, even when the marijuana was homegrown and for personal use only.[133] His concurrence urged so sweeping a view of the commerce power that Justice Ginsburg prominently cited it in three separate places in her subsequent opinion supporting the constitutionality of the Affordable Care Act.[134] In that later case, however, decided several years after *Raich*, Scalia returned

---

[129] Seminole Tribe of Florida v. Florida, 517 U.S. 44, 69 (1996) (Rehnquist, C.J., joined by Scalia). Scalia would use the text of the amendment, however, when it served his purpose. College Savings Bank v. Florida Prepaid Postsecondary Education Expense Board, 527 U.S. 666, 689 (1999) (Scalia, J.).

[130] "Though its precise terms bar only federal jurisdiction over suits brought against one State by citizens of another State or foreign state, we have long recognized that the Eleventh Amendment accomplished much more." *College Savings Bank*, 527 U.S. at 669 (Scalia, J.) (citing precedents beginning in 1890, including *Seminole Tribe*).

[131] United States v. Lopez, 514 U.S. 549 (1995) (Rehnquist, C.J., joined by Scalia, J.) (limiting the commerce power to channels and instrumentalities of interstate commerce as well as to activities that "substantially affected" interstate commerce).

[132] Gonzales v. Raich, 545 U.S. 1, 33 (2005) (Scalia, J., concurring in the judgment). When asked about the contradiction between *Lopez* and *Raich* at a Federalist Society meeting, Scalia refused to answer. "Oh no," he responded. "Get another question." BISKUPIC, AMERICAN ORIGINAL, 9.

[133] *Raich*, 545 U.S. at 7 (Stevens, J.).

[134] National Federation of Independent Business v. Sibelius, 567 U.S. at 618 (two references), 619 (Ginsburg, J., concurring in the judgment in part and dissenting in part). Ginsburg also cited Scalia's article on "The Rule of Law" against him. *Id.* at 644.

to the conservative fold and adopted a narrower position that would have invalidated the hotly contested measure—the paramount achievement of Democratic president Barack Obama.[135] Scalia's aberrant behavior in *Raich* suggested to some that he was using the case to show himself less conservative and to thereby increase his chances of being selected to replace the recently deceased Rehnquist as chief justice.[136] Whatever his motive in *Raich*, there seemed no plausible originalist, textualist, or traditionalist explanation for his embarrassing flip-flops.[137] His subsequent return to the conservative fold in the Affordable Care Act case, however, was wholly consistent with his political and ideological views.

Scalia's assertion of a sweeping commerce power in *Raich*, moreover, was doubly embarrassing for him. Not only was it inconsistent with the other restrictive opinions on the Commerce Clause that he joined before and after it, but it was also inconsistent with his scornful view of the Necessary and Proper Clause. In *Raich* he relied on that clause to support his defense of an extremely broad commerce power, arguing that "the authority to enact laws necessary and proper for the regulation of interstate commerce is not limited to laws governing intrastate activities that substantially affect interstate commerce."[138] Only eight years earlier, writing for the Court, he had mocked a dissent for being so baseless that it "of course resorts to the last, best hope of those who defend ultra vires congressional action, the Necessary and Proper Clause."[139]

Further, in construing the Eleventh Amendment Scalia not only abandoned textualism but also embarrassed himself on originalist grounds. To

[135] *Sibelius*, 567 U.S. at 646 (Scalia, J., dissenting).

[136] MURPHY, SCALIA, 321–33, esp. 324–25. Considering Rehnquist's possible successor, Scalia's personal friend, Vice President Dick Cheney, and other conservatives initially pushed him forward for promotion to the center chair. PETER BAKER, DAYS OF FIRE: BUSH AND CHENEY IN THE WHITE HOUSE 417 (2013); JEFFREY TOOBIN, THE NINE: INSIDE THE SECRET WORLD OF THE SUPREME COURT 280 (2007). Scalia feared that he was too old for the appointment, but he nonetheless admitted that he wanted it. JOAN BISKUPIC, THE CHIEF: THE LIFE AND TURBULENT TIMES OF CHIEF JUSTICE JOHN ROBERTS 139, 160, 173 (2019).

[137] Conservative law professor Randy Barnett, litigating the conservative challenge to the Affordable Care Act, offered an analysis that attempted to explain why, in spite of *Raich*, Scalia could still vote to invalidate the statute, as he subsequently did. Randy Barnett, *Understanding Justice Scalia's Concurrence*, in Raich, THE VOLOKH CONSPIRACY, March 9, 2012. In a critical comment, a lawyer at the Cato Institute could only suggest that "Scalia's preference for rules carried the day in *Raich*." Mark Moller, *What Was Scalia Thinking?*, *available at* https://www.cato.org/publications/commentary/what-was-scalia-thinking (last consulted Aug. 27, 2019).

[138] *Raich*, 545 U.S. at 34–35 (Scalia, J., concurring in the judgment). "Where necessary to make a regulation of interstate commerce effective, Congress may regulate even those intrastate activities that do not themselves substantially affect interstate commerce." *Id.* at 35.

[139] Printz v. United States, 521 U.S. 898, 923 (1997) (Scalia, J.).

provide an originalist cover for his views, he relied on a line of precedents that began not in the eighteenth or early nineteenth century but only in 1890. At that time, when the Court was scuttling Reconstruction and sanctioning both Southern bond repudiation and racial segregation and disenfranchisement, the justices had enhanced state independence by elevating the Eleventh Amendment to a newly prominent position in *Hans v. Louisiana*.[140] There, the Court protected the white "redeemer" governments of the South by confecting a dubious originalist justification for ignoring the amendment's text. *Hans* proclaimed that the states enjoyed a preconstitutional sovereign immunity that barred the federal courts from hearing suits brought against them.[141] In embracing an interpretation that contradicted the text of the Eleventh Amendment, Scalia claimed that he was content to rest on the "venerability of an answer consistently adhered to for almost a century," that is, the post-Reconstruction answer that *Hans* created in 1890.[142] He accepted *Hans* as authoritative even though it was consistent with neither the text the Founders had adopted nor the Court's own early nineteenth-century precedents. Instead, he declared that such "a venerable precedent" should control because it had been "embedded within our legal system for over a century."[143] He rejected, of course, the many precedents that established the dormant Commerce Clause even though they were even more "venerable" and "embedded" in the legal system.[144] Indeed, Scalia himself traced the origin of the latter doctrine back to the Marshall Court and its formal adoption by the Court to 1873, nearly two decades prior to *Hans*.[145] Nonetheless, on

---

[140] Hans v. Louisiana, 134 U.S. 1 (1890) (Bradley, J.).

[141] On the highly questionable and unconvincing nature of *Hans*, *see* Edward A. Purcell, Jr., *The Particularly Dubious Case of* Hans v. Louisiana: *An Essay on Law, Race, History, and "Federal Courts,"* 81 N.C. L. REV. 1927 (2003).

[142] Pennsylvania v. Union Gas Co., 491 U.S. 1, 29, 31–33 (1989) (quote at 34) (Scalia, J., concurring in part and dissenting in part). Although early on he was somewhat uncertain about *Hans*, Welch v. Texas Department of Highways & Public Transportation, 483 U.S. 468, 495–96 (1987) (Scalia, J., concurring in part and concurring in the judgment), he subsequently embraced it fully. On Scalia's abandonment of textualism in the area, *see* ROSSUM, ANTONIN SCALIA'S JURISPRUDENCE, 106–14.

[143] *College Savings Bank*, 527 U.S. at 689 (Scalia, J.). In *Union Gas*, 491 U.S. at 34–35 (Scalia, J., dissenting), he offered practical reasons to support his decision to defend *Hans* on stare decisis grounds.

[144] The dormant Commerce Clause had been established long before *Hans* in 1890. The doctrine was suggested in *Cooley v. Board of Wardens*, 53 U.S. 299, 319–20 (1851) (Curtis, J.), and stated clearly in the *Case of State Freight Tax*, 82 U.S. 232, 279–80 (1873) (Strong, J.), and in *Bowman v. Chicago and Northwestern Railway Co.*, 125 U.S. 465, 485–87 (1888) (Matthews, J.). Fourteen years before *Hans*, the Court had used it to void a state law prohibiting racial segregation in interstate carriers. *Hall v. DeCuir*, 95 U.S. 485, 487–90 (1876) (Waite, C.J.). "The Court's dormant Commerce Clause docket expanded considerably in the period following the Civil War." Barry Cushman, *Federalism*, *in* THE CAMBRIDGE COMPANION TO THE UNITED STATES CONSTITUTION 203 (Karen Orren & John W. Compton eds., 2018).

[145] *Tyler Pipe*, 483 U.S. at 260 (Scalia, J., concurring in part and dissenting in part).

the dormant Commerce Clause—where he sought to limit federal judicial power—"venerability" simply disappeared as a relevant consideration.

In spite of the bold assurance that marked his opinions, Scalia's text-based reasoning was also on occasion simply arbitrary.[146] In *Tennessee v. Lane*, for example, the Court upheld an exercise of congressional power under Section 5 of the Fourteenth Amendment, setting aside the sovereign immunity of the states and enforcing a provision of the Americans with Disabilities Act. Scalia strove repeatedly to limit congressional power under Section 5,[147] and in *Lane* he dissented and relied on the section's text which, he stressed, granted Congress the power "to *enforce*, by appropriate legislation" the amendment's other provisions. Acknowledging that he had italicized the word "enforce," he argued that

> one does not, within any normal meaning of the term, "enforce" a prohibition by issuing a still broader prohibition directed to the same end. One does not, for example, "enforce" a 55-mile-per-hour speed limit by imposing a 45-mile-per-hour speed limit—even though that is indeed directed to the same end of automotive safety and will undoubtedly result in many fewer violations of the 55-mile-per-hour limit.[148]

Contrary to that assertion, however, and as he himself could not avoid admitting implicitly, governments could quite reasonably choose to "enforce" a fifty-five-mile-per-hour speed limit by posting a forty-five-mile-per-hour limit. The simple and virtually universally known fact was that people commonly drove their cars at speeds somewhat above posted limits, regularly exceeding them by five or even ten miles per hour. The word "enforce," in other words, simply did not carry the necessarily rigid and exact meaning that

---

[146] *E.g.*, Morales v. Trans World Airlines, Inc., 504 U.S. 374 (1992) (Scalia, J.) (finding preemption by construing phrase "relating to" broadly rather than narrowly when latter interpretation was entirely plausible); CBOCS West, Inc. v. Humphries, 553 U.S. 442, 457, 460 (2008) (Thomas, J., dissenting, joined by Scalia, J.) ("When an individual is subjected to reprisal because he has complained about racial discrimination, the injury he suffers is not on account of his race; rather, it is the result of his conduct"). In the former case, three justices (Stevens, Rehnquist, and Blackmun) dissented and Souter did not participate; in the latter case, the other seven justices joined the majority opinion. *See also* Feltner v. Columbia Pictures TV, 523 U.S. 340, 355 (1998) (Scalia, J., concurring); Dastar Corp v. Twentieth Century Fox Film Corp., 539 U.S. 23 (2003) (Scalia, J.).

[147] *E.g.*, Nevada Department of Human Resources v. Hibbs, 538 U.S. 721, 741 (2003) (Scalia, J., dissenting).

[148] Tennessee v. Lane, 541 U.S. 509, 554, 558 (2004) (Scalia, J., dissenting).

Scalia insisted upon, and it surely did not carry such a restricted meaning from logical or linguistic necessity.[149]

Equally striking, the Court had long recognized the obvious and unexceptionable contrary principle of valid law enforcement. "The inclusion of a reasonable margin to insure effective enforcement," declared conservative Justice George Sutherland, "will not put upon a law, otherwise valid, the stamp of invalidity."[150] Indeed, in a different doctrinal context where he was seeking to protect gun rights—one of his most fervent passions—Scalia himself invoked the same contrary principle. In that context he maintained that it was common for statutory and constitutional provisions "to go further than is necessary for the principal purpose involved."[151] His acknowledgment of that principle in a gun-rights case demonstrated once again that the results he sought determined which legal arguments he would use and which he would ignore or dismiss.

Worse, Scalia's crabbed interpretation of the word "enforce" in *Tennessee v. Lane* was particularly egregious for another reason. It flatly contradicted his own principle of proper constitutional interpretation that he had announced in his book, *A Matter of Interpretation*. "In textual interpretation, context is everything," he had written, "and the context for the Constitution tells us not to expect nit-picking detail, and to give words and phrases an expansive rather than narrow interpretation."[152] His argument by italics in *Lane* violated that principle and illustrated as well his characteristic use of italics as a handy tool for manipulating the meaning of texts.[153] To limit the power of Congress in enforcing the Fourteenth Amendment with effective civil rights statutes, he was willing to use whatever arguments came to mind.

Scalia's acceptance of a comparative textualist argument showed similar ideological opportunism. As a general matter he sought to limit the

---

[149] Over the protest of four dissenting justices, Scalia used a similar narrowing and restrictive technique to deny enforcement of Title VI of the Civil Rights Act of 1964. Alexander v. Sandoval, 532 U.S. 275, 285–86 (2001) (Scalia, J.) (denying the Department of Justice power to adopt, pursuant to statutory authority, a regulation that created a private cause of action to challenge laws having a disparate racial impact).

[150] *Euclid*, 272 U.S. 365, 388–89 (1926) (Sutherland, J.).

[151] Transcript of Oral Argument, District of Columbia v. Heller, No. 07-290 (Mar. 18, 2008), at 56.

[152] ANTONIN SCALIA, A MATTER OF INTERPRETATION: FEDERAL COURTS AND THE LAW 37 (1997) [hereafter SCALIA, MATTER]. Scalia stated the same principle two years earlier. Scalia, *Common Law Courts*, 111.

[153] Scalia employed a similarly arbitrary argument-by-italics in an effort to bar a plaintiff from compelling action by a federal agency pursuant to a statutory right to sue. Federal Election Commission v. Akins, 524 U.S. 11, 29, 30–31 (1998) (Scalia, J., dissenting). He adopted a similar argument by italics in *Bush v. Gore*, 531 U.S. 98, 111, 112 (2000) (Rehnquist, C.J., joined by Scalia, J.). Scalia used italics with great frequency. *See, e.g., Printz*, 521 U.S. at 932 (Scalia, J.).

Equal Protection Clause as much as possible to racial issues.[154] When he did so in order to reject affirmative action, he argued from the interrelated nature of the three Civil War amendments. The purpose of "the Civil War Amendments," he declared, was to prohibit all legal oppression on the basis of race or color.[155] While the Thirteenth abolished "slavery" and "involuntary servitude," Scalia insisted more broadly that the Fourteenth demonstrated "the Constitution's focus upon the individual" and the Fifteenth "its rejection of dispositions based on race."[156] Together, he maintained, they meant that the Constitution barred government from using racial classifications regardless of benevolent motives and required it to focus solely on individual behavior and merit. In contrast, when he sought to limit the Fourteenth Amendment to racial issues for an entirely different purpose—to restrict as much as possible congressional efforts to enforce other types of civil rights claims—he ignored the textual argument based on the interrelated nature of the three amendments. If the Thirteenth abolished "slavery" and "involuntary servitude" and the Fifteenth rejected "dispositions based on race," it was apparent on its textual face that the Fourteenth Amendment was neither limited to racial matters nor reasonably implied any such limitation. Quite the contrary. Its express terms extended the rights it established to "[a]ll persons born or naturalized in the United States."[157] Further, Scalia acknowledged that "the Fourteenth Amendment, unlike the Fifteenth, is not limited to denial of the franchise and not limited to the denial of other rights on the basis of race."[158] He used the Civil War amendments in tandem to condemn affirmative action, in other words, but he ignored their in-tandem implication when he sought to restrict congressional power to enforce the Fourteenth Amendment's Equal Protection Clause more broadly in areas beyond racial discrimination.

In condemning affirmative action plans, moreover, Scalia gave a pointedly and unnecessarily narrow construction to both the original meaning of

[154] *E.g.*, United States v. Virginia, 518 U.S. 515, 566 (1996) (Scalia, J., dissenting) (Equal Protection Clause not relevant to alleged gender discrimination claim); Coleman v. Court of Appeals of Maryland, 566 U.S. at 44 (Scalia, concurring in the judgment) ("outside of the context of racial discrimination (which is different for stare decisis reasons), I would limit Congress's §5 power to the regulation of conduct that *itself* violates the Fourteenth Amendment," at 45) (emphasis in original). *Accord* Tennessee v. Lane, 541 U.S. at 561–65 (Scalia, J., dissenting).

[155] Richmond v. J.A. Croson Co., 488 U.S. 469, 520, 522 (Scalia, J., concurring in the judgment, citing Ex parte Virginia, 100 U.S. 339, 345 (1880) (Strong, J.).

[156] Adarand Constructors v. Pena, 515 U.S. 200, 239 (1995) (Scalia, J., concurring in part and concurring in the judgment).

[157] U.S. CONST. amend. 14, sec. 1.

[158] Tennessee v. Lane, 541 U.S. at 555 (Scalia, J., dissenting).

the Civil War amendments and his proclaimed interpretative principle that "context is everything."[159] On this issue he simply ignored the relevant historical context and the compelling evidence that showed how the combined social policies of federal, state, and local governments had fostered racial segregation and inequality over much of the twentieth century.[160] That, in turn, enabled him to deny that African-Americans in the late twentieth century had been harmed by "unlawful racial discrimination."[161] On that historically faulty factual premise he could view the original understanding of the Civil War amendments—an understanding that clearly authorized affirmative action to remedy the consequences of racial discrimination and abuse—as irrelevant to contemporary issues of racial discrimination.[162]

Further, his position on affirmative action demonstrated once again both his jurisprudential inconsistency and the influence of his personal values on his constitutional rulings. In a 1979 law review article he attacked affirmative action vigorously and across the board, charging that racial "entitlement" of any kind evoked "Nazi Germany." "I am, in short," he proclaimed, "opposed to racial affirmative action for reasons of both principle and practicality."[163]

[159] SCALIA, MATTER, 37. *Accord* Scalia, *Common Law Courts*, 111. *See* Gil Seinfeld, *The Good, The Bad, and the Ugly: Reflections of a Counter-Clerk*, 114 MICH. L. REV.: FIRST IMPRESSIONS 111, 117–20 (2016).

[160] *See, e.g.*, RICHARD ROTHSTEIN, THE COLOR OF LAW: A FORGOTTEN HISTORY OF HOW OUR GOVERNMENT SEGREGATED AMERICA (2017) ("Racial segregation in housing was not merely a project of southerners in the former slaveholding Confederacy. It was a nationwide project of the federal government in the twentieth century, designed and implemented by its most liberal leaders," at xii); KENNETH T. JACKSON, CRABGRASS FRONTIER: THE SUBURBANIZATION OF THE UNITED STATES (1985) ("The result, if not the intent, of the public housing program of the United States was to segregate the races, to concentrate the disadvantaged in inner cities, and to reinforce the image of suburbia as a place of refuge from the problems of race, crime, and poverty," at 219). *See generally* IRA KATZNELSON, WHEN AFFIRMATIVE ACTION WAS WHITE: AN UNTOLD STORY OF RACIAL INEQUALITY IN TWENTIETH-CENTURY AMERICA (2005).

[161] "Individuals who have been wronged by unlawful racial discrimination should be made whole; but under our Constitution there can be no such thing as either a creditor or a debtor race. That concept is alien to the Constitution's focus upon the individual." *Adarand*, 515 U.S. at 239 (Scalia, J., concurring in part and concurring in the judgment). *Accord Croson*, 488 U.S. at 526 (Scalia, J., concurring in the judgment).

[162] The Freedman's Bureau furnished special protections for ex-slaves and provided them with any number of goods and services, including food, clothing, schools, courts, and grants of confiscated Southern land. *See, e.g.*, THE FREEDMEN'S BUREAU: RECONSTRUCTING THE AMERICAN SOUTH AFTER THE CIVIL WAR (Paul A. Cimbala & Hans L. Trefousse eds., 2005); THE FREEDMEN'S BUREAU AND RECONSTRUCTING: RECONSIDERATIONS (Paul A. Cimbala & Randall M. Miller eds., 1999); ERIC FONER, RECONSTRUCTION: AMERICA'S UNFINISHED REVOLUTION, 1863–1877 (1988); LEON F. LITWACK, BEEN IN THE STORM SO LONG: THE AFTERMATH OF SLAVERY (1979); W.E. BURGHARDT DU BOIS, THE FREEDMEN'S BUREAU (1901); Eric Schnapper, *Affirmative Action and the Legislative History of the Fourteenth Amendment*, 71 VA. L. REV. 753 (1985); Stephen A. Siegel, *The Federal Government's Power to Enact Color Conscious Laws: An Originalist Inquiry*, 92 NW. U. L. REV. 477 (1998).

[163] Antonin Scalia, *Commentary: The Disease as Cure*, 1979 WASH. U. L.Q. 147, 153, 154, 156 (1979).

Seven years later in his Senate confirmation hearing he acknowledged that the article expressed "policy views of mine at the time," but he distinguished those views sharply from the position he would take when interpreting the Constitution. The article, he assured the Senate Judiciary Committee, expressed only his personal opinion about affirmative action, "not its constitutionality." "I didn't think [affirmative action] was a good idea," he explained, but "those policy views will not inform my decisions from the Supreme Court." Quite explicitly, moreover, he seemed to assure the committee that he would accept affirmative action plans if they had congressional approval. "Those views have nothing to do with the way I will apply whatever affirmative action laws are enacted by the Congress." His personal position, he reiterated, "has nothing to do with whether I would enforce [affirmative action] vigorously if it's passed by Congress."[164]

Once on the Court, however, much as he had done in abandoning his claimed commitment to deference on federalism issues, he charted a steady course away from the assurances he had given the judiciary committee and moved to enforce his own contrary "policy views." In his very first year on the high bench he rejected the Court's interpretation of Title VII that approved a local government agency's affirmative action plan. His opinion, however, seemed to accept the legitimacy of the congressional statute itself and fault the Court for misconstruing it. "A statute designed to establish a color-blind and gender-blind workplace," he protested, "has thus been converted into a powerful engine of racism and sexism, not merely *permitting* intentional race- and sex-based discrimination, but often making it, through operation of the legal system, practically compelled."[165]

Then, two years later in *City of Richmond v. Croson*, he concurred in the Court's decision to strike down the affirmative action plan of a Southern city. There, in a separate Janus-like solo opinion he maintained consistency with his statements to the judiciary committee while at the same time seeming to reject them absolutely. On one hand, consistent with the assurances he had given, he agreed that the city's plan was unconstitutional because state and local governments were properly subject to a stricter constitutional standard than was the federal government. It "is one thing to permit racially based

---

[164] *Hearings before the Committee on the Judiciary, United States Senate, Ninety-Ninth Congress, Second Session, on the Nomination of Judge Antonin Scalia, to be Associate Justice of the Supreme Court of the United States* (Aug. 5–6, 1986), 76, 94, 96, 95 [hereafter *Scalia Hearings*]. *See id.* at 45.

[165] Johnson v. Transportation Agency, 480 U.S. 616, 657, 677 (1987) (Scalia, J., dissenting) (emphasis in original).

conduct by the Federal Government," he explained, but it was "quite another to permit it by the precise entities against whose conduct in matters
of race that [Fourteenth] Amendment was specifically directed."[166] On the
other hand, seeming to repudiate those same assurances, he announced in
his opinion's first paragraph that he agreed with the statement of Alexander
Bickel, an uncompromising opponent of affirmative action, that all "discrimination on the basis of race is illegal, immoral, unconstitutional, inherently
wrong, and destructive of democratic society."[167] For emphasis, in the same
introductory paragraph he also quoted Justice John Marshall Harlan's dissent in *Plessy v. Ferguson* declaring that the Constitution should be "color-
blind"[168] Both quotes supported his "policy view" that affirmative action
plans should be unconstitutional in all cases.

Following *Croson*, Scalia moved to enforce that absolute anti-affirmative
action principle. The very next year he voted to invalidate a federal affirmative action plan, contradicting the seemingly deferential view toward federal action that he had expressed in both *Croson* and his Senate confirmation
testimony.[169] Then, in 1995 he joined a majority in *Adarand Constructors
v. Pena* to strike down another federal affirmative action plan. This time,
again writing separately, he fully embraced the absolute anti-affirmative-
action position he had floated in *Croson*. The government, he declared, "can
never have a 'compelling interest' in discriminating on the basis of race" for
affirmative action purposes.[170] Thus, eight years after ascending the high
bench, he proclaimed that affirmative action was unconstitutional across the
board, regardless of the governmental branch or agency that sponsored it.

---

[166] *Croson*, 488 U.S. at 521–22 (Scalia, J., concurring in the judgment). In a part of her opinion that
only Rehnquist and White joined, O'Connor made the same point: "What appellant ignores is that
Congress, unlike any State or political subdivision, has a specific constitutional mandate to enforce
the dictates of the Fourteenth Amendment." *Id.* at 490.

[167] *Croson*, 488 U.S. at 521 (Scalia, J., concurring in the judgment), quoting ALEXANDER M.
BICKEL, THE MORALITY OF CONSENT 133 (1975). "If the Constitution prohibits exclusion of blacks
and other minorities on racial grounds, it cannot permit the exclusion of whites on similar grounds;
for it must be the exclusion on racial grounds which offends the Constitution, and not the particular
skin color of the person excluded." *Id.* at 132–33.

[168] *Croson*, 488 U.S. at 521 (Scalia, J., concurring in the judgment), quoting *Plessy v. Ferguson*, 163
U.S. 537, 552, 559 (1896) (Harlan, J., dissenting).

[169] Metro Broadcasting, Inc. v. Federal Communications Commission, 497 U.S. 547 (1990) (Scalia,
J., joining the separate dissents of both O'Connor, J. and Kennedy, J.) (both dissents requiring strict
scrutiny of federal affirmative action plans and holding the federal action unconstitutional).

[170] *Adarand*, 515 U.S. at 239 (Scalia, J., concurring in part and concurring in the judgment). *See,
e.g.*, Scalia's later opinion in *Grutter v. Bollinger*, 539 U.S. at 346 (Scalia, J., concurring in part and
dissenting in part).

As a Supreme Court justice, Scalia's shifting position on affirmative action supported three conclusions. First, his affirmative action opinions between 1987 and 1995 were, like much of his constitutional jurisprudence, inconsistent. Second, those opinions ended with the absolute conclusion that affirmative action was always unconstitutional. Third, those opinions traced a course that made his interpretation of the Constitution after 1995 identical to the personal "policy views" he had announced in 1979—the precise policy views that he had assured the Senate Judiciary Committee would not affect his constitutional decision-making.[171]

On a more general level, Scalia regularly proclaimed his respect for popular lawmaking authority,[172] but he had no qualms about rejecting that authority when he decided to invalidate a statute.[173] In *City of Boerne v. Flores*, for example, he ended a concurrence by insisting on the principle that it was not the Court but "the people, through their elected representatives" who should rule.[174] In the same case, however, he voted with the majority to invalidate a congressional statute enacted under Section 5 of the Fourteenth Amendment.[175]

In spite of his customary rhetoric heralding the right of the people to rule through their democratically elected legislatures, Scalia joined the other four conservative justices in voiding many legislative measures. In the years immediately following *Boerne*, they invalidated seven separate federal statutes on state sovereignty grounds alone,[176] in the process severely limiting and essentially overruling a line of precedents extending from 1880 into the 1980s that upheld expansive congressional powers under all three of the Civil War amendments.[177] Those precedents surely came well within the "venerability"

[171] One might think that Scalia's testimony before the judiciary committee showed a lack of candor. "From his first days on the Court, Scalia waged a fierce campaign to end affirmative action." EVAN THOMAS, FIRST: SANDRA DAY O'CONNOR 259 (2019). At least one law review article has raised the question whether Scalia committed perjury when discussing the issue. James L. McAlister, *A Pigment of the Imagination: Looking at Affirmative Action Through Justice Scalia's Color-Blind Rule*, 77 MARQ. L. REV. 327, 345 n.152 (1994).

[172] Booth v. Maryland, 482 U.S. 496, 519, 520 (1987) (Scalia, J., dissenting).

[173] Scalia sometimes expressed his scorn for legislative behavior. "It is no indication whatever of the invalidity of the constitutional rule which we announce, that it produces unhappy consequences when a legislature lacks foresight, and acts belatedly to remedy a deficiency in the law." Plaut v. Spendthrift Farm, 514 U.S. 211, 237 (1995) (Scalia, J.).

[174] City of Boerne v. Flores, 521 U.S. 507, 537, 544 (1997) (Scalia, J., concurring in part).

[175] *City of Boerne*, 521 U.S. at 536 (Kennedy, J., joined by Scalia, J.).

[176] ROSSUM, ANTONIN SCALIA'S JURISPRUDENCE, 113.

[177] *See, e.g.*, Ex parte Virginia, 100 U.S. 339 (1880) (Strong, J.) (Fourteenth Amendment); Katzenbach v. Morgan, 384 U.S. 641 (1966) (Brennan, J.) (Fourteenth Amendment); South Carolina v. Katzenbach, 383 U.S. 301 (1966) (Warren, C.J.) (Fifteenth Amendment); Jones v. Alfred H. Mayer Co., 392 U.S. 409 (1968) (Stewart, J.) (Thirteenth Amendment); Fitzpatrick v. Bitzer, 427 U.S. 445 (1976) (Rehnquist, C.J.) (Fourteenth Amendment); Runyon v. McCrary, 427 U.S. 160 (1976)

principle he found compelling when he wished to justify staying with *Hans* and using the Eleventh Amendment to limit federal judicial power. Once again, however, he refused to apply that same "venerability" principle when it cut against his effort to limit congressional power under the Fourteenth Amendment.[178]

On top of that, the decisions Scalia joined limiting congressional power mocked another principle of statutory construction that he cited on other occasions. "The cardinal principle of statutory construction," he declared in *Edwards v. Aguillard*, "is to save and not to destroy."[179] In *Edwards*, however, he was not considering the constitutionality of congressional power to enforce broad civil rights legislation but rather defending a religiously inspired state statute that required the teaching of "creation science." He was willing to "save and not to destroy" a statute that compelled the teaching of a fundamentalist religious doctrine in public schools, but unwilling to do the same for statutes that sought to protect many other kinds of civil rights.[180] Indeed, he had no use for that principle—or for other similarly generous principles of statutory construction[181]—when he voted to void such major congressional enactments as the Violence Against Women Act, the Bipartisan Campaign Reform Act, and the Voting Rights Act of 1965, all statutes that conflicted with his ideological commitments.[182]

Moreover, when one or more of the conservative justices joined the Court's liberals in upholding the power of Congress under the Fourteenth Amendment, Scalia dissented, offering unusually weak grounds for his position[183] and urging severe restrictions on that

(Stewart, J.) (Thirteenth Amendment); City of Rome v. United States, 446 U.S. 156 (1980) (Marshall, J.) (Fifteenth Amendment).

[178] Scalia did not seek to formally overrule the earlier cases but to limit them severely outside of the context of race. *See, e.g.,* Tennessee v. Lane, 541 U.S. at 561–65 (Scalia, J., dissenting).

[179] Edwards v. Aguillard, 482 U.S. 578, 610, 626 (1987) (Scalia, J., dissenting, quoting NLRB v. Jones & Laughlin Steel Corp., 301 U.S. 1, 30 (1937) (Hughes, C.J.)).

[180] *E.g.,* Kimel v. Florida Board of Regents, 528 U.S. 62 (2000) (O'Connor, J., joined by Scalia, J.) (denying congressional power to impose damages remedies on states under the Age Discrimination in Employment Act); Board of Trustees of the University of Alabama v. Garrett, 531 U.S. 356 (2001) (Rehnquist, C.J., joined by Scalia, J.) (same under the Americans with Disabilities Act); *Coleman*, 566 U.S. at 44 (Scalia, J., concurring) (same under a provision of the Family and Medical Leave Act).

[181] He also ignored, for example, "the doctrine of constitutional doubt," a doctrine "which counsels us to interpret statutes, if possible, in such fashion as to avoid grave constitutional questions." Federal Election Commission v. Akins, 524 U.S. 11, 29, 32 (Scalia, J., dissenting).

[182] United States v. Morrison, 529 U.S. 598 (2000) (Rehnquist, C.J., joined by Scalia, J.); Citizens United v. Federal Election Commission, 558 U.S. 310 (2010) (Kennedy, J., joined by Scalia, J.); Shelby County v. Holder, 570 U.S. 529 (2013) (Roberts, C.J., joined by Scalia, J.).

[183] As one scholar who studied his jurisprudence in the area concluded, Scalia relied on arbitrary dictionary definitions, mischaracterized precedents, ignored the significance of the Necessary and

power.[184] By 2011 he maintained that in some areas the Court should no longer even give deference to Congress, and he charged the legislative branch with "extravagant assertions of congressional power." Most of those assertions involved "efforts to eliminate or control powers belonging to one of the other two branches," while some involved "the assertion of a general police power that has never been given to the federal government and belongs only to the states."[185]

His contrasting and excessively sweeping rhetoric in two cases decided a day apart in 2013 illustrated the pervasive fact that his jurisprudence sacrificed methodological and rhetorical consistency to the demands of political ideology. In *Shelby County v. Holder*[186] he joined a 5–4 majority that invalidated a provision of the Voting Rights Act of 1965. Although Congress had repeatedly re-enacted the statute—most recently by overwhelming majorities—Scalia baselessly charged in the oral argument that "this is not the kind of a question you can leave to Congress." His reasoning was rawly antidemocratic and contrary to his repeated claims about the rights of popular government. Senators and representatives, he declared, voted for the statute only because they were otherwise "going to lose votes" in seeking re-election.[187] Consequently, he voted to invalidate the statute.

In contrast, the very next day in *United States v. Windsor* he castigated the Court's 5–4 decision to invalidate a provision of the Defense of Marriage Act. The case, he proclaimed, was

about the power of our people to govern themselves, and the power of this Court to pronounce the law. Today's opinion aggrandizes the latter, with the predictable consequence of diminishing the former. We have no

---

Proper Clause, betrayed the federalism principles he proclaimed in his confirmation hearing, and rejected the clear purpose of the Fourteenth Amendment to give Congress the primary role in determining how to enforce the Fourteenth Amendment. Rossum, ANTONIN SCALIA'S JURISPRUDENCE, 122–24.

[184] *Coleman*, 566 U.S. at 45 (2012) (Scalia, J., concurring in the judgment) (statutes must be tightly tailored to Fourteenth Amendment rights or focused exclusively on racial discrimination); Tennessee v. Lane, 541 U.S. at 560 (Scalia, J., dissenting) (no merely "prophylactic" legislation allowed under Fourteenth Amendment). In addition, he sought to deny the power of Congress unless its measures satisfied extreme and unprecedented evidentiary requirements for nationwide application. *Hibbs*, 538 U.S. at 741–44 (Scalia, J., dissenting).

[185] SCALIA SPEAKS, 216.

[186] Shelby County v. Holder, 570 U.S. 529 (2013) (Roberts, C.J., joined by Scalia, J.).

[187] Transcript of oral argument, Shelby County v. Holder, No. 12-96 (Feb. 27, 2013), 47.

power to decide this case. And even if we did, we have no power under the Constitution to invalidate this democratically adopted legislation.[188]

The dramatically contrasting rhetoric in *Shelby County* and *Windsor* was due to the fact that the two statutes at issue served radically different social and political purposes. Scalia voted to invalidate the Voting Rights Act of 1965, a monumental civil rights measure that had enabled millions of minority citizens to vote and that served as a barrier to Republican efforts to suppress minority and other Democratic leaning voting blocks. In contrast, he decried the invalidation of the Defense of Marriage Act, a statute that Congress had passed to block legal recognition of gay marriages by the federal government. Constitutionally inconsistent rhetoric; ideologically consistent results.

Countless other inconsistencies also plagued Scalia's judicial work. His decisions addressing problems of constitutional retroactivity were themselves contradictory and inconsistent with "the traditional common-law understanding of rights he embraces in other contexts."[189] He abandoned both originalist reasoning and principles of separation of powers when he justified judicial deference to federal agencies on the ground that they were required by the twentieth-century demands of "the modern administrative state."[190] He abjured reliance on foreign and international law in construing the Constitution, but to defend executive power he was willing to cite a leading Court precedent that relied centrally on principles of international law.[191] He condemned the use of legislative history

---

[188] United States v. Windsor, 570 U.S. at 778 (Scalia, J., dissenting). When Scalia felt differently about a state action, his rhetoric was quite different. Rejecting a constitutional limitation that the Court placed on death penalty prosecutions, he dissented in *South Carolina v. Gathers*, 490 U.S. 805, 823, 825 (1989), declaring that "I would think it a violation of my oath to adhere to what I consider a plainly unjustified intrusion upon the democratic process." *Accord Edwards*, 482 U.S. at 626 (Scalia, J., dissenting).

[189] ROSSUM, ANTONIN SCALIA'S JURISPRUDENCE, 188 ("Scalia's willingness to give *Ring* [*v. Arizona*, 536 U.S. 584] only prospective effect not only contradicts the traditional common-law understanding of rights he embraces in other contexts but also encourages the very policymaking tendencies of the colleagues he elsewhere attacks"). On Scalia's retroactivity decisions, *see id.* at 184–89. *Accord* DORSEN, UNEXPECTED, 37; Caleb Nelson, *The Legitimacy of (Some) Federal Common Law*, 101 VA. L. REV. 1, 57–62 (2015).

[190] Antonin Scalia, *Judicial Deference to Administrative Interpretations of Law*, 1989 DUKE L.J. 511, 516 (1989).

[191] *Compare* Roper v. Simmons, 543 U.S. 551, 607, 622–28 (2005) (Scalia, J., dissenting and opposing reliance on foreign and international law sources in construing Constitution), *with* Webster v. Doe, 486 U.S. at 614–15 (Scalia, J., dissenting, quoting *United States v. Curtiss-Wright Export Corp.*, 299 U.S. 304, 316–20 (1936), which relied on international law to support independent and extra-constitutional foreign-affairs power of president). *See* Edward A. Purcell, Jr., *Understanding Curtiss-Wright*, 31 L. & HIST. REV. 653, 659–60, 714 (2013). Scalia could also cite to foreign law when it supported his position. Lafler v. Cooper, 566 U.S. 156, 175, 185 (2012) (Scalia, J., dissenting). Justice

absolutely,[192] but he not only declared it "a significant factor in interpreting a statute" in his confirmation hearing[193] but occasionally cited it in his opinions on the Court when it seemed to support his views.[194]

In condemning legislative history, moreover, Scalia was ready to pre-judge a basketful of constitutional issues. Drawing on legislative history "is not just wrong," he insisted in the most sweeping terms; "it violates consti-tutional requirements of nondelegability, bicameralism, presidential par-ticipation, and the supremacy of judicial interpretation in deciding the case presented."[195] So much for his proclaimed emphasis on the need for judi-cial restraint and the necessity of avoiding constitutional issues whenever possible.

Scalia's inconsistencies hardly stopped there. He was willing to loosen standing requirements to allow defendants in state court actions under Section 1983 to carry appeals to the Court, but he was unwilling to do the same for plaintiffs in state court actions asserting federal law challenges to state laws that deprived schools of funding and raised local taxes.[196] In *Smith* he construed the Free Exercise Clause to deny protection to a small Native American religious group,[197] but in a later case he construed the Establishment Clause to uphold a clergy-led prayer at a public school grad-uation on the ground that "maintaining respect for the religious observ-ance of others is a fundamental civil virtue that governments (including the public schools) can and should cultivate."[198] He was willing to infer a causal

Ginsburg noted that on rare occasions Scalia cited foreign legal sources. RUTH BADER GINSBURG, MY OWN WORDS 254 (2016).

[192] SCALIA, READING, 388. *See, e.g.*, National Endowment for the Arts v. Finley 524 U.S. 569, 590, 594 (Scalia, J., concurring in the judgment) ("More fundamentally, of course, all this legislative his-tory has no valid claim upon our attention at all"); Samantar v. Yousuf, 560 U.S. 305, 326, 326–29 (Scalia, J., concurring in the judgment); Wisconsin Public Intervenor v. Mortier, 501 U.S. 597, 616, 617–23 (1991) (Scalia, J., concurring in the judgment).

[193] *Scalia Hearings*, at 65. *Accord id.*, at 105–06.

[194] *Edwards*, 482 U.S. at 624–27, 636–39 (Scalia, J., dissenting); *Lucas*, 505 U.S. at 1028 n.15 (Scalia, J.).

[195] SCALIA, READING, 388.

[196] *Compare* Camreta v. Greene, 563 U.S. 692, 714 (2011) (Scalia, J. concurring, allowing standing to prevailing defendant on ground that "our precedents, strange though they may be," controlled), *with* ASARKO v. Kadish, 490 U.S. 605, 634 (1989) (Rehnquist, joined by Scalia, concurring in part and dissenting in part, denying standing for appeal to the Court on ground that plaintiffs below lacked standing to bring their state-court suit originally in federal court). Scalia seemed similarly inconsistent in applying his ideas on standing in voting rights cases. Christopher S. Elmendorf & Edward B. Foley, *Symposium: How We Vote: Electronic Voting and Other Voting Practices in the United States: Gatekeeping vs Balancing in the Constitutional Law of Elections: Methodological Uncertainty on the High Court*, 17 WM. & MARY BILL RTS. J. 507, 533–34 (2008).

[197] *Smith*, 494 U.S. 872 (1990) (Scalia, J.).

[198] Lee v. Weisman, 505 U.S. at 638 (Scalia, J., dissenting).

relationship in the absence of record evidence to support a decision enabling defendants to defeat tort claims,[199] but unwilling to infer far more likely
causal relationships that would allow plaintiffs to assert claims challenging
employment discrimination and government intrusions under the Foreign
Intelligence Surveillance Act.[200]

The inconsistencies in the arguments and assertions Scalia used were
strikingly apparent in the area of election law. He criticized those who
supported gay rights by explaining that their growing "political power" was
based on certain social facts—their ardent concern, geographical concentra-
tion, and "high disposable income"—that gave them "political power much
greater than their numbers."[201] When he insisted that corporations had a
First Amendment right to funnel as much money as they wished into political campaigns, however, he gave no weight to the far more obvious and compelling social facts that gave corporations "political power" that far exceeded
their numbers.[202] Similarly, when he opposed all restrictions on campaign
finances, he stressed the great danger that incumbent legislators would exploit such restrictions by enacting self-serving laws to advance their own
interests.[203] When, however, he opposed claims that partisan redistricting,
gerrymandering, and state and local election laws were being exploited by
self-serving—and Republican—legislators, he dismissed those very same
dangers as irrelevant.[204]

[199] Boyle v. United Technologies Corp., 487 U.S. 500 (1988) (Scalia, J.).

[200] Wal-Mart Stores, Inc. v. Dukes, 564 U.S. 338 (2011) (Scalia, J.); Clapper v. Amnesty
International, 568 U.S. 398 (2013) (Alito, J., joined by Scalia). *See also* Franklin v. Massachusetts, 505
U.S. 788, 823, 824–25 (1992) (Scalia, J. concurring in part and concurring in the judgment).

[201] Romer v. Evans, 517 U.S. 620, 636, 645–46 (1996) (Scalia, J., dissenting).

[202] *Austin*, 494 U.S. at 679 (Scalia, J., dissenting). The Court largely adopted the position Scalia
set out in his *Austin* dissent in *Citizens United v. Federal Elections Commission*, 558 U.S. 310 (2010)
(Kennedy, J., joined by Scalia, J.). "[T]o exclude or impede corporate speech is to muzzle the principal agents of the modern free economy." *Id.* at 393 (Scalia, J., concurring). For decades "Scalia had
hammered" on the view "that corporations have the First Amendment right to spend whatever they
want to influence the outcomes of elections." HASEN, JUSTICE OF CONTRADICTIONS, 114. For one response to Scalia's ideologically shaped vision of First Amendment speech rights, *see* BERT NEUBORNE,
MADISON'S MUSIC: ON READING THE FIRST AMENDMENT (2015).

[203] "The incumbent politician who says he welcomes full and fair debate is no more to be believed
than the entrenched monopolist who says he welcomes full and fair competition. Perhaps the
Michigan Legislature was genuinely trying to assure a 'balanced' presentation of political views; on
the other hand, perhaps it was trying to give unincorporated unions (a not insubstantial force in
Michigan) political advantage over major employers. Or perhaps it was trying to assure a 'balanced'
presentation because it knows that with evenly balanced speech incumbent officeholders generally
win." *Austin*, 494 U.S. at 692–93 (Scalia, J., dissenting).

[204] HASEN, JUSTICE OF CONTRADICTIONS, 120–21. *See id.* at 114–32 (comparing Scalia's opinions in
those areas). Scalia similarly invoked the danger of self-serving legislators when he argued against the
use of legislative history. It was "no wonder that one of the routine tasks of the Washington lawyer-
lobbyist is to draft language that sympathetic legislators can recite in a pre-written 'floor debate'—or,
even better, insert into a committee report." SCALIA SPEAKS, 239.

Finally, addressing the scope of the Court's own appellate jurisdiction, Scalia was inconsistent there as well. When opportunities arose to cut back on liberal state court rulings that protected the constitutional rights of criminal defendants, he defended an expansive view of that jurisdiction. The Court's "principal responsibility under current practice" and "a primary basis" for its constitutional jurisdiction, he insisted, was "to ensure the integrity and uniformity of federal law."[205] Yet where his policy goals were different and he consequently wished to block appeals, he readily ignored what he had previously called the "primary basis" for the Court's jurisdiction and the importance of ensuring "the integrity and uniformity of federal law." In those cases he announced a contrary principle. "[D]eclaring the compatibility of state or federal laws with the Constitution," he then maintained, "is not only not the 'primary role' of this Court, it is not a separate, free-standing role *at all*."[206] Indeed, Scalia was the only justice to join Rehnquist's separate opinion in another case that declared it "a rather unremarkable proposition" that in some instances "state courts will remain free to decide important questions of federal statutory and constitutional law without the possibility of review in this Court."[207] Even the very nature of the Court's constitutional role and the importance of "the integrity and uniformity of federal law" varied according to Scalia's personal goals and values.

When considered separately, Scalia's individual opinions may seem to apply a coherent jurisprudence, but when considered comparatively and across the board they suggest a far different conclusion. They show that his jurisprudence was elastic and malleable, that he applied it inconsistently and erratically, and that he commonly used it to reach results reflecting his own political, religious, cultural, and ideological convictions. Never did he adequately explain, for example, why originalist sources were supposedly

---

[205] Kansas v. Marsh, 548 U.S. 163, 182, 183 (2006) (Scalia, J., concurring). The Court applied the rule established in *Michigan v. Long*, 463 U.S. 1032 (1980) (O'Connor, J.), which was based on the "important need for uniformity in federal law." *Id.* at 1040. Generally, the rule served conservative goals by allowing the Court to cut back on the constitutional rights of criminal defendants in state courts, and Scalia applied it regularly. *E.g.*, Ohio v. Robinette, 519 U.S. 33 (1996) (Rehnquist, C.J., joined by Scalia, J.); Arizona v. Evans, 514 U.S. 1 (1995) (Rehnquist, C.J., joined by Scalia, J.). *See, e.g.*, Edward A. Purcell, Jr., *The Story of Michigan v. Long: Supreme Court Review and the Workings of American Federalism, in* FEDERAL COURTS STORIES 115–39 (Vicki C. Jackson & Judith Resnik eds., 2010). *Compare, e.g.*, Scalia's views with those of Justice Stevens in *Michigan v. Long*, 463 U.S. 1032, 1065 (Stevens, J., dissenting), and Arizona v. Evans, 514 U.S. 1, 18 (1995) (Stevens, J., dissenting).

[206] *Windsor*, 570 U.S. at 781 (Scalia, J., dissenting) (emphasis in original).

[207] *ASARCO*, 490 U.S. at 636 (Rehnquist, C.J., concurring in part and dissenting in part, joined only by Scalia, J.).

determinative in some cases but irrelevant in others.[208] Nor why it was proper for him to bow to stare decisis in some cases and areas but not in others.[209] Nor why "venerability" demanded respect for some precedents but not for others. Nor why the significance of both history and tradition changed from one case to another. Nor why sometimes neither was even relevant. Nor why some inferences from the Constitution's text and structure were proper and others not. Nor why some words in the text—"speech," "press," "Arms,"[210] "search," "property," "executive Power," and "person, house, paper, or effect"—were to be construed loosely and expansively, while many others—"Cases," "Controversies," "religion," "liberty," "Treaty," "enforce," "confrontation," "due process," "judicial Power," "equal protection," and "cruel and unusual punishments"—were to be construed narrowly and restrictively.

During a debate in 2005 with Nadine Strossen, the president of the American Civil Liberties Union, Scalia responded to a question about the meaning of the word "religion" in the Establishment Clause and made the decisive point exactly. "It depends," he explained, "on how generalized you want to get."[211] True. And the Constitution contained no rules whatsoever for determining the level of generalization proper for its many broad, capacious,

---

[208] He attempted to explain this inconsistency by claiming that in his earlier years on the bench parties did not make originalist arguments in their briefs and scholars had not yet produced relevant originalist research. SCALIA, READING, 401–02.

[209] Scalia acknowledged that the doctrine of precedent was a "pragmatic *exception*" to his originalism, SCALIA, MATTER, 140 (emphasis in original), but he commonly failed to explain adequately, or often at all, why the exception applied most of the times when he relied on it. For his statement of common ideas about following or rejecting stare decisis, *see* SCALIA, READING, 87, 411–14. In one opinion, for example, he wrote that "I adhere to my view" of the issue "our contrary precedents notwithstanding." Stern v. Marshall, 564 U.S. 462, 503 (2011) (Scalia, J., concurring). In the oral argument of another case he declared that "I think that [*United States v. Katz*, 389 U.S. 347 (1967)] was wrong," but stated that "it's been around for so long, we are not going to overrule that." TRIBE & MATZ, UNCERTAIN JUSTICE, 234. In other opinions he followed precedents even though he thought them dubious or wrong. *E.g.*, Shady Grove Orthopedic Associates v. Allstate Insurance Co., 559 U.S. at 412–14 (Scalia, J.) (refusing to depart from a precedent that was "hard to square" with a controlling statute but had been accepted for "nearly seven decades"); *Camreta*, 563 U.S. at 714 (Scalia, J. concurring) (following "our precedents, strange though they may be"). In an Eighth Amendment case he commented that two other cases that "find no proper basis" in the Constitution nonetheless "have some claim to my adherence because of the doctrine of *stare decisis*." He rejected them there, not because they had no basis in the Constitution but because there were "irreconcilable" with another Supreme Court decision whose foundation he thought was "probably" unsound. Walton v. Arizona, 497 U.S. 639, 656, 670 672–73 (1990) (Scalia, J., concurring in part and concurring in the judgment).

[210] The word "Arms" in the Second Amendment, Scalia declared, "extends, prima facie, to all instruments that constitute bearable arms even those that were not in existence at the time of the founding." District of Columbia v. Heller, 554 U.S. at 582 (Scalia, J.).

[211] *The State of Civil Liberties*, C-Span video (at approximately 43:15 of the tape), *available at* https://www.c-span.org/video/?194843-1/state-civil-liberties&start=NaN&start=3018 (last consulted Aug. 28, 2019).

and undefined terms. In Scalia's jurisprudence, applied through a range of varying and serviceable rhetorical moves, it was his own personal values and goals that regularly made that determination.

The ultimately personal nature and ideological thrust of Scalia's juris-prudence seems particularly evident in light of his interpretation of the Equal Protection Clause. "Our salvation is the Equal Protection Clause," he declared, because it "requires the democratic majority to accept for them-selves and their loved ones what they impose on you and me."[212] That state-ment sounded a noble principle of justice and equality, but in applying it Scalia carefully narrowed its meaning and the scope of the "salvation" it promised. He insisted that the Court could not interpret the Equal Protection Clause to undermine "those constant and unbroken national traditions that embody the people's understanding of ambiguous constitutional texts." It had no basis for striking down any practice that "bears the endorsement of a long tradition of open, widespread, and unchallenged use."[213] Thus, he held that the clause did not protect certain groups—women and gays, for example[214]—even though those groups had long suffered abuse and discrim-ination at the hands of other dominant groups. Curiously echoing the harsh religious doctrine of predestination, he preached that the clause could not bring "salvation" to those who most needed it, but only to those who were already saved.

[212] Cruzan v. Director, Missouri Department of Health, 497 U.S. 261, 292, 300 (1990) (Scalia, J., concurring).

[213] United States v. Virginia, 518 U.S. at 568 (Scalia, J. dissenting). The second quote in the text above was a quote that Scalia cited from his own prior dissent in *Rutan*, 497 U.S. at 95.

[214] On women's rights, *see, e.g.*, J.E.B., 511 U.S. at 127 (1994) (Blackmun, J.). There, Scalia dissented from the Court's decision prohibiting gender discrimination in the use of peremptory challenges in jury selection. He protested that "to pay conspicuous obeisance to the equality of the sexes, the Court imperils a practice that has been considered an essential part of fair jury trial since the dawn of the common law. The Constitution of the United States neither requires nor permits this vandalizing of our people's traditions." *Id.* at 156, 163. On gay rights, *see, e.g., Obergefell*, 135 S. Ct. at 2626 (Scalia, J., dissenting). There, he dissented from the Court's decision to uphold same-sex marriage. "We have no basis for striking down a practice [limiting marriage "to one man and one woman"] that is not expressly prohibited by the Fourteenth Amendment's text, and that bears the endorsement of a long tradition of open, widespread and unchallenged use dating back to the Amendment's ratification." *Id.* at 2628.

6

A Manipulative
Jurisprudence: Unprincipled
and Expedient Reasoning

Stage-Managing James Madison: The "Father of the Constitution" as Originalist Authority

James Madison was understandably one of the Founders, if not the principal Founder, Scalia cited commonly and repeatedly in attempting to support his interpretations of the Constitution's original public meaning. His treatment of Madison, however, was typical of his jurisprudential reasoning. It was inconsistent, selective, and result-driven. Seeking originalist authority for his strict textualism, for example, Scalia quoted Madison's statement in 1821 that "the debates and incidental decisions of the Convention can have no authoritative character."[1] Seeking to bolster his interpretation of the original meaning of the Elections Clause, however, he invoked statements Madison made at that very convention.[2] An understandable partisan ploy, of course, but on originalist grounds hardly a principled one. Basically, Scalia quoted Madison when useful, ignored him when not, and twisted his meaning when necessary.

In both *Morrison v. Olson* and *United States v. Printz*, Scalia cited Madison in praise of separation of powers, but in both he ignored Madison's statements in *Federalist No. 37* that stressed the "obscurity" that marked both the meaning and operation of separation of powers.[3] Similarly, when he argued

---

[1] ANTONIN SCALIA & BRYAN A. GARNER, READING LAW: THE INTERPRETATION OF LEGAL TEXTS 371 (2012) [hereafter SCALIA, READING] (citing James Madison to Thomas Richie, Sept. 15, 1821, 9 THE WRITINGS OF JAMES MADISON 71 n.1 (Gaillard Hunt ed., 1910) [hereafter MADISON, WRITINGS].

[2] Arizona v. Inter Tribal Council of Arizona, Inc., 570 U.S. 1, 17 (2013) (Scalia, J.); Vieth v. Jubelirer, 541 U.S. 267, 275 (2004) (Scalia, J., announcing the judgment of the Court).

[3] Morrison v. Olson, 487 U.S. 654, 697 (1988) (Scalia, J., dissenting) (citing Madison's *Federalist No. 47*); United States v. Printz, 521 U.S. 898, 921–22 (1997) (Scalia, J.) (citing Madison's *Federalist No. 51*); THE FEDERALIST PAPERS No. 37, at 224 (Madison) (Clinton Rossiter ed., originally published in 1961, with Introduction and Notes by Charles R. Kessler, 2003) [hereafter FEDERALIST PAPERS].

Antonin Scalia and American Constitutionalism. Edward A. Purcell, Jr., Oxford University Press (2020).
© Edward A. Purcell, Jr.
DOI: 10.1093/oso/9780197508763.001.0001

that eighteenth-century common law was stable and that the courts lacked the power to change it,[4] he passed over Madison's statement in the same essay that the "precise extent of the common law" remained "still to be clearly and finally established in Great Britain."[5]

Again, in his book *Reading Law* Scalia cited Madison as an authority for his own "Fixed Meaning Canon." "Words," Scalia declared, "must be given the meaning they had when the text was adopted."[6] In support, he quoted from another letter that Madison wrote late in his life stating that "[w]e must take the meaning of the Constitution as it has been solemnly fixed."[7] On that issue, however, Scalia ignored Madison's argument to the contrary in *Federalist No. 37*, a source contemporaneous with the founding and hence far more authentically originalist. "All new laws, though penned with the greatest technical skill, and passed on the fullest and most mature deliberation," Madison wrote in 1788, "are considered as more or less obscure and equivocal until their meaning be liquidated and ascertained by a series of particular discussions and adjudications."[8]

When their ideas conflicted, moreover, Scalia literally had no use for Madison. In touting his textualism, Scalia passed over Madison's considered views on the inevitable imprecisions and inherent ambiguities in language, qualities that Madison identified as adding "a fresh embarrassment" to all efforts to communicate clearly. "No language is so copious as to supply words and phrases for every complex idea," Madison pointed out, "or so correct as not to include many equivocally denoting different ideas." Thus, Madison argued, there was an "unavoidable inaccuracy" in language, especially when it addressed political ideas of "complexity and novelty." The problem was deeply perplexing and wholly inescapable. "When the Almighty himself condescends to address mankind in their own language," Madison famously concluded, "his meaning, luminous as it must be, is rendered dim and doubtful by the cloudy medium through which it is communicated."[9]

Similarly, when Scalia defended religion as a critical support for democracy, he paid no attention to Madison's contrary view on the subject. "Americans,

---

[4] James B. Beam Distilling Co. v. Georgia, 501 U.S. 529, 548, 549 (1991) (Scalia, J., concurring in the judgment).

[5] FEDERALIST PAPERS No. 37, at 224 (Madison) (explaining reasons for "obscurity" in separation of powers practice).

[6] SCALIA, READING, 78.

[7] SCALIA, READING, 80, citing James Madison to C.E. Haynes, Feb. 21, 1821, 9 MADISON, WRITINGS, 443.

[8] FEDERALIST PAPERS No. 37, at 225 (Madison).

[9] FEDERALIST PAPERS No. 37, at 225 (Madison).

from the settlers to the founding generation," Scalia declared, "believed vehe-mently in the importance of religion to the welfare of democracy."[10] Madison repudiated that claim. In his famous "Memorial and Remonstrance Against Religious Assessments," written in 1785, Madison contradicted Scalia's be-nign vision on two counts. First, he explained that using religion for political purposes corrupted religion itself. Those who would "employ Religion as an engine of Civil policy," he declared, committed "an unhallowed perversion of the means of salvation." Second, and precisely contrary to Scalia's asser-tion about religion and democracy, Madison charged that religion caused deplorable political and social results. For almost fifteen centuries "the legal establishment of Christianity [has] been on trial," Madison explained, and its "fruits" were available for all to see. "More or less in all places, pride and indo-lence in the Clergy; ignorance and servility in the laity; in both, superstition, bigotry and persecution."[11] Those views Scalia ignored.

Further, Madison's discussion in the "Memorial and Remonstrance" as well as in his other writings pointed toward a strict position of church-state separation that required government to take no account of religion what-ever.[12] Scalia, in contrast, believed that the Establishment Clause allowed governments to support religion in general. He ignored Madison as an au-thority on that issue as well.[13]

When he was forced to deal with Madison's "Memorial and Remonstrance" because parties or other justices invoked it, Scalia responded in two ways. First, he dismissed it as irrelevant[14] and as "written before the Federal

---

[10] ANTONIN SCALIA, SCALIA SPEAKS 34 (Christopher J. Scalia & Edward Whelan eds., 2017) [here-after SCALIA SPEAKS]. Id. at 71, 73. "[T]hose who adopted our Constitution," Scalia declared, cer-tainly "believed that the public virtues inculcated by religion are a public good." Lamb's Chapel v. Center Moriches Union Free School District, 508 U.S. 384, 397, 400 (1993) (Scalia, J., dissenting).

[11] JAMES MADISON, THE COMPLETE MADISON: HIS BASIC WRITINGS 302 (Saul K. Padover ed., 1953) [hereafter MADISON, COMPLETE]. Madison's "Memorial and Remonstrance" did not reject re-ligion or deny the existence of a "Creator" but simply argued that religion and government should be kept separate. Id. at 299–300.

[12] See, e.g., James Madison to Edward Livingston, July 10, 1822, in 9 MADISON, WRITINGS, 101–02 ("Every new & successful example therefore of a perfect separation between ecclesiastical and civil matters, is of importance."). See VINCENT PHILLIP MUNOZ, GOD AND THE FOUNDERS: MADISON, WASHINGTON, AND JEFFERSON 48 (2009) (Madison "concluded that government must remain blind to religion as such," and a "Madisonian approach to the First Amendment would require the govern-ment to neither privilege religion nor punish citizens on account of their religion"). Accord id. at 121.

[13] Scalia similarly failed to cite Madison as authority on another issue. Madison urged an open welcome to "new sects" that could arise even when they advocated "absurd opinion or overheated imaginations." James Madison to Edward Everett, March 19, 1823, in 9 MADISON, WRITINGS, at 127. In contrast, Scalia urged an original meaning of the Establishment Clause that limited its protection to "traditional" and preferably monotheistic religions.

[14] Hein v. Freedom From Religion Foundation, Inc., 551 U.S. 587, 618, 634 (2007) (Scalia, J., con-curring in the judgment); McCreary County v. American Civil Liberties Union, 545 U.S. 844, 886,

Constitution had been proposed."[15] The fact, however, was that Madison continued to hold the views he expressed in the "Memorial and Remonstrance" and repeated them emphatically in 1787. "Religion itself," he warned the delegates at the Constitutional Convention, "may become a motive to persecution & oppression."[16] Further, in the middle of the ratification debates he continued to express the same disdain for religion in the public sphere. The "strongest of religious ties" did not prevent those in government from joining "without remorse in acts against which their consciences would revolt," he wrote to Thomas Jefferson. When "kindled into enthusiasm," religion fired dangerous passions, but even in "its coolest state" it "has been much oftener a motive to oppression than a restraint from it."[17] Indeed, in *Federalist No. 10* he echoed that same conviction when he insisted that "neither moral nor religious motives can be relied on as an adequate control" over political passions and the dangers of "factions."[18] Those were, in fact, Madison's truly "originalist" views, and Scalia simply refused to acknowledge them.

His second response to the "Memorial and Remonstrance" was to simply avert his glance and look elsewhere. He tried to trump Madison's views about the dangers that religion posed for popular government by heralding other statements Madison made, especially one in his first inaugural address where the new president placed his confidence "in the guardianship and guidance of that Almighty Being whose power regulates the destiny of nations."[19] Unlike the charges Madison leveled in the "Memorial and Remonstrance" and repeated subsequently, statements of that type Scalia could and did use. They supported his claims that the nation had traditionally made "public acknowledgment of God"[20] and that "prayer has been a prominent part of governmental ceremonies and proclamations."[21] Unlike Madison's many efforts to alert Americans to the threats that religion posed to republican government, the inaugural statement and a few others served Scalia's purpose, so they merited recognition as originalist authorities. Madison's more typical

---

896 (2005) (Scalia, J., dissenting); City of Boerne v. Flores, 521 U.S. 507, 537, 541–42 (1997) (Scalia, J., concurring in part).

[15] *McCreary*, 545 U.S. at 895 (Scalia, J., dissenting).
[16] 1 THE RECORDS OF THE FEDERAL CONVENTION OF 1787 135 (Max Farrand ed., 1911) (James Madison, June 6, 1787).
[17] James Madison to Thomas Jefferson, Oct. 24, 1787, in 5 MADISON, WRITINGS (1904), 30–31.
[18] FEDERALIST PAPERS NO. 10, at 75 (Madison).
[19] *McCreary*, 545 U.S. at 888 (Scalia, J., dissenting); Lee v. Weisman, 505 U.S. 577, 631, 634 (1992) (Scalia, J., dissenting).
[20] *McCreary*, 545 U.S. at 896 (Scalia, J., dissenting).
[21] Lee v. Weisman, 505 U.S. 577, 631, 633 (1992) (Scalia, J., dissenting).

and surely more deeply felt warnings about the political dangers of religion did not.

Indeed, Scalia's use of Madison's public proclamations as president was flawed for another reason. As Andrew Koppelman pointed out, Madison subsequently concluded that his presidential invocations of the Deity were "a mistake."[22] Scalia breathed no word of that Madisonian confession.

Similarly, when Scalia addressed the scope of the Eleventh Amendment, he again ignored Madison, this time turning a blind eye to Madison's famous theory of the "extended republic."[23] Determined to bar individual claimants from suing states in federal court, Scalia accepted an interpretation of the Eleventh Amendment that gave it a scope far broader than its text would allow. "The inherent necessity of a tribunal for peaceful resolution of disputes between the Union and the individual States, and between the individual States themselves," he explained in *Pennsylvania v. Union Gas Co.*, "is incomparably greater, in my view, than the need for a tribunal to resolve disputes on federal questions between individuals and the States." He reasoned that the Founders had abrogated state sovereign immunity in the first two classes of cases because of the "inherent necessity of a tribunal" for their "peaceful resolution."[24] In contrast, he reasoned that they had refused to abrogate that immunity in the last class of cases—and did so purposely in the Eleventh Amendment—because such individual suits against states were simply much less important and therefore not "necessary." Because the Constitution did not "require that private individuals be able to bring claims against the Federal Government for violation of the Constitution or laws [citations omitted]," he concluded, "it is difficult to see why it must be interpreted to require that private individuals be able to bring such claims against the States."[25]

Contrary to Scalia's contention, however, it was not at all difficult to see why the Constitution should be interpreted to require such suits against states. Madison's classic theory of the "extended republic" provided a cogent and convincing reason for doing so. Articulated most fully in the famous *Federalist No. 10* and re-emphasized later in *Federalist No. 51*, Madison's

[22] ANDREW KOPPELMAN, DEFENDING AMERICAN RELIGIOUS NEUTRALITY 64 (2013).

[23] Madison set out his theory in *Federalist Papers No. 10* and used the phrase "extended republic" to describe it in *id.* NO. 14, at 99, and No. 51, at 322. I am indebted for this general point to RALPH A. ROSSUM, ANTONIN SCALIA'S JURISPRUDENCE: TEXT AND TRADITION 111–12 (2006).

[24] Pennsylvania v. Union Gas Co., 491 U.S. 1, 29, 33 (1989) (Scalia, J., concurring in part and dissenting in part).

[25] *Union Gas*, 491 U.S. at 33–34 (Scalia, J., concurring in part and dissenting in part).

theory held that "small" states were likely to fall under the domination of a single "faction" and consequently suffer injustice and "oppression" while an "extended republic"—one large enough to include a wide variety of "factions" willing and able to hold one another in check—promised "greater security" and was likely to block "unjust or dishonorable purposes."[26] If Rhode Island were separated from the union and "left to itself," Madison warned accordingly, it would soon suffer from "the insecurity of rights" and "reiterated oppressions."[27] Consequently, if the greatest danger to individual liberty and republican government lurked in "small states" rather than in large ones, there was a powerful reason for allowing individual suits against states even if such suits were not allowed against the "extended" federal republic. In those relatively small states individuals were especially vulnerable to oppression and abuse, according to Madison, and hence allowing them to sue states for infringing their federal rights was not only "necessary" but essential for the preservation of liberty. For his purposes in *Union Gas*, however, Scalia had no use for Madison's reasoning.

The fact that Scalia ignored Madison's "extended republic" theory in *Union Gas* was particularly revealing. He cited the *Federalist* frequently, including both *No. 10* and *No. 51*,[28] and only a few months before *Union Gas* he had deployed Madison's theory of the "extended republic" explicitly and effectively in *City of Richmond v. Crosson*.[29] In that case he quoted *Federalist No. 10* and its warnings about the acute dangers of oppression in "small" states. In *Union Gas*, where Madison's theory contradicted Scalia's desired result, it was not useful to him and he ignored it, but in *Crosson* it was extremely useful. There, it allowed him to support his argument condemning the affirmative action plan of a local government and to thereby advance a cause that he pursued relentlessly, that of ending affirmative action programs.

Indeed, Scalia's selective use of Madison was again apparent six years later in *Adarand Constructors, Inc. v. Pena*. There, Scalia broadened his

---

[26] FEDERALIST PAPERS NO. 10, at 78 (Madison); *id.*, No. 51, at 322 (Madison).

[27] FEDERALIST PAPERS NO. 51, at 322 (Madison).

[28] *E.g.*, Zitovsky v. Kerry, 135 S. Ct. 2076, 2116, 2124 (No. 49), 2125 (No. 47) (2015) (Scalia, J., dissenting); Inter Tribal Council, 570 U.S. at 16 (No. 52) (2013) (Scalia, J.); Arizona v. United States, 567 U.S. 387, 416, 417 (No. 42) (2012) (Scalia, J., concurring in part and dissenting in part); Freytag v. Commissioner, 501 U.S. 868, 892, 906 (No. 48 & No. 49), 907 (No. 51) (1991) (Scalia, J., concurring in part and concurring in the judgment); Hamdi v. Rumsfeld, 542 U.S. 507, 554, 568 (No. 45) (2004) (Scalia, J., dissenting).

[29] *E.g.*, City of Richmond v. Crosson, 488 U.S. 469, 520, 523–24 (1989) (Scalia, J., concurring in the judgment). Three years later Scalia again cited *Federalist No. 10* and Madison's theory that the dangers of "factionalism decrease as the political unit becomes larger." Norman v. Reed, 502 U.S. 279, 296, 299–300 (1992) (Scalia, J., dissenting).

constitutional rejection of affirmative action from state and local efforts to those of the federal government. Regardless of benign purposes, he declared, "the concept of racial entitlement" could only "reinforce and preserve" the thinking "that produced race slavery, race privilege and race hatred." It made no difference, in other words, which level of government engaged in affirmative action, for every such effort was "alien to the Constitution's focus upon the individual."[30] Expanding his rejection of affirmative action to include federal programs as well as state and local ones, he no longer had any use for Madison's theory of the "extended" republic and its claim that the new national government was designed to protect the interests and rights of minority groups. "The struggle for racial justice," he had intoned earlier in *Croson*, where his target had been a local affirmative action plan, "has historically been a struggle by the national society against oppression in the individual States."[31] In *Adarand*, however, he turned a blind eye to such ideas because, as in *Union Gas*, they cut against his desired result. Consequently, in *Union Gas* and *Adarand*—contrary to his reasoning in *Crosson*—he ignored Madison, the tenth *Federalist*, and the claimed virtues of the "extended republic."

Sometimes, too, when Scalia quoted Madison, he simply misused his statements. Scalia insisted that "whether for hobby, hunting, or self-defense, Americans believe strongly in the right to own a gun," and he loved to quote Madison's *Federalist No. 46* to support his claim. Unlike governments in America, Scalia quoted Madison as stating, the governments of Europe were "afraid to trust the people with arms." Immediately following that quote, Scalia asserted that "I hope this country never falls into such a state."[32] But Madison's statement in *Federalist No. 46* did not mean, as Scalia implied, that Madison was supporting Scalia's belief in a personal right to own and possess firearms. Rather, Madison made his statement in the course of arguing that state militias would prevent the new national government from posing any serious military threat to the states. The national government could raise no more than "twenty-five or thirty thousand men," Madison maintained, and in the event it sought to oppress the states, "a militia amounting to near half a million of citizens with arms in their hands" would be ready to oppose them. Because of both the larger numbers and local affections of the state militias,

[30] Adarand Constructors, Inc. v. Pena, 515 U.S. 200, 239 (1995) (Scalia, J. concurring in part and concurring in the judgment).

[31] *Croson*, 488 U.S. at 522 (Scalia, J., concurring in the judgment).

[32] SCALIA SPEAKS, 32, 63 (quoting *Federalist No. 46*, at 296). *See id.* at 258.

Madison continued, it "may well be doubted" whether they "could ever be conquered by such a proportion of regular [federal] troops."[33] Madison's statement, in other words, addressed "arms" in a structural constitutional context that linked them to the institutional function of the state militias as protectors of the states, not to any individual right for "hobby, hunting, or self-defense."

Worse, Scalia not only misused *Federalist No. 46* to suggest that Madison supported his belief in an individual right to possess firearms, but he also refused to cite or quote another passage in the same essay that positively contradicted that idea. The Second Amendment referred to "the right of the people to keep and bear Arms."[34] Those who urged the individual right interpretation that Scalia advocated construed the phrase "bear Arms" to mean a general individual right to possess firearms, while those who urged the militia interpretation that he opposed construed the phrase more specifically to mean the right and obligation of military service.[35] In *Federalist No. 46*, Madison used the phrase in the latter sense. Discussing the ability of a nation to support a standing army, Madison explained that only "one twenty-fifth part" of the population—physically able, military-age males—would be "able to bear arms."[36] Scalia ignored Madison's usage on that point.

Along similar lines, Scalia also misused Madison's *Federalist No. 48*. In a law review article advancing his claim that standing was based on Article III, he cited a passage from that essay that neither stated nor even implied that proposition.[37] Further, in *Lujan v. Defenders of Wildlife* he used the same *Federalist* essay in an equally misleading manner. There, he quoted Madison's statement that the "landmarks" of federal judicial power were "less uncertain" than those defining the limits of federal legislative and executive powers. On its face Madison's statement meant only that the scope of the judicial power was somewhat more clearly delimited than the scope of the executive power and especially of the legislative power, the latter being "more extensive, and less susceptible of precise limits" than the power of either of

---

[33] FEDERALIST PAPERS NO. 46, at 296 (Madison).

[34] U.S. CONST. amend. 2.

[35] *Compare, e.g.,* District of Columbia v. Heller, 554 U.S. 570, 589–90 (2008) (Scalia, J.), *with id.* at 636, 660–61 (Stevens, J., dissenting).

[36] FEDERALIST PAPERS NO. 46, at 296 (Madison). In the *Federalist No. 46* Madison did not capitalize the word "arms." In *District of Columbia v. Heller,* 554 U.S. 570, 595, to make a different point Scalia quoted from the same paragraph in *Federalist No. 46* in which the phrase "bear arms" appears.

[37] Antonin Scalia, *The Doctrine of Standing as an Essential Element of the Separation of Powers,* 17 SUFFOLK U. L. REV. 881 (1982). The quote from the *Federalist* referred only to the comparative reach of the three national branches. *See* FEDERALIST PAPERS NO. 48, at 306–07 (Madison).

the other two branches.[38] Scalia, however, transformed that statement into one that purportedly affirmed a specific constitutional certainty, that Article III imposed a constitutional limit on the judicial power. Using Madison's word "landmarks" to create a nonexistent link between Madison's alleged views and his own, Scalia announced that "[o]ne of those landmarks" of judicial power was the Article III "doctrine of standing."[39] Thus, without explicitly making the anachronistic claim that Madison agreed that the doctrine of standing was a requirement of Article III, Scalia used the word "landmarks" to imply that Madison did hold that view. Madison's essay, however, made no such claim.

It was no surprise, moreover, that Scalia cited no support whatever for his sly insinuation about the import of *Federalist No. 48*. It was, in fact, virtually inconceivable that Madison saw standing as an Article III requirement. That idea was a product only of the twentieth century, and the Court did not begin to adopt it until the 1920s.[40]

A comparison of two of Scalia's most famous opinions further illustrates his willingness to twist Madison's words to serve his own purposes, even when—as in these two cases—the results Scalia sought were themselves contradictory. In *Morrison v. Olson* Scalia urged the Court to invalidate the Independent Counsel Act on the ground that it violated the powers of the executive. In contrast, in *United States v. Windsor* he urged the Court to refuse to invalidate the Defense of Marriage Act on the ground that there were no properly adverse parties before the Court.

Scalia invoked the very same sentence from Madison's *Federalist No. 49* in both of his opinions, but he used its words to support two contrary arguments. Madison's sentence read:

> The several departments being perfectly co-ordinate by the terms of their common commission, neither of them, it is evident, can pretend to an exclusive or superior right of settling the boundaries between their respective powers.[41]

---

[38] Lujan v. Defenders of Wildlife, 504 U.S. 555, 560 (1992) (Scalia, J.) (citing *Federalist No. 48*). *See* FEDERALIST PAPERS NO. 48, at 307, 306 (Madison).

[39] *Defenders*, 504 U.S. at 560 (Scalia, J.).

[40] EVAN TSEN LEE, JUDICIAL RESTRAINT IN AMERICA: HOW THE AGELESS WISDOM OF THE FEDERAL COURTS WAS INVENTED 39–40, 68, 77 (2011).

[41] FEDERALIST PAPERS NO. 49, at 311 (Madison).

In *Morrison*, attacking a congressional statute that limited the executive, Scalia used the quote to support the Court's authority to intervene on the ground that when "the political branches are (as here) in disagreement, neither can be presumed correct."[42] Thus, he implied, Madison's sentence referred to congressional-executive disputes and supported his position that the Court stood apart from the other two branches and was therefore designed to decide such disputes independently and without the deference usually accorded congressional enactments. In *Windsor*, however, seeking to protect a congressional statute when the executive refused to defend it, he used the same sentence to support his claim that the three branches were coequal and, therefore, that none of them could claim the power to decide conflicts between the other two.[43] In *Morrison* he used Madison's sentence to justify judicial intervention; in *Windsor* he used it to deny the propriety of such intervention.

A subtle change that Scalia made in quoting the words from *Federalist No. 49* suggested that he knew full well that he was twisting Madison's words for inconsistent purposes. In *Morrison* he quoted the sentence in full, including the key phrase "neither of them." That phrase seemed to imply a reference to only two branches. As so construed, it supported Scalia's interpretation that Madison was referring only to congressional-executive disputes, that is, to disputes involving only the two "political branches." That reading supported Scalia's argument in *Morrison* that the Court stood apart from the other two branches and was therefore properly situated to intervene in the case and, in doing so, should show no deference to Congress.

To support the opposite conclusion in *Windsor*, Scalia quoted only parts of that same sentence and dropped Madison's phrase "neither of them." In its place he inserted his own pointedly different paraphrase, "none of which." Thus, quoting key phrases from the sentence in *Federalist No. 49* (placed in italics in the following quotation), Scalia wrote that the Founders understood the dangers of power

and so created branches of government that would be "*perfectly co-ordinate by the terms of their common commission,*" none of which branches "*could*

---

[42] *Morrison*, 487 U.S. at 704–05 (Scalia, J., dissenting). Scalia introduced the quote by stating that the "reason" for his position "is stated concisely by Madison." *Id.* at 705 (Scalia, J., dissenting).

[43] United States v. Windsor, 570 U.S. 744, 778, 779–80 (2013) (Scalia, J., dissenting).

pretend to an exclusive or superior right of settling the boundaries between their respective powers."[44]

The words that Scalia inserted between the two quoted parts of Madison's sentence, namely the paraphrase "none of which," suggested that Madison's sentence referred not just to two branches but to all three branches, thus including the judiciary as well as the legislative and executive within its prescription. That interpretation, in turn, meant that Madison was arguing that the judicial branch was just like the legislative and executive branches in that "none" of the three could properly intervene in a dispute over the boundaries that marked the powers of the other two branches. With that paraphrase, Madison's sentence supported Scalia's argument in *Windsor* that the Court should not properly intervene in the case.

As for Madison's actual position in *Federalist No. 49*, it seems that Scalia got it wrong in *Morrison* and right in *Windsor*. First, Madison's essay addressed disputes over the boundaries of all three of the "several" federal branches, not just legislative-executive disputes. The paragraph in the *Federalist* that contains the quoted sentence makes no references to individual branches but refers instead to the "several branches" and then to the "several departments" of government.[45] Second, as an originalist and textualist matter, the word "neither" did not necessarily refer to only two things because in the eighteenth century it was still used to refer to more than two.[46] Thus, the meaning Scalia apparently sought to imply with that word in *Morrison* was anachronistic and ill-founded. Third, later in the same essay Madison noted specifically the danger of "a combination of two of the departments against the third."[47] That warning suggested that any such "combination" would be improper and thereby meant that in legislative-executive disputes the Court was not authorized to throw its weight on the side of either of the other two branches.

---

[44] *Windsor*, 570 U.S. 744, 778, 779–80 (2013) (Scalia, J., dissenting) (italics added by the author and not in the original).

[45] FEDERALIST PAPERS NO. 49, at 310–11 (Madison).

[46] " 'Neither': B. pron. 2. Not any one (of more than two). Now rare." OXFORD ENGLISH DICTIONARY ONLINE, June 2018, *available at* http://www.oed.com/view/Entry/125948 (last consulted June 14, 2018). In apparently assuming that "neither" referred only to two things, Scalia violated his own warning about such anachronistic readings. "It would be quite wrong for someone to ascribe to Queen Anne's 18th-century words their 21st-century meanings." SCALIA, READING, 78.

[47] FEDERALIST PAPERS NO. 49, at 311 (Madison). "If the legislative authority, which possesses so many means of operating on the motives of the other departments, should be able to gain to its interest either of the others, or even one third of its members, the remaining department could derive no advantage from its remedial provision." *Id.* at 311.

Further, neither *Federalist No. 49* nor Madison's essays that directly followed made the point that Scalia claimed in *Morrison*. *No. 49* noted that the theoretically proper solution to such interbranch conflicts was "an appeal to the people themselves" who "can alone declare [the Constitution's] true meaning," but it quickly scotched that idea because "there appear to be insuperable objections" to it.[48] Then, after explaining those "insuperable objections" in the remainder of *No. 49* and the first part of *No. 50*, Madison proceeded to dismiss the efficacy of another possibility, a special council to resolve interbranch disputes made up of members of the legislative and executive branches.[49] Finally, in *Federalist No. 51*, the climactic essay in the famous sequence, Madison identified his solution to the problem of interbranch disputes—the checking power given each branch in the Constitution's structure of separated and divided powers. The "great security," Madison explained, "consists in giving to those who administer each department the necessary constitutional means and personal motives to resist encroachments of the others."[50] Thus, contrary to Scalia's claim in *Morrison*, Madison was not arguing in *Federalist No. 49* that the Supreme Court was the proper authority to resolve congressional-executive disputes. Rather, he was arguing that each branch was to check the others when one or both of them sought to encroach on its powers but that none of the branches was authorized to intervene and decide disputes between the other two.

Madison's contrasting view of the Court's role in resolving federalism conflicts, as opposed to separation-of-powers conflicts, confirmed that conclusion. In *Federalist No. 39* he declared explicitly that the U.S. Supreme Court would have authority to decide the "boundary" between national and state powers.[51] In the Virginia ratifying convention he made the same point once again, defending the Court's authority in federalism disputes and terming it "necessary and expedient."[52] In neither his *Federalist* essays nor in the ratification debate did he ever claim that role for the Court in boundary disputes between Congress and the executive.[53]

---

[48] FEDERALIST PAPERS No. 49, at 311 (Madison).

[49] FEDERALIST PAPERS No. 49, at 311–14 (Madison), and No. 50, at 314–15 (Madison).

[50] FEDERALIST PAPERS No. 51, at 318–19 (Madison).

[51] FEDERALIST PAPERS No. 39, at 242 (Madison).

[52] 3 THE DEBATES IN THE SEVERAL STATE CONVENTIONS ON THE ADOPTION OF THE FEDERAL CONSTITUTION 532 (Jonathan Elliot ed., 1888).

[53] Madison's views about the Supreme Court subsequently changed, as did many of his other views. *See, e.g.,* ROBERT A. BURT, THE CONSTITUTION IN CONFLICT, ch. 2 (1992); Jack N. Rakove, *Judicial Power in the Constitutional Theory of James Madison,* 43 WM. & MARY L. REV. 1513 (2002).

Were any doubt remaining that in *Morrison* Scalia misused *Federalist No. 49*, Madison's immediately preceding essay, *No. 48*, would dispel it.

> It is agreed on all sides, that the powers properly belonging to one of the departments ought not to be directly and completely administered by either of the other departments. It is equally evident, that none of them ought to possess, directly or indirectly, an overruling influence over the others, in the administration of their respective powers.[54]

Thus, contrary to Scalia's use of *Federalist No. 49* in *Morrison*, *Federalist No. 48* made it clear that Madison was not arguing that the Court had the power to intervene and decide the case without showing deference to Congress. Scalia, moreover, was well aware of that explicit language in *No. 48* because he quoted it in an opinion he had written only two years earlier while still a judge on the court of appeals.[55]

Over the centuries, of course, the Supreme Court has intervened in separation-of-powers disputes between the two political branches, and as a general matter Americans have come to assume that in at least many situations it has the constitutional right and authority to do so.[56] Although that view has become widely accepted and even regarded as necessary to preserve the constitutional order, it was not the view that Madison expressed during the ratification debates. To the extent that Scalia's argument in *Morrison* made sense, then, it made sense in light of contemporary assumptions, not originalist ones and certainly not those of Madison in the years when the Constitution was being drafted and ratified.

---

[54] FEDERALIST PAPERS No. 48, at 305 (Madison). In another opinion Scalia cited *Federalist No. 39* to suggest that Madison supported the argument that the states and their officials could not be controlled by federal authority while ignoring his declaration that the U.S. Supreme Court was supreme on federalism issues. Printz v. United States, 521 U.S. 898, 920–21 (1997) (Scalia, J.).

[55] Synar v. United States, 626 F. Supp. 1374, 1402 (1986). The opinion was per curiam issued by a special three-judge district court, Scalia sitting with two district judges. Scalia took the lead in drafting the court's opinion, based the decision on his ideas of separation of powers, and voided a congressional statute that infringed the powers of the executive. *See* JOAN BISKUPIC, AMERICAN ORIGINAL: THE LIFE AND CONSTITUTION OF SUPREME COURT JUSTICE ANTONIN SCALIA 91, 377 n.34 (2009); BRUCE ALLEN MURPHY, SCALIA: A COURT OF ONE 113–16 (2014). Adopting Scalia's general approach, the Supreme Court affirmed the district court ruling in *Bowsher v. Synar*, 478 U.S. 714 (1986).

[56] The classic case is United States v. Nixon, 418 U.S. 683 (1974) (Burger, C.J.). The law has developed to allow the Court to decide whether structural arrangements, although agreed to by both the legislative and executive branches, are nonetheless unconstitutional. For Scalia's view supporting that principle, *see* National Labor Relations Board v. Noel Canning, 134 S. Ct. 2550, 2592, 2593–95 (2014) (Scalia, J., concurring in the judgment).

Scalia's treatment of Madison illustrates his inconsistent and sometimes misleading use of originalist sources and the fact that his own ideological goals determined his selection of sources. The contrary uses he made of Madison in *Morrison* and *Windsor* confirm that conclusion with particular clarity. In those two cases he used the same passage and ostensibly the same constitutional principle to justify two contrary conclusions, the propriety of judicial action in one and the impropriety of judicial action in the other. In *Morrison* the judicial action he urged would protect executive power, and in *Windsor* the judicial inaction he urged would protect an anti-gay statute. The cases revealed one paramount consistency, not principled respect for Madison as an original authority but only a determination to deploy his words whenever possible as weapons of partisan expedience.

Anything Goes: *Shelby County* and *Boyle*

In *Shelby County v. Holder*[57] Scalia joined the Court's four other conservatives in overturning a critical provision of the Voting Rights Act of 1965, one of the three paramount legislative achievements of the civil rights movement of the 1960s. There, the five-justice conservative majority dismissed substantial record evidence supporting the statute, stretched precedents to create a novel right of states to equal treatment, and without explanation privileged that principle of state equality over the principle that all citizens have a right to vote and that governments have a duty to honor that right.[58] As a practical matter, the decision enabled and encouraged Republican efforts to enact state voter restriction laws that promised to have a disproportionately negative impact on certain categories of Democratic-leaning voters, including blacks, other minorities, and the elderly. At the time of the decision, moreover, those probable political results were widely recognized and well

---

[57] Shelby County v. Holder, 570 U.S. 529 (2013) (Roberts, C.J., joined by Scalia, J.).
[58] *See* Edward A. Purcell, Jr., *Reflections on the Fiftieth Anniversary of the March and the Speech: History, Memory, Values*, 59 N.Y.L. Sch. L. Rev. 17, 47, 50–51 (2014–15) [hereafter Purcell, *Reflections*]. For an analysis of the Court's inadequate and badly flawed review of the factual record supporting the Voting Rights Act, *see* Morgan Kousser, *Do the Facts of Voting Rights Support Chief Justice Roberts's Opinion in* Shelby County, 1 Transatlantica (2015), *available at* http://journals.openedition.org/transatlantica/7462 (last consulted July 31, 2019) [hereafter Kousser, *Do the Facts*]. Scalia had previously cited the Voting Rights Act as justified by its showing of intentional voting discrimination in the covered states. Nevada Department of Human Resources v. Hibbs, 538 U.S. 721, 741, 741–42 (2003) (Scalia, J., dissenting); Tennessee v. Lane, 541 U.S. 509, 554, 564 (2004) (Scalia, J., dissenting).

documented, a fact that cast the majority's decision in a most disturbing partisan light.[59] Indeed, three years after *Shelby County*, for the presidential election of 2016, in "heavily black and Latino counties" that had previously been protected by the Voting Rights Act "there were 868 fewer polling places" than there had been in 2012.[60]

Scalia's decision to join the majority, however, was particularly egregious. His vote in *Shelby County* stands as one of the most embarrassing and compromised actions of his judicial career.

First, Scalia told the Senate Judiciary Committee during his confirmation hearings that he was committed to showing deference to Congress. More to the point, he stressed to an unusual extent that federalism issues presented "most often a question of prudence" and that maintaining the proper federalism balance was "essentially the function of the Congress." Thus, he assured the committee, federal-state issues were "most often a question for this body to decide, when it wishes to displace State law, and when not." And, he added emphatically, "[w]hen it does so, that is the end of the matter."[61] In *Shelby County* he contradicted that commitment.

That contradiction, moreover, was unusually acute in *Shelby County*. Record evidence strongly justified the statute, and the well-known political context highlighted the fact that the voting rights of many citizens were in immediate danger.[62] Equally important, Congress passed the Voting Rights Act under its power granted in Section 2 of the Fifteenth Amendment, a provision that conferred on Congress a special and quite specific power over the states to protect voting rights. If any matter required special judicial deference to Congress, a measure designed to protect voting rights under the authority of the Fifteenth Amendment would stand at the top of the list.

---

[59] *See* Purcell, *Reflections*, 51–55. Beginning in 2017, the Trump administration continued the Republican efforts on the national level. The Department of Justice used the Voting Rights Act as a rationalization for changing department policy on the National Voter Registration Act and supporting state efforts to remove registered voters from the rolls. David Cole, *Trump's Inquisitor*, 65 N.Y. REV. OF BOOKS (Apr. 19, 2108), at 18.

[60] Michael Tomasky, *Fighting to Vote*, 65 N. Y. REV. BOOKS 8 (Nov. 8, 2018) (citing report of the Leadership Conference for Civil Rights).

[61] *Hearings before the Committee on the Judiciary, United States Senate, Ninety-Ninth Congress, Second Session, on the Nomination of Judge Antonin Scalia, to be Associate Justice of the Supreme Court of the United States* (Aug. 5–6, 1986), 33, 81 [hereafter *Scalia Hearings*]. Scalia privileged the text of a congressional statute over general "federalism" concerns in *City of Columbus v. Ours Garage and Wrecker Service*, 536 U.S. 424, 442, 447–50 (Scalia, J., dissenting).

[62] Justice Ginsburg highlighted much of the salient evidence in the record. Shelby County v. Holder, 570 U.S. 529, 559 (2013) (Ginsburg, J., dissenting). On recent Republican efforts to restrict voting, especially after *Shelby County, see* ALLAN J. LICHTMAN, THE EMBATTLED VOTE IN AMERICA: FROM THE FOUNDING TO THE PRESENT 189–230, 247–49 (2018).

Second, more than the other conservative justices, Scalia had repeatedly stressed the importance of judicial restraint in favor of honoring legislative judgments as the voice of democracy. On that score, the Voting Rights Act seemed unusually secure. Congress had re-enacted it five times between 1970 and 2006 with ever-growing majorities in both Houses.[63] Rather than crediting the statute's overwhelming popular support, however, Scalia chose to mock it. He expressed his disdain for those who voted for the act on the wholly incongruous and, in democratic terms, facially absurd ground that they did so only because they feared that "they are going to lose votes if they do not reenact the Voting Rights Act." His comment scorned the fundamental principle of popular government that he had so often and so fervently proclaimed on and off the bench when it suited his purposes. Accusing Congress of perpetuating "racial entitlement," he concluded with a peremptory assertion that "this is not the kind of a question you can leave to Congress."[64]

Third, Scalia's willingness to go along with the majority's analysis of the record flouted yet another of his proclaimed principles, this one distinctly his own. In large part the majority's decision to invalidate the statute rested on what it claimed was the inadequacy of the record Congress had compiled to support its re-enactment,[65] a highly questionable assessment at best given the more than substantial evidence in the record.[66] For Scalia, however, the majority's dismissal of the evidence in the record contradicted his previous insistence that the Court should not scrutinize the legislative records that underlay congressional measures. Two years before *Shelby County* he had assured the Tea Party Caucus of the House of Representatives that he spurned efforts to inquire into the factual bases of congressional legislation.

> I have refused to join opinions that make the constitutionality of legislation depend upon the nature of the hearings conducted by Congress, and the

---

[63] On the history of the act, *see, e.g.*, MICHAEL WALDMAN, THE FIGHT TO VOTE (2016); GARY MAY, BENDING TOWARD JUSTICE: THE VOTING RIGHTS ACT AND THE TRANSFORMATION OF AMERICAN DEMOCRACY (2013); MARSHA J. DARLING, THE VOTING RIGHTS ACT OF 1965: RACE, VOTING, AND REDISTRICTING (CONTROVERSIES IN CONSTITUTIONAL LAW) (2013); RACE, VOTING, AND REDISTRICTING AND THE CONSTITUTION: SOURCES AND EXPLORATIONS ON THE FIFTEENTH AMENDMENT, ENFORCING AND CHALLENGING THE VOTING RIGHTS ACT OF 1965, VOL. 2 (Marsha J. Darling ed., 2001); DAVID J. GARROW, PROTEST AT SELMA: MARTIN LUTHER KING, JR. AND THE VOTING RIGHTS ACT OF 1965 (1978).

[64] Transcript of oral argument, Shelby County v. Holder, No. 12-96 (Feb. 27, 2013), 16–17, 46–47 (quotes at 47, 48) [hereafter Oral Argument in *Shelby County*].

[65] *Shelby County*, 570 U.S. at 551–55 (Roberts, C.J.).

[66] *Shelby County*, 570 U.S. at 569–85 (Ginsburg, J., dissenting); Kousser, *Do the Facts*.

adequacy of those hearings to support the findings set forth in the prologue to the statute. I have referred to that process as reviewing the Congress's homework, a function inappropriate for our court.[67]

Reviewing "Congress's homework," of course, was exactly what he and the other conservatives did in *Shelby County.*

Indeed, only the year before *Shelby County* Scalia had criticized the Court's "congruence and proportionality" test of congressional power under the Fourteenth Amendment on the precise ground that it unwisely required the justices to "scour the legislative record in search of evidence that supports the congressional action." The insurmountable objection to such evidentiary review, he explained, was that such "grading of Congress's homework is a task we are ill suited to perform and ill advised to undertake."[68] Yet, in *Shelby County* he was willing to undertake that same "ill advised" task for which he and the Court were "ill suited" to perform and—in spite of the more than substantial evidence in the record—to grade the congressional effort a failure.

Finally, and even worse, Scalia contradicted himself in an even more fundamental way. The Court's "congruence and proportionality" test required statutes to have a tightly tailored relation to the specific evil that Congress sought to remedy, and initially Scalia and the other conservatives had used it to invalidate civil rights statutes.[69] When the Court at last applied it to uphold a civil rights statute, however, Scalia suddenly rejected the test and excoriated it as "flabby" and indeterminate. Its amorphous nature, he thundered in a solo dissent, made it "a standing invitation to judicial arbitrariness and policy-driven decisionmaking." It had "no demonstrable basis in the text

[67] SCALIA SPEAKS, 213–14.
[68] Coleman v. Court of Appeals of Maryland, 566 U.S. 30, 44–45 (2012) (Scalia, J., concurring in the judgment). In an earlier case Scalia similarly criticized the test because it required the courts to "regularly check Congress's homework" and was "ill advised." Tennessee v. Lane, 541 U.S. 509, 554, 558 (2004) (Scalia, J., dissenting). Scalia's vote in *Shelby County* also contradicted his action in another case where he refused to inquire into the legislative record behind a congressional action to determine whether a revenue bill had originated in the Senate or the House. DAVID M. DORSEN, THE UNEXPECTED SCALIA: A CONSERVATIVE JUSTICE'S LIBERAL OPINIONS 153–54 (2017) (citing *United States v. Munoz-Flores*, 495 U.S. 385, 408, where Scalia concurred in the judgment).
[69] *E.g.*, Kimel v. Florida Board of Regents, 528 U. S. 62 (2000) (O'Connor, J., joined by Scalia, J.); Board of Trustees v. Garrett, 531 U.S. 356 (2001) (Rehnquist, C.J., joined by Scalia, J.). The test originated in *City of Boerne v. Flores*, 521 U.S. 507 (1997) (Kennedy, J., joined in relevant part by Scalia, J.).

of the Constitution and cannot objectively be shown to have been met or failed."[70]

In *Shelby County*, however, agreeing to serve as the decisive fifth vote for invalidation, Scalia accepted an alternate test that the conservative justices devised to justify voiding the act, a test that only required the legislation to be "sufficiently related" to the evil to be remedied.[71] On its face a "sufficiently related" test was vaguer, more indeterminate, and far more readily open to subjective application and purposeful manipulation, than the obviously stricter "congruence and proportionality" test.[72] Equally, as Scalia had said of the "congruence and proportionality" test, the virtually meaningless "sufficiently related" test had "no demonstrable basis" in the Constitution and surely invited—indeed, encouraged—"judicial arbitrariness and policy-driven decisionmaking." Yet Scalia embraced the latter test and found it adequately objective, demanding, and constitutionally grounded to serve as a justification for invalidating the Voting Rights Act. If the other conservative justices acted on highly questionable grounds in *Shelby County*, Scalia not only did the same but also—unlike the other four—betrayed his own delegitimizing analysis of the more specific and demanding "congruence and proportionality" test.

Worst of all, Scalia knew that *Shelby County*'s "sufficiently related" test was amorphous, easily manipulable, and "a standing invitation to judicial arbitrariness and policy-driven decisionmaking." Many years earlier he himself had, as a last resort, sought refuge in that same test in *Boyle v. United Technologies Corp.* to create a new federal common-law rule to limit the liability of government military contractors.[73] There, in a tort suit brought by the father of a Marine helicopter pilot killed in a crash, he had strained for legal cover by grasping at anything he could possibly use. Over the protest of four dissenting justices and with no support from any originalist or textualist source, he turned to the "sufficiently related" test to link two wholly unrelated things.

---

[70] Tennessee v. Lane, 541 U.S. at 557–58 (Scalia, J., dissenting). Rehnquist, joined by Kennedy and Thomas, also dissented, but they did not join Scalia's dissent rejecting the "congruence and proportionality" test. *Id.* at 538 (2004).

[71] *Shelby County*, 570 U.S. at 551, quoting *Northwest Austin Municipal Utility District Number One v. Holder*, 557 U.S. 193, 204 (2009) (Roberts, C.J., joined by Scalia, J.).

[72] Before Scalia joined the Court, Rehnquist noted for a plurality that the "sufficiently related" test required "great deference" to the legislature. Michael M. v. Superior Court of Sonoma County, 450 U.S. 464, 470 ("great deference"), 473 ("sufficiently related") (1981) (Rehnquist, J.). *See* Purcell, *Reflections*, 48 n.150.

[73] Boyle v. United Technologies Corp., 487 U.S. 500 (1988) (Scalia, J.).

In *Boyle*, to support his unprecedented decision, Scalia proclaimed a Rube Goldberg–like connection between the tort claim at issue in the case and a rule of state law involving privity of contract. The plaintiff's tort claim was not based on any contract, and it raised no issue of contractual privity. The real-world connection between the tort claim and the state contract law was virtually non-existent: the claim arose from a crash that caused the death of the pilot; the crash and death had allegedly been caused by the defective design of the helicopter; the defendant had designed and manufactured the helicopter; the U.S. government had bought the helicopter from defendant pursuant to a contract between them; and the crash occurred in Virginia which used to have a law requiring privity of contract. Neither the plaintiff nor his deceased Marine son were parties to the contract, and the government was not a party to the suit. Moreover, the contract contained no provision relevant to the claim, and the suit implicated no contractual term, warranty, or condition. Even more arresting, the state contract law that Scalia cited had been abrogated by the state eighteen years before the crash and was not even in force when the Marine pilot was killed.[74] Yet Scalia found that the state contract law was somehow relevant and furnished some kind of support for his innovative lawmaking because it was "sufficiently related" to the tort claim.[75]

If an abandoned rule of state contract law was "sufficiently related" to the tort claim in *Boyle*, then the challenged statutory provision in *Shelby County* was surely "sufficiently related" to the evils Congress sought to remedy in the Voting Rights Act. Yet in *Shelby County* Scalia agreed to apply the test and to find that the two were not "sufficiently related."[76] His two contrasting applications demonstrated conclusively that the test was wholly indeterminate, easily manipulable, and virtually boundless. Accordion-like, it could be expanded or contracted at will. In *Boyle* Scalia chose to stretch the test endlessly to find a "sufficient" connection between two wholly unrelated things, while in *Shelby County* he agreed to contract it ruthlessly to deny a "sufficient" connection between two intimately related things. His contrary applications

---

[74] *Boyle*, 487 U.S. at 505.
[75] Defendant's potential "liability may be styled one in tort, but it arises out of performance of the contract—and traditionally has been regarded as sufficiently related to the contract that until 1962 Virginia [where the injury occurred] would generally allow design defect suits only by the purchaser and those in privity with the seller." *Boyle*, 487 U.S. at 505.
[76] Scalia could easily find a "lack of nexus" between means and ends when necessary to achieve his goal of protecting private property. *E.g.*, Nollan v. California Coastal Commission, 483 U.S. 825, 837 (1987) (Scalia, J.).

of the test supported only one conclusion: to invalidate the Voting Rights Act he was willing to resort to a "flabby" test that invited "judicial arbitrariness and policy-driven decisionmaking" and use that test to achieve a fervently desired result that he was resolutely determined to reach.

Beyond its illuminating relationship to *Shelby County*, Scalia's opinion in *Boyle* also illustrated more generally both his result orientation and his ability to conjure up essentially baseless legal arguments when necessary to advance his purposes. Perhaps most striking, it demonstrated his willingness to expand federal judicial power—in contrast to his general efforts to limit it—when he needed that power to serve his own policy goals. Accordingly, in restating the controlling constitutional principle in *Boyle*, he implied the legitimacy of a substantially broadened federal common law that went well beyond the limits established in *Erie Railroad Co. v. Tompkins*, the prime modern authority on the scope of federal judicial lawmaking and the paramount limiting precedent that loomed over the Court in *Boyle*.

Erie had announced a straightforward rule. "Except in matters governed by the federal Constitution or by acts of Congress, the law to be applied in any case is the law of the state."[77] To reach the result he sought in *Boyle*, Scalia subtly but radically altered that limitation. The Court could preempt state law and replace it with federal common law, he explained, in areas "committed by the Constitution and laws of the United States to federal control."[78] *Erie*, of course, had famously held that the word "laws" included not just constitutions and statutes but judicial decisions as well.[79] Thus, Scalia's reformulation in *Boyle* expanded *Erie's* limitation on judicial lawmaking from areas where the Constitution and statutes controlled to areas where the Constitution and "laws"—that is, judicial decisions as well as statutes—controlled. Scalia's expansion thus meant that the courts had the power to preempt state law and make federal common law even when the Constitution and statutes did not authorize or even undergird their action. That, in turn, meant that judicial decisions alone could provide a sufficient basis for federal judicial lawmaking. In *Boyle* Scalia's designing substitution of "Constitution and laws" for *Erie's* "Constitution and statutes" justified him in using judicial precedents as his authority for creating a broadened federal common law. Jettisoning his repeated claims of deference to Congress, his effort to protect

---

[77] Erie Railroad Co. v. Tompkins, 304 U.S. 64, 78 (1938) (emphasis added) (Brandeis, J.).

[78] *Boyle*, 487 U.S. at 504 (emphasis added).

[79] *Erie*, 304 U.S. at 78–80.

government contractors from tort suits made Congress wholly unnecessary for federal judicial lawmaking.

Not once did Scalia even mention *Erie* in his opinion, while in dissent Justice William Brennan understandably cited it six times.[80] Not once did Scalia mention the principle of judicial restraint. Not once did he refer to the principle of deference to the legislature. Not once did he mention the principle of separation of powers. Not once, finally, did he mention the fact that over the previous years Congress had repeatedly rejected bills introduced to establish the kind of government contractor defense that he was determined to create.[81] *Erie*, restraint, separation of powers, deference to the legislature, and the principle of "interpreting not legislating" were all instruments for other occasions.

Indeed, to support his lawmaking in *Boyle*, Scalia pressed his position even further, advancing the startling proposition that judicial decisions could carry a broader preemptive force than congressional statutes.

> The conflict with federal policy [established by judicial decisions] need not be as sharp as that which must exist for ordinary pre-emption when Congress legislates "in a field which the States have traditionally occupied" [cite omitted]. Or to put the point differently, the fact that the area in question *is* one of unique federal concern changes what would otherwise be a conflict that cannot produce pre-emption into one that can.[82]

That claim not only extended federal judicial power into areas beyond the scope of existing congressional legislation, but it also contradicted the text-based theory of preemption that he himself had asserted only two months earlier. "There is no federal pre-emption *in vacuo*, without a constitutional text or a federal statute to assert it."[83] To create a government contractor defense, however, more judicial power was needed than that text-based principle would allow. Scalia simply abandoned his previously announced principle and the textual limitation it imposed.

---

[80] *Boyle*, 487 U.S. at 516, 517 (3 cites), 518, 519 (Brennan, J., dissenting, joined by Marshall and Blackmun, JJ.). Stevens dissented separately. *Id.* at 530.

[81] *Boyle*, 487 U.S. at 515 & n.1 (Brennan, J., dissenting, pointing out that Congress had refused to authorize such a defense "and conspicuously so, having resisted a sustained campaign by Government contractors to legislate for them some defense," citing six bills introduced to create such a tort defense in the previous decade, none of which were enacted). *See also id.* at 531 (Brennan, J., dissenting).

[82] *Boyle*, 487 U.S. at 507–08 (emphasis in original).

[83] Puerto Rico Department of Consumer Affairs v. Isla Petroleum Corp., 485 U.S. 495, 503 (1988) (Scalia, J.).

Drawing on nothing but judicial precedents in *Boyle*, then, Scalia identi-fied a "concern" or "interest" that was "uniquely" or "peculiarly" federal[84] and asserted that protecting that federal interest provided a necessary basis for creating a government contractor defense. On their face, the precedents he cited had no proper application to the issue in *Boyle*. One line addressed gov-ernment contracts and the other the immunity of federal officials, and *Boyle* involved neither a government contract nor a federal official.

In addressing the precedents involving government contracts, Scalia not only cited the irrelevant and long-abandoned state contract law that he contended was "sufficiently related" to the tort claim at issue, but he egre-giously misconstrued the Court's most recent precedent that he cited in sup-port. *United States v. Little Lake Misere Land Co.*,[85] he claimed, established the proposition that "obligations to and rights of the United States under its contracts are governed exclusively by federal law."[86] The Court in *Little Lake Misere*, however, had expressly refused to make that ruling and, in fact, had refused even to make a much narrower ruling. "The Government urges us to decide, virtually without qualification, that *land acquisition agreements* of the United States should be governed by federally created federal law," *Little Lake* explained. "We find it unnecessary to resolve this case on such broad terms."[87]

In addressing precedents involving official immunity Scalia cited cases where the Court had protected federal employees from state suits that chal-lenged actions the officials had taken within the scope of their federal au-thority. Acknowledging that *Boyle* presented no such facts, he claimed that the precedents were relevant by raising the level of generality. Government employees were "like" government contractors because both "implicated the same interest in getting the Government's work done."[88] His recourse to that high and abstract level of generality was entirely arbitrary. It violated his "most specific level" principle and ignored as well the numerous legal and practical differences that distinguished government employees from private contractors and, consequently, made the legitimate "interest" of the United States government in each substantially different.[89]

[84] *Boyle*, 487 U.S. at 504 ("uniquely federal interests") and 505 ("peculiarly federal concern").
[85] United States v. Little Lake Misere Land Co., 412 U.S. 580 (1973) (Burger, C.J.).
[86] *Boyle*, 487 U.S. at 504.
[87] *Little Lake Misere*, 412 U.S. at 595 (emphasis added).
[88] *Boyle*, 487 U.S. at 505 & n.1.
[89] Brennan identified some of the many significant differences in his dissent. *Boyle*, 487 U.S. at 522–24.

Further, and even more revealing, his move raising the level of generality contradicted the approach he adopted in civil rights cases. There, he repeatedly rejected plaintiffs' efforts to use higher levels of generality to show that "established law" overcame the qualified immunity that defendants invariably asserted.[90] In those cases—where a higher level of generality favored plaintiffs, not defendants—he insisted that precedents must be construed on "a more particularized" and fact-specific level,[91] a highly restrictive level that commonly defeated plaintiffs' civil rights claims. The "level of generality," he fully understood, could easily be raised or lowered to achieve whatever results he desired.

Thus, even assuming that judicial decisions properly provided authority for the Court to make law beyond the scope of constitutional and statutory provisions, the precedents Scalia cited applied only by strained analogy. Indeed, Scalia essentially admitted as much, claiming no more than the vaguest relevance for them. The issue in *Boyle*, he wrote, merely "borders upon" them.[92]

To justify the government contractor defense, however, Scalia needed to do still more. The existence of a "uniquely federal interest" was only "a necessary, not a sufficient, condition" for making federal common law. A "significant conflict" between that interest and state law was also necessary.[93] To establish such a conflict he resorted to yet another strained analogy, this time citing an exception in the Federal Tort Claims Act (FTCA). That act, Scalia explained, "authorized damages to be recovered against the United States for harm caused by the negligent or wrongful conduct of Government employees," and the exception barred claims that arose from the performance of "a discretionary function or duty." Like the judicial precedents he had cited earlier, however, neither the act nor the exception applied of its own force to any claim in *Boyle*. No government employee had caused any "harm," and no claim was being asserted against the United States. Once again he was forced to acknowledge his stretch. Unable to claim that the statute and exception actually applied, he offered the notion that the statute merely "suggests

---

[90] Anderson v. Creighton, 483 U.S. 635, 639–640 (1987) (Scalia, J.) (rejecting the tactic of raising "the level of generality," at 639, to expand the scope of a legal rule); Hope v. Pelzer, 536 U.S. 730, 748, 752–53 (2002) (Thomas, J., dissenting, joined by Scalia, J.) (same). *See also* Brosseau v. Haugen, 543 U.S. 194, 201 (2004) (Scalia, J., concurring in Court's opinion rejecting high level of generality and requiring highly particularized level of analysis in determining immunity of government officials).

[91] *Anderson*, 483 U.S. at 640 (Scalia, J.).

[92] *Boyle*, 487 U.S. at 504.

[93] *Boyle*, 487 U.S. at 507.

the outlines" of a conflict that could exist between state law and the "uniquely federal interest" at stake. The conflict he proposed was that allowing state law to impose liability on government contractors would likely have an impact on "discretionary" functions because federal officials would be constrained in their decisionmaking by concern about the increased costs the government could face in procuring equipment. "The financial burden of judgments against the contractors would ultimately be passed through, substantially if not totally, to the United States itself."[94]

Scalia's claim of such a "financial burden" was unsupported by the record in the case and at most hypothetical and potential.[95] More important, it would not necessarily even prove true. As Justice Brennan pointed out in dissent, the tort system was designed to compel manufacturers to make safer products, and potential tort liability could induce government contractors to do just that. Even if the government were forced to pay more for safer equipment, its net costs could balance out or even decline if the safer equipment led to fewer equipment failures and personal injuries. Such safer equipment could reduce the financial burden of providing medical care to injured soldiers, paying death benefits to beneficiaries, reassigning and relocating replacement personnel, purchasing additional replacement equipment, and refilling the ranks by recruiting and training larger numbers of new recruits. The Court, Brennan pointed out, "therefore has no basis for its assumption that tort liability will result in a net burden on the Government (let alone a clearly excessive net burden) rather than a net gain."[96]

Left entirely unsaid in Scalia's opinion, moreover, was the underlying fact that the U.S. government had no legal right, or even any plausible claim of right, to acquire equipment at some special lower cost. Earlier in the year the Court itself had seemed to affirm that proposition in a tax case,[97] and several years later Scalia himself rejected the argument that federal common law was necessary because application of state law would put additional financial burdens on the United States by depleting a federal insurance fund. There is "no federal policy that the fund should always win," he declared. "Our cases have previously rejected 'more money' arguments remarkably similar to the

[94] *Boyle*, 487 U.S. at 511, 511–12, 512–13.

[95] *Compare Boyle*, 487 U.S. at 511–12 (Scalia, J.), *with id.* at 530 (Brennan, J., dissenting).

[96] *Boyle*, 487 U.S. at 530–31 (Brennan, J., dissenting).

[97] South Carolina v. Baker, 485 U.S. 505, 521 (1988), cited in *Boyle*, 487 U.S. at 527 (Brennan, J., dissenting).

one made here."[98] That "more money" argument was precisely the argument he used in *Boyle*.

Finally, it was revealing that Scalia did not honor the fact that the question of the desirability of a government contractor defense required a complex, fact-based judgment that cried out for deference to the expertise and policy authority of Congress. No judicially cognizable rule or clear legal line could satisfactorily deal with such a complex issue, and any sound approach required a judgment based on the careful balancing of any number of practical considerations. As Justice Stevens pointed out in his dissent, only three days before *Boyle* came down Scalia had acknowledged that decisions involving such complex, fact-based policy judgments required judicial deference to Congress.[99]

In that earlier case, *Schweiker v. Chilicky*, Scalia signed on to Justice O'Connor's opinion maintaining that "Congressional competence at 'balancing governmental efficiency and the rights of [individuals]' "[100] and the complex nature of such policy issues compelled the Court to defer to the practical judgment of the legislature. Not surprisingly, in *Chilicky* Scalia was pursuing a different ideological goal and, as he commonly did, simply accepted whatever arguments served in the situation. In *Chilicky* he sought to deny the propriety of judicial lawmaking in an area—creating rights of action for injured or otherwise aggrieved individuals—where he wanted the Court to make no law. In *Boyle*, however, where he did want the Court to make law, he used that very same argument about the significance of practical policy considerations to support a conclusion opposite to the one he had approved in *Chilicky*. The selection of military equipment, he reasoned in *Boyle*,

> often involves not merely engineering analysis but judgment as to the balancing of many technical, military, and even social considerations, including specifically the trade-off between greater safety and greater combat effectiveness.[101]

It was on that basis that he maintained that the FTCA's "discretionary" exception was relevant in *Boyle* and supported judicial lawmaking there. *Chilicky*

---

[98] O'Melveny & Myers v. Federal Deposit Insurance Corp., 512 U.S. 79, 88 (1994) (Scalia, J.).

[99] *Boyle*, 487 U.S. at 532 (Stevens, J., dissenting).

[100] Schweiker v. Chilicky, 487 U.S. 412, 425 (1987) (O'Connor, J., joined by Scalia, J.) (quoting *Bush v. Lucas*, 462 U.S. 367, 388 (1983) (Stevens, J.).

[101] *Boyle*, 487 U.S. at 511.

and *Boyle* served radically different social purposes, and Scalia accepted the argument for judicial deference in *Chilicky* and rejected it in *Boyle* not for any reason of originalism, textualism, or traditionalism—and surely not for any reason of logic or precedent—but only for a reason of policy. In the two cases, he simply sought to achieve different results.

On a variety of levels, then, *Boyle* demonstrated Scalia's willingness to manipulate established legal sources and deploy inconsistent reasoning to serve his own policy goals. When those goals required him to assert a creative judicial power, he readily did so and was more than willing to make an exception to his general campaign to limit that power. More commonly, however, when such creative judicial power conflicted with his policy goals, he denied its legitimacy. Thus, it was no surprise that he found no such power in *Chilicky*, nor was it a surprise that only seven months after creating a federal common-law defense in *Boyle*, he proposed a "categorical" rule that federal courts should never use their power to imply rights of action for injured individuals.[102] A creative judicial power existed to protect government contractors from tort suits, he decided, but not to protect ordinary individuals injured by governmental and corporate violations of the Constitution and federal statutes.

Both separately and together, *Shelby County* and *Boyle* exemplified the fact that neither originalism nor textualism but ideologically based judicial decision-making marked large swaths of Scalia's actual jurisprudence. Consistent with his political and social views, *Shelby County* limited the ability of civil rights plaintiffs to protect their right to vote, while *Boyle* prevented tort claimants from suing private corporations. Both struck at two of Scalia's favorite targets; both contradicted his own most frequently heralded jurisprudential principles; and both illustrated his willingness to twist authorities for his own purposes. Like his contrary uses of Madison in *Morrison* and *Windsor*, his behavior in *Shelby County* and *Boyle* revealed central characteristics of his jurisprudence, its inconsistent, nonoriginalist, and result-driven nature.

---

[102] Thompson v. Thompson, 484 U.S. 174, 188, 191 (1988) (Scalia, J., concurring).

7

An Arbitrary Jurisprudence: *Heller*

The most personal opinion that Scalia wrote for the Court likely came in *District of Columbia v. Heller*.[1] It "is my legacy opinion," he proudly announced. "[I]t is the best example of the technique of constitutional interpretation, which I favor: that is to say it is a good example of originalism."[2] *Heller* was "originalism's high-water mark," declared one commentator, while another thought it showed Scalia "at the peak of his legal influence."[3]

Scalia's opinion for a five-justice majority in *Heller* deployed a variety of textual and historical arguments to identify what he announced as "the original understanding of the Second Amendment." On that basis, he held that the amendment protected an individual constitutional right to possess handguns in the home for self-defense and voided a conflicting prohibition in the District of Columbia Code.[4] In typical Scalian style his opinion was well written, forcefully argued, and replete with both irrelevant flourishes and flashy insults hurled at those who disagreed with him.[5]

The opinion provoked extensive and severe scholarly criticism aimed at his highly selective use of historical materials, inadequate understanding of political and cultural contexts, and inattention to the historical changes that marked the late eighteenth and nineteenth centuries.[6] The massive evidence

---

[1] District of Columbia v. Heller, 554 U.S. 570 (2008) (Scalia, J.).

[2] BRUCE ALLEN MURPHY, SCALIA: A COURT OF ONE 390 (2014) [hereafter MURPHY, SCALIA].

[3] Adam J. White, *The American Constitutionalist: Antonin Scalia, 1936–2016*, 21 THE WEEKLY STANDARD (Feb. 29, 2016), 24, 25; JOAN BISKUPIC, AMERICAN ORIGINAL: THE LIFE AND CONSTITUTION OF SUPREME COURT JUSTICE ANTONIN SCALIA 344–45 (2009) [hereafter BISKUPIC, AMERICAN ORIGINAL].

[4] *Heller*, 554 U.S. at 625, 635.

[5] *E.g.*, "[I]t is not the role of this Court to pronounce the Second Amendment extinct," Scalia proclaimed grandly. *Heller*, 554 U.S. at 636. He termed Stevens's position in dissent "grotesque," *id.* at 587, "unknown this side of the looking glass," *id.* at 589, and "worthy of the Mad Hatter," *id.* at 589.

[6] For a sample of works providing general support for Scalia's individual right interpretation, *see, e.g.,* JOYCE LEE MALCOLM, TO KEEP AND BEAR ARMS: THE ORIGINS OF AN ANGLO-AMERICAN RIGHT (1994); LEONARD LEVY, ORIGINS OF THE BILL OF RIGHTS (1999); STEPHEN P. HALBROOK, THE FOUNDERS' SECOND AMENDMENT: ORIGINS OF THE RIGHT TO BEAR ARMS (2008); DAVID E. YOUNG, THE FOUNDERS' VIEW OF THE RIGHT TO BEAR ARMS (2007); ROBERT J. SPITZER, THE POLITICS OF GUN CONTROL (2004); David T. Hardy, *The Rise and Demise of the "Collective Right" Interpretation of the Second Amendment*, 59 CLEV. ST. L. REV. 315 (2011); James A. Hanretta, *Collective Responsibilities, Private Arms, and State Regulations: Toward the Original Understanding*, 73 FORDHAM L. REV. 529

Antonin Scalia and American Constitutionalism. Edward A. Purcell, Jr., Oxford University Press (2020).
© Edward A. Purcell, Jr.
DOI: 10.1093/oso/9780197508763.001.0001

that scholars unearthed and the sophisticated analyses they produced justify four basic conclusions.[7] First, there are many varieties of historical evidence that could be used in attempts to support different interpretations
of the amendment's meaning. That evidence shows that a person genuinely
determined to construe the amendment according to its original meaning
could not know with any real certainty what that meaning was or whether
there was any specific and shared understanding of it at all.[8] Second, though
Scalia's version drew support from some selected pieces of historical evidence, it was most likely wrong. The bulk of the available historical research
undermines it, and most scholars who have studied the issue have rejected
it.[9] Third, the evidence does not come close to providing the clarity and confidence necessary to justify the pronouncement of a novel, sweeping, extremely controversial, and arguably exceptionally dangerous constitutional

(2004); Robert E. Shalhope, *The Ideological Origins of the Second Amendment*, 69 J. AM. HIST. 599
(1982).

    For a sample of works challenging or contradicting Scalia's individual right interpretation,
see, e.g., Brief of Amici Curiae Jack N. Rakove et al., in Support of Petitioners, District of Columbia
v. Heller (brief signed by fifteen historians who specialized in eighteenth- and early-nineteenth-
century history) [hereafter Rakove Brief]; Brief for Professors of Linguistics and English in
Support of Petitioners, District of Columbia v. Heller (brief signed by three language specialists)
[hereafter Linguistics Brief]; PATRICK J. CHARLES, THE SECOND AMENDMENT: THE INTENT AND
ITS INTERPRETATION BY THE STATES AND THE SUPREME COURT (2009) [hereafter CHARLES,
SECOND AMENDMENT]; JOHN MASSARO, NO GUARANTEE OF A GUN: HOW AND WHY THE SECOND
AMENDMENT MEANS EXACTLY WHAT IT SAYS (2009); SAUL CORNELL, A WELL-REGULATED
MILITIA: THE FOUNDING FATHERS AND THE ORIGINS OF GUN CONTROL IN AMERICA (2006); H.
RICHARD UVILLER & WILLIAM G. MERKEL, THE MILITIA AND THE RIGHT TO BEAR ARMS, OR, HOW
THE SECOND AMENDMENT FELL SILENT (2002); David Thomas Konig, *Why the Second Amendment
Has a Preamble: Original Public Meaning and the Political Culture of Written Constitutions in
Revolutionary America*, 56 U.C.L.A. L. REV. 1295, 1326–37 (2009); Cass Sunstein, *Second Amendment
Minimalism: Heller as Griswold*, 122 HARV. L. REV. 246 (2008); Paul Finkelman, *"A Well-Regulated
Militia": The Second Amendment in Historical Perspective*, 76 CHI-KENT L. REV. 195 (2000); Lawrence
Delbert Cress, *An Armed Community: The Origins and Meaning of the Right to Bear Arms*, 71 J. AM.
HIST. 22 (1984); Lawrence Delbert Cress, *The Second Amendment and the Rights to Bear Arms: An
Exchange*, 71 AM. HIST. REV. 587 (1984). It is worth noting, too, that Scalia's opinion presented an an-
tiseptic view of the Second Amendment that ignored the extent to which gun laws and practices were
used in the United States to enforce slavery, white supremacy, and racist policies. ROXANNE DUNBAR-
ORTIZ, LOADED: A DISARMING HISTORY OF THE SECOND AMENDMENT (2018).
    [7] Two years after the decision, Justice Stephen Breyer identified some of the more recent literature
showing that *Heller*'s "historical account was flawed." McDonald v. City of Chicago, 561 U.S. 742, 912,
914–16 (2010) (Breyer, J., dissenting).
    [8] Jack N. Rakove, *The Second Amendment: The Highest State of Originalism*, 76 CHI-KENT L. REV.
103 (2000). For a qualified defense of the individual right view followed by several critical responses
written just prior to *Heller, see Forum: Rethinking the Second Amendment*, 25 L. & HIST. REV. 139
(2007).
    [9] *See, e.g.*, Saul Cornell, *Originalism on Trial: The Use and Abuse of History in* District of Columbia
v. Heller, 69 OHIO ST. L.J. 626 (2008). For a historical critique of *Heller*'s individual rights model, *see*
Patrick J. Charles, *The Second Amendment in Historiographical Crisis: Why the Supreme Court Must
Reevaluate the Embarrassing Standard Model Moving Forward*, 39 FORDHAM URB. L.J. 1727 (2012).

right. Finally, as a general matter, positions on the meaning of the Second Amendment correlate strongly with their advocates' political affiliations and ideological passions.[10]

Thus, in *Heller*, one thing was crystal clear: neither preexisting "law" nor sound historical scholarship dictated its conclusions. Taken at their most convincing, Scalia's arguments were no more plausible than those of the dissent, and they provided a particularly dubious basis for creating a new constitutional right. His "opinion was a selective incorporation of the evidence to ensure the Second Amendment protected an individual right," one Second Amendment scholar concluded, and it "clearly shows that politics had seeped into the United States' highest court."[11]

As a technical matter, Scalia could have handled the issue in *Heller* quite differently than he did. His specific holding, after all, was itself quite narrow, voiding only "the District's ban on handgun possession in the home" and "its prohibition against rendering any lawful firearm in the home operable for the purpose of immediate defense."[12] That minimalist ruling could have been based on the proposition that the District's regulation was so completely disabling, intrusive into the home, and potentially endangering to personal safety as to be unreasonable and therefore void under due process, privileges or immunities, the Ninth Amendment, or even some slightly expanded right of personal privacy in the home. For obvious reasons, however, those grounds were unacceptable to Scalia on their own terms and likely equally unacceptable to the other conservative justices as well.

Alternatively, Scalia could have invalidated the District's measure by placing his decision on a formally different but still relatively narrow basis. He could have based it on straightforward "reasonableness" grounds, acknowledging that governments had broad authority to regulate firearms

---

[10] Early on, a few liberal scholars suggested that the Second Amendment could support an individual right interpretation. Sanford Levinson, *The Embarrassing Second Amendment*, 99 YALE L.J. 637 (1989) (arguing that the individual right interpretation is at least a plausible interpretation of the amendment); AKHIL REED AMAR, THE BILL OF RIGHTS: CREATION AND RECONSTRUCTION 18, 216–17, 221–23 (1998) (arguing that the amendment's meaning in 1791 did not support an individual right interpretation but that the Fourteenth Amendment modified its meaning to confer such a right) [hereafter AMAR, BILL OF RIGHTS].

[11] CHARLES, SECOND AMENDMENT 10. Scalia's majority opinion "went through great lengths to incorporate legal sources that supported its predetermined conclusion. Unfortunately, the sources it used did not actually support their contentions for the majority consistently made wrongful inferences of the fact, left out important commentary, or placed citations and quotes out of context." *Id.* at 69. "An original and textual construction of the Second Amendment does not support the Supreme Court majority determination in *Heller.*" *Id.* at 89.

[12] *Heller*, 554 U.S. at 635 (Scalia, J.).

but concluding that the regulation at issue was too intrusive and potentially endangering to pass a reasonableness test. Scalia's opinion actually referred to many of those practical considerations. It emphasized the dire threat posed by intruders in the home,[13] acknowledged that the Second Amendment had limits,[14] declared two parts of the regulation invalid under "any standard of scrutiny,"[15] and allowed the rest of the District's handgun licensing regulation to stand.[16] The opinion, in other words, could have upheld plaintiff's right to possess operable firearms in his home while at the same time stressing the power of government to regulate such firearms broadly and reasonably. In the oral argument, in fact, Scalia seemed to suggest that exact point. Guiding the attorney attacking the District's regulation, he corrected his response to a question from Justice Stevens. "You would just say [the Second Amendment] is not being infringed," Scalia prompted, "if reasonable limitations are placed upon it."[17] Indeed, if the history of gun laws in America proved anything conclusively, it was that the regulation of firearms had from the nation's beginning been widespread and often severely restrictive.[18]

Neither of those possible narrow grounds attracted Scalia, however, for he had a far more sweeping and personally compelling goal in mind. He was determined to rule on the Second Amendment, create a new individual constitutional right to own and use firearms, and place that right on the firmest, broadest, and most unchallengeable ground possible. He was responding enthusiastically to the individuals and groups who had initially brought *Heller* to the courts and who were animated by the goal of gaining Second Amendment protection for gun rights as part of their concept of constitutional "liberty."[19] In *Heller* Scalia and the other conservative justices were

[13] *Heller*, 554 U.S. at 599, 628, 630 n.28, 636. The regulation at issue was particularly dangerous because it extended "to the home, where the need for defense of self, family, and property is most acute." *Id.* at 628. *Accord id.* at 629. At the oral argument he pointed to the same dangers. Transcript of Oral Argument, District of Columbia v. Heller, No. 07-290 (Mar. 18, 2008), 42 [hereafter Oral Argument in *Heller*]. *See also id.* at 83.

[14] *Heller*, 554 U.S. at 595, 626–27, 636.

[15] *Heller*, 554 U.S. at 628.

[16] *Heller*, 554 U.S. at 635. The plaintiff below had sought to enjoin the District from enforcing its licensing requirement, *id.* at 630–31, but the Court merely ordered that the District must allow him to register his handgun and must grant him a license to carry it in his home. *Id.* at 635.

[17] Oral Argument in *Heller*, 77. *See also id.* at 53. Throughout the argument Scalia stepped in to guide the attorney. CHARLES, SECOND AMENDMENT, 8–9.

[18] *See, e.g.,* PATRICK J. CHARLES, ARMED IN AMERICA: A HISTORY OF GUN RIGHTS FROM COLONIAL MILITIA TO CONCEALED CARRY (2018) [hereafter CHARLES, ARMED]; MICHAEL WALDMAN, THE SECOND AMENDMENT: A BIOGRAPHY (2014) [hereafter WALDMAN, SECOND AMENDMENT]; ADAM WINKLER, GUNFIGHT: THE BATTLE OVER THE RIGHT TO BEAR ARMS IN AMERICA (2011) [hereafter WINKLER, GUNFIGHT].

[19] MARCIA COYLE, THE ROBERTS COURT: THE STRUGGLE FOR THE CONSTITUTION, ch. 7 (2103) [hereafter COYLE, ROBERTS COURT].

ready to follow those gun-rights advocates, and they voted specifically to grant certiorari on that Second Amendment issue.[20] Their decision, Marcia Coyle wrote, revealed "an aggressive conservative Court taking on a long-sought objective on the conservative political agenda."[21]

Scalia was not only determined to establish a fundamental constitutional principle affirming his belief that the Second Amendment guaranteed a specifically individual right to own and use firearms, but he also wanted to push to the periphery ideas about any flexible "reasonableness" standard and the general power of the government to "regulate" firearms.[22] He was determined to use his opinion not just to construe the Second Amendment but to emphasize that the individual right it recognized severely limited the power of governments to regulate guns. "The very enumeration of the right," he declared in *Heller*, "takes out of the hands of government—even the Third Branch of Government—the power to decide on a case-by-case basis whether the right is really worth insisting upon." Scalia used his opinion, in other words, to exalt the Second Amendment and establish a broad principle that would satisfy, nourish, and further energize the Republican right in general and the gun-rights movement in particular. The "enshrinement of constitutional rights," he intoned, "necessarily takes certain policy choices off the table."[23]

The giveaway as to Scalia's animating purpose in *Heller* came at the very outset of his opinion when he made his key move by essentially begging the question. The Second Amendment provided: "A well regulated Militia, being necessary to the security of a free State, the right of the people to keep and bear Arms, shall not be infringed."[24] Scalia simply bifurcated the text, as if the amendment's two clauses were hardly related. The militia clause was merely

---

[20] The Court granted the petition "limited to the following question: Whether the following provisions—D.C. Code §§ 7-2502.02(a)(4), 22-4504(a), and 7-2507.02—violate the Second Amendment rights of individuals who are not affiliated with any state-regulated militia, but who wish to keep handguns and other firearms for private use in their homes?" *Heller*, 552 U.S. 1035 (2007) (per curiam).

[21] Coyle, Roberts Court, 151.

[22] The Court in *Heller* failed to decide a critical issue. If the Second Amendment did establish an individual right, what level of scrutiny should be used to protect it? Did the amendment establish a right that was constitutionally the same as the rights in the First Amendment? Did it require, in other words, strict scrutiny? Scalia suggested that some higher level of scrutiny applied, 554 U.S. at 628 & n.27, but the justices in the majority apparently could not agree on the level that was proper and left the issue unsettled.

[23] *Heller*, 554 U.S. at 634, 636.

[24] U.S. Const. amend. 2.

"prefatory," he claimed, while the rights clause was "operative."[25] Then, he drew the conclusion he had embedded in the two premise bearing labels he had assigned the clauses. A "prefatory clause does not limit or expand the scope of the operative clause."[26] Bingo! By fiat, cutting the second clause free from the first, he neatly jettisoned the express textual and contextualizing limit that the Constitution placed on the right to "keep and bear Arms."[27] Thus textually unbound, Scalia felt free to define the right in the "operative" clause as broadly as he wished. A personal, individual right to possess firearms for self defense, he announced immediately thereafter, was the "*central component*" of the Second Amendment.[28]

Indeed, to reach his desired result he also jettisoned the "most specific level" of meaning principle that he used to interpret the rights that he sought to narrow or deny.[29] Surely, the "most specific level" of meaning of the right protected by the Second Amendment was the right and duty to bear arms by serving in the militia. In *Heller*, however, Scalia had no use for such a specific level of meaning so he simply returned that interpretive principle to the jurisprudential closet for other occasions.

---

[25] *Heller*, 554 U.S. at 577. Scalia reduced the "prefatory" clause further by later terming it a mere "prologue," at 554 U.S. 578 n.4, a move he also made in the oral argument. Oral Argument in *Heller*, 45.

[26] *Heller*, 554 U.S. at 578. For a critique of Scalia's key move, *see, e.g.*, David Thomas Konig, *Why the Second Amendment Has a Preamble: Original Public Meaning and the Political Culture of Written Constitutions in Revolutionary America*, 56 U.C.L.A. L. REV. 1295, 1326–37 (2009) ("Justice Scalia's ahistorical reliance on present-day settled rules of construction disqualifies his dismissal of the controlling force of the preamble," at 1331). As an original matter "we can sensibly read the phrase *the people* in the amendment's main clause as synonymous with the *militia*, thereby eliminating the grammatical and analytic tension that would otherwise exist between the two clauses." AMAR, BILL OF RIGHTS 216. Many historians and linguists agree that the two clauses are "logically and linguistically dependent." William G. Merkel, The District of Columbia v. Heller *and Antonin Scalia's Perverse Sense of Originalism*, 13 LEWIS & CLARK L. REV. 349, 365 (2009) (citing "Rakove Brief"); "Linguistics Brief."

[27] *E.g.*, in United States v. Miller, 307 U.S. 174, 178 (1939) (McReynolds, J.), the Court held that the militia clause restricted the "keep and bear Arms" clause. Dissenting in *Heller*, Stevens relied heavily and elaborately on *Miller*, *Heller*, 554 U.S. at 636, 637–79 (Stevens, J., dissenting), while Scalia tried to distinguish the case. *Id.* at 621–26. The claim that "the public understanding of 'bear arms' included the carrying of private arms for self defense is not supported by the historical record." Nathan Kozuskanich, *Originalism, History, and the Second Amendment: What Did Bearing Arms Mean to the Founders*, 10 U. PA. J. CONST. L. 413, 446 (2008). Massive digital searches of archives of late-eighteenth-century sources "prove that Americans consistently employed 'bear arms' in a military sense, both in times of peace and in times of war, showing that the overwhelming use of 'bear arms' had a military meaning." *Id.* at 416. *Accord* Nathan Kozuskanich, *Originalism in a Digital Age: An Inquiry into the Right to Bear Arms*, 29 J. EARLY AM. REPUB. 585 (2009). Madison himself used the phrase "bear arms" in this sense. *See* THE FEDERALIST PAPERS No. 46, at 296 (Madison) (Clinton Rossiter ed., originally published in 1961, with Introduction and Notes by Charles R. Kessler, 2003) [hereafter FEDERALIST PAPERS].

[28] *Heller*, 554 U.S. at 599 (emphasis in original). *Accord id.* at 628.

[29] Michael H. v. Gerald D., 491 U.S. 110, 127 n.6 (Scalia, J.).

Still, he faced a nagging problem. The text of the amendment did, after all, contain that awkward "prefatory" clause, so it presumably had to mean something. To negate the slightest limitation it might be thought to impose, he imagined a harmless role for it that by no stretch of the imagination could justify a limit on gun rights. All that was necessary, he explained, was that "our reading of the operative clause" must be "consistent with [the militia clause's] announced purpose."[30] To render the purpose of the militia clause totally harmless, he first—and wholly inaccurately—redefined the concept of a "well-regulated" militia to mean merely "well trained," a redefinition that obscured the amendment's express textual affirmation of government power to "regulate" the right to bear arms.[31] Then, he shrank the purpose of the militia clause to a virtually meaningless extreme, declaring that it was designed only "to prevent elimination of the militia."[32] So defined, the clause could not bar any law dealing with firearms unless the law would literally mean the abolition of state militias. That definition meant that no law encouraging the use of firearms or expanding their availability could possibly run afoul of the "prefatory" clause, for such laws could not possibly require the "elimination" of the militia.

The manifestly arbitrary nature of Scalia's textualism was similarly apparent at another point. Given the amendment's "prefatory clause," he noted, the "structure of the Second Amendment is unique in our Constitution." But when he turned to construe the phrase "right of the people," which appeared in the First and Fourth Amendments as well as the Second Amendment, he ignored the Second Amendment's special textual characteristics—its "prefatory" clause and "unique" structure—and concluded that the three uses of the phrase "right of the people" carried the same meaning. "All three of these instances," he announced, "unambiguously refer to individual rights, not collective rights."[33] That was simply not true. The militia clause made clear that the phrase "right of the people" did not carry the same meaning as that in the other two amendments because only military-age males could serve in the militia and "bear

---

[30] *Heller*, 554 U.S. at 578.

[31] *Heller*, 554 U.S. at 597; Oral Argument in *Heller*, 26. *See* William G. Merkel, The District of Columbia v. Heller *and Antonin Scalia's Perverse Sense of Originalism*, 13 Lewis & Clark L. Rev. 349, 361 and sources cited at n.45. (2009); Patrick J. Charles, *The Constitutional Significance of a "Well-Regulated Militia" Asserted and Proven with Commentary on the Future of Second Amendment Jurisprudence*, 3 Northeastern L.J. 67 (2011); Paul Finkelman, *It Really Was About a Well Regulated Militia*, 59 Syracuse L. Rev. 267 (2008).

[32] *Heller*, 554 U.S. at 599.

[33] *Heller*, 554 U.S. at 577, 579.

Arms."[34] Indeed, one year after the Second Amendment was ratified, Congress added yet another restriction in the Militia Act of 1792, further limiting militia service to military-age male citizens who were "white."[35] Thus, Scalia disregarded the significance of the Second Amendment's "unique" structure—and the significance of its militia-based restriction "bear Arms" that appeared in the "operative" clause itself—when he wished the amendment to be "like" other amendments. It was "unique" when he wished it to be unique, but otherwise it was not unique at all.

Scalia's opinion went even further in its creativity by adding a surprisingly adaptive twist to Second Amendment law. His immediate goal, after all, was to provide constitutional protection for private handguns in the home, and he could hardly fail to acknowledge that such protection was far removed from anything connected to modern militias. "It may well be true today that a militia, to be as effective as militias in the 18th century, would require sophisticated arms that are highly unusual in society at large," he acknowledged with considerable understatement. "Indeed, it may be true that no amount of small arms could be useful against modern-day bombers and tanks." Such modern conditions, however, were not relevant to the meaning of the Second Amendment. "[T]he fact that modern developments have limited the degree of fit between the prefatory clause and the protected right cannot change our interpretation of the right."[36]

If that last assertion was stock originalism, what followed it was not. "There are many reasons that a citizen may prefer a handgun for home defense," Scalia continued, and "handguns are the most popular weapon chosen by Americans for self-defense in the home."[37] In the oral argument he emphasized the same point when he declared that the dispositive issue was not "the dictionary definition of arms" but what weapons were "nowadays commonly held."[38] Thus, he argued, modern preferences for handguns in the home—a consideration entirely unrelated to militia matters and hardly in the mind of the Founders—determined the nature and scope of the Second Amendment right. Although "modern developments" could not alter "our interpretation of the right," they could do something just as good. They could transform the content of the right itself by infusing into it "popular"

[34] See, e.g., FEDERALIST PAPERS No. 46, at 296 (Madison). Madison did not capitalize the word "arms."
[35] 1 Stat. 271 (May 8, 1792).
[36] Heller, 554 U.S. at 627–28.
[37] Heller, 554 U.S. at 629.
[38] Oral Argument in Heller, 47.

preferences for guns that were "nowadays commonly held." That was a highly elastic bit of originalism, one that was adaptive, evolutionary, politically expedient, and hardly shaped by anything the Founders had prescribed.[39] Indeed, it contradicted Scalia's claim about the methodology of originalism itself. "Words in the Constitution were not to be interpreted in the abstract," he insisted, "but rather according to the understandings that existed when they were adopted."[40] His reasoning in *Heller* contradicted that principle.[41]

Scalia's position in *Heller* was rife with such inconsistent and problematic claims.[42] If preferences "nowadays commonly held" could determine anew the content of the right to bear arms, for example, why could they not equally determine the content of rights involving "liberty," "equality," "due process," and "cruel and unusual punishments"? Indeed, why could they not control the meaning of constitutional provisions that supported rights involving abortion, homosexuality, gender equality, and assisted suicide? Scalia's opinion gave no answer to such questions.

Equally obvious, Scalia's opinion was inconsistent with most of his proclaimed jurisprudential principles. It rejected judicial restraint, negated local legislative authority, asserted federal judicial power aggressively and creatively, disregarded the police powers of the states in a critical area marked by diverse and substantial local concerns, and ignored any structural analysis of the Second Amendment's place in the overall constitutional design.[43] More broadly, it was inconsistent with his efforts to bar the creation of new individual rights in so many other areas without the clearest constitutional or statutory warrant, a test that the Second Amendment—absent Scalia's ploy of severing half of its text and ignoring most relevant historical scholarship— simply did not meet. Indeed, Scalia's opinion conflicted with the very goal

[39] Examining *Heller*'s sources and logic, "we discover a ruling exquisitely attuned to the living constitutionalism that Scalia so vehemently disdains." LAURENCE TRIBE & JOSHUA MATZ, UNCERTAIN JUSTICE: THE ROBERTS COURT AND THE CONSTITUTION 172 (2014). *See* Reva Siegel, *Comment: Dead or Alive: Originalism as Popular Constitutionalism in* Heller, 122 HARV. L. REV. 191 (2008) [hereafter Siegel, *Comment*].

[40] ANTONIN SCALIA, SCALIA SPEAKS: REFLECTIONS ON LAW, FAITH, AND LIFE WELL LIVED 198 (Christopher J. Scalia & Edward Whelan eds., 2017) [hereafter SCALIA SPEAKS].

[41] Scalia stated that the amendment "extends, prima facie, to all instruments that constitute bearable arms, even those that were not in existence at the time of the founding," *Heller*, 554 U.S. at 582.

[42] As Reval Siegel noted, Scalia's opinion and the sources he invoked produced many "temporal oddities." Siegel, *Comment*, 196. Further, he seemed to say that he was deciding *Heller* under a "rationality" standard, but at the same time he suggested that he was using some unspecified but stricter standard. *Compare Heller*, 554 U.S. at 628, *with* 628 n.27. For Breyer's critique of Scalia's treatment of the applicable standard, *see id.* at 687–91. *See* CHARLES, SECOND AMENDMENT, 9–10.

[43] *See generally* DAVID C. WILLIAMS, THE MYTHIC MEANINGS OF THE SECOND AMENDMENT: TAMING POLITICAL VIOLENCE IN A CONSTITUTIONAL REPUBLIC (2003).

and purpose he had proclaimed for his originalism, the contention that it would severely limit the ability of the courts to make their own law.[44]

Less obviously, Scalia's position was also in tension with many of his other positions and pronouncements. When he construed congressional power under the Fourteenth Amendment, a power he sought to restrict, he insisted that the power was limited to enforcing the precise rights the amendment created and should not be construed to reach any additional rights.[45] In contrast, when he construed the "operative" clause of the Second Amendment, a right he sought to defend, he adopted a far more liberal and expansive assumption. It was "not at all uncommon," he insisted in the oral argument in *Heller*, "for a legislative provision or a constitutional provision to go further than is necessary for the principal purpose involved."[46] The terms of the Fourteenth Amendment's first section limited congressional power under its fifth section, in other words, but the specific terms of the Second Amendment's first section did not similarly limit the individual rights created under its second section.

Along the same lines, Scalia justified the breadth and generality of his opinion in *Heller* by noting that "this case represents this Court's first in-depth examination of the Second Amendment."[47] That meant that *Heller* was essentially a case of first impression and that the Court could therefore construe the amendment largely free from the limits of precedent. In contrast, when he addressed the issue of congressional power to abrogate the Eleventh Amendment immunity of states, another congressional power he disfavored, he chastised the justices who disagreed with him on the ground that they could not cite "a single Supreme Court case, over the past 200 years" to support their position. "How strange," he commented sarcastically, that "such a useful power" supposedly existed even though it "should never have been approved and rarely (if ever) have been asserted" in any prior case.[48]

---

[44] Scalia claimed that his method of dealing with the Second Amendment was "an objective approach that reaches conclusions by applying neutral rules to verifiable evidence." *McDonald*, 561 U.S. at 800 (Scalia, J., concurring). In contrast, he charged, "the historical analysis of the principal dissent in *Heller* is as valid as the Court's only in a two-dimensional world that conflates length and depth." *Id.* at 804 n.9.

[45] Coleman v. Court of Appeals of Maryland, 132 S. Ct. 1327, 1338 (2012) (Scalia, J., concurring in the judgment) ("outside of the context of racial discrimination (which is different for stare decisis reasons), I would limit Congress's [section] 5 power to the regulation of conduct that *itself* violates the Fourteenth Amendment"). *Accord* Tennessee v. Lane, 541 U.S. 509, 554, 558, 560 (2004) (Scalia, J., dissenting) (same).

[46] Oral Argument in *Heller*, 56.

[47] *Heller*, 554 U.S. at 635.

[48] Pennsylvania v. Union Gas Co., 491 U.S. 1, 29, 40 (1989) (Scalia, J., concurring in part and dissenting in part).

If a constitutional principle had not been confirmed by the Court in over two centuries, in other words, it must be unsound and even fanciful. Because he admitted that *Heller* was the Court's "first in-depth examination of the Second Amendment" after more than two hundred years, the exact same argument applied to the principle at issue there. On that basis the claim of an individual right to possess firearms would be equally unsound and frivolous. But in *Heller* Scalia ignored his earlier argument for an obvious reason. Unlike his use of it in the prior case, in *Heller* it cut against the result he sought.[49]

Heller is particularly significant for understanding Scalia's jurisprudence for four fundamental reasons. First, and most obvious, it demonstrated how indeterminate both his textualism and his originalism were and how easily both could be manipulated to reach the results he desired.[50] Contrary originalist arguments advanced by the four dissenting justices were based on extensive historical sources that were at least as soundly based and convincing as Scalia's.[51] As a result, Judge J. Harvey Wilkinson, a political conservative and a friend of Scalia's, drew the obvious and fatal conclusion. "While *Heller* can be hailed as a triumph of originalism," Wilkinson wrote, "it can just as easily be seen as the opposite—an exposé of original intent as a theory no less subject to judicial subjectivity and endless argumentation as any other."[52] That, indeed, was exactly the nature of Scalia's originalism.

[49] "[N]o actual case came before the Court involving firearms during the antebellum period." Karen O'Connor & Graham Barron, *Madison's Mistake? Judicial Construction of the Second Amendment*, in THE CHANGING POLITICS OF GUN CONTROL 76 (John M. Bruce & Clyde Wilcox eds., 1998).

[50] Scalia's use of the constitutional text assumed that the Framers had systematically thought through all the issues they addressed, agreed on a consistent and comprehensive theory of government, and meant the exact same thing each time they adopted a particular word or phrase, an entirely implausible if not unbelievable assumption. *See, e.g., Heller*, 554 U.S. at 579 (Scalia, J.). Examining the Second Amendment in the context of federalism, Richard Epstein remarked that one relevant consideration, "like everything else in this debate, is suggestive but not conclusive." Richard Epstein, *A Structural Interpretation of the Second Amendment: Why Heller Is (Probably) Wrong on Originalist Grounds*, 59 SYRACUSE L. REV. 171, 180 (2008). Richard Posner went further. Done properly, "the 'originalist' method would have yielded the opposite result." The Second Amendment "creates no right to the private possession of guns for hunting or other sport, or for the defense of person or property." Richard A. Posner, *In Defense of Looseness*, THE NEW REPUBLIC, Aug. 27, 2008, *available at* https://newrepublic.com/article/62124/defense-looseness (last consulted June 7, 2019) [hereafter Posner, *In Defense*]. For an excellent and largely sympathetic analysis of *Heller, see* Lawrence B. Solum, District of Columbia v. Heller *and Originalism*, 103 Nw. L. REV. 923 (2009).

[51] *See, e.g., Heller*, 554 U.S. at 636 (Stevens, J., dissenting), and 681 (Breyer, J., dissenting). Similarly, in *Lee v. Weisman*, 505 U.S. 577 (1992), Souter developed a historical analysis of the Establishment Clause, *id.* at 609 (Souter, J., concurring), that countered Scalia's historical analysis of the clause, *id.* at 631; and in *Seminole Tribe of Florida v. Florida*, 517 U.S. 44 (1996), Souter did the same with the historical analysis of the Eleventh Amendment, *id.* at 100 (Souter, J., dissenting), effectively challenging the position in the opinion of Chief Justice Rehnquist that Scalia silently joined.

[52] J. Harvey Wilkinson, *Of Guns, Abortions, and the Unraveling Rule of Law*, 95 U. VA. L. REV. 253, 256 (2009).

It was just another interpretative theory that allowed or welcomed "judicial subjectivity," as his opinion in *Heller* so convincingly demonstrated.

Second, Scalia's opinion in *Heller* rested on a highly questionable constitutional judgment. The historical evidence he cited was carefully selected, sharply disputed, and often of dubious relevance, while the historical evidence against him was at least as substantial and extensive.[53] Consequently, it was profoundly unwise—and a violation of principles of judicial restraint— to create a fundamental constitutional right on the basis of such an uncertain and contested historical record. Further, no bright line or clear constitutional test—guides that Scalia commonly proclaimed as necessary for proper judicial analysis when it served his purpose—informed his evaluation of the mass of conflicting evidence. His concept of "tradition," moreover, could not possibly tip the balance in his favor, for as common as guns were in the American past their strict regulation was at least equally common and quite likely more so. Indeed, the Court's own "tradition"—its precedents dealing with gun control measures—weighed heavily against him.[54]

Scalia's judgment in *Heller* was even more questionable for other reasons as well. As the historical materials were at best debatable, two obvious conclusions followed. One was that before ruling on the issue the Court should have given substantial consideration to the practical consequences of any decision it might make.[55] The other was that those practical consequences would surely vary greatly from state to state and locality to locality. On neither of those issues did *Heller* present an adequate record for decision.[56]

Further, Scalia's individual right theory did nothing to settle the law but promised only to bring to the courts a potentially endless stream of cases challenging gun laws of all kinds and at all levels of government. In addition, Scalia's individual right theory immediately suggested an even broader

[53] The four dissenting justices emphasized that point. *See Heller*, 554 U.S. at 636 (Stevens, J., dissenting, joined by Souter, Ginsburg, and Breyer, JJ.) and 681 (Breyer, J., dissenting, joined by Stevens, Souter, and Ginsburg, JJ.).

[54] *E.g., Miller*, 307 U.S. at 178 (McReynolds, J.); Presser v. Illinois, 116 U.S. 252, 266–68 (1886) (Woods, J.); United States v. Cruikshank, 92 U.S. 542, 553 (1875) (Waite, C.J.). Scalia did, nonetheless, claim that "tradition" supported the Court's position on the Second Amendment. *McDonald*, 561 U.S. at 792 (Scalia, J., concurring).

[55] For an enlightening debate over judicial methodology, *compare* Stevens's thoughtful and sophisticated approach to the Second Amendment in *McDonald*, 561 U.S. at 858 (Stevens, J., dissenting), *with* Scalia's defense of originalism and charge of subjectivity against Stevens's approach, *id.* at 791 (Scalia, J., concurring).

[56] "*Heller* gives short shrift to the values of federalism, and to the related values of cultural diversity, local preference, and social experimentation." Richard A. Posner, *In Defense of Looseness*, THE NEW REPUBLIC, Aug. 27, 2008, *available at* https://newrepublic.com/article/62124/defense-looseness (last consulted June 7, 2019).

potential sweep for the Second Amendment, the possibility that it might be made to apply to the states through the Fourteenth Amendment. That possibility was inconsistent with both the overwhelming mass of historical evidence about the amendment's original meaning and Supreme Court precedents going back to 1876. *Heller*'s logic, however, suddenly made incorporation of the Second Amendment against the states seem possible,[57] a result that the five conservatives brought about only two years later.[58] Given all those considerations, there seemed little reason to adopt the individual right theory beyond the intensely felt promptings of personal desire and ideological commitment.

Third, *Heller* demonstrated that a judge's firm belief that he or she was strictly objective and rigorously principled could easily mask the subjective values and goals that could inspire legal judgments.[59] The decisive personal fact was that Scalia was in love with guns. From his early boyhood he delighted in having and using them, happily recalling rabbit hunting with his grandfather and proudly telling a reporter that there was "a photo of me holding a rabbit and his twelve-gage shotgun."[60] More than half a century later he fondly announced that "I still have his gun." Indeed, he boasted that he kept his grandfather's gun even though it was "entirely corroded about six inches down from the end of the barrel." Along the same line, he regularly enjoyed recounting memories of his years at a military high school when he was on the school's rifle team and rode the New York subways carrying his .22 caliber target rifle with him. The school's "varsity team was really pretty good," he recalled warmly; "it used to beat the West Point plebes."[61]

More to the point was the way that Scalia's love of guns and hunting influenced his broader thinking. Only two years before *Heller* he addressed the National Wild Turkey Foundation, where he announced happily that "I'm a turkey hunter." Not only that, he told the group proudly, he was also a deer hunter, a duck hunter, and a boar hunter as well.[62] Hunting "is a sport

---

[57] In *Heller*, 554 U.S. at 620–21, Scalia noted that the Court had held in *Cruikshank*, 92 U.S. at 553, that the Second Amendment did not apply to the states.

[58] *McDonald*, 561 U.S. 742 (Alito, J., joined by Scalia, J.).

[59] Scalia continued to defend his *Heller* opinion long after it came down. COYLE, ROBERTS COURT, 209.

[60] Jennifer Senior, *In Conversation: Antonin Scalia*, NEW YORK MAGAZINE, Oct. 6, 2013, *available at* http://nymag.com/nymag/features/antonin-scalia-2013-10/index4.html (last consulted June 6, 2019). "Since his days as a boy hunting rabbits with his grandfather on Long Island, Scalia has enjoyed guns for recreation." BISKUPIC, AMERICAN ORIGINAL, 345.

[61] SCALIA SPEAKS, 56. He was proud of the military training he received in high school and cherished his sense of still belonging to "the Regiment," *see id.* at 307–17.

[62] SCALIA SPEAKS, 62.

that I very much enjoy."[63] In fact, over his years on the Court Scalia took literally dozens if not hundreds of hunting trips, largely with Republican political figures and donors, and the year before he decided *Heller* he traveled to Nuremberg, Germany, to accept an award at the World Forum for the Future of Sports Shooting Activities.[64] At the Court he "turned his chambers into a veritable museum of taxidermy, with his kills mounted and displayed on the walls," Jeffrey Toobin reported. A huge elk's head dominated the room, while a wooden decoy duck sat on a table in front of the sofa where he entertained visitors.[65]

Most immediately telling, Scalia praised what he termed the "hunting culture" and rooted its vitality and survival in "a broader culture that is not hostile toward firearms." To protect that hunting culture, he exhorted his audience, it was necessary to protect that "broader culture" by introducing young people to the value of guns and the pleasure of their use. "If you can't get them into hunting, get them into skeet shooting, or anything that shows that guns are not things that are used only by bad people."[66] For Scalia the general availability of firearms was a great social good, and the wrong-headed idea that guns were associated "with nothing but crime" was "what had to be changed."[67]

Indeed, in the years immediately preceding *Heller* Scalia invoked the Second Amendment and proclaimed a national belief in "the right to own a gun," a belief that he was convinced distinguished America from Europe. "Should we," he asked rhetorically, "revise the Second Amendment because of what these other countries think?"[68] Only the year before he wrote *Heller* he answered that question with a resounding negative. "I hope this country never falls into such a state."[69] Those deeply held personal convictions about

---

[63] BISKUPIC, AMERICAN ORIGINAL, 345. For the extremes Scalia went to in arranging hunting trips, *see* MURPHY, SCALIA 298–304 (Scalia arranged for hunting trip with Vice President Dick Cheney and got ride on Cheney's Air Force Two at time when Cheney was named litigant in a case before the Court), and for the ethical dispute that Scalia's trip with Cheney caused, *see id.*, 252–66.

[64] Stephen R. Bruce, *"Any Good Hunting?" When a Justice's Impartiality Might Reasonably be Questioned* (Oct. 5, 2016) (reference to the award appears at p. 2), *available at* https://ssrn.com/abstract=2782170 or http://dx.doi.org/10.2139/ssrn.2782170 (last consulted June 15, 2019) [hereafter Bruce, *Any Good Hunting?*].

[65] JEFFREY TOOBIN, THE NINE: INSIDE THE SECRET WORLD OF THE SUPREME COURT 200-01 (2007).

[66] SCALIA SPEAKS, 63.

[67] BISKUPIC, AMERICAN ORIGINAL, 346.

[68] SCALIA SPEAKS 32, 258. Scalia opposed using foreign and international law sources in construing American law and condemned what he called "this follow-the-foreign-crowd requirement." *McDonald*, 561 U.S. at 800 (Scalia, J., concurring).

[69] SCALIA SPEAKS, 63.

the value of guns and the virtues of the "hunting culture" were surely compelling considerations that determined his position in *Heller*.[70] Indeed, they
suggested that Scalia had in effect already decided *Heller* before the case ever
reached the Court. He made all of the statements quoted in this paragraph in
2006 and 2007, shortly before *Heller* was argued in March 2008 and decided
in June of that year.

Another statement he made shows even more conclusively that his mind
was firmly made up before the Court agreed to hear the case or he had read
the extensive briefs that parties and amici submitted. On the day that the
District of Columbia Circuit struck down the gun regulation at issue in
Heller, Scalia said as much to a fellow hunting enthusiast. "[I]t takes four
votes on the Supreme Court to hear a case, and it takes five to win it," he con-
fided. "If I don't think we have the five to win it, there won't be four to hear
it."[71] His determination was steeled and his course charted long before the
Court had received the first filing in the case. Only sometimes was Scalia an
originalist, but at all times he was a passionate lover of guns.

Finally, and more broadly, *Heller* demonstrated that originalism was essentially a method of constitutional change and, consequently, a tool of political
movements that sought to bring about that change. Repeatedly in American
history, from Jeffersonian attacks on the Marshall Court to the rhetoric of
the Warren Court itself and on to contemporary Republican attacks on
"liberal judicial activism," political movements pressing for constitutional
change commonly did so by appealing to the supposed "original" ideas of the
Founders.[72] Scalia exemplified that practice, and his success in *Heller* would
have been inconceivable absent the modern gun rights movement, the fierce
pro-gun political campaigns that the National Rifle Association (NRA) had
been mounting for four decades, and the ideological transformation of the
post-Reagan Republican Party that seated *Heller*'s five-justice conservative
majority on the Court.

Although the importance of guns in American culture grew during
the nineteenth century, well into the twentieth century there was virtually no dispute about the constitutional power of federal, state, and local
governments to regulate gun ownership and prohibit possession of certain

---

[70] *Heller* "is evidence that the Supreme Court, in deciding constitutional cases, exercises a free-
wheeling discretion strongly flavored with ideology." Posner, *In Defense*.

[71] Bruce, *"Any Good Hunting?,"* 2.

[72] *See, e.g.,* FRANK B. CROSS, THE FAILED PROMISE OF ORIGINALISM 98 (2013); JACK M. BALKIN,
LIVING ORIGINALISM 11 (2011); EDWARD A. PURCELL, JR., ORIGINALISM, FEDERALISM, AND THE
AMERICAN CONSTITUTIONAL ENTERPRISE: A HISTORICAL INQUIRY 183–86 (2007).

kinds of firearms. Supreme Court rulings and popular culture both reflected that basic assumption. In 1939, for example, in *United States v. Miller* the archconservative James C. McReynolds wrote for a unanimous Supreme Court in ruling that the Second Amendment was intended to ensure "a well-regulated militia," not an individual right to possess firearms.[73] That same year Warner Brothers released *Dodge City*, a popular Western starring Errol Flynn as a sheriff charged with bringing law and order to a violent Kansas town. One of the first and most effective actions the movie hero took was to bar cowboys from bringing guns into the central city and, equally unsurprising, he succeeded in his task of bringing law and order to the community. In fact, that aspect of the movie reflected historical events. "Dodge City, Kansas, for example," Justice Breyer noted in his *Heller* dissent, "joined many western cattle towns in banning the carrying of pistols and other dangerous weapons in response to violence accompanying western cattle drives."[74]

Perhaps even more revealing, twenty years after *Dodge City* Warner Brothers released another Western, *Rio Bravo*, this one starring John Wayne—another classic movie hero who had become the popular symbol of rugged and armed American individualism. Playing another sheriff equally charged with establishing law and order in a violent town, Wayne decided similarly to bar cowboys from entering town with their guns, and he also succeeded in his task. Both movies were box-office successes, and both reflected—in line with the Court's decision in *Miller*—the common-sense view that prevailed up through the middle decades of the twentieth century about the wisdom and necessity of regulating gun possession to secure the public safety.[75]

Attitudes began to change, however, in the 1970s when the NRA moved from cautious and largely behind the scenes efforts limiting or moderating gun regulations to a far more public, militant, and extreme campaign to

[73] "In the absence of any evidence tending to show that possession or use of a 'shotgun having a barrel of less than eighteen inches in length' at this time has some reasonable relationship to the preservation or efficiency of a well regulated militia, we cannot say that the Second Amendment guarantees the right to keep and bear such an instrument. Certainly it is not within judicial notice that this weapon is any part of the ordinary military equipment or that its use could contribute to the common defense." *Miller*, 307 U.S. at 178 (McReynolds, J.). Justice Douglas did not participate.

[74] *McDonald*, 561 U.S. at 937 (Breyer, J., dissenting). For a study of the "myth" of Dodge City and its place in American history, *see* ROBERT R. DYKSTRA & JO ANN MANFRA, DODGE CITY AND THE BIRTH OF THE WILD WEST (2017).

[75] Not withstanding his adherence to Scalia's opinion in *Heller*, Chief Justice John Roberts seemed to accept that common-sense view. "A basic step in organizing a civilized society is to take that sword out of private hands and turn it over to an organized government, acting on behalf of all the people." Robertson v. Watson, 560 U.S. 272, 282–83 (2010) (Roberts, C.J., dissenting).

delegitimize gun regulation, advance a virtually untrammeled individual right to possess firearms, and anchor its public relations and lobbying efforts on the Second Amendment.[76] A new leadership generation adopted a near absolute opposition to restrictions of any kind, forged a large and devoted single-issue political base, methodically raised and spent tens of millions of dollars to advance its goals, and orchestrated vigorous lobbying efforts at the local, state, and national levels. The "fervor of its activist members," an ex-NRA official lamented, "is just as inflexible as that of Muslim, Christian, or Jewish zealots."[77] Their efforts increasingly bore fruit, blocking most legislative proposals to restrict gun sales or ban certain kinds of weapons from the market. In large letters on the facade of its headquarters in Fairfax, Virginia, the NRA inscribed the words "the right of the people to keep and bear arms, shall not be infringed."[78] Nothing else. Going one better than Scalia in *Heller*, the NRA literally excised the militia clause from the Second Amendment.

The NRA's efforts proved especially successful within the Republican Party. As one element in its contemporaneous turn toward a hard right-wing ideology that cut across many issues,[79] Republicans began to defend gun rights with increasing fervor, criticizing gun registration proposals and defending gun manufacturers against lawsuits that it termed "frivolous," which meant any lawsuit seeking to impose liability on anyone who produced or sold firearms. While the party's 1972 platform supported gun control and focused in particular on the desirability of restricting "cheap handguns," those

---

[76] The material in the following paragraph is drawn from CHARLES, ARMED; WALDMAN, SECOND AMENDMENT; WINKLER, GUNFIGHT; EMILIE RAYMOND, DEAD HANDS: CHARLTON HESTON AND AMERICAN POLITICS (2006); Jill Lepore, *Battleground America: One Nation, under the Gun*, THE NEW YORKER, Apr. 23, 2012, *available at* https://www.newyorker.com/magazine/2012/04/23/battleground-america (last consulted Apr. 16, 2018) [hereafter Lepore, *Battleground*]; and Ronald G. Shaiko & Marc A. Wallace, *Going Hunting Where the Ducks Are: The National Rifle Association and the Grass Roots, in* THE CHANGING POLITICS OF GUN CONTROL 155–71 (John M. Bruce & Clyde Wilcox eds., 1998).

[77] RICHARD FELDMAN, RICOCHET: CONFESSIONS OF A GUN LOBBYIST 2 (2008) [hereafter FELDMAN, RICOCHET]. "I'd been forced to recognize that, despite its sacrosanct facade, the NRA is actually a cynical, mercenary political cult. It is obsessed with wielding power while relentlessly squeezing contributions from its members, objectives that overshadow protecting Constitutional liberties." *Id.*

[78] Michael Waldman, *How the NRA Rewrote the Second Amendment, available at* https://www.brennancenter.org/analysis/how-nra-rewrote-second-amendment (last consulted July 17, 2019).

[79] For the evolution of the Republican Party and its ideology since the 1960s, *see, e.g.*, JOSEPH CRESPINO, STROM THURMOND'S AMERICA (2012); ROBERT O. SELF, ALL IN THE FAMILY: THE REALIGNMENT OF AMERICAN DEMOCRACY SINCE THE 1960s (2012); GEOFFREY KABASERVICE, RULE AND RUIN: THE DOWNFALL OF MODERATION AND THE DESTRUCTION OF THE REPUBLICAN PARTY: FROM EISENHOWER TO THE TEA PARTY (2012); JOSEPH CRESPINO, IN SEARCH OF ANOTHER COUNTRY: MISSISSIPPI AND THE CONSERVATIVE COUNTERREVOLUTION (2007); ROBERT O. SELF, AMERICAN BABYLON: RACE AND THE STRUGGLE FOR POSTWAR OAKLAND (2003).

positions disappeared completely in the following years. In both 1976 and 1980 the party's platforms defended "the right of citizens to keep and bear arms."[80]

In 1980, as part of its new aggressiveness, the NRA for the first time endorsed a presidential candidate, Republican Ronald Reagan.[81] The move paid off handsomely, as the Reagan administration and the Republican Party quickly became loyal supporters of the NRA's positions. In 1982, for example, the Republican-controlled Senate, led by Orrin Hatch of Utah as Chair of the Senate Judiciary Committee's Subcommittee on the Constitution, stepped to the plate. He produced a report on the history of the Second Amendment that claimed to discover "clear—and long-lost—proof that the Second Amendment of our Constitution was intended as an individual right of the American citizen" for the "protection of himself, his family, and his free-doms."[82] Beginning in 1984 Republican platforms defended an explicitly "constitutional right to keep and bear arms,"[83] and the gun-rights ideology became critically important in considering judicial nominees.[84] Republican presidents would not nominate nor Republican Senates confirm candidates who failed to demonstrate strong support for the Second Amendment or re-ceive the endorsement of the NRA.[85]

By the 1990s the contrasting political identifications of the two major political parties on the gun issue were marked in sharp relief. In 1992 the Democratic platform supported gun control for the first time, while the Republicans hit a new low in their rhetoric. They charged that "those who seek to disarm citizens in their homes are the same liberals who tried to disarm our Nation during the Cold War."[86] In control of both the presidency

[80] Republican Party Platforms are the American Presidency Project, *available at* https://www.presidency.ucsb.edu/documents/app-attributes/party-platforms (last consulted July 12, 2019) [here-after *American Presidency Project*].

[81] Lepore, *Battleground*, 18.

[82] Siegel, Comment, 216. *See also* Robert Leider, *Our Non-Originalist Right to Bear Arms*, 89 IND. L.J. 1587 (2014); David C. Williams, *Civil Republicanism and the Citizen Militia: The Terrifying Second Amendment*, 101 YALE L.J. 551 (1991).

[83] *American Presidency Project*.

[84] Lee Epstein, Jeffrey A. Segal, & Chad Westerland, *The Increasing Importance of Ideology in the Nomination and Confirmation of Supreme Court Justices*, 56 DRAKE L. REV. 609 (2008) ("The rule now is that Presidents name Justices who share their political ideology. If Presidents could put them-selves on the bench, they would; however, they cannot, so they find the closest possible surrogates," at 615).

[85] The administration, for example, withdrew the nomination of Andrew Frey, who served as Reagan's deputy solicitor general, when two conservative senators discovered that he had made donations to the National Coalition to Ban Handguns. David M. O'Brien, *The Reagan Judges: His Most Enduring Legacy?*, *in* THE REAGAN LEGACY: PROMISE AND PERFORMANCE 69 (Charles O. Jones ed., 1988).

[86] *American Presidency Project*.

and Congress, Democrats in 1994 passed laws requiring background checks for gun purchases in the so-called "Brady bill" and then enacted a ban on assault weapons.

In contrast, Republicans continued to push their pro-gun campaign. In 2000 they announced that the constitutional right to bear arms was necessary because "self-defense is a basic human right," and they attacked proposals for national gun registration as "a violation of the Second Amendment and an invasion of privacy."[87] Four years later, when they controlled both the presidency and Congress, they allowed the assault weapon ban to expire. In the presidential campaign the same year they added claims to their platform that directly foreshadowed *Heller*. Their 2004 platform asserted that there was "an individual right to own guns" and that the right "is explicitly protected by the Constitution's Second Amendment." The amendment enabled "law-abiding citizens throughout the country to own firearms in their homes for self-defense." Indeed, as if wooing Scalia himself personally and longingly, the platform declared in a gratuitous but highly evocative non sequitur that "Our Party honors the great American tradition of hunting."[88]

Changes in federal and state court decisions evidenced the growing impact of the gun rights movement.[89] Prior to 2001 no federal court had adopted the individual right interpretation, while ten had adopted the militia-based collective right interpretation. Only in 2001 did a federal court adopt the individual right theory, while two others followed before *Heller*. Similarly, between 1968 and 1980 ten state courts had adopted the collective right interpretation. Prior to 1988 only one had adopted the individual right interpretation, and only one other did so before 2000. Between 2000 and *Heller* in 2008, however, another five followed. The law was changing, and those changes flowed from the powerful and concentrated drive of the modern gun-rights movement and the ideological transformation of the Republican Party.

Heller followed along in due course, and in its wake the Republican platform in 2008 was openly celebratory and rawly partisan.[90] "We applaud the

---

[87] "In 2000 the NRA exploited the white hot anger and frustration that gun owners and conservatives felt after eight years of Clinton/Gore firearms restrictions and bans." FELDMAN, RICOCHET, 274.

[88] *American Presidency Project.*

[89] The material in the following paragraph is drawn from CHARLES, SECOND AMENDMENT, 6, 179 n.10, 180 n.13.

[90] While *Heller* was before the Court, it caused some disagreement in the Bush administration. The Justice Department supported the individual right interpretation but thought that the Court should compromise on its decision and remand the case so that the lower court could develop a "more flexible" standard of review. Some in the administration opposed the remand idea but the president, informed of the dispute at the last minute, decided not to intervene. Among those opposing any

Supreme Court's decision in Heller," it announced. Then, turning to the politically negative, it declared that Republicans "are astounded that four justices of the Supreme Court believe that individual Americans have no individual right to bear arms to protect themselves and their families."[91] With *Heller* in the bank, the NRA and its supporters consistently proclaimed their reliance on the individual constitutional right that Scalia found in the Second Amendment. In 2012 the party's pro-gun rhetoric raged on unabated, and in 2016 Republican presidential candidate Donald Trump repeatedly affirmed that individual right and avidly sought the support of "Second Amendment people."[92]

Scalia's opinion in *Heller* and the ready agreement of the other four conservative justices—all appointed by Reagan and his Republican successors—were the products of that political movement and the consequent ideological transformation that had remade the Republican Party and its ideology over the preceding forty years. Ultimately, then, *Heller* is a monument to irony. If it was Scalia's "legacy opinion," that legacy was the opposite of what he assumed. *Heller* did not demonstrate the objectivity of originalism and textualism but their inadequacy and manipulability. It did not return the Constitution to any original understanding but adopted the late twentieth-century formulation promoted by the militant gun-rights movement. It did not flow from jurisprudential principles but from systematic Court-packing driven by political change, party power, and ideological fervor.

Finally, *Heller* did not do honor to Scalia himself. Rather, it showed that the scourge of "subjective" and "activist" liberal judges exemplified in nearly perfect form the very judicial failings that he regularly attributed to them.[93]

---

compromise was Scalia's hunting companion, Vice President Dick Cheney, who agreed—without consulting the White House—to sign an amicus brief drafted by those who opposed the compromise. PETER BAKER, DAYS OF FIRE: BUSH AND CHENEY IN THE WHITE HOUSE 578–79 (2013). The brief was signed overwhelmingly by Republicans, 46 senators and 182 members of the House. On the Democratic side, 9 senators and 67 representatives signed, largely though not exclusively members from midwestern, southern, and western states.

[91] *American Presidency Project*.
[92] Benjamin Pomerance, *Justices Denied: The Peculiar History of Rejected United States Supreme Court Nominees*, 80 ALB. L. REV. 627 (2017). During the campaign Trump not only appealed to "Second Amendment people" but also seemed to many to suggest that they might even consider using their firearms against rival presidential candidate Hillary Clinton were she to win the election. Nick Corasaniti & Maggie Haberman, *Donald Trump Suggests "Second Amendment People" Could Act Against Hillary Clinton*, N.Y. TIMES, Aug. 9, 2016, *available at* https://www.nytimes.com/2016/08/10/us/politics/donald-trump-hillary-clinton.html.
[93] *E.g.*, "Seldom has an opinion of this Court rested so obviously upon nothing but the personal views of its members." Atkins v. Virginia, 536 U.S. 304, 337, 338 (2002) (Scalia, J., dissenting). A standard proposed by Stevens was essentially "subjective" and "incapable of restraining judicial whimsy" and an approach that "does nothing to stop a judge from arriving at any conclusion he sets out to reach." *McDonald*, 561 U.S. at 793, 795, 799 (Scalia, J., concurring).

8

An Ignored Jurisprudence: *Bush v. Gore*

Bush v. Gore was extraordinary by any standard.[1] It confronted the Court with difficult and in some ways unprecedented legal issues and, more important, subjected the justices to exceptional political pressures. The Court agreed to hear an appeal from a decision of the Florida Supreme Court that would allow it to decide whether and on what terms the recount of the state's vote in the 2000 presidential election would continue. Its ruling could, and did, determine who would become president of the United States.

The only ordinary characteristic of the Court's final decision was the lineup of the justices. The five conservatives voted to terminate the recount and thereby ensure that Republican candidate George W. Bush won the election. The four liberal justices—two Democrats and two Republicans—dissented, suggesting various methods for allowing the recount to continue and thereby keeping alive the hopes of Democratic candidate Al Gore.

The case produced six opinions. A majority—the five conservatives and two of the liberals—ruled in a per curiam opinion that the ongoing recount did not meet the requirements of the Equal Protection Clause, but the seven justices split over the consequences of that holding. The five conservatives concluded that there was not sufficient time left to continue the recount and declared the election over, while the two liberals concluded that the recounts should continue under newly articulated and constitutionally adequate standards. Three of the five conservatives, Chief Justice Rehnquist joined by Justices Scalia and Thomas, filed a concurring opinion, while each of the four liberals—including the two who joined the majority opinion on the equal protection issue—filed separate dissents.

Because the case was so exceptional, it presented a defining test for Scalia and his jurisprudence. As he repeatedly insisted, his originalism was designed to guide and limit the Court, especially in cases when personal preferences might prove unusually strong. His jurisprudence promised rigorous methods that would ensure judicial neutrality, eliminate improper

---

[1] Bush v. Gore, 531 U.S. 98 (2000) (per curiam).

Antonin Scalia and American Constitutionalism. Edward A. Purcell, Jr., Oxford University Press (2020).
© Edward A. Purcell, Jr.
DOI: 10.1093/oso/9780197508763.001.0001

activism, and prevent the justices from imposing their own personal views on the law. The Court's duty, he preached, lay "in ascertaining an objective law."[2] Although the case raised unusually difficult legal issues, many of which fairly divided reasonable minds, it also led to a clear result in terms of evaluating Scalia and his jurisprudence. It showed that he was willing to allow political expedience to overcome his fundamental jurisprudential principles and that he could easily narrow, twist, or simply ignore them when necessary.

Scalia joined both the majority opinion and Rehnquist's concurrence, and both were inconsistent with almost every element of his jurisprudence. As a general matter, neither opinion relied on originalism; both resorted to textualism sporadically and unpersuasively;[3] and both baldly flouted long-established electoral traditions.[4] Indeed, the majority opinion itself acknowledged the dubious nature of the Court's intervention. "None are more conscious of the vital limits on judicial authority than the Members of this Court," it claimed, and "none stand more in admiration of the Constitution's design to leave the selection of the President to the people, through their legislatures, and to the political process."[5] The "Constitution's design" that the per curiam claimed so fulsomely to admire was exactly what Scalia and the others who joined it refused to honor and follow.

The majority's equal protection argument was roundly scorned, even by conservatives who defended the Court's decision.[6] It was so baseless, in

[2] Planned Parenthood of Southeastern Pennsylvania v. Casey, 505 U.S. 833, 979, 1000 (1992) (Scalia, J., dissenting).

[3] The majority opinion made the December 12 cutoff date in the federal election statute (3 U.S.C. Sec. 5) mandatory rather than—as the statutory text made unquestionably clear—a matter of state option. It did so by relying on one statement of the Florida Supreme Court while at the same time ignoring the same court's other language and specific ruling that made undeniable its commitment to have the recount continue past that date. Bush v. Gore, 531 U.S. at 110–11; id. at 124–28 (Stevens, J., dissenting); id. at 130 (Souter, J., dissenting). For its part, the concurrence adopted a theory based on Article II that was essentially an arbitrary argument by italics, emphasizing one word in the provision at the expense of two other words and thereby giving the text one meaning rather than another. Compare id. at 112–13 (Rehnquist, C.J., concurring), with id. at 123–24 (Stevens, J. dissenting) and 142 (Ginsburg, J., dissenting).

[4] In his dissent Stevens noted that the "intent of the voter" standard had long been used in the election statutes of a majority of the states. Bush v. Gore, 531 U.S. at 124 and n.2 (Stevens, J., dissenting). "Before election 2000 it had never occurred to anyone that [the "intent of the voter" standard] might raise federal constitutional issues. In fact, differential treatment of ballots seemed to be an inevitable part of the traditional U.S. commitment to state and county-based election processes." HOWARD GILLMAN, THE VOTES THAT COUNTED: HOW THE COURT DECIDED THE 2000 PRESIDENTIAL ELECTION 186 (2001) [hereafter GILLMAN, VOTES THAT COUNTED]. Accord ALAN M. DERSHOWITZ, SUPREME INJUSTICE: HOW THE HIGH COURT HIJACKED ELECTION 2000, at 128 (2001) [hereafter DERSHOWITZ, SUPREME INJUSTICE].

[5] Bush v. Gore, 531 U.S. at 111 (per curiam).

[6] "Any equal protection challenge to the Florida recount procedure quickly runs into insurmountable difficulties." Richard A. Epstein, "In Such Manner as the Legislature Thereof May Direct": The

fact, that the justices initially refused even to consider it on November 24 when they agreed to hear two other claims that Bush advanced.[7] Most conclusive, the equal protection argument the per curiam adopted was based on a glaring doctrinal contradiction. The Court—Scalia fully agreeing— had expressly held that a violation of the Equal Protection Clause required proof of "intent" to discriminate.[8] In *Bush v. Gore* there was no evidence whatever that any official had intentionally sought to deprive anyone of the right to vote or had intentionally refused to count anyone's vote. Indeed, eight years later, concurring in a case with the opposite political salience—where he upheld a restrictive Republican-backed Indiana voter identification law—Scalia invoked that very principle. "Insofar as our election-regulation cases rest upon the requirements of the Fourteenth Amendment," he insisted, voters had no valid claim "without proof of discriminatory intent."[9]

Further, in terms of Scalia's originalism and textualism, the equal protection argument he accepted ignored the fact that the Founders had explicitly granted Congress—not the judiciary—the power to determine the results of disputed presidential elections.[10] If anything was clear about the Constitution's original public meaning, it was that a combination of a popular vote, a specially selected body called the Electoral College, and ultimately the Congress of the United States would determine who would win the presidency. None of the Founders considered the matter appropriate for the judiciary.[11] "It is extremely difficult," Cass Sunstein concluded in striking

---

Outcome in Bush v. Gore *Defended* [hereafter Epstein, In Such Manner], *in* VOTE: BUSH, GORE, AND THE SUPREME COURT 14 (Cass R. Sunstein & Richard A. Epstein eds., 2001) (defending the Court's decision on its Article II theory) [hereafter VOTE].

[7] CHARLES L. ZELDEN, BUSH V. GORE: EXPOSING THE HIDDEN CRISIS IN AMERICAN DEMOCRACY 100–01 (abridged & updated ed. 2010) [hereafter ZELDEN, BUSH V. GORE]. In denying certiorari on the equal protection claim, the Court initially agreed to hear one claim based on due process and 3 U.S.C. Sec. 5 and a second one based on Article II.

[8] *See, e.g.,* Washington v. Davis, 426 U.S. 229, 236–41, 247–48 (1976) (White, J.); Village of Arlington Heights v. Metropolitan Housing Development Corp., 429 U.S. 252, 264–65 (1977) (Powell, J.); McClesky v. Kemp, 481 U.S. 279, 297–98 (1987) (Powell, J., joined by Scalia).

[9] Crawford v. Marion County Election Board, 553 U.S. 181, 204, 207 (2008) (Scalia, J., concurring). *Accord* Schuette v. Coalition to Defend Affirmative Action, 572 U.S. 291, 316, 318, 329–32 (2014) (Scalia, J., concurring in the judgment).

[10] U.S. CONST. art. II, sec. 1, paras. 3 & 4; amend. 12. On the evolution of the presidential electoral system and the origins of the Twelfth Amendment, *see* TADAHISA KURODA, THE ORIGINS OF THE TWELFTH AMENDMENT: THE ELECTORAL COLLEGE IN THE EARLY REPUBLIC, 1787–1804 (1994).

[11] *See, e.g.,* THE FEDERALIST PAPERS No. 68 (Hamilton) (Clinton Rossiter ed., originally published in 1961, with Introduction and Notes by Charles R. Kessler, 2003) [hereafter FEDERALIST PAPERS];

understatement, "to justify the equal protection holding in *Bush v. Gore* on originalist grounds."[12]

Moreover,electoral tradition firmly established over the previous two centuries underwrote the exact same conclusion.[13] Congress had decided the outcome in the country's three previous disputed presidential elections in 1800, 1828, and 1876.[14] Until November 24, 2000, the day when the Court surprisingly agreed to hear an appeal in the case, "it was widely understood and accepted that any problems associated with the appointment of presidential electors would be handled by state officials as they saw fit and then reviewed by the U.S. Congress," Howard Gillman explained. "This practice dated from the beginning of the Republic, and it was the process that was clarified in the Electoral Count Act of 1887," a statute that remained in force in the 2000 election.[15]

The novel Article II ground advanced in Rehnquist's concurrence was equally inconsistent with Scalia's jurisprudential principles. According to Gillman, it "had never previously been theorized or articulated in the history of U.S. constitutional law." The concurrence, however, used Article II to justify rejecting the long-established—and nonjudicial—process that had existed since the Constitution's ratification.[16]

Shlomo Slonim, *The Electoral College at Philadelphia: The Evolution of an Ad Hoc Congress for the Selection of a President*, 73 J. Am. Hist. 35 (1986).

[12] Cass R. Sunstein, *Does the Constitution Enact the Republican Party Platform? Beyond* Bush v. Gore, *in* Question of Legitimacy, 184. "There is no reason to think that by adopting the Equal Protection Clause, the nation thought that it was requiring clear and specific standards in the context of manual recounts in statewide elections. In fact, it is controversial to say that the Fourteenth Amendment applies to voting at all. The failure of Justices Scalia and Thomas to suggest the relevance of originalism, their preferred method, raises many puzzles." Cass R. Sunstein, Order Without Law, *in* Vote, 213 n.39 (2001).

[13] In oral argument Souter emphasized that in Electoral Count Act of 1887 Congress "has committed the determination of the issues [Bush] raise[s] and the consequences to follow from them to the Congress." Gillman, Votes That Counted, 87. Even a strong defender of Rehnquist's concurrence acknowledged that there "were several groups of elected officials who, according to our laws and traditions, would have been more legitimate arbiters of the 2000 presidential election than the judges." Steven G. Calabresi, *A Political Question, in* Bush v. Gore: The Question of Legitimacy 129 (Bruce Ackerman ed., 2002) [hereafter Calabresi, *Political Question*].

[14] In the first two elections Congress decided the issue on its own, and in the third it charged a special commission composed of five senators, five representatives, and five members of the Supreme Court to decide the issue. Thus, even though five members of the Court participated in the 1876 decision, they did so only under the authority of Congress and only as a minority of the commission members. *See* Charles Fairman, Five Justices and the Electoral Commission of 1877 (1988).

[15] Gillman, Votes That Counted, 191.

[16] Gillman, Votes That Counted, 186, 191. The Court had previously addressed the Article II issue once before, more than a hundred years earlier, in *McPherson v. Blacker*, 146 U.S. 1 (1892) (Fuller, C.J.), an essentially unknown precedent that was easily distinguished from the issue in *Bush v. Gore*.

Further, while neither originalist nor traditionalist grounds supported the Article II claim,[17] the textual ground that Rehnquist relied on was arbitrary on its face. The chief justice quoted the relevant constitutional language in Article II as providing that "each State shall appoint, in such Manner as the *Legislature* thereof may direct" its presidential electors. Acknowledging that he had added the italics,[18] Rehnquist construed the provision to mean that the U.S. Constitution gave exclusive authority in the area to the state legislature and hence that neither a state constitution, popular referendum, or supreme court ruling could alter the electoral provisions its legislature had made.

In dissent, Justice Stevens countered with the obvious textual response. He simply italicized different words. Stevens quoted Article II as mandating that "each *state* shall appoint, in such Manner as the Legislature *thereof* may direct" the state's electors.[19] Thus, the text of Article II, he maintained, did not confer power specifically on the state legislature but on the sovereign state itself, presumably acting in the first instance through its lawmaking branch as it normally would. Moreover, pointing out the obvious and long-settled law, Stevens explained that the Constitution accepted the states as they were organized according to their own constitutions, and Article V of the Florida constitution specifically subjected the measures its legislature enacted to judicial review by its courts. And "nothing in Article II of the Federal Constitution," Stevens continued, "frees the state legislature from the constraints in the state constitution that created it."[20]

When Scalia accepted Rehnquist's italics over Stevens's, he not only accepted a textual interpretation that was arbitrary but also one that conflicted with another of his prior positions. Only a few years earlier he had joined the Court in holding that states had the sovereign right to structure their governments as they wished.[21] In signing on to the concurrence, he ignored

---

[17] Richard Posner, who elaborated a pragmatic justification for the Article II theory, acknowledged that the constitutional text itself was unclear in its meaning. RICHARD A. POSNER, BREAKING THE DEADLOCK: THE 2000 ELECTION, THE CONSTITUTION, AND THE COURTS 153–54 (2001) [hereafter POSNER, BREAKING]. His overtly pragmatic construction, he acknowledged, was "not compelled by case law, legislative history, or constitutional language," and it would provide a "new principle" of constitutional law. *Id.* at 156, 174. "One thing courts do all the time is find contemporary functions for old legal categories." *Id.* at 154.

[18] Bush v. Gore, 531 U.S. at 112 (Rehnquist, C.J., concurring, joined by Scalia, J.).

[19] Bush v. Gore, 531 U.S. at 123 (Stevens, J., dissenting). In her dissent, Justice Ginsburg also deployed the counter-italics argument. Article II, she explained, provided that "Each *State* shall appoint, in such Manner as the Legislature *thereof* may direct," presidential electors. *Id.* at 142 (Ginsburg, J., dissenting) (emphasis in original).

[20] Bush v. Gore, 531 U.S. at 124 (Stevens, J., dissenting).

[21] Gregory v. Ashcroft, 501 U.S. 452 (1991) (O'Connor, J., joined by Scalia, J.).

that principle and the further fact that Florida had expressly structured its government to grant its courts the power of judicial review over the actions of its legislature. More striking and revealing, he had reasoned quite differently about state sovereignty when he found it useful in rejecting an affirmative action plan. Then, referring to what he termed "the rule of structural state sovereignty," he had summarized a line of Court cases by declaring that "we have emphasized the near-limitless sovereignty of each State to design its governing structure as it sees fit." In support, he quoted a prior case declaring that "a State is afforded wide leeway when experimenting with the appropriate allocation of state legislative power."[22]

The subsequent alteration that the three concurring justices made to their Article II theory, moreover, clearly suggested that they were simply determined to support Bush. Initially, at the first oral argument Scalia joined Rehnquist in arguing that Article II made the statutes of the state legislature supreme over the state's own constitution. They maintained, that is, that the U.S. Constitution itself gave exclusive and untrammeled authority specifically and solely to the state legislature and that the state constitution and state supreme court could do nothing to alter that constitutional mandate.[23] Thus, their initial formulation of the Article II argument concluded, when the state supreme court invoked the state constitution in rendering its decision about the state statute, it was violating the U.S. Constitution. That interpretation rested on an arbitrary and historically implausible construction of Article II, but it at least stated a rule that was clean and clear.

On remand, however, the Florida Supreme Court refused to rely on the state constitution and instead declared that it was merely construing the legislature's election statutes under its normal and supreme judicial authority to construe state law. Faced with the state court's reliance on that fundamental and well-recognized constitutional principle, Rehnquist and Scalia did not concede that their Article II theory was now irrelevant. Rather, they simply reconceived it to strike at the new target. As Abner S. Greene pointed out, the concurrence shifted its argument from the claim that the state constitution could not trump Article II to the claim that the state supreme court could not interpret the state's election statutes in a way that substantially changed the legislature's electoral design.[24] As reformulated, the theory provided a

---

[22] *Schuette*, 572 U.S. at 327 (Scalia, J., concurring in the judgment).

[23] GILLMAN, VOTES THAT COUNTED, 86–92; ZELDEN, BUSH V. GORE, 105–08.

[24] *See* ABNER S. GREENE, UNDERSTANDING THE 2000 ELECTION: A GUIDE TO THE LEGAL BATTLES THAT DECIDED THE PRESIDENCY 94–99, 107–08 (2001).

vague standard to judge a question defined as one of relative degree and thus opened the way for a subjective and result-driven ruling.[25] Consequently, the concurrence was able to apply its reformulated version of the Article II theory to do exactly what Rehnquist and Scalia had attempted to do with their earlier version of it, namely to ensure Bush's election.[26]

In spite of its legal flaws, as a political matter the Article II theory not only supported Bush but also offered another distinct advantage. It played nicely to the standard Republican rhetoric that denounced "activist" and "liberal" courts. It enabled the concurrence to invoke the party's "legislating rather than interpreting" line of attack and portray the actions of the Florida Supreme Court as simply more examples of abusive liberal activism. Thus, in spite of the theory's novelty, ambiguity, and shifting form, Republicans were groomed to give it a ready and warm embrace.

Beyond the contradictions between Scalia's principles and the two questionable constitutional theories he endorsed in *Bush v. Gore*, both the per curiam and the concurrence violated most of his other jurisprudential principles as well. First was Scalia's insistence that, absent clear justification, the Court had no business interfering with normal democratic processes.[27] On its face, *Bush v. Gore* interfered with normal democratic processes both in terminating the recounts intended to determine what voters had actually decided and in intruding into a fundamental political issue that the Constitution allocated to Congress. Similarly, Scalia had also invoked the rule of "constitutional doubt" to limit the Court's review of statutes on the ground that, if the issue

---

[25] The next year Scalia acknowledged the well-established rule that a "reasonable reading of state law by the State's highest court is binding upon us." Rogers v. Tennessee, 532 U.S. 451, 467,469 (2001) (Scalia, J., dissenting). Thus, under the later version of the Article II theory the concurrence had to show that the Florida Supreme Court had construed the state's election laws in a wholly unreasonable manner.

[26] The dissents defended the state court's interpretation of state law as fair and reasonable. *See* Bush v. Gore, 531 U.S. at 127–28 (Stevens, J., dissenting); *id.* at 130–33 (Souter, J., dissenting); *id.* at 135–36 (Ginsburg, J., dissenting); *id.* at 149–52 (Breyer, J., dissenting). Under the subjective test of degree that the concurrence applied, commentators varied widely in their judgments as to the relative legitimacy and propriety of the state supreme court's rulings and tended to follow ideological sympathies. Rejecting the Article II argument, *see, e.g.*, DERSHOWITZ, SUPREME INJUSTICE (the charge that the state court "changed Florida law" was "to put it bluntly, nonsense," at 87); David A. Strauss, *What Were They Thinking*, in VOTE ("the Florida Supreme Court's decision was consistent with the plain language of the contest statute" at 201). Supporting the Article II argument, *see, e.g.*, Epstein, "*In such Manner*," in VOTE (there are "key mistakes of the Florida Supreme Court that support the charge that it created its own electoral scheme," at 21); Calabresi, *Political Question* ("I would hold that the Florida Supreme Court's erratic behavior clearly violated Article II of the U.S. Constitution," at 136).

[27] "The Court should return this matter [abortion] to the people—where the Constitution, by its silence on the subject, left it." Stenberg v. Carhart, 530 U.S. 914, 953, 956 (1992) (Scalia, J., dissenting). *Accord., e.g.*, Dickerson v. United States, 530 U.S. 428, 444 (2000) (Scalia, J., dissenting).

was "a close one," the Court should not intervene.[28] The same rule should have applied when the Court faced a novel, reasonably contested, and obviously "close" question of constitutional law, as it surely did in *Bush v. Gore*. Indeed, both Congress and the Florida legislature offered ready political remedies in the case and, from a political point of view, remedies that seemed promising for Bush.[29] Scalia, however, was too determined and too impatient to wait for other institutions to perform their duties.

Second, Scalia repeatedly condemned what he considered ad hoc and un-principled decisions that lacked the safeguards of generality.[30] The "rule of law" was "the law of rules," he preached. When "I adopt a general rule . . . I not only constrain lower courts, I constrain myself as well." It was essential to the rule of law that "I have committed myself to the governing principle," he declared, insisting that "the establishment of broadly applicable general principles is an essential component of the judicial process."[31] He proclaimed the same ideal of generality from the high bench. "The Supreme Court of the United States," he insisted, "does not sit to announce 'unique' dispositions."[32] Six years earlier he had condemned the Court when it announced what he regarded as "a special rule to govern only" one single party.[33]

Yet in *Bush v. Gore*, he accepted the Court's embarrassing and unavoid-ably partisan proclamation of what can only fairly be termed its "Bush-only"

---

[28] *See, e.g.*, Federal Election Commission v. Akins, 524 U.S. 11, 29, 32 (1998) (Scalia, J., dissenting).

[29] "If the constitutional crisis rationale is not a simple post hoc rationalization of an otherwise inex-cusable decision then it most represents simple impatience with democratic processes. . . . [F]orcing politicians to work through a presidential selection process without the roadmap of a crystal clear legal process is not a crisis; it is democracy." GILLMAN, VOTES THAT COUNTED, 195.

[30] *See, e.g.*, Morrison v. Olson, 487 U.S. 654, 697, 733 (1988) (Scalia, J., dissenting) ("This is not analysis; it is ad hoc judgment"); Dickerson v. United States, 530 U.S. at 455) (Scalia, J., dissenting) ("The issue, however, is not whether court rules are 'mutable'; they assuredly are. It is not whether, in the light of 'various circumstances,' they can be 'modified'; they assuredly can. The issue is whether, as mutated and modified, they must make sense. The requirement that they do so is the only thing that prevents this Court from being some sort of nine-headed Caesar, giving thumbs-up or thumbs-down to whatever outcome, case by case, suits or offends its collective fancy.").

[31] Antonin Scalia, *The Rule of Law as a Law of Rules*, 56 UNIV. CHI. L. REV. 1175, 1179, 1185 (1989). "The chances that frail men and women will stand up to their unpleasant duty are greatly increased if they can stand behind the solid shield of a firm, clear principle enunciated in earlier cases." *Id.* at 1180. "It is no indication whatever of the invalidity of the constitutional rule which we announce, that it produces unhappy consequences," he wrote in another case. Rather, unhappy consequences were "the routine result of constitutional rules." Plaut v. Spendthrift Farm, 514 U.S. 211, 237 (1995) (Scalia, J.). *See. e.g.*, Herrera v. Collins, 506 U.S. 390, 427 (1993) (Scalia, J., concurring).

[32] United States v. Virginia, 518 U.S. 515, 566, 596 (1996) (Scalia, J., dissenting). He continued: "Its principal function is to establish *precedent*—that is, to set forth principles of law that every court in America must follow. As we said only this Term, we expect both ourselves and lower courts to adhere to the '*rationale* upon which the Court based the results of its earlier decisions." *Id.* (emphasis in orig-inal) (quoting Seminole Tribe of Florida v. Florida, 517 U.S. 44, 66–67 (1996).

[33] Board of Education of Kiryas Joel Village School District v. Grumet, 512 U.S. 687, 732, 748 (1994) (Scalia, J., dissenting).

rule: "Our consideration," the per curiam stated, "is limited to the present circumstances."[34] That "Bush-only" rule contradicted Scalia's fundamental jurisprudential principle of generality and, as Richard Posner concluded, "made the opinion seem thoroughly unprincipled."[35] In reality, of course, it may well have been the "Bush-only" rule that made the equal protection rationale palatable to Scalia and the other conservative justices, especially Rehnquist and Thomas. That preclusive rule seemed designed to guarantee that the majority's equal protection rationale could not be applied to any other claim that involved voting rights and elections brought by any other party under any other circumstance.[36] It was, and was intended to be, a "unique" disposition.

Third, Scalia repeatedly insisted on "judicial restraint" when there was a constitutional ground for refusing to act, and in *Bush v. Gore* the "political question" doctrine provided a compelling ground for just such a refusal. That doctrine called for the Court to decline to hear cases when, among other reasons, there was a "textually demonstrable constitutional commitment of the issue to a coordinate political department."[37] In *Bush v. Gore*, the constitutional commitment of the election issue to the legislature was manifest and express. The "technical legal case for treating the matter as a 'political question' was particularly powerful," noted Laurence H. Tribe. "The requisite

---

[34] Bush v. Gore, 531 U.S. at 109 (per curiam). The best the Court could do in attempting to justify its Bush-only rule was to say that "the problem of equal protection in election processes generally presents many complexities." *Id.*

[35] Richard A. Posner, Bush v. Gore *as Pragmatic Adjudication* [hereafter Posner, Pragmatic Adjudication], *in* BADLY FLAWED ELECTION 209 (Ronald Dworkin ed., 2002) [hereafter BADLY FLAWED].

[36] *See, e.g.,* ZELDEN, BUSH V. GORE, 237–39 (suggesting that the three concurring justices joined the majority for tactical reasons to secure the result and that they likely accepted the equal protection rationale precisely because the majority agreed to limit its reach solely to the case at hand).

[37] Powell v. McCormack, 395 U.S. 486, 518 (1969) (Warren, C.J.), quoting *Baker v. Carr,* 369 U.S. 186, 217 (1962) (Brennan, J.). In *Baker* the Court had identified six characteristics of a "political question" that rendered a dispute nonjusticiable:

> It is apparent that several formulations which vary slightly according to the settings in which the questions arise may describe a political question, although each has one or more elements which identify it as essentially a function of the separation of powers. Prominent on the surface of any case held to involve a political question is found a textually demonstrable constitutional commitment of the issue to a coordinate political department; or a lack of judicially discoverable and manageable standards for resolving it; or the impossibility of deciding without an initial policy determination of a kind clearly for nonjudicial discretion; or the impossibility of a court's undertaking independent resolution without expressing lack of the respect due coordinate branches of government; or an unusual need for unquestioning adherence to a political decision already made; or the potentiality of embarrassment from multifarious pronouncements by various departments on one question.

Id. at 217.

textual commitment to a political branch could hardly be clearer."[38] Even
Steven Calabresi, a Federalist Society conservative, a defender of the Article
II theory, and one of Scalia's greatest admirers, acknowledged that fact. The
"problem with *Bush v. Gore*," he conceded, "is that the case raised a political
question that ought to have been decided by Congress."[39]

Fourth, Scalia also ignored his long proclaimed commitment to the doctrine of separation of powers, "the cornerstone of our Constitution."[40] "The
nonjusticiability of a political question," the Court had explained in *Baker
v. Carr*, "is primarily a function of the separation of powers."[41] That structural doctrine, Scalia repeatedly declared, was a fundamental principle of the
Constitution, one that was essential to preserving the Constitution's guarantee
of liberty and democracy.[42] Yet in *Bush v. Gore*, he passed over it in silence and
supported judicial intervention into the political process.

Fifth, Scalia turned a blind eye to his own repeated assertions that the courts
had no valid basis for overriding "those constant and unbroken national
traditions that embody the people's understanding of ambiguous constitutional
texts."[43] Florida law had long used the "clear intent of the voter" as its standard
for hand-counted votes, and that standard also bore "the endorsement of many
states over a long period of time" and had "never previously been challenged."[44]
Yet, in joining the majority opinion, Scalia rejected that long-established tradition and the vote-counting practice it authenticated.

Sixth, and perhaps doctrinally most glaring, Scalia failed to apply the
requirement of standing—the "Essential Element of the Separation of
Powers"[45]—that he had vigorously championed for virtually his entire career.[46] The equal protection claim that he accepted was a claim that could

[38] Laurence H. Tribe, *Freeing eroG v. hsuB from Its Hall of Mirrors, in* BADLY FLAWED, 141.

[39] Calabresi, *Political Question*, 137. "All six of those characteristics [listed in *Baker v. Carr*] suggest
that the Court should have stayed its hand." *Id.,* at 138.

[40] Antonin Scalia, *Bicentennial Institute Proceedings*, 28 ADMIN. L. REV. 686, 693 (1976).

[41] Baker v. Carr, 369 U.S. at 210 (Brennan, J.).

[42] "The principle of separation of powers is central to the American system of government.
The Framers of the American Constitution believed that that principle—as popularized by
Montesquieu—was the single most important guarantee of freedom." ANTONIN SCALIA, SCALIA
SPEAKS: REFLECTIONS ON LAW, FAITH, AND LIFE WELL LIVED 223 (Christopher J. Scalia & Edward
Whelan eds., 2017). *See Hearings before the Committee on the Judiciary, United States Senate on the
Nomination of Judge Antonin Scalia, to be Associate Justice of the Supreme Court of the United States*,
99th Cong., 2d Sess. (Aug. 5–6, 1986), 32; Morrison v. Olson, 487 U.S. at 697 (Scalia, J., dissenting).

[43] United States v. Virginia, 518 U.S. at 568 (Scalia, J., dissenting).

[44] DERSHOWITZ, SUPREME INJUSTICE, 128; GILLMAN, VOTES THAT COUNTED, 186.

[45] Antonin Scalia, *The Doctrine of Standing as an Essential Element of the Separation of Powers*, 17
SUFFOLK U. L. REV. 881 (1983) [hereafter Scalia, *Doctrine of Standing*].

[46] *E.g.*, Scalia, *Doctrine of Standing*; Lujan v. Defenders of Wildlife, 504 U.S. 555, 560–61 (1992)
(Scalia, J.).

only be raised by a Florida voter, and Bush clearly was not a Florida voter. Well-settled law that Scalia had repeatedly and emphatically affirmed held that no claim could proceed absent a showing of particular and individualized harm to the claimant,[47] and it was obvious that Bush could claim no equal protection harm over his own vote since he had cast that vote in Texas, not Florida. Well-settled law equally held that—absent limited exceptions not relevant—a party could not raise the claims of other individuals who were able to allege a sufficient injury. Thus, Bush could not raise the claim of any Florida voters, all of whom in any event also lacked standing to bring suit under the Court's well-settled doctrine.[48] Yet Scalia agreed to allow Bush to raise the equal protection claim and ignored what he had long preached as the Constitution's "core" requirement of standing.

Finally, Scalia and the four other conservatives violated their commitment to "federalism." They had repeatedly trumpeted the importance of federalism and the foundational nature of state sovereignty, and they had issued a series of decisions over the preceding decade that limited federal power and enhanced the independence of the states.[49] Yet in *Bush v. Gore* they used the Equal Protection Clause to overrule the Florida Supreme Court, turning their backs on their "pro-federalism" principles. Indeed, only a decade earlier four of the conservative justices who shut down the recount—Scalia, Rehnquist, O'Connor, and Kennedy—had joined the Court's opinion in *Gregory v. Ashcroft* affirming the fundamental principle that the sovereign

[47] Scalia repeatedly insisted that standing required plaintiff to show a "tangible injury and concrete harm." Powers v. Ohio, 499 U.S. 400, 417, 427 (1991) (Scalia, J., dissenting). More to the point, he also insisted that a plaintiff could assert only his own injury, not the injury of anyone else. "Indeed, we do not even recognize third-party standing in the litigation context—that is, permit a civil or criminal litigant to upset an adverse judgment because the process by which it was obtained involved the violation of someone else's rights—even when the normal injury-in-fact standard is amply met." *Id.* at 428. *See* United States v. Hays, 515 U.S. 737 (1995) (O'Connor, J., joined by Scalia, J.) (there is "no authority for the proposition that an equal protection challenge may go forward in federal court absent that showing of individualized harm, and we decline appellees' invitation to approve that proposition in this litigation," at 747).

[48] Standing required a "demonstrable, particularized injury" by the claimant. Warth v. Seldin, 422 U.S. 490, 508 (1975) (Powell, J.). Opposition to any general government action or policy that did not directly harm a person was insufficient for standing. *E.g.*, Allen v. Wright, 468 U.S. 737 (1984) (O'Connor, J.); Massachusetts v. Mellon and Frothingham v. Mellon, 262 U.S. 447 (1923) (Sutherland, J.).

[49] For major "pro-federalism" decisions of the five conservatives before *Bush v. Gore*, all of which Scalia joined, *see, e.g.*, United States v. Lopez, 514 U.S. 549 (1995) (Rehnquist, C.J.) (Commerce Clause); Seminole Tribe of Florida v. Florida, 517 U.S. 44 (1996) (Rehnquist, C.J.) (Eleventh Amendment); Alden v. Maine, 527 U.S. 706 (1999) (Kennedy, J.) (Tenth and Eleventh Amendments); United States v. Morrison, 529 U.S. 598 (2000) (Rehnquist, C.J.) (Fourteenth Amendment). For Scalia's views on federalism, *see, e.g.*, ANTONIN SCALIA, A MATTER OF INTERPRETATION: FEDERAL COURTS AND THE LAW 28–29 (1997).

status of the states meant that they could organize their governments in whatever manner they wished. "Through the structure of its government, and the character of those who exercise government authority," they had then declared, "a State defines itself as a sovereign."[50]

In their Article II theory Rehnquist, Scalia, and Thomas also contradicted their federalism principles, though in a narrower and more nuanced way. They set aside the decision of the Florida Supreme Court by honoring what they termed the statutory mandate of the Florida legislature.[51] Thus, on one hand they did respect and defer to state law, but on the other hand they used federal power to intrude into state government and determine a decisive issue of state law by favoring one of its branches over another. In federalism terms, however, that intrusion was quite real, as Justice Ginsburg pointed out in dissent. Rehnquist's "solicitude for the Florida Legislature," she noted, "comes at the expense of the more fundamental solicitude we owe to the legislature's sovereign"—the state itself.[52]

The opinions Scalia joined in *Bush v. Gore* highlighted two basic truths about American constitutionalism. First, the Article II theory illustrated the fact that separation of powers existed at both state and national levels and that simplistic dichotomies between "states" and "nation" considered as block entities were often misleading and sometimes irrelevant. The concurrence did not impose federal law over state law but rather used federal law to impose the law of one state branch over the law of another state branch. It exemplified the fact that different federal branches could support different state branches at different times and on different issues and that the institutionalization of separated powers at both the state and national levels added yet another level of complexity to the shifting governmental relations that marked American constitutionalism.[53]

Second, both the equal protection theory and the Article II theory illustrated another truth. When Americans, including Supreme Court justices, felt the need for federal power with sufficient keenness, they were invariably

---

[50] *Gregory*, 501 U.S. at 460 (O'Connor, J., joined by Scalia, J.). Citing *Gregory*, Justice Ginsburg made this point in *Bush v. Gore*, 531 U.S. at 141 (Ginsburg, J., dissenting).

[51] "This inquiry does not imply a disrespect for state *courts* but rather a respect for the constitutionally prescribed role of state *legislatures.*" Bush v. Gore, 531 U.S. at 115 (Rehnquist, C.J., concurring, joined by Scalia, J.) (emphasis in original).

[52] "Were the other Members of this Court as mindful as they generally are of our system of dual sovereignty, they would affirm the judgment of the Florida Supreme Court." 531 U.S. at 142–43 (Ginsburg, J., dissenting).

[53] *See, e.g.,* EDWARD A. PURCELL, JR., ORIGINALISM, FEDERALISM, AND THE AMERICAN CONSTITUTIONAL ENTERPRISE: AN HISTORICAL INQUIRY, esp. ch. 6 (2000).

able to find some constitutional basis for justifying the assertion of that power. Scalia recognized that instrumentalist truth when he noted that federalism principles could be used to support either national or state power and that the "trick" was to apply them "wisely."[54] Like the Court's other conservatives, he defended federalism and state sovereignty, but despite his formal claims, he was no rigid rule follower. Like the stiffly rule-bound British colonel in *The Bridge on the River Kwai*, he repeatedly stressed the importance of rules and regularity, but unlike the colonel he always understood what he was ultimately trying to accomplish.

Had there been any doubt about what was driving Scalia, he made his political goal starkly apparent three days before the Court issued its final judgment in the case. Then, the justices addressed Bush's motion to stay the ongoing recount, a motion designed to defeat Gore as a practical matter before the Court could even reach the merits of his legal claim. The stay required a finding of "irreparable harm" as well as a consideration of the "balance of equities." The Court split 5–4, with the five conservatives agreeing to issue the stay and, in effect, ending the election in Bush's favor and mooting the pending case. The four liberals dissented, provoking Scalia to take the unusual step of writing a solo opinion in an effort to justify the stay. Counting votes of "questionable legality," he announced, would "threaten irreparable harm to [Bush], and to the country, by casting a cloud upon what [Bush] claims to be the legitimacy of his election."[55]

It was an astonishingly flawed and biased attempt at justification, an effort so partisan and unconvincing in its reasoning that not one of the other four conservatives was willing to join it. Scalia's opinion ignored the fact that, by stopping the recount, the stay itself would cast a cloud over Bush's claim to the presidency, and it equally ignored the fact that there would be no "cloud" at all if the recount was merely allowed to run its course. Even more obviously biased, it assumed that the "harm" Bush claimed was greater than the "harm" that Gore could claim[56] and that protecting Bush's claim was more important than accurately determining the election's winner. Further, it also assumed that the "harm" to Bush was "irreparable" even though any one of

---

[54] Antonin Scalia, *The Two Faces of Federalism*, 6 HARV. J.L. & PUB. POL'Y 19, 22 (1982).

[55] ZELDEN, BUSH V. GORE, 136–38. Neither Scalia's opinion on the stay motion nor the opinion of the dissenters appears in *U.S. Reports*. They are available online through Wikisource via Google search: "Bush v. Gore stay order."

[56] In a different context Scalia noted that the "value of any prophylactic rule" had to be "assessed not only on the basis of what is gained, but also on the basis of what is lost." Minnick v. Mississippi, 498 U.S. 146, 156, 161 (Scalia, J., dissenting).

several quite real possibilities—an accurate recount, resolution by Congress, or a final decision by the Court on the merits in a matter of only days—could obviate the harm.[57] Moreover, as the four dissenters noted, "counting every legally cast vote cannot constitute irreparable harm" in an election, and it was the very stay the Court agreed to issue that "will inevitably cast a cloud on the legitimacy of the election."[58]

Thus, it was no wonder that the other conservative justices refused to join Scalia's opinion.[59] In no other situation, Jeffrey Toobin wrote, would the Court ever "have considered something so vague as the casting of clouds as amounting to a genuine legal harm, much less one that required the extraordinary step of issuing a stay."[60] Scalia, however, was "in a white heat," reported one insider, and he "didn't even see the need for oral arguments."[61] Two days after Scalia released his stay opinion, the *Washington Post* reported that "no member of the court played a more pivotal role than Scalia, who, by his public words and private actions, has clearly been a driving force in the court's approach to the election."[62] In the stay opinion, Joan Biskupic explained, "Scalia saw the case through the eyes of the Republican candidate" and "was ready to put himself on the line in the bluntest terms."[63] His stay opinion evidenced his total commitment to Bush's cause and his unyielding desire for the Republicans to regain the presidency and maintain conservative control over the Court.

[57] ZELDEN, BUSH V. GORE 192–96.

[58] Scalia's opinion, Howard Gillman wrote, "was as close to an overtly partisan assessment of the conflict as we would officially hear from the Supreme Court." Margaret Jane Radin added that "Scalia's opinion will now live forever in the pages of the *U.S. Reports* where it will embarrass the Court for the rest of its history." Margaret Jane Radin, *Can the Rule of Law Survive* Bush v. Gore?, *in* QUESTION OF LEGITIMACY, 114. The action of the "five Republican members of the Court" was "nothing more than a naked expression of these justices' preferences for the Republican Party." *Id.*

[59] The strongest legal justification for the stay was the likelihood that the five conservatives had already decided that Gore had little or no chance of prevailing on the merits. On that basis, a stay might have been warranted. Equally, however, it would have meant that the five had already decided the case before the Court had received the final briefs and heard the final arguments. *See* Sunstein, *Order Without Law, in* VOTE, 210–11; David A. Strauss, *What Were They Thinking, in id.* at 189–91. Alan Dershowitz reported that he had been "reliably informed that work had already begun on the opinion giving the election to Bush *before* any briefs were received or any arguments heard." DERSHOWITZ, SUPREME INJUSTICE, 51.

[60] JEFFREY TOOBIN, THE NINE: INSIDE THE SECRET WORLD OF THE SUPREME COURT 163 (2007) [hereafter TOOBIN, THE NINE].

[61] EVAN THOMAS, FIRST: SANDRA DAY O'CONNOR 328 (2019).

[62] JOAN BISKUPIC, AMERICAN ORIGINAL: THE LIFE AND CONSTITUTION OF SUPREME COURT JUSTICE ANTONIN SCALIA 238 (2009) [hereafter BISKUPIC, AMERICAN ORIGINAL]. Scalia not only drove the conservative effort to issue the stay, but he also pressed to hear Bush's appeal immediately and to summarily reverse the state supreme court without any oral argument. He was "itching to shut down the recount as soon as possible." TOOBIN, THE NINE, 162.

[63] BISKUPIC, AMERICAN ORIGINAL, 237, 238.

For years after *Bush v. Gore* came down, Scalia's stock response to those who questioned his actions was blunt and unyielding. "Get over it."[64] That peremptory back of the hand was probably the best indication of his deep embarrassment over his judicial performance in *Bush v. Gore*. Indeed, in private he reputedly referred to the majority opinion he had joined as "a piece of shit."[65]

On the relatively rare public occasions when he tried to defend his performance in the case his comments ranged from the misleading to the patently false. On one such occasion, for example, he blamed the Court's action on Gore and his decision to challenge the Florida vote,[66] failing to note that Bush had been the first to bring the election issue to the courts in an early effort to stop the Florida recounts.[67] On another occasion, after telling an audience at Wesleyan University to "Get over it" and again blaming Gore for everything, he claimed misleadingly that the case "was a 7–2 decision" that "wasn't even close."[68] On yet another occasion he claimed falsely that there was "no way that we could turn down the petition for certiorari."[69]

The fact that Scalia did not write separately in the case, as he had similarly failed to do in *Clinton v. Jones*,[70] was another indication that he recognized that his actions betrayed his jurisprudential principles. Commonly, Scalia wrote separately when he joined an opinion with which he did not entirely agree or one that failed to make some point he thought important.[71] Commonly, too, and even more relevant in this case, he often wrote separately when he found that he could support the Court's judgment but not its

---

[64] BRUCE ALLEN MURPHY, SCALIA: A COURT OF ONE 278 (2014).

[65] ZELDEN, BUSH V. GORE, 237.

[66] *Justice Antonin Scalia: Al Gore to Blame for US Election Mess*, THE TELEGRAPH, June 26, 2008, *available at* https://www.telegraph.co.uk/news/worldnews/northamerica/usa/2200495/Justice-Antonin-Scalia-Al-Gore-to-blame-for-2000-us-election-mess.html (last consulted July 2, 2019).

[67] While Gore filed the suits that ultimately came to the Court, Bush had initiated the candidate's recourse to legal action. BISKUPIC, AMERICAN ORIGINAL, 250.

[68] Ian Millhiser, *Scalia Rewrites History, Claims 5–4 Bush v. Gore Decision "Wasn't Even Close,"* *available at* https://thinkprogress.org/Scalia-rewrites-history-claims-5-4-bush-v-gore-decision-wasnt-even-close (last consulted July 2, 2019). *See* BISKUPIC, AMERICAN ORIGINAL, 247–51.

[69] Interview, *The Originalist*, CALIFORNIA LAWYER (Dec. 2010), at 33.

[70] Clinton v. Jones, 520 U.S. 681 (1997). *See* chapter 4.

[71] In *Herrera*, 506 U.S. at 427, for example, Scalia concurred even though he stated expressly that "I nonetheless join the entirety of the Court's opinion." *Id.* at 428. *See, e.g.*, Minneci v. Pollard, 565 U.S. 118 (2012) (Scalia, J. concurring); Gonzales v. Raich, 545 U.S. 1, 33 (2005) (same); Correctional Services Corp. v. Malesko, 534 U.S. 61 (2001) (same); Good News Club v. Milford Central School, 533 U.S. 98, 120 (2001) (same); Cruzan v. Director, Missouri Department of Health, 497 U.S. 261, 292 (1990) (same).

opinion.[72] In *Bush v. Gore*, however, he remained discreetly silent, voicelessly taking refuge behind the words of others.

Finally, Scalia had other reasons to feel embarrassed about the case and his actions. One was that he had been badly burned by criticism aimed at his partisan-sounding solo concurrence defending the Court's decision to stay the recount order of the Florida Supreme Court.[73] Another was that his judicial neutrality seemed compromised by the fact that two of his sons were closely tied to the Bush campaign. One was a partner in the law firm that represented Bush before the Court itself, and the other had taken a position with a Florida law firm that Bush suddenly retained—the day after Scalia's son joined it—to represent him in the state.[74] A third reason for embarrassment was the headline fact that Scalia himself had become closely and personally identified with Bush and his presidential campaign because the candidate had praised him specifically as the kind of justice he wanted to appoint to the Court.[75]

In his biography of Scalia, Bruce Allen Murphy made a compelling case that Scalia must have entertained the strongest personal motivations in *Bush v. Gore.*

For Scalia, winning the battle of *Bush v. Gore* meant everything. The man who had endorsed him and his brand of originalism would be sitting in the White House. For the next four years and possibly eight years President Bush, aided by legions of former and present members of the same Federalist Society that Scalia had helped to create and support over the years, some of them sitting in the Justice Department, would be sending conservative, possibly originalist-oriented jurists to the federal judiciary. Any vacancies on the Supreme Court would be filled with those who would

---

[72] *E.g.*, Hein v. Freedom from Religion Foundation, Inc., 551 U.S. 587, 618 (2007) (Scalia, J., concurring in the judgment); Burson v. Freeman, 504 U.S. 191, 214 (1992) (same); Lamb's Chapel v. Center Moriches Union Free School District, 508 U.S. 384, 397 (1993) (same); Franklin v. Gwinett County Public Schools, 503 U.S. 60, 76 (1992) (same); National Endowment for the Arts v. Finley, 524 U.S. 569, 590 (1998) (same).

[73] Alan Dershowitz indicted Scalia for remaining silent. He "even lacked the courage to try to justify what he was doing by writing a separate opinion on the merits—which he often does when he feels that his actions require explanation." DERSHOWITZ, SUPREME INJUSTICE, 132.

[74] GILLMAN, VOTES THAT COUNTED, 136. At the same time Justice Thomas's wife was working at a conservative think tank collecting resumes for possible appointment in a future Bush administration. *Id.*

[75] *See* chapter 1.

tip the voting direction in Scalia's favor, and who might also follow his brand of textualism and originalism.[76]

Richard Posner offered a more abstract and delicate analysis of the justices' behavior that nonetheless pointed toward a similar conclusion. Although he fairly suggested that all of the justices might have been unusually sensitive to the practical significance of the case,[77] he nonetheless could not avoid raising questions about Scalia's behavior in particular.[78] Joining the majority opinion "was a particular embarrassment for the Court's most conservative justices, Scalia and Thomas," Posner pointed out, for they "have gone out of their way in opinions and (in Scalia's case) in speeches and articles, to embrace a concept of adjudication that is inconsistent with the majority opinion that they joined." In addition, Posner continued, Scalia worsened the Court's "self-inflicted wound" because he wrote "an unconvincing opinion in support of the stay." That action cast him "as the ringleader of a conservative cabal determined to elect Bush." Most pointedly, he noted that Scalia's acceptance of the "Bush-only" rule "invited charges of hypocrisy, or worse." Acknowledging that there was "insufficient evidence" to clearly prove that devastating charge, Posner nonetheless concluded that it seemed "plausible."[79]

On a broad institutional level, *Bush v. Gore* showed the overall importance of political and social context in shaping and undergirding American constitutional law. It was probably critical that the five conservative justices knew they had the practical institutional freedom to assert jurisdiction over the case and to confer the presidency on Bush. The Republican Party was united behind its candidate and equally united behind the five conservative justices as well, and it controlled almost all the government institutions, both state

---

[76] MURPHY, SCALIA, 279–80. Exemplifying the general academic response to *Bush v. Gore*, Robert Post declared that he was "stung by distrust of the Court's good faith" and that the conservative justices "seemed bent on achieving a blatantly extralegal objective." Robert Post, *Sustaining the Premise of Legality: Learning to Live with* Bush v. Gore, *in* QUESTION OF LEGITIMACY, 100, 109.

[77] "I doubt that any of the Justices has so debased a conception of the judicial office as to try *deliberately* to swing the election to his preferred Presidential candidate. But the undeniable interest that a judge, especially a Justice of the U.S. Supreme Court, has in who his colleagues and successors will be is likely to have alerted the Justices to features of *Bush v. Gore* that might otherwise have eluded them. The conservative Justices may have been more sensitive to arguments based on Article II and the equal protection clause than they otherwise would have been, and the liberal Justices more sensitive to the weaknesses of those arguments than they otherwise would have been. . . . [J]udges who have different values and experience are sensitive to different features of a case." POSNER, BREAKING, 180.

[78] Posner noted that the concurring justices "did not defend [their opinion] very cogently," POSNER, BREAKING, 161, and that the concurrence was not "convincing," Posner, *Pragmatic Adjudication*, 205.

[79] Posner, *Pragmatic Adjudication*, 212, 206, 213. The quoted phrase "Bush-only" in the text is not Posner's but the author's.

and federal, that could potentially challenge their action. More broadly, since the late nineteenth century the Court had steadily, if unevenly, gained in power and prestige, and the American people had come to accept its authoritative role as essential. Evidencing that fact, public opinion surveys taken late in the process showed that almost three-quarters of those polled supported a judicial resolution of the dispute.[80] Those underlying social conditions meant that the Court could act without substantial political or institutional challenge and that its decision would, as a practical matter, surely be accepted as final.

On the personal level, *Bush v. Gore* showed that Scalia was almost certainly animated by a compelling personal goal and that he was prepared to jettison virtually all of his principles to achieve it. His originalism, textualism, and traditionalism disappeared under the pressure of personal and political desire. Both he and his methods once again failed to deliver on their claims of neutrality, objectivity, and fidelity.

---

[80] GILLMAN, VOTES THAT COUNTED, 196–99. For Republican Party efforts to support Bush at both the federal and state levels, *see* ZELDEN, BUSH V. GORE, 98–100.

9

An Abandoned Jurisprudence

The Nature of the Federal Judicial Power

In his campaign to severely limit the federal judiciary and overturn the legacy of the Warren Court, Scalia developed a highly restrictive, albeit selective, understanding of the nature of the Article III judicial power.[1] Although he claimed that his interpretation, like his general jurisprudence, was "originalist," it was anything but. In fact, to justify his view and achieve the practical results he desired, he abandoned originalism altogether.

Central to his efforts to limit the federal judicial power was his claim that the federal courts were not "common-law" courts and that they consequently lacked "common-law" powers to make law. Common-law reasoning, he believed, was the tool of an activist and unrestricted judiciary. Since England's thirteenth-century Year Books "any equivalence between custom and common law had ceased to exist, except in the sense that the doctrine of *stare decisis* rendered prior judicial decisions 'custom.'"[2] By that early date the common law had become simply whatever the judges decided, and judge-made law was inherently subjective and creative.

In Scalia's view those characteristics made common-law reasoning a threat to democracy as well as to his goal of narrowing the power of the federal

---

[1] His radical opinion in *Boyle v. United Technologies*, 487 U.S. 500 (1988), favoring corporate defendants over tort plaintiffs, was a major exception to his general effort to limit the federal judicial power. *See* chapter 6. In addition, Scalia parted with two of the other conservative justices in defending the long-established authority of the federal courts to enjoin state officials who engaged in allegedly unconstitutional acts. *Compare* Idaho v. Coeur d'Alene Tribe of Idaho, 521 U.S. 261 (Kennedy, J., joined by Rehnquist, C.J.) (1997) (seeking to limit that power substantially), *with id.* at 288–97 (O'Connor, J., joined by Scalia and Thomas, JJ., concurring in part and concurring in the judgment) (defending the traditional scope of that power). For Scalia's acceptance and use of that injunctive power, *see, e.g.*, Virginia Office of Protection and Advocacy v. Stewart, 563 U.S. 247 (2011) (Scalia, J.); New Orleans Public Service, Inc. v. Council of the City of New Orleans, 491 U.S. 350 (1989) (Scalia, J.).

[2] Antonin Scalia, *Common-Law Courts in a Civil-Law System: The Role of United States Federal Courts in Interpreting the Constitution and Laws*, The Tanner Lectures on Human Values, Princeton University, Mar. 8 and 9, 1995, at 80 [hereafter Scalia, *Common-Law Courts*]. Scalia repeated his argument in his subsequent book. *See* ANTONIN SCALIA, A MATTER OF INTERPRETATION: FEDERAL COURTS AND THE LAW 3–47 (1997) [hereafter SCALIA, MATTER].

Antonin Scalia and American Constitutionalism. Edward A. Purcell, Jr., Oxford University Press (2020).
© Edward A. Purcell, Jr.
DOI: 10.1093/oso/9780197508763.001.0001

judiciary.[3] The common law inspired a mindset that was "exhilarating," he explained, because it "consists of playing king—devising, out of the brilliance of one's own mind, those laws that ought to govern mankind."[4] Thus, the "*practical* threat" of common-law reasoning was that "under the guise or even the self-delusion of pursuing unexpressed legislative intents, common-law judges will in fact pursue their own objectives and desires."[5] Consequently, he insisted, the federal judicial power conferred by Article III granted "no common-law powers."[6]

In denying that the federal courts held common-law powers, Scalia targeted most intently the Court's practice of implying private rights of action for damages from provisions of the Constitution and federal statutes. Under the Warren Court, such implied rights of action began to proliferate, and Scalia maintained that the practice constituted illegitimate judicial lawmaking.[7] In the late 1970s conservatives on the Court began to oppose the practice,[8] and when he arrived on the high bench he readily joined their effort.

Vigorously pushing an extreme position, Scalia flatly rejected the Court's precedents that supported implied causes of actions and denied the law-making power they asserted. In his first term on the Court in 1987 he wrote for a five-justice majority to deny a cause of action under the Constitution in an outrageous instance of military abuse,[9] one so egregious that Justice O'Connor dissented and denounced the army's conduct as "so far beyond the bounds of human decency that as a matter of law it simply cannot be considered a part of the military mission."[10] The next year in *Thompson*

---

[3] When one takes a "realistic view of what common-law courts do, the uncomfortable relationship of common-law lawmaking to democracy (if not to the technical doctrine of the separation of powers) becomes apparent." Scalia, *Common-Law Courts*, 86. *See also id.* at 85.

[4] Scalia, *Common-Law Courts*, 79–80, 83–86 (quote at 83). *Accord* ANTONIN SCALIA, SCALIA SPEAKS: REFLECTIONS ON LAW, FAITH, AND LIFE WELL LIVED 173–78 (Christopher J. Scalia & Edward Whelan eds., 2017) [hereafter SCALIA SPEAKS].

[5] Scalia, *Common-Law Courts*, 93 (emphasis in original). *Accord* SCALIA, MATTER, 17–18.

[6] SCALIA SPEAKS, 231.

[7] *E.g.*, J.I. Case Co. v. Borak, 377 U.S. 426 (1964) (Clark, J.) (implying cause of action for damages from federal statute); Bivens v. Six Unknown Named Agents of Federal Bureau of Narcotics, 403 U.S. 388 (1971) (Brennan, J.) (implying cause of action for damages from constitutional provision).

[8] Justice Powell spearheaded the effort starting with *Cannon v. University of Chicago*, 441 U.S. 677, 730 (1979) (Powell, J., dissenting). The next year Justice Rehnquist rejected the Court's creation of implied constitutional causes of action on the ground that "federal courts do not have the authority to act as general courts of common law absent authorization by Congress." Carlson v. Green, 446 U.S. 14, 31, 44 (Rehnquist, J., dissenting).

[9] United States v. Stanley, 483 U.S. 669 (1987) (Scalia, J.).

[10] *Stanley*, 483 U.S. at 709 (O'Connor, J., dissenting). In the case the army deceived soldiers who volunteered to participate in a program supposedly intended to test protective clothing but designed in fact to study the effects of LSD. Plaintiff alleged that he was given LSD without his knowledge on four occasions and that the drug caused severe damage to him and his family. *Id.* at 671.

v. Thompson, Scalia urged an absolute ban on all implied causes of action. The Court, he declared, should adopt "the categorical position that federal private rights of action will not be implied."[11] He derided the Warren Court's leading precedent supporting the judicial power to imply such rights of action as "a relic of the heady days in which this Court assumed common-law powers to create causes of action."[12] Because the federal courts were not "common-law courts," he insisted, they had no authority to create private causes of action.[13] Consistently over the decades he sought to block the recognition of new implied causes of action and to narrow or overturn those that had previously been established.[14]

In his ardor to discredit implied causes of action, Scalia even misstated the law. "There is even greater reason to abandon [the practice] in the constitutional field," he wrote, "since an 'implication' imagined in the Constitution can presumably not even be repudiated by Congress."[15] The Court, however, had expressly held the contrary and never changed that position.[16]

More fundamentally, Scalia once again molded the supple principles of separation of powers to serve his particular political goals. The very purpose of the separation of powers, he repeatedly proclaimed, was to protect individual liberties by creating a system of checks and balances in the federal government. Divided national power was designed to ensure that the

[11] Thompson v. Thompson, 484 U.S. 174, 188, 191 (1988) (Scalia, J., concurring in the judgment).

[12] Correctional Services Corp. v. Malesko, 534 U.S. 61, 75 (2001) (Scalia, J., concurring). The "relic" was *Bivens*, 403 U.S. 388 (1971) (Brennan, J.). Scalia and Thomas both quoted Scalia's "relic" charge in subsequent cases: Wilkie v. Robbins, 551 U.S. 537, 568 (2007) (Thomas, J., joined by Scalia, J., concurring); Minneci v. Pollard, 565 U.S. 118, 131 (2012) (Scalia, J., joined by Thomas, J., concurring).

[13] "Raising up causes of action where a statute has not created them may be a proper function for common-law courts, but not for federal tribunals." Lampf, Pleva, Lipkind, Prupis & Petigrow v. Gilbertson, 501 U.S. 350, 364, 365 (1991) (Scalia, J., concurring in part and concurring in the judgment). *Accord* Alexander v. Sandoval, 532 U.S. 275, 286–87 (2001) (Scalia, J.); *Malesko*, 534 U.S. at 75 (Scalia, J., concurring).

[14] *E.g., Sandoval*, 532 U.S. 275 (Scalia, J.); Stoneridge Investment Partners, LLC v. Scientific-Atlanta, Inc., 552 U.S. 148 (2008) (Kennedy, J., joined by Scalia, J.); Gebser v. Lago Vista Independent School District, 524 U.S. 274 (1998) (O'Connor, J., joined by Scalia, J.); Franklin v. Gwinnett County Public Schools, 503 U.S. 60, 76, 77–78 (1992) (Scalia, J., concurring in the judgment). Dissenting in *Sandoval*, Justice Stevens suggested with his usual consummate judicial delicacy that "today's decision is the unconscious product of the majority's profound distaste for implied causes of action." *Sandoval*, 532 U.S. at 317 (Stevens, J., dissenting). Deferring to the Court's settled doctrines, Scalia joined in affirming the existence of an implied cause of action under the First Amendment when the Court made the elements of a retaliatory prosecution claim especially demanding. Hartman v. Moore, 547 U.S. 250 (2006) (Souter, J.).

[15] *Malesko*, 534 U.S. at 75 (Scalia, J., concurring).

[16] *E.g., Bivens*, 403 U.S. at 397 (no constitutional cause of action if Congress creates another remedy that is equally availing) (Brennan, J.); Bush v. Lucas, 462 U.S. 367, 377–78 (1983) (Stevens, J.) (Congress has power to limit or bar implied constitutional causes of action); Schweiker v. Chilicky, 487 U.S. 412, 423 (1988) (O'Connor, J.) (same).

abuses of one branch could be blocked or remedied by the counter action of another branch. Without the separation of powers, he declared, "our Bill of Rights would be worthless."[17] Those precious rights "are the *reasons*" why provisions for the separation of powers exist, and it was those provisions that "convert the Bill of Rights from a paper assurance to a living guarantee."[18] Yet determined to restrict the federal courts and bar the creation of judicial remedies for aggrieved individuals, he refused to honor that checking principle and enforce what he proclaimed as the very purpose of separation of powers. Scorning all implied causes of action, he turned his back on the idea that the judicial power should check the other two branches when they failed to protect the people's rights against the abuses and transgressions of federal officials. It was a perfect example of subjectivity and result orientation in manipulating the principles of separation of powers. He chose to sever the Constitution's provisions for separated national powers from their defining institutional purpose as "checking" mechanisms and to enforce the former while ignoring the latter.

Although the Court moved in Scalia's direction on implied causes of action, it did not adopt his absolute position.[19] On one hand, the justices began to limit ever more strictly the creation of new implied causes of action and restrict some of those already created. On the other hand, they sometimes reaffirmed their power to imply causes of action despite conservative objections. Absent a congressional directive on the subject, the Court declared in 1983, "the federal courts must make the kind of remedial determination that is appropriate for a common-law tribunal."[20] A quarter century later, a majority reaffirmed that principle. In considering whether to imply a new cause of action, the Court announced in 2007, "the federal courts must make the kind of remedial determination that is appropriate for a common-law tribunal."[21]

In maintaining that the federal judicial power did not authorize such judicial lawmaking, Scalia's contentions were filled with inconsistencies and

---

[17] Morrison v. Olson, 487 U.S. 654, 697 (1988) (Scalia, J., dissenting).

[18] SCALIA SPEAKS, 163 (emphasis in original).

[19] In implying constitutional causes of action, the second Justice Harlan saw the Court acting "in the great tradition of the common law." *Bivens*, 403 U.S. at 420 (Harlan, J., concurring in the judgment).

[20] Bush v. Lucas, 462 U.S. at 378 (Stevens, J.).

[21] *Wilkie*, 551 U.S. at 550 (Souter, J.). Because the Court denied plaintiff's claim in the case, Scalia joined a concurrence by Thomas that reiterated their rejection of the Court's power to imply causes of action and urged that the precedents upholding those rights of action be confined narrowly to their facts. *Id.* at 568 (Thomas, J., concurring, joined by Scalia, J.).

contradictions. Most obvious, he did not actually mean what he said, for he also believed that the federal courts could make some kinds of "common-law" rules.[22] Strikingly, six months after he urged an absolute ban on judge-made causes of action in *Thompson*, he wrote his exceptionally dubious and ill-reasoned opinion in *Boyle v. United Technologies Corp.* There, he created out of whole cloth a novel federal judge-made defense against state-law tort claims to protect companies producing equipment for the military.[23] While seeking to narrow or eliminate damages remedies for injured persons, in other words, he was nonetheless ready to strain beyond limits to create common-law rules protecting business and the military.[24]

More important, as a textual matter Article III did not support his position on the limited nature of the federal judicial power and in fact repudiated it. In contrast to the vesting clause of Article I, the vesting clauses of Articles II and III paralleled one another. Article I granted Congress only the specific "Powers herein granted," while Articles II and III granted "executive" and "judicial" powers that were textually unqualified. The former granted the "executive Power" to "a President of the United States," and the latter granted the "judicial Power" to the Supreme Court and whatever "inferior Courts" Congress established.[25] Textually, the difference between the three vesting clauses meant that Congress was limited to powers specifically conferred but that the executive and judiciary were granted their respective powers in full.[26] Thus, the constitutional text supported the proposition that the "judicial Power of the United States" granted federal courts the power to do everything properly done by English and American courts, certainly including the common-law courts the Founders knew so well. Indeed, in a later case when it served a different purpose and one that he favored, Scalia asserted that very

[22] *E.g.*, Norfolk Southern Railway v. Kirby, 543 U.S. 14 (O'Connor, J., joined by Scalia, J.) (extending judge-made admiralty law to accident occurring on land); Semtek International, Inc. v. Lockheed Martin Corp., 531 U.S. 497 (2001) (Scalia, J.) (holding federal common law controlling on issue of res judicata effect of dismissal in a federal diversity action); Musick, Peeler & Garrett v. Employers Insurance of Wassau, 508 U.S. 286 (1993) (Kennedy, J., joined by Scalia, J.) (creating a right of action for contribution from joint 10b-5 tortfeasors).

[23] *Boyle*, 487 U.S. 500 (Scalia, J.). *See* chapter 6.

[24] Scalia's narrow view of the judicial power did not, of course, invariably favor corporate interests. *See, e.g.*, Stewart Organization, Inc. v. Ricoh Corp., 487 U.S. 22, 33 (1988) (Scalia, J., dissenting) (denying federal judicial power to use 28 U.S.C. Section 1404 to set aside state law that made forum-selection clauses unenforceable).

[25] U.S. CONST. art. II, sec. 1; art. III, secs. 1–2.

[26] Although there were other textual differences between Articles II and III, both gave their respective branches authority over federal law. Article II imposed on the executive the duty to "take Care that the [federal] Laws be faithfully executed," while Article III extended the "judicial Power" to "all Cases, in Law and Equity" arising under the Constitution, laws, and Treaties of the United States.

principle. "What those who framed and ratified the Constitution had in mind when they entrusted the 'judicial Power' to a separate and coequal branch of the Federal Government," he declared, "was the judicial power they were familiar with—that traditionally exercised by English and American courts."[27]

Contradicting his own position on the federal judiciary's lack of common-law powers, in fact, Scalia accepted that textual argument and agreed that both the executive and judiciary held "all" of their respective powers. In his effort to protect and expand executive power, he insisted that the vesting clause in Article II "does not mean *some* of the executive power, but *all* of the executive power."[28] To support that argument, he cited the parallel language in the vesting clause of Article III. Were Congress to "consider a statute giving to non–Article III judges just a tiny bit of purely judicial power in a relatively insignificant field," even with substantial control in the Article III courts, he maintained, the Court would reject it and "say that our 'constitutionally assigned duties' include *complete* control over all exercises of the judicial power."[29] Three years later he repeated the point. The text of Article III was "unequivocal," and it conferred on the federal courts "not '*Some* of the judicial Power of the United States,' or even '*Most of* the judicial Power of the United States'" but all of that power.[30] Thus, on his own principles, Article III granted the federal judiciary "all" of the "judicial Power of the United States" and, as a result, all of the common-law powers traditionally exercised by English and American courts. After the Constitution itself, the Founders looked to the common law as the most important source of law that courts could draw on, and that power included the common-law power to create causes of action and to shape appropriate remedies to enforce the law.[31]

Worse for his position, Scalia advanced an "originalist" view that actually contradicted his claim that the judicial power did not include common-law

---

[27] Arizona State Legislature v. Arizona Independent Redistricting Commission, 135 S. Ct. 2652, 2694 (2015) (Scalia, J., dissenting).

[28] Morrison v. Olson, 487 U.S. 654, 697, 705 (1988) (Scalia, J., dissenting) (emphasis in original). *See id.* at 697–98, 709–10, 719–20 (comparing the language and meaning of the power granted by the three articles and the parallels between Articles II and III).

[29] *Morrison,* 487 U.S. at 709–10 (Scalia, J., dissenting) (emphasis in original).

[30] Freytag v. Commissioner, 501 U.S. 868, 892, 908 (1991) (Scalia, J., concurring in part and concurring in the judgment) (italics in the original).

[31] G. EDWARD WHITE, THE MARSHALL COURT AND CULTURAL CHANGE, 1815–1835, at 112 (1988) [hereafter WHITE, MARSHALL COURT]. *See id.* at 6–7, 154; Stewart Jay, *Origins of Federal Common Law: Part One,* 133 U. PA. L. REV. 1003–1116 (1985); Stewart Jay, *Origins of Federal Common Law: Part Two,* 133 U. PA. L. REV. 1231–1333 (1985) [hereafter Jay, *Origins,* pt. 2]; Donald H. Zeigler, *Rights Require Remedies: A New Approach to the Enforcement of Rights in the Federal Courts,* 38 HASTINGS L.J. 665, 667–77 (1987).

powers. "The judicial power of the United States," he declared in *James B. Beam Distilling Co. v. Georgia*, "must be deemed to be the judicial power as understood by our common-law tradition."[32] More than two decades later he again equated the proper understanding of the Article III judicial power with the common-law understanding of judicial power. Addressing two of the Court's justiciability doctrines, he declared that "[b]oth doctrines have equivalently deep roots in the common-law understanding, and hence the constitutional understanding, of what makes a matter appropriate for judicial disposition."[33] His concluding phrase, "and hence the constitutional understanding," said it all. The common-law understanding was the constitutional understanding.

There was no question that common-law courts could "make law" and create private rights of action. In fact, the creation of such actions—much of the common-law writ system and most of the actions it came to recognize—constituted a major part of the common-law tradition.[34] Sir William Blackstone, whom Scalia cited repeatedly as a high originalist authority, made that point explicitly. "For wherever the common law gives a right or prohibits an injury, it also gives a remedy by action," he declared in his famous *Commentaries on the Laws of England*; "and therefore, wherever a new injury is done, a new method of remedy must be pursued."[35] Indeed, quoting Blackstone as authority, Chief Justice John Marshall had made the same point in *Marbury v. Madison*.[36] Reluctantly, Scalia seemed even to admit as much when he conceded that creating "causes of action where a statute has not created them may be a proper function for common-law courts."[37]

[32] James B. Beam Distilling Co. v. Georgia, 501 U.S. 529, 548, 549 (1991) (Scalia, J., concurring in the judgment).

[33] Lexmark International, Inc. v. Static Control Components, Inc., 572 U.S. 118 (2014) (Scalia, J.) (criticizing concept of "prudential" standing and suggesting that justiciability doctrines may all be of constitutional stature).

[34] E.g., In spite of the common law's early commitment to a rigid writ system, "eventually a means was found of introducing new remedies through a relatively formless action, so that Holt C.J. could declare in 1703 that wherever there was a right a remedy must be found." J.H. BAKER, AN INTRODUCTION TO ENGLISH LEGAL HISTORY 53 (4th ed. 2007) [hereafter BAKER, INTRODUCTION]. "Habeas corpus did not evolve. Judges made it." PAUL D. HALLIDAY, HABEAS CORPUS: FROM ENGLAND TO EMPIRE 9 (2010). For the early development of common-law actions, *see* SIR FREDERICK POLLOCK & FREDERIC WILLIAM MAITLAND, THE HISTORY OF ENGLISH LAW BEFORE THE TIME OF EDWARD I (2d ed., two volumes, with introduction and bibliography by S.F.C. Milsom 1968).

[35] 3 WILLIAM BLACKSTONE, BLACKSTONE'S COMMENTARIES ON THE LAWS OF ENGLAND 97 (Wayne Morrison ed., 2001) (in original edition, published in 1770, the quote appears at page 123).

[36] "The government of the United States has been emphatically termed a government of laws, and not of men. It will certainly cease to deserve this high appellation, if the laws furnish no remedy for the violation of a vested legal right." Marbury v. Madison, 5 U.S.137, 193 (1803) (Marshall, C.J.).

[37] *Sandoval*, 532 U.S. at 286–87 (Scalia, J.), citing *Lampf*, 501 U.S. at 365 (Scalia, J., concurring in part and concurring in judgment). Notwithstanding his recognition of the power of common-law

Thus, in spite of his fear of the subjective and creative nature of common-law reasoning, Scalia recognized that as an originalist he had to acknowledge the relevance of the common-law tradition to an understanding of the federal judicial power. To incorporate the common law into his overall jurisprudence, then, he sought to turn it into a rigid and unchanging body of concepts and doctrines that could serve as a bulwark for his appeals to "tradition." Accordingly, while he argued that the common law had divorced itself from custom and practice as early as the thirteenth century, he also claimed that by the eighteenth century the common law had disavowed its power to change its rules and that it consequently provided a stable, coherent, and highly restrictive normative baseline that could be used to limit the federal courts.[38] Thus, although he maintained that common-law reasoning "was not the way of construing a democratically adopted [constitutional] text,"[39] he nonetheless felt free to repeatedly invoke what he claimed to be unchanging common-law rules and precedents in construing—for the purpose of rigidly restricting—the Constitution's meaning.[40]

Consequently, when he wrote in *James B. Beam* that "the judicial Power of the United States" was "the judicial power as understood by our common-law tradition," he immediately defined that power to fit his restrictive goal. The judicial power granted in Article III, he explained, was "the power 'to say what the law is'" but "not the power to change it."[41] Properly understood, the established rules, concepts, and writs of the eighteenth-century common law itself—in contrast to dangerous and antidemocratic common-law

---

courts to create causes of action, Scalia followed his statement by repeating his contention that such power was "not for federal tribunals." *Id.*

[38] Rogers v. Tennessee, 532 U.S. 451, 467, 472–78 (2001). *Accord* Boumediene v. Bush, 553 U.S. 723, 826, 832 (2008) (Scalia, J., dissenting) ("The writ [of habeas corpus] as preserved in the Constitution could not possibly extend farther than the common law provided when that Clause was written"). Scalia did acknowledge that tradition could be "living," and he allowed for the possibility of some apparently slight flexibility, in the interpretation of other constitutional provisions. "The Equal Protection Clause and other provisions of the Constitution, unlike the Due Process Clause, are not an explicit invocation of the 'law of the land,' and might be thought to have some counter-historical content." Pacific Mutual Life Insurance Co. v. Haslip, 499 U.S. 1, 24, 38, 39–40 (1991) (Scalia, J., concurring in the judgment).

[39] Scalia, *Common-Law Courts*, 113.

[40] In *County of Riverside v. McLaughlin*, 500 U.S. 44 (1991) (O'Connor, J.), for example, Scalia dissented, arguing that the Fourth Amendment's prohibition of unreasonable seizures "preserves for our citizens the traditional protections against unlawful arrest afforded by the common law." *Id.* at 59, 60. The Court dismissed his common-law authorities on the ground that they came "from the early 1800's" and contained only a "vague admonition" that provided "no more support" for the "inflexible standard" that he offered. *Id.* at 54–55.

[41] *James B. Beam*, 501 U.S. at 549 (Scalia, J., concurring in the judgment).

reasoning—constituted a firm constraining force that cabined judicial subjectivity and creativity. Not surprisingly, then, Scalia used that interpretation of the common law to restrict actions under the federal civil rights laws[42] and to limit rights under the Due Process Clause which, he explained, was to be "understood as an embodiment of common-law tradition."[43] On that restrictive theory of an unchanging common-law, he argued that due process was limited only to procedures that were "deeply rooted in traditional custom and practice"[44] and that courts could recognize no "substantive" due process rights unless they were "'so rooted in the traditions and conscience of our people as to be ranked as fundamental.'"[45]

In *Rogers v. Tennessee*, for example, where the Court upheld a more flexible interpretation of due process, Scalia castigated the majority for claiming that its decision was "a routine exercise of common law decisionmaking."[46] Though he acknowledged ruefully that the majority's claim was "an accurate enough description of what modern 'common law decisionmaking' consists of," he denied that its claim was "an accurate description of the theoretical model of common-law decisionmaking accepted by those who adopted the Due Process Clause." That originalist model did not allow courts to change the common law but merely allowed them to apply it to new situations. "What is important here is that it was an undoubted point of principle, at the time the Due Process Clause was adopted, that courts could not 'change' the law."[47] Thus, he rejected what he considered early

---

[42] *Compare* Scalia's majority opinion in *Heck v. Humphrey*, 512 U.S. 477 (1994), *with* the four-justice opinion rejecting the majority's reasoning, *id.* at 491 (Souter, J., concurring in the judgment). O'Connor, who joined Souter's concurrence in *Heck*, had previously maintained that the congressional policy underlying Section 1983 should prevail over ambiguous or unhelpful common-law precedents. Smith v. Wade, 461 U.S. 30, 92 (1983) (O'Connor, J., dissenting). Scalia joined in a similar use of the common law to trump statutory policy arguments, provoking dissents from the Court's liberals. *See* Newton v. Rumery, 480 U.S. 386 (1987) (Powell, J., joined by Scalia) (using common-law contract principles to narrow scope, meaning, and significance of Section 1983).

[43] Shafer v. South Carolina, 532 U.S. 36, 55 (2001) (Scalia, J., dissenting).

[44] Montana v. Egelhoff, 518 U.S. 37, 48 (1996) (Scalia, J., announcing judgment of the Court in a plurality opinion). *See id.* at 47–51 for Scalia's broader discussion of the issue. "I affirm that no procedure firmly rooted in the practices of our people can be so 'fundamentally unfair' as to deny due process of law." *Haslip*, 499 U.S. at 38 (Scalia, J., concurring in the judgment).

[45] Reno v. Flores, 507 U.S. 292, 303 (1993) (Scalia, J.). "In my view, it is not for the Members of this Court to decide from time to time whether a process approved by the legal traditions of our people is 'due' process, nor do I believe such a rootless analysis to be dictated by our precedents." *Haslip*, 499 U.S. at 27–28 (Scalia, J., concurring in the judgment).

[46] *Rogers*, 532 U.S. at 472 (Scalia, J., dissenting, quoting the majority's language). *See* RALPH A. ROSSUM, ANTONIN SCALIA'S JURISPRUDENCE: TEXT AND TRADITION 167–69 (2006).

[47] *Rogers*, 451 U.S. at 472, 477 (Scalia, J., dissenting). To the extent that Scalia had in mind the Due Process Clause of the Fourteenth Amendment, ratified in 1868, he still misconstrued the English doctrine of precedent, which did not reach its most rigid and formalistic stage until later in the nineteenth century. BAKER, INTRODUCTION, 199–201; A.H. MANCHESTER, A MODERN LEGAL HISTORY

thirteenth- and fourteenth-century ideas about the common law as well as later twentieth-century ideas about it. Instead, to define the limits of the federal judicial power he invoked what he identified as specifically seventeenth- and eighteenth-century "originalist" ideas that purportedly understood the common law as relatively static, unchanging, and strictly bound by preexisting traditions.[48]

As elsewhere, however, in dealing with the nature of the common law in the eighteenth century, Scalia was a highly selective and quite unreliable historian. At the time of the nation's founding the common law was hardly static, unchanging, or rigidly bound by tradition. To the contrary, it was undergoing a substantial evolution in England, and the doctrine of stare decisis was not regarded as rigorously binding.[49] English lawyers and judges enjoyed a "degree of flexibility" that gave them "the opportunity to attempt to ensure that the common law kept pace with social change."[50] Indeed, the eighteenth-century common-law courts made "utilitarian adjudications in cases, acting flexibly with a view to particular justice," Michael Lobban explained. With decisions shaped by "a constant feeding from society," they administered "a flexible system of adjudication responding to society's problems."[51] Between about 1700 and 1750, for example, the English courts began to expand the action of trespass on the case to include actions for a variety of kinds of negligence, a development that was accelerated later in the century by the growing number of injuries that accompanied the expansion of carriage and stagecoach traffic on the English roads.[52] Similarly, in the 1770s Lord Mansfield was in the process of remolding the common law of contracts. Acknowledging that the contract doctrine of consideration had become "a matter of great consequence to trade and commerce," he set about trying to

OF ENGLAND AND WALES 1750–1950, at 28–29 (1980) [hereafter MANCHESTER, MODERN LEGAL HISTORY]; ALAN HARDING, A SOCIAL HISTORY OF ENGLISH LAW 355–58 (1966); ROBERT STEVENS, LAW AND POLITICS: THE HOUSE OF LORDS AS A JUDICIAL BODY, 1800–1976, at 87–90 (1978) [hereafter STEVENS, LAW AND POLITICS].

[48] In his dissent in *Rogers*, Scalia cited in support of his position only one seventeenth-century source, Sir Francis Bacon, and one eighteenth-century source, Sir William Blackstone. *Rogers*, 451 U.S. at 472.

[49] C.H.S. FIFOOT, HISTORY AND SOURCES OF THE COMMON LAW 406–43 (1949); BAKER, INTRODUCTION, 199–200.

[50] MANCHESTER, MODERN LEGAL HISTORY, 28.

[51] MICHAEL LOBBAN, THE COMMON LAW AND ENGLISH JURISPRUDENCE 1760–1850, at 78–79 (1991) [hereafter LOBBAN, COMMON LAW].

[52] BAKER, INTRODUCTION, 410–12.

fit the concept to changing commercial practices.[53] Well into the nineteenth century, in fact, English practice regarding precedent remained flexible and diverse, avoiding any rigid doctrine of stare decisis and leaving considerable leeway for judges to shape the law to meet changing conditions.[54]

In the colonies the legal situation was even more fluid, especially after the final break with England in 1776 when the tumultuous revolutionary period profoundly disrupted traditional patterns of behavior and altered assumptions about the nature of both law and the courts.[55] The newly independent states passed statutes "receiving" the common law as local law subject to the control of their legislatures, while their courts continued to adapt common-law principles to new domestic conditions. In the process those courts established a variety of local common-law rules, picked among the English precedents they would accept, and often allowed juries to decide the law as well as the facts.[56] The American common law, G. Edward White explained, "was an ideology of adapting general principles to changing specific circumstances" and "of instituting change by gradual adaptation rather than by sudden positivist edict."[57] At the founding, then, the common law was neither static in conception nor unchanging in fact, and the revolutionary era spurred profound changes in ideas about the nature of courts and the powers they exercised.[58] Indeed, Americans disagreed about the very nature of the common law and its relation to their new constitutional order.[59]

[53] MANCHESTER, MODERN LEGAL HISTORY, 272. Henry Paul Monaghan, *Symposium: Doing Originalism*, 104 COLUM. L. REV. 32, 37 (2004) [hereafter Monaghan, *Doing Originalism*] ("Moses v. Macferlan [97 Eng. Rep. 676, K.B. 1760, a decision of Lord Mansfield] thus shows that but a few years prior to the adoption of the Constitution common law institutions were still evolving"). For a general summary of Mansfield's impact, *see* LOBBAN, COMMON LAW, 98–114.

[54] STEVENS, LAW AND POLITICS, ch. 3 & 114–30.

[55] *See, e.g.,* GORDON S. WOOD, THE CREATION OF THE AMERICAN REPUBLIC, 1776–1787 (1998 ed.).

[56] WILLIAM E. NELSON, AMERICANIZATION OF THE COMMON LAW, ch. 1 (1975); KUNAL M. PARKER, COMMON LAW, HISTORY, AND DEMOCRACY IN AMERICA, 1790–1900: LEGAL THOUGHT BEFORE MODERNISM, ch. 3 (2011) [hereafter PARKER, COMMON LAW]; F.W. Hall, *The Common Law: An Account of Its Reception in the United States*, 4 VAND. L. REV. 791 (1951). *See, e.g.,* THE FEDERALIST PAPERS NO. 84, at 511–12 (Hamilton) (Clinton Rossiter ed., originally published in 1961, with Introduction and Notes by Charles R. Kessler, 2003).

[57] WHITE, MARSHALL COURT, 51–52.

[58] GORDON S. WOOD, EMPIRE OF LIBERTY: A HISTORY OF THE EARLY REPUBLIC, 1789–1815, at 400–32 (2009) [hereafter WOOD, EMPIRE]. Intercolonial and then interstate conflict-of-laws issues heightened Americans' awareness of local divergencies in the common law that the courts were developing and hence of the changing nature of the common law. William E. Nelson, *The American Revolution and the Emergence of Modern Doctrines of Federalism and Conflict of Laws, in* LAW IN COLONIAL MASSACHUSETTS, 1630–1800, at 419–67 (1984). Legal reformers like Thomas Jefferson criticized the common law on the ground that it was too uncertain and changing and thus that it needed to be replaced by legislative codes. David Thomas Konig, *Legal Fictions and the Rule(s) of Law: The Jeffersonian Critique of Common-Law Adjudication, in* THE MANY LEGALITIES OF EARLY AMERICA 97–117 (Christopher L. Tomlins & Bruce H. Mann eds., 2001).

[59] PARKER, COMMON LAW, ch. 3.

"The most we can conclude from a survey of jurisdictional theory" in the late eighteenth and early nineteenth century, concluded one scholar of the early federal common law, was "that it was generally conceded that federal courts had what we would term significant common-law powers."[60]

Thus, Scalia failed in his effort to establish a sound originalist understanding of the federal judicial power that would severely limit the federal courts and deny them lawmaking powers, including the right to imply private rights of action for damages. Neither eighteenth-century ideas about the nature of the common law nor originalist sources generally supported his severely restrictive view. When the Founders adopted the common law, Paul Freund noted, they must also have adopted the intrinsic "dynamic element" that it contained.[61] Indeed, late in his career Scalia seemed to acknowledge his error and abandon his earlier position on the nature of the common law, if not his view of the federal judicial power. "Ours is a common-law tradition in which judicial improvisation has abounded," he acknowledged. As late as the nineteenth century, he continued, the absence of statutes meant that "the law was the product of judicial invention."[62]

Scalia, however, did not merely fail to provide a plausible originalist justification for his claim that the Article III judicial power did not confer common-law powers on the federal courts. Nor did he merely abandon his claim about the unchanging nature of the eighteenth-century common law. Rather, pressing to limit the federal judicial power generally, he abandoned originalism entirely.

The undeniable obstacle that Scalia faced was the fact that from the nation's earliest days the federal courts had asserted a variety of common-law powers to make law and announce new judge-made rules, including approving damages remedies against those who broke the law or committed

---

[60] Jay, *Origins*, pt. 2, 1323. The Jeffersonian Republicans had been critical of the federal courts, but by the first decade of the nineteenth century many of them "came to understand that a strong independent judiciary and a flexible common law were crucial." Wood, Empire, 431. There is much scholarly disagreement about the exact nature and scope of the "original" common-law powers of the federal courts. *See, e.g.*, Anthony J. Bellia & Bradford R. Clark, *The Original Source of the Cause of Action in Federal Courts: The Example of the Alien Tort Statute*, 101 Va. L. Rev. 609, 688 (2015) ("In the Process Acts, early Congresses directed federal courts to apply the same causes of action that local state courts applied in cases at law"); John F. Preis, *How the Federal Cause of Action Relates to Rights, Remedies, and Jurisdiction*, 67 Fla. L. Rev. 849, 874 (2015) ("In sum, federal courts in the nineteenth century enforced federal statutory and constitutional rights through ordinary common law writs").

[61] Monaghan, *Doing Originalism*, 37. Reporting Freund's comments, Monaghan noted that Freund was speaking in particular about the writ of habeas corpus.

[62] Antonin Scalia & Bryan A. Garner, Reading Law: The Interpretation of Legal Texts 3 (2014).

common-law torts.[63] They enforced their own independent judgments on "general" common-law principles and rights of action,[64] and they applied their own broader principles and flexible remedies in what they conceived of as a constitutionally based equity jurisdiction that also allowed them to create private rights of action.[65] Further, as Scalia admitted,[66] many of the Founders, including John Marshall as late as 1800,[67] thought that the federal courts even had common-law powers to define and adjudicate judge-made crimes. They believed, that is, that the federal courts had an inherent judicial power to declare certain acts criminal without legislative authorization or statutory definition of the crime. In the 1790s every member of the Supreme Court except Justice Samuel Chase upheld criminal convictions based on such judge-made common-law crimes.[68] Finally, the federal courts also saw the "law of nations" as part of their lawmaking powers, and they enforced it

---

[63] *See, e.g.*, Little v. Barreme, 6 U.S. 170 (1804) (Marshall, C.J.); Wise v. Withers, 7 U.S. 331 (1806) (Marshall, C.J.); Raborg v. Peyton, 15 U.S. 385 (1817) (Story, J.); Gelston v. Hoyt, 16 U.S. 246 (1818) (Story, J.); Tracy v. Swartwout, 35 U.S. 80 (1836) (Mcclean, J.); Mitchell v. Harmony, 54 U.S. 115 (1851) (Taney, C.J.).

[64] *See, e.g.*, WHITE, MARSHALL COURT; RANDOLPH BRIDWELL & RALPH U. WHITTEN, THE CONSTITUTION AND THE COMMON LAW: THE DECLINE OF THE DOCTRINES OF SEPARATION OF POWERS AND FEDERALISM (1977); William P. LaPiana, Swift v. Tyson *and the Brooding Omnipresence in the Sky: An Investigation of the Idea of Law in Antebellum America*, 20 SUFFOLK U. L. REV. 771 (1986); Michael G. Collins, *Before* Lochner—*Diversity Jurisdiction and the Development of General Constitutional Law*, 74 TULANE L. REV. 163 (2000); Ann Woolhandler, *The Common Law Origins of Constitutionally Compelled Remedies*, 107 YALE L.J. 77 (1997).

[65] "[A]nchoring federal practice in English practice, the federal courts developed an equity jurisprudence independent of the states, whereby a party could often invoke equity on certain fact patterns without regard to whether state legal remedies might address the problem." Consequently, the law applied in federal equity courts "was frequently either federal or general law rather than state law." Ann Woolhandler & Michael G. Collins, *The Article III Jury*, 87 VA. L. REV. 587, 617, 619 (2001). *See, e.g.*, Kristin Collins, *"A Considerable Surgical Operation": Article III, Equity, and Judge-Made Law in the Federal Courts*, 60 DUKE L.J. 249 (2010) [hereafter K. Collins, *"Considerable Surgical"*]; Kristin Collins, *"Government by Injunction": Legal Elites and the Making of the Modern Federal Courts, in* 3 CRITICAL ANALYSIS OF LAW 335 (2016) [hereafter K. Collins, *"Government by Injunction"*]; Ann Woolhandler, *The Common Law Origins of Constitutionally Compelled Remedies*, 107 YALE L.J. 77 (1997).

[66] *Rogers*, 532 U.S. at 467 (Scalia, J., dissenting) (referring to "the framing era's acceptance of common-law crimes," adding that "[a]t the time of the framing, common-law crimes were considered unobjectionable," and acknowledging that "the notion of a common-law crime is utterly anathema today," at 476). For early attitudes toward a federal common law of crimes, *see* WHITE, MARSHALL COURT, 121, 137–54, 458; Gary Rowe, *The Sound of Silence*, 101 YALE L.J. 919 (1992); Kathryn Preyer, *Jurisdiction to Punish: Federal Authority, Federalism and the Common Law of Crimes in the Early Republic*, 4 L. & HIST. REV. 223 (1986). Thomas Jefferson, for example, condemned the idea of common-law crimes, but as president he sought to use the power against his political enemies. LEONARD W. LEVY, JEFFERSON AND CIVIL LIBERTIES: THE DARKER SIDE 57–67 (1963).

[67] WHITE, MARSHALL COURT, 458.

[68] JEAN EDWARD SMITH, JOHN MARSHALL: DEFINER OF A NATION 284 (1996).

with their own judge-made rules as part of the laws of the United States in cases that fell within their jurisdiction.[69]

In 1793, for example, four of the five justices on the Supreme Court—all authentic Founders—agreed in *Chisholm v. Georgia* that the courts needed no legislative authorization to enforce their own judge-made cause of action for breach of contract against a state.[70] In seriatum opinions they rejected the need for legislative authorization and upheld plaintiff's action for assumpsit on the basis of the Court's jurisdiction under the Constitution and the judicial power to recognize common-law damages actions. "We have seen," wrote Justice James Wilson, "that on the principles of general jurisprudence, a State, for the breach of a contract, may be liable for damages."[71] Justice James Iredell, the sole dissenter, did not deny the judicial power to create such causes of action. Rather, he maintained only that suits against sovereign states were not recognized at common law.[72]

Only gradually and long after the Founding did those original understandings of the common-law powers of the federal judiciary disappear. The Eleventh Amendment, ratified in 1798, denied the federal courts jurisdiction over certain suits against states, including the kind of action that *Chisholm* recognized, but it did not purport to deny their substantive common-law power to create such judge-made causes of action for damages against parties other than states.[73] The first of the original federal judicial lawmaking powers to be terminated was the power to create common-law crimes, but that did not occur until 1812, more than two decades after the Founding.[74] The original understandings of the other lawmaking powers of the federal judiciary persisted and even expanded into the early twentieth

[69] BLACKSTONE IN AMERICA: SELECTED ESSAYS OF KATHRYN PREYER 195 (Mary Sarah Bilder, Maeva Marcus, & R. Kent Newmyer eds., 2009); INTERNATIONAL LAW IN THE U.S. SUPREME COURT: CONTINUITY AND CHANGE 27–32 (David L. Sloss, Michael D. Ramsey, & William S. Dodge eds., 2011) [hereafter INTERNATIONAL LAW IN THE U.S. SUPREME COURT].

[70] Chisholm v. Georgia, 2 U.S. 419 (1793). The bench constituted an all-time great originalist Court. Of the four justices in the majority, two (James Wilson and John Blair, Jr.) had been delegates to both the Constitutional Convention and their state ratifying conventions; the third (William Cushing) had presided over the Massachusetts ratifying convention; and the fourth (John Jay) was a delegate to the New York ratifying convention and one of the authors of *The Federalist Papers*. The dissenter (James Iredell), equally a Founder, led the fight to adopt the Constitution in the North Carolina ratifying convention.

[71] *Chisholm*, 2 U.S. at 465 (Wilson, J.).

[72] *Chisholm*, 2 U.S. at 429 (Iredell, J.). *See* AKHIL REED AMAR, AMERICA'S CONSTITUTION: A BIOGRAPHY 333–34 (2006).

[73] U.S. CONST. amend. 11.

[74] United States v. Hudson and Goodwin, 11 U.S. 32 (1812) (Johnson, J.). *See* BRUCE ACKERMAN, THE FAILURE OF THE FOUNDING FATHERS: JEFFERSON, MARSHALL, AND THE RISE OF PRESIDENTIAL DEMOCRACY, ch. 10 (2005).

century before they, too, were finally discarded.[75] The idea that the federal courts possessed a special constitutionally based equity power lasted into the 1930s[76] before morphing into the more limited idea that federal equity powers, though vast, were neither conferred directly by the Constitution nor free from congressional restriction.[77] The power of the federal courts to make "general" common-law rules and apply them while ignoring the common-law rules of the states remained in effect until 1938, when the Court suddenly and surprisingly repudiated it in *Erie Railroad Co. v. Tompkins*. There, the Court declared that enforcing their "general" common-law rules was an "unconstitutional assumption of powers" by the federal judiciary.[78] The idea that the federal courts could enforce the "law of nations" as part of the federal judicial power declined in the nineteenth century, faded in importance for a variety of reasons during the early twentieth century, and after 1938 was gradually and partially subsumed into a new post-*Erie* federal common law.[79] Thus, as an originalist matter, both judicial authorities and traditional practices conclusively contradicted Scalia's claim about the limited lawmaking authority inherent in the "original" federal judicial power.

In truth, Scalia's position was based not on any original understanding but on later and for the most part twentieth-century understandings. He admitted as much when he acknowledged that the kind of federal judicial lawmaking authority he accepted was entirely different from the judicial lawmaking authority that the Founders had recognized. The "creation of post-Erie federal common law is rooted in a positivist mindset utterly foreign to the American common-law tradition of the late 18th century," he admitted,

[75] For the Court's use of implied causes of action for both equitable and legal relief, *see e.g.*, Michael G. Collins, *"Economic Rights," Implied Constitutional Actions, and the Scope of Section 1983*, 77 GEO. L.J. 1493, 1517–25 (1989) [hereafter M. Collins, *"Economic Rights"*]; Ann Woolhandler, *Patterns of Official Immunity and Accountability*, 37 CASE WESTERN L. REV. 396, 448–49 (1987) [hereafter Woolhandler, *Patterns*].

[76] *E.g.*, "The principles of equity exist independently of and anterior to all Congressional legislation." United States v. Detroit Timber and Lumber Co., 200 U.S. 321, 339 (1906) (Brewer, J.). By the 1920s the Court had also developed the rule that federal equity was insulated from state power and that new state law remedies at law could not oust federal equity jurisdiction. EDWARD A. PURCELL, JR., BRANDEIS AND THE PROGRESSIVE CONSTITUTION: ERIE, THE JUDICIAL POWER, AND THE POLITICS OF THE FEDERAL COURTS IN TWENTIETH-CENTURY AMERICA 44, 323 n.34 (2000) [hereafter PURCELL, BRANDEIS].

[77] In the Norris-LaGuardia Act of 1932, for example, Congress substantially restricted federal equity in labor disputes, and the Court upheld the statute six years later in *Lauf v. Shinner*, 303 U.S. 323 (1938) (Roberts, J.). *See, e.g.*, K. Collins, *"Considerable Surgical"*; K. Collins, *"Government by Injunction."*

[78] Erie Railroad Co. v. Tompkins, 304 U.S. 64, 79 (1938) (Brandeis, J., quoting Holmes, J., dissenting in *Black & White Taxicab and Transfer Co. v. Brown & Yellow Taxicab & Transfer Co.*, 276 U.S. 518, 532, 533 (1928)).

[79] INTERNATIONAL LAW IN THE U.S. SUPREME COURT, chs. 3, 7, 11.

and the federal judicial power to make common-law rules that he accepted was "far removed" from the common-law ideas of the Founders.[80] Thus, he explained quite correctly, "today's federal common law is not our Framers' general common law."[81]

Even *Erie*, moreover, which became the touchstone for understanding the lawmaking powers of the federal courts, provided no support for Scalia's claim that the national courts lacked the power to imply causes of action. Although *Erie* extinguished the idea that the federal courts had the power to ignore state common-law rules by making their own independent judgments of "general" common-law principles, it did not purport to deny all their law-making powers. It terminated federal judicial lawmaking authority in areas beyond the power of the national government, but it left room for judicial lawmaking in areas committed by the Constitution to national authority.[82] After *Erie* the federal courts continued to make substantive rules of law in civil actions but limited their efforts to areas they regarded as properly con-trolled by federal constitutional or statutory provisions.[83] Even in criminal cases they continued to apply—though to a far more limited extent—many of their own judge-made rules to supplement statutory law.[84] Scalia himself wrote or joined opinions in civil cases that accepted the power of the federal courts to create such judge-made rules,[85] and he agreed that even in crim-inal cases the Due Process Clause left federal courts free to adapt, refine, and re-evaluate applicable judge-made rules as long as they did not apply any changes retroactively.[86]

---

[80] Sosa v. Alvarez-Machain, 542 U.S. 692, 739, 745 (2004) (Scalia, concurring in part and concur-ring in the judgment).

[81] *Sosa*, 542 U.S. at 746 (Scalia, concurring in part and concurring in the judgment).

[82] *Compare* the two opinions Brandeis handed down on the same day: *Erie*, 304 U.S. at 78–80 (Brandeis, J.) *with* Hinderlider v. La Plata River & Cherry Creek Ditch Co., 304 U.S. 92, 110 (1938) (Brandeis, J.). *See generally* PURCELL, BRANDEIS, 186–90.

[83] *See, e.g.*, Henry P. Monaghan, *The Supreme Court, 1974 Term: Forward: Constitutional Common Law*, 89 HARV. L. REV. 1 (1975); Caleb Nelson, *The Legitimacy of (Some) Federal Common Law*, 101 VA. L. REV. 1 (2015); Anthony J. Bellia, Jr. & Bradford R. Clark, *General Law in Federal Court*, 54 WM. & MARY L. REV. 655 (2013).

[84] After 1812 the federal courts lacked power to define common-law crimes, but they nonethe-less applied common-law ideas in criminal cases to define defenses such as mistake, entrapment, and duress. They did so on the theory that "Congress in enacting criminal statutes legislates against a background of Anglo-Saxon common law." United States v. Bailey, 444 U.S. 394, 415 n.11 (1980) (Rehnquist, J.). *See, e.g.*, Dan M. Kahan, *Lenity and Federal Common Law Crimes*, 1994 SUP. CT. REV. 345, 367–89.

[85] *Boyle*, 487 U.S. 500 (Scalia, J.); *Semtek*, 531 U.S. 497 (Scalia, J.); *Kirby*, 543 U.S. 14 (O'Connor, J., joined by Scalia, J.); *Musick, Peeler*, 508 U.S. 286 (Kennedy, J., joined by Scalia, J.). *See also* O'Melveny & Myers v. Federal Deposit Insurance Corp., 512 U.S. 79 (1994) (Scalia, J.) (acknowledging power of federal courts to make federal common law though construing the power narrowly and refusing to make law in the case).

[86] *Rogers*, 532 U.S. at 481 (Scalia, J., dissenting).

Although some conservative justices suggested that implying causes of action contravened *Erie*,[87] that case did not support their claim and was, to the contrary, quite consistent with the principle that the federal judicial power authorized the creation of private rights of action.[88] First, in implying a cause of action the Court was creating no new substantive law or right but merely providing a practical remedy for the violation of some preexisting and authoritative constitutional or congressional command. As the Court explained in 1982, if federal law was violated, then "federal courts, following a common-law tradition, regarded the denial of a remedy as the exception rather than the rule."[89]

Second, in implying causes of action the Court was only enforcing constitutional or statutory provisions that were authentically "federal" law, not "general" common-law principles that were beyond federal authority and under *Erie* properly subject to state control. Such judge-made causes of action were authentically "federal" because they were based either on a federal constitutional provision or a federal statute, the two authoritative sources of law that *Erie* expressly excluded from its limitation on the federal judicial power. "Except in matters governed by the Federal Constitution or by Acts of Congress," *Erie* specified, "the law to be applied in any case is the law of the State."[90] Further, those two positive sources of law were of far greater legitimacy and authority than the mere judge-made legal sources—the judicial identification of allegedly "uniquely federal interests"—that Scalia himself was willing to accept as legitimate authority for federal judicial lawmaking.[91]

Third, *Erie* drew no distinction between law and equity, and in its wake the Court quickly applied its principles equally to suits in equity.[92] Consequently,

[87] *E.g.*, "The determination by federal courts of the scope of such a remedy [implied from the Constitution] involves the creation of a body of common law analogous to that repudiated in Erie and Hudson & Goodwin." *Carlson*, 446 U.S. at 39 (Rehnquist, J., dissenting). *Accord Cannon*, 441 U.S. at 745–77 (Powell, J., dissenting) (suggesting that *Erie* meant that implying causes of action was unconstitutional).
[88] For a contrary view, *see, e.g.*, George D. Brown, *Of Activism and Erie—Implication Doctrine's Implications for the Nature and Role of the Federal Courts*, 69 IOWA L. REV. 617 (1984).
[89] Merrill Lynch, Pierce, Fenner & Smith, Inc. v. Curran, 456 U.S. 353, 374–75 (1982) (Stevens, J.). In support, the Court cited *Texas & Pacific Railway Co. v. Rigsby*, 241 U.S. 33 (1916) (Pitney, J.).
[90] *Erie*, 304 U.S. at 78 (Brandeis, J.).
[91] *Boyle*, 487 U.S. at 504 (Scalia, J.). *See also id.* at 505, 507 (1988) (Scalia, J., citing *Texas Industries, Inc. v. Radcliffe Materials, Inc.*, 451 U.S. 630, 640 (1981) (Burger, C.J.). The category of "uniquely federal interests" was both vague and subject to judicial manipulation. Scalia used the concept in *Boyle* to protect government military contractors, but he could readily deny a "uniquely federal interest" when he wished to avoid federal law and uphold a highly restrictive state law that targeted suspected illegal immigrants. Arizona v. United States, 567 U.S. 387, 416, 430 (2012) (Scalia, J., concurring in part and dissenting in part).
[92] *See Erie*, 304 U.S. at 72, n.2 (Brandeis, J.). Immediately after it announced its decision in *Erie*, the Court applied it to a suit in equity. "Inevitably, therefore, the principle of Erie R. Co. v. Tompkins,

since the federal courts had long implied causes of action for injunctive relief against those who threatened to violate federal law,[93] it furnished no reason to deny implied causes of action for legal relief against those who had already violated federal law and injured someone in the process. Unlike the "extraordinary" nature of equitable remedies, moreover, an award of damages was the ordinary remedy of the common law, a remedy available without the special requirements necessary to obtain equitable relief.[94] Further, such a damages award made perfect sense because it was the only remedy that would commonly provide relief to those who had already suffered injury.[95]

Finally, as long as the Court implied causes of action for the violation of positive federal law, *Erie* created no substantial separation-of-powers problem. Congress could always alter or reject such judge-made remedies or substitute its own remedial scheme in their place.[96] To make that obvious, the Court recognized that Congress could alter or eliminate implied causes of

an action at law, was promptly applied to a suit in equity. Ruhlin v. N. Y. Life Ins. Co., 304 U.S. 202." Guaranty Trust Co. v. York, 326 U.S. 99, 107 (1945) (Frankfurter, J.) (holding that *Erie* applied to suits in equity).

[93] An injunction remedy was available against private parties when the normal requirements of equity jurisdiction were met, and it was available against state officials under *Ex parte Young,* 209 U.S. 123 (1908) (Peckham, J.). "In determining whether the doctrine of Ex parte Young avoids an Eleventh Amendment bar to suit, a court need only conduct a 'straightforward inquiry into whether [the] complaint alleges an ongoing violation of federal law and seeks relief properly characterized as prospective.'" *Verizon Maryland,* 535 U.S. at 645 (Scalia, J., quoting *Idaho v. Coeur D'Alene,* 521 U.S. at 296 (O'Connor, J., concurring, joined by Scalia and Thomas, JJ.)). For the long established availability of such relief, *see* M. Collins, *"Economic Rights,"* 1517–25; Woolhandler, *Patterns,* 448–49. For his part, Scalia sought to limit the availability of such injunctive relief by emphasizing that the *Ex parte Young* remedy was based on traditional equity, not on the Constitution, and consequently that the Court could construe congressional statutes to limit or foreclose its availability and that its availability could also be limited by the exercise of judicial discretion. Armstrong v. Exceptional Child Center, Inc., 135 S. Ct. 1378 (2015) (Scalia, J.).

[94] Equitable remedies were not available unless, among other considerations, there was "no adequate remedy at law" and the injury defendant threatened would be "irreparable." *See, e.g.,* eBay, Inc. v. MercExchange, LLC, 547 U.S. 388, 391 (2006) (Thomas, J.).

[95] In implied cause-of-action cases plaintiffs were almost invariably seeking damages for defendants' past acts, and hence equitable relief would provide no practical remedy for their injuries. Concurring in *Bivens,* Justice Harlan made this precise point: "[I]f a general grant of jurisdiction to the federal courts by Congress is thought adequate to empower a federal court to grant equitable relief for all areas of subject-matter jurisdiction enumerated therein, see 28 U.S.C. § 1331 (a), then it seems to me that the same statute is sufficient to empower a federal court to grant a traditional remedy at law." *Bivens,* 403 U.S. at 405 (Harlan, J., concurring). Justice Rehnquist disputed the point, claiming that the equity precedents had no bearing on the issue of damages actions. *Carlson,* 446 U.S. at 42–44 (Rehnquist, J., dissenting).

[96] *See, e.g., Chilicky,* 487 U.S. at 423 (O'Connor, J.); Bush v. Lucas, 462 U.S. at 372–73, 378 (Stevens, J.).

AN ABANDONED JURISPRUDENCE 219

action even when the Court based those rights of action on the Constitution itself.[97]

Thus, Scalia's oft-repeated claim that the federal judicial power did not authorize the creation of implied causes of action for damages drew no support from *Erie* and, more fundamentally, constituted an abandonment of originalism, something he was ready to do when originalism no longer served his purposes. The original public meaning of the federal judicial power was drawn from the common-law tradition, as he acknowledged, and following that tradition federal judges had for a century and a half employed various common-law powers and practices to make law, including implying remedies for those injured by the violation of a federal statute or threatened with injury by the violation of a constitutional provision.[98] Quite to the point, he openly acknowledged that the late twentieth-century federal common-law power that he accepted and applied was "not our Framers' general common law."[99]

In 2004 Scalia made his abandonment of originalism explicit. In *Sosa v. Alvarez-Machain*,[100] he sought to prevent the federal courts from incorporating elements of customary international law into the post-*Erie* federal common law and to deny their power to create new causes of action under that law.[101] In *Sosa* a Mexican citizen had sued Mexican and American defendants under the Alien Tort Statute,[102] claiming that the defendants had violated his rights under international law by kidnapping him, transporting him to the United States, and arresting him there for the murder of a federal agent. Six justices agreed that the Alien Tort Statute allowed federal courts to hear claims based on customary international law, but they also ruled that

<hr>

[97] *Bivens*, 403 U.S. at 396–97 (Brennan, J.); Bush v. Lucas, 462 U.S. at 377–78 (Stevens, J.). Scalia, of course, saw common-law lawmaking by the federal courts as posing a separation-of-powers problem. Scalia, *Common-Law Courts*, 85–86. For commentary on the principle's application, including an introductory essay by Scalia, *see Symposium: Separation of Powers as a Safeguard of Federalism*, 83 NOTRE DAME L. REV. 1417 (2008).

[98] "A disregard of the command of the statute is a wrongful act, and where it results in damage to one of the class for whose especial benefit the statute was enacted, the right to recover the damages from the party in default is implied, according to a doctrine of the common law expressed in 1 Com. Dig., tit." *Rigsby*, 241 U.S. at 39 (Pitney, J.). The classic example of the implied right to equitable relief against government officials is *Ex parte Young*, 209 U.S. 123 (1908) (Peckham, J.).

[99] *Sosa*, 542 U.S. at 746 (Scalia, J., concurring in part and concurring in the judgment).

[100] *Sosa*, 542 U.S. 692 (2004) (Souter, J.).

[101] The discussion of Scalia's opinion in *Sosa* is drawn from Edward A. Purcell, Jr., *History, Ideology, and* Erie v. Tompkins, *in* INTERNATIONAL LAW IN THE U.S. SUPREME COURT 499–504. On *Sosa* itself, *see* the careful analysis in John O. McGinnis, Sosa *and the Derivation of Customary International Law* in *id.* at 481–93.

[102] 28 U.S.C. Section 1350.

customary international law provided for only three quite narrow causes of action and that, for a variety of prudential reasons, the courts should create new ones under its aegis only in exceptional circumstances. Under that principle, they denied plaintiff's claim.[103]

Scalia concurred in the judgment denying relief, but he disputed the Court's conclusion that it had power to create new claims under customary international law. In doing so, he based his opinion on *Erie*, the case that rejected the Founders' views of the lawmaking powers of the federal courts and, in Scalia's own words, made an "avulsive change" in original and traditional understandings of the lawmaking power of the federal courts.[104] He argued that the majority in *Sosa* wholly misconstrued the nature of the federal judicial power and transgressed the fundamental principles that *Erie* established. *Erie* not only "extirpated" the old "general" federal common law, he maintained, but it also established two basic principles: first, that federal courts could only make law when they were operating under authentically "federal" authority and, second, that a mere statutory grant of jurisdiction did not by itself confer substantive lawmaking power over cases within that jurisdiction.[105] Thus, he argued, *Erie* established that the Court had no power to create new causes of action based on either customary international law or the congressional grant of jurisdiction that the federal courts exercised under the Alien Tort Statute.

Scalia's *Erie* arguments were sound and powerful, but they were twentieth-century arguments that rejected original understandings. In *Sosa* Scalia not only embraced *Erie* and its "avulsive change" in federal jurisprudence, but he did so on explicitly nonoriginalist grounds. Because there had been many other changes in both customary international law and federal common law since 1789, he argued, it was necessary for him to address the issue of a federal lawmaking power anew and consider it in its modern historical context.[106] Thus, he not only accepted an "avulsive change" that rejected the Founders' view of the common law but also accepted the idea that legal concepts and principles had to be altered to meet changed historical conditions. His position expressly abandoned originalism.

---

[103] *Sosa*, 542 U.S. at 712, 725–28, 732–33 736–37 (Souter, J.).

[104] *Sosa*, 542 U.S. at 744, 749 (Scalia, J., concurring in part and concurring in the judgment).

[105] *Sosa*, 542 U.S. at 741 ("extirpated"), 742, 744 (federal authority required), and 744 (jurisdictional statute insufficient for substantive lawmaking) (Scalia, J., concurring in part and concurring in the judgment).

[106] *Sosa*, 542 U.S. at 744–46, 749–50 & n.* (Scalia, J., concurring in part and concurring in the judgment).

Recognizing his jurisprudential inconsistency, Scalia made an unconvincing and far-fetched attempt to deny that abandonment by offering an entirely ahistorical and speculative theory to reconcile his use of *Erie* with his purported originalism. He imagined that the Founders would have agreed with his views if they had been confronted by the changed historical conditions that the modern Court faced. "Despite the avulsive change of *Erie*," he hypothesized, "the Framers who included reference to 'the Law of Nations' in Article I, § 8, cl. 10, of the Constitution would be entirely content with the post-*Erie* system I have described."[107] Thus, if any originalism remained in his jurisprudence dealing with the federal judicial power, it was a purely imaginary originalism wholly inconsistent with the historically based originalist jurisprudence that he constantly promoted. In truth, however, it was not originalism at all, but a version of "living" constitutionalism based first on the principle that rules and ideas should change as conditions changed, and second on the hypothetical contention that the Founders would agree with such changes if only they were still around some two hundred years later.

In relying on *Erie*, moreover, Scalia even misconstrued the original understanding of the original doctrine that *Erie* had repudiated. While acknowledging that *Erie* changed the nature of federal judicial lawmaking power, he ignored the fact that the "general" law that *Erie* "extirpated" had itself been evolving and was not, as Scalia seemed to suggest, a fixed category of unchanging elements. In fact, between 1789 and 1938 the content of "general" law underwent massive changes. Its scope expanded in some ways and narrowed in others. In one direction the pre-*Erie* "general" law ballooned broadly over the decades as courts pushed more than two dozen common-law fields into its realm, leading the Court in 1888 to confess embarrassment at its inability to clearly define and limit its scope.[108] In the other direction the scope of the "general" law was also reduced during the same years as state legislatures created increasing numbers of "local" statutory laws that trumped "general" common-law rules in the federal courts and narrowed some of the issues it governed.[109]

---

[107] *Sosa*, 542 U.S. at 749 (Scalia, J., concurring in part and concurring in the judgment).

[108] Bucher v. Cheshire Railroad Co., 125 U.S. 555, 583 (1888) (Miller, J.). On the expansion of "general" law, *see, e.g.*, ARMISTEAD M. DOBIE, HANDBOOK OF FEDERAL JURISDICTION AND PROCEDURE 557–78 (1928).

[109] EDWARD A. PURCELL, JR., LITIGATION AND INEQUALITY: FEDERAL DIVERSITY JURISDICTION IN INDUSTRIAL AMERICA, 1870–1958, at 60 (1992).

By far most telling, however, the Court itself narrowed the scope of the "general" law by transforming some of the issues it encompassed into authentically "federal" issues by finding that they fell within the reach of congressional statutes and constitutional provisions. Examples abounded. Admiralty law was part of the "general" maritime law in the eighteenth century, but by the early twentieth century the Court had transformed it into "federal" law based on the Constitution and a statutory grant of jurisdiction.[110] Similarly, the law of interstate disputes had been regarded as a matter of "general" law based in part on customary international law, but in the early twentieth century the Court incorporated that matter into "federal" law on the basis of another jurisdictional statute and implications from the constitutional structure.[111] Again, issues of personal jurisdiction and conflicts of laws were considered subjects of "general" law until the Court partially constitutionalized both areas in the nineteenth century.[112] Finally, beginning in the 1890s the Court used the Fourteenth Amendment to constitutionalize the "general" law of limitations on government that had developed during the preceding decades.[113] Thus, over the course of more than a century the Court shifted many subjects from the category of "general" law into the category of authentically "federal" law by deciding that they properly came within the constitutional authority of the national government. What *Erie* did, then, was "extirpate" the category of "general" law, but it did not define the content of that category. *Erie* neither repudiated the Court's prior incorporations of "general" law issues into the "federal" law category nor prohibited the Court from making new incorporations in the future as long as the incorporated issues fell within the constitutional authority of the national government.

Thus, what *Erie* did was complex, but for the substantive rules of customary international law and the rights of action it authorized it did nothing that was conclusive. It determined that some elements placed within the category of "general" law in 1938, such as ordinary contracts and torts, were beyond the lawmaking authority of the national government and hence beyond the lawmaking authority of the federal judiciary.[114] It did not, however,

---

[110] *E.g.*, Southern Pac. Co. v. Jensen, 244 U.S. 205 (1917) (McReynolds, J.); Chelentis v. Luckenbach Steam Ship Co., 247 U.S. 372 (1918) (McReynolds, J.); Knickerbocker Ice Co. v. Stewart, 253 U.S. 149 (1920) (McReynolds, J.).

[111] *E.g.*, Kansas v. Colorado, 206 U.S. 46 (1907) (Brewer, J.); *Hinderlider*, 304 U.S. 92 (Brandeis, J.).

[112] *See, e.g.*, Michael D. Ramsey, *Customary International Law in the Supreme Court, 1901–1945*, in INTERNATIONAL LAW IN THE U.S. SUPREME COURT, 235–36.

[113] Michael G. Collins, *October Term, 1896—Embracing Due Process*, 45 AM. J. LEGAL HIST. 71 (2001).

[114] *Erie*, 304 U.S. at 78 (Brandeis, J.).

determine that all the various issues covered by customary international law were necessarily and forever "general," nor did it determine that the Court was powerless to incorporate any of them into "federal" law if there were proper constitutional or statutory bases for asserting federal control over them. Indeed, *Erie* could not have done so because such a ruling would have contradicted its fundamental premise that the constitutional authority of the federal government marked the outer boundary of the lawmaking power of the federal judiciary. Thus, contrary to Scalia's assertion, *Erie* left untouched the Court's long-exercised power to incorporate selected issues of customary international law as long as those elements fell within federal lawmaking power.

After *Erie*, in fact, the Court continued to make judgments about whether it should incorporate issues covered by the old "general" law into post-*Erie* "federal" common law. It decided that conflict-of-laws rules should not be incorporated,[115] for example, but that personal jurisdiction rules should be.[116] Similarly, while *Erie* determined that the old "general" commercial law fell for the most part outside of federal authority, it nonetheless held in *Clearfield Trust Co. v. United States*[117] that one part of that commercial common law— the part governing the commercial paper of the federal government—lay within federal power and thus was properly part of post-*Erie* federal judge-made law. Again, in 1897 the Court had regarded the "act of state" doctrine as a matter of "general" law,[118] but in 1964 it incorporated that doctrine into post-*Erie* and authentically "federal" judge-made law.[119]

Scalia's efforts to limit the federal judicial power and deny the lawmaking authority of the federal courts were particularly illuminating, for they threw into clear relief both the inconsistent nature of his jurisprudential reasoning and the consistent nature of the social and political results he sought. His jurisprudence in the area rejected the original understanding of both the nature of the common law and the scope of the federal judicial power, and in their place it embraced the "avulsive change" that *Erie* wrought and accepted its distinctly nonoriginalist, twentieth-century positivism. His social and political goals in the area, however, were the same as those he pursued in so many other areas. He sought to restrict the power of the federal courts, deny

---

[115] Klaxon v. Stentor Electric Manufacturing Co., 313 U.S. 487 (1941) (Reed, J.).
[116] International Shoe Co. v. Washington, 326 U.S. 310 (1945) (Stone, C.J.).
[117] Clearfield Trust Co. v. United States, 318 U.S. 363 (1943) (Douglas, J.).
[118] Underhill v. Hernandez, 168 U.S. 250 (1897) (Fuller, C.J.).
[119] Banco Nacional de Cuba v. Sabbatino, 376 U.S. 398 (1964) (Harlan, J.).

their authority to provide remedies for those injured by violations of federal law, bar a wide variety of individual claimants from the courts, relieve business and government of liability for many of their wrongdoings, and repudiate another central element of the Warren Court's legacy.

Scalia's jurisprudence addressing the federal judicial power was anything but originalist, textualist, or traditionalist. It demonstrated the fact that, when originalism did not serve his purposes, he was more than ready to abandon it. His originalism, textualism, and traditionalism, like his other rhetorical tools, were for occasions when useful, and for the most part it was his personal goals and values that identified those occasions.

PART III
HISTORICAL FIGURE

10

The Methodological Fallacy

Introduction: Antonin Scalia as a Historical Figure

There seems little doubt that Antonin Scalia will go down in American constitutional history as one of the U.S. Supreme Court's most outspoken, important, and influential justices. He brought originalism to the fore in debates
over constitutional interpretation and forced judges, lawyers, and scholars
to consider it seriously, whether they accepted or rejected it. Similarly with
textualism, an interpretive approach that he made newly prominent and perhaps even dominant in statutory interpretation. He was equally influential
on many substantive legal issues, and his forceful arguments helped reshape
the law in a variety of areas from basic structural issues about the powers of
government to the individual rights protected by the Bill of Rights and the
Fourteenth Amendment.

To what extent his contributions to constitutional and statutory interpretation will continue to exert a powerful influence and to what extent the specific legal positions he advanced will prevail are questions only the future can
answer. To the extent that the controversial issues he addressed remain in the
forefront of legal and political debate, his ideas and opinions will likely remain vital and perhaps prove triumphant. To the extent that those issues fade
in importance, change in political salience, or fragment contemporary party
coalitions, they may wane in influence, come to serve new rhetorical uses, or
exert an appeal to unanticipated groups and unexpected causes.

Notwithstanding unknowable future developments, Scalia's overall career
and jurisprudence have a clarion significance that is identifiable at present
and will surely stand the test of time. Whatever the future holds and however
his reputation rises or falls, he will remain an unusually illuminating figure
because he exemplified in striking form three fundamental and intrinsic
characteristics of American constitutionalism: the inherent inadequacy of
formal and mechanical methods of interpretation, the fusion of constitutional jurisprudence with the personal and political, and the dynamic and
living nature of American constitutionalism itself.

Antonin Scalia and American Constitutionalism. Edward A. Purcell, Jr., Oxford University Press (2020).
© Edward A. Purcell, Jr.
DOI: 10.1093/oso/9780197508763.001.0001

This chapter examines Scalia's paradigmatic role in exemplifying the first of those characteristics, while the following two chapters consider the second and third.

The Methodological Fallacy

The multitude of issues Scalia faced on the bench tested his methods of originalism and textualism, and his resulting actions on the Supreme Court over some thirty years support two overarching conclusions. One is that his methods were largely indeterminate, highly elastic, easily manipulable, and readily ignored. The second is that they exemplified the methodological fallacy that recurs among many American constitutionalists, the wholly understandable but nonetheless fatally mistaken claim that there is some determinate method or methods that can reliably and consistently produce correct interpretations of the Constitution on reasonably contested issues.

Scalia's jurisprudence was one more attempt in the long line of efforts that began in 1789 to claim interpretive authority to pronounce the "correct" meaning of the Constitution, and in more recent history it represented yet another attempt to overcome the skeptical and relativistic insights that triumphed with the coming of legal realism in the early twentieth century. By the end of World War II most American legal thinkers acknowledged the uncertainties that marked much of the law, especially constitutional law, and they recognized that judges exercised varying degrees of discretion in interpreting and applying legal rules and principles. They recognized, too, that personal, political, and ideological influences could and did help shape the ways that judges exercised that discretion. The challenge that jurisprudential theorists faced was to develop effective ways to eliminate or somehow reasonably constrain that discretion and thereby preserve the ideal and practice of a fair and orderly rule of law under an authoritative written Constitution.

Most of those commentators quickly came to recognize that the law could not eliminate judicial discretion entirely, and they focused their efforts on developing theories and methods to minimize and channel that discretion. In the 1940s Justice Felix Frankfurter urged a stringent version of "judicial restraint," while Justice Hugo L. Black urged an originalism tied closely to the text of the Constitution.[1] Later generations of theorists—from Learned

---

[1] See, e.g., JAMES F. SIMON, THE ANTAGONISTS: HUGO BLACK, FELIX FRANKFURTER AND CIVIL LIBERTIES IN MODERN AMERICA (1989).

Hand, Herbert Wechsler, and Henry Hart, Jr., through Alexander M. Bickel, John Hart Ely, and Ronald Dworkin to untold numbers of others who followed in later decades—advanced a variety of theories purporting to integrate the reality of judicial discretion with the normative demands of a knowable and predetermined constitutional rule of law.[2]

The challenge those theorists faced was hardly a matter of mere abstract or academic concern, and in the 1950s it became a central and continuing focus in national politics. Critics of the Supreme Court had from the early days of the republic charged the justices with distorting or ignoring the Constitution to serve their own political goals, but such accusations became ever more common in the second half of the twentieth century with the emergence of the Warren Court and its explosive decision ending school segregation in *Brown v. Board of Education*.[3] From that point on criticism of the Court—and the whole federal judiciary— escalated and sometimes reached savage levels. "The Warren Court became Richard Nixon's quarry," Laura Kalman wrote. "He used it to win election in 1968 and to unify, shape, and broaden the modern Republican Party."[4] With Nixon's presidential campaign Republicans began regularly denouncing the Court for "legislating" rather than "interpreting" the law,[5] and the Court came to feature prominently as an issue in national elections. Republicans consistently condemned "judicial activism," while Democrats tacked between defending the Court's decisions and countering with charges that the "real" judicial activists were the Court's conservative justices.

Beginning in the 1970s Scalia jumped feet first into the debate. "[E]ver since the presidential candidacy of Richard Nixon," he agreed, "use of the judicial appointment power has been a prominent *election* issue." In his view the reason was simple and the villain clear. Judicial liberals and their ideas of a "living Constitution" had politicized the law and the courts, especially the federal courts. Consequently, "Nixon and subsequent Republican

---

[2] *See generally* NEIL DUXBURY, PATTERNS OF AMERICAN JURISPRUDENCE (1995); Edward A. Purcell, Jr., *Alexander M. Bickel and the Post-Realist Constitution*, 11 HARV. CIV. RIGHTS/CIV. LIB. L. REV. 521 (1976). For a view of the jurisprudential landscape from the vantage point of the early 1980s before Scalia took his seat on the Court, *see, e.g.*, Dallin H. Oaks, *Judicial Activism*, 7 HARV. J.L. & PUB. POL'Y 1 (1984).

[3] Brown v. Board of Education of Topeka, Kansas, 347 U.S. 483 (1954) (Warren, C.J.).

[4] LAURA KALMAN, THE LONG REACH OF THE SIXTIES: LBJ, NIXON, AND THE MAKING OF THE CONTEMPORARY SUPREME COURT, ix (2017).

[5] *See, e.g.*, JAMES F. SIMON, IN HIS OWN IMAGE: THE SUPREME COURT IN RICHARD NIXON'S AMERICA (1973).

presidential candidates have promised to appoint so-called non-activist judges to the Supreme Court," he explained, "and their Democratic opponents have promised to appoint justices who will uphold *Roe v. Wade*, which is synonymous with judicial activism."[6]

In responding to ideas of a "living Constitution" and what he condemned as the politicization of law and the courts, Scalia sought to demonstrate that his jurisprudence provided a way to severely restrict and perhaps even largely eliminate judicial discretion. Originalism and textualism, he repeatedly maintained, offered a way to counter judicial "subjectivity" and ensure an "objective" application of the law. Scorning tests that involved "inherently political, moral judgment," he claimed that his originalism was the "antithesis" of such methods, "an objective approach that reaches conclusions by applying neutral rules to verifiable evidence."[7] If judges honestly applied that approach, their decisions would no longer be infected with personal values but would, instead, flow properly from the established law that the Constitution and statutes ordained. Those methods promised to resolve the central dilemma of American constitutionalism. "The most important" reason for rejecting ideas of a "living Constitution," he declared, was that "only the traditional view that the meaning of the Constitution does not change places any real constraints upon the decisions of future members of Congress or future judges."[8]

The seemingly straightforward, plausible, and highly appealing nature of his claims made his originalist jurisprudence appear to many wholly credible and practically necessary. The idea that the Constitution had a predetermined and true meaning that Americans could discover and faithfully follow was immensely heartening and seemed to guarantee that republican government and individual freedoms would forever prevail in the United States. Indeed,

---

[6] ANTONIN SCALIA, SCALIA SPEAKS: REFLECTIONS ON LAW, FAITH, AND LIFE WELL LIVED 226 (emphasis in original), 227 (Christopher J. Scalia & Edward Whelan eds., 2017) [hereafter SCALIA SPEAKS]. To Scalia's credit, he called the Republican nominees "so-called non-activist judges."

[7] McDonald v. City of Chicago, 561 U.S. 742, 791, 800 (2010) (Scalia, J., concurring). Scalia made slightly different claims about the "objective" nature of originalism, but at a minimum he insisted that it was far better than any nonoriginalist method. The "question to be decided is not whether the historically-focused method is a *perfect means* of restraining aristocratic judicial Constitution-writing; but whether is it the *best means available* in an imperfect world," he declared from the high bench. "I think it beyond all serious dispute that it is much less subjective, and intrudes much less upon the democratic process" than do approaches based on the idea of a "living Constitution." *Id.* at 803–04 (emphasis in original). *Accord* SCALIA SPEAKS, 210–12; ANTONIN SCALIA & BRYAN A. GARNER, READING LAW: THE INTERPRETATION OF LEGAL TEXTS 89 (2014) [hereafter SCALIA, READING]. Scalia's attack on both legislative history and the use of foreign law was based on the same goal of minimizing judicial discretion. SCALIA SPEAKS, 234–42, 253–57.

[8] SCALIA SPEAKS, 221.

the idea seemed to promise the continuation of the nation's popular form of government and to ensure its operation under a secure and unchallengeable rule of law. The force and certainty with which Scalia urged his jurisprudential theories, moreover, helped convince many that he had, indeed, found the philosopher's stone of American constitutional law.

He had not. "Certitude," Justice Oliver Wendell Holmes, Jr., famously noted, "is not the test of certainty."[9] The problem was not that Scalia's methods were illegitimate or unhelpful in interpreting the Constitution and statutes but that they were limited, imprecise, and wholly inadequate to accomplish what he promised. They could not eliminate judicial discretion, and—perhaps more important—they could easily be used to disguise and expand that discretion. They could not guarantee an objectively "correct" interpretation of the law, and they could not resolve large numbers of legal issues, especially those that divided the Founders themselves and those that changing times and conditions continually brought to the Court. Most important, those methods were themselves not "objective," for originalism and textualism—and Scalia's versions of traditionalism as well—provided flexible and manipulable standards that possessed no predefined authoritative character and prescribed no exact or disciplined operational "method." Indeed, all three were interpretive approaches that judges and commentators had used for centuries in diverse and shifting ways, along with other interpretive methods, just as Scalia in fact used them. Revealingly, he wrote a weighty book identifying seventy separate "canons"—that is, general guidelines for addressing textual problems—for interpreting constitutional and statutory sources, a book that not only implicitly acknowledged the discretion that existed in textual interpretation but also seemed to offer inconsistent instructions for interpreting and applying those canons.[10]

---

[9] Oliver Wendell Holmes, Jr., *Natural Law, in* OLIVER WENDELL HOLMES, JR., COLLECTED LEGAL PAPERS 311 (1920).

[10] SCALIA, READING. *See* BRUCE ALLEN MURPHY, SCALIA: A COURT OF ONE, ch. 26 (2014) [hereafter MURPHY, SCALIA]. For a highly critical evaluation of Scalia's book on the "canons" of interpretation, *see* Richard A. Posner, *The Incoherence of Antonin Scalia,* THE NEW REPUBLIC, Aug. 24, 2102; and for a brief sample of the extended controversy that developed over the book, *see* Bryan A. Garner & Richard A. Posner, *How Nuanced Is Justice Scalia's Judicial Philosophy? An Exchange,* THE NEW REPUBLIC, Sept. 10, 2012; Ed Whelan, *Richard A. Posner's Badly Confused Attack on Scalia/Garner—* Part 1, NATIONAL REVIEW, Aug. 31, 2012; Richard Posner, *Richard Posner Responds to Antonin Scalia's Accusation of Lying,* THE NEW REPUBLIC, Sept. 20, 2012. On inherent problems with the canons of statutory construction, *see, e.g.,* Karl Llewellyn, *Remarks on the Theory of Appellate Decision and the Rules or Canons About How Statutes Are to Be Construed,* 3 VAND. L. REV. 395 (1950); MICHAEL SINCLAIR, KARL LLEWELLYN'S DUELING CANONS IN PERSPECTIVE (2014); Anita S. Krishnakuman, *Dueling Canons,* 65 DUKE L.J. 909 (2016).

Originalism and textualism may, of course, sometimes provide sound and efficacious answers to constitutional questions. On particular issues the text might be quite explicit or the relevant historical evidence overwhelming, consistent, and legitimately on point.[11] Those questions, however, are the ones that in virtually all instances have long been settled.

Originalism and textualism, however, could not and did not resolve the perennial questions that Americans have repeatedly debated over the course of the nation's history, nor could they resolve most of the novel and unsettled ones that arose from divisive new contexts, conditions, and challenges.[12] Though some present and future judges will surely employ Scalia's rhetoric and some will also support his substantive views and values, it seems highly doubtful that any of them will follow his proclaimed methods with any consistency.[13] Like Scalia himself, they will likely do so for the most part only when those methods prove useful in advancing their own "conscientious and informed convictions." Indeed, of the conservative justices with whom Scalia served on the Court only Justice Thomas accepted originalism as a general interpretive method, and even he disagreed with Scalia's constitutional interpretations on many issues. Quite noticeably, the other justices on the Court—including the other conservatives—kept a considerable distance from originalism while acknowledging its shortcomings.[14]

Despite Scalia's many confident assertions, his career demonstrated that his jurisprudence was not objective and that he used it in his own particular,

---

[11] For advocacy of a truly informed and sophisticated historical originalism, *see, e.g.*, Saul Cornell, *Reading the Constitution, 1787–91: History, Originalism, and Constitutional Meaning*, 37 L. & HIST. REV. 821 (2019).

[12] Over the course of the nineteenth century, for example, religious conflict was one of the forces that drove fundamental changes in constitutional law and pushed it far from the views of the Founders and their "original" ideas. *See, e.g.*, SARAH BARRINGER GORDON, THE MORMON QUESTION: POLYGAMY AND CONSTITUTIONAL CONFLICT IN NINETEENTH CENTURY AMERICA (2002); Nathan B. Oman, *Natural Law and the Rhetoric of Empire: Reynolds v. United States, Polygamy, and Imperialism*, 88 WASH. U. L. REV. 661 (2011).

[13] Some originalists would surely disagree. The "judges who were nurtured in the Federalist Society," wrote originalist John O. McGinnis, were "likely to continue a revolution of formalism in both statutory and constitutional interpretation." John O. McGinnis, *Meet the Federalist Society Caucus*, available at https://lawliberty.org/2018/11/21/meet-the-federalist-society-caucus (last consulted July 20, 2019).

[14] "I don't know how much progress I've made on originalism," Scalia acknowledged in 2013. Although it had become "more respectable" generally, "there's still only two justices up here who are thoroughgoing originalists." Jennifer Senior, *In Conversation: Antonin Scalia*, NEW YORK MAGAZINE, Oct. 6, 2013, *available at* http://nymag.com/nymag/features/antonin-scalia-2013-10/index7.html (last consulted July 20, 2019). When Scalia appealed to originalism in a First Amendment case involving video games, for example, conservative Justice Samuel Alito poked fun at his effort. "Well, I think what Justice Scalia wants to know is what James Madison thought about video games. Did he enjoy them?" LAURENCE TRIBE & JOSHUA MATZ, UNCERTAIN JUSTICE: THE ROBERTS COURT AND THE CONSTITUTION 142 (2014).

inconsistent, and purposeful ways. Infusing his own specific content into un-exceptionable generalizations and guiding their interpretation and applica-tion, his personal views and values gave those generalities their particular form and determined their practical meaning. Sometimes his jurisprudence led to legal and political conclusions that were persuasive or at least plausible, but at other times they supported conclusions that were neither necessary nor impersonal. In most cases they reflected not the results of a truly "objec-tive" method but only the results of impressive technical skills warped by the compelling gravitational pull of his own political, social, and moral views.

Scalia's jurisprudence incorporated a number of principles that seemed plausible at first glance but dubious on reflection and often arbitrary in ap-plication. First, and most fundamental, was his foundational claim about "original public meaning" itself, a claim that seemed commonsensical but seldom withstood careful scrutiny on contested issues. The history of rati-fication and the nation's earliest decades demonstrated that the text of the Constitution simply did not answer a good many critical questions. Beyond agreement about the meaning of certain specific provisions, the Founders shared little consensus on a sweeping range of issues.[15] It was for that reason that, immediately after ratification, the members of the founding generation split and their conflicts turned the decade of the 1790s into one of extended partisan strife.[16] Throughout the nation's subsequent history, disputes over many of those same constitutional issues—and an ever multiplying number of new ones that the Founders could never have imagined—continued to erupt. Claims by later generations about the Constitution's "original public meaning" represented for the most part merely shrewd practical formulations confected to serve their changing contemporary purposes. Thus, the foundational truth was that there was simply no "original public meaning" that provided clear, correct, and specifically directive answers to

[15] See, e.g., JACK N. RAKOVE, ORIGINAL MEANINGS: POLITICS AND IDEAS IN THE MAKING OF THE CONSTITUTION (1996).

[16] "Translating the words of the Constitution into practice, it would appear, was an act of crea-tivity hardly less impressive or disputatious than framing the document in the first place. The neces-sities of governing, rather than quieting disagreements over the Constitution, only escalated the debate." R. KENT NEWMYER, JOHN MARSHALL AND THE HEROIC AGE OF THE SUPREME COURT 70 (2001). For disputes that immediately arose in the early Congresses, see JONATHAN GIENAPP, THE SECOND CREATION: FIXING THE AMERICAN CONSTITUTION IN THE FOUNDING ERA (2018) [hereafter GIENAPP, SECOND CREATION], and on the extreme partisanship and political violence of the 1790s, see, e.g., JAMES ROGER SHARP, AMERICAN POLITICS IN THE EARLY REPUBLIC: THE NEW NATION IN CRISIS (1993); John R. Howe, Jr., Republican Thought and Political Violence of the 1790s, 19 AM. Q. 147 (1967); Marshall Smelser, The Federalist Period as an Age of Passion, 10 AM. Q. 391 (1958).

most, if not all, of the legitimately contested constitutional questions that persisted or newly arose.

Second, Scalia advanced a "purpose principle" positing that originalism was the Constitution's methodological requirement because the very point of a written constitution was to prevent change. Consequently, he maintained, the Constitution's original meaning must always prevail. "A constitution is designed to provide not flexibility but rigidity," he insisted, and above all "*it does not change*."[17] Indeed, he emphasized, "its whole purpose is to prevent change—to embed certain rights in such a manner that future generations cannot take them away."[18] His "purpose principle" was both arbitrary and overgeneral.

It was arbitrary because the Constitution served not just one purpose but many. It sought to create a central government capable of acting with "energy," establish a complex governmental structure to channel that energy, mandate adherence to core republican political principles, enshrine certain fundamental human values, and achieve the highly practical and desirable social goals identified in its Preamble. All those purposes demonstrated that the Constitution was also and necessarily designed to enable the nation to deal with the problems it would face in an unknowable future and to meet whatever new conditions and challenges that future might bring. Thus, contrary to Scalia's assertions, the Constitution had many purposes, and one of its paramount purposes was to enable succeeding generations to adapt its provisions to meet those new challenges and fulfill those animating purposes.

Scalia's "purpose principle" was overgeneral because the Constitution was not designed to prevent all changes but only some changes. Indeed, it specifically mandated some changes,[19] and it authorized many others, including

[17] SCALIA SPEAKS, 207, 368 (emphasis in original). *Accord id.* at 221, 227, 265. The Constitution "has a fixed meaning ascertainable through the usual devices familiar to those learned in the law." Antonin Scalia, *Originalism: The Lesser Evil*, 57 U. CINCINNATI L. REV. 849, 854 (1989). Scalia, for example, scorned the Court's earlier statement that the Eighth Amendment "must draw its meaning from the evolving standards of decency that mark the progress of a maturing society." Trop v. Dulles, 356 U.S. 86, 101 (1958) (Warren, C.J.). That statement, he declared, "has caused more mischief to our jurisprudence, to our federal system, and to our society than any other that comes to mind." Glossip v. Gross, 135 S. Ct. 2726, 2746, 2749 (2015) (Scalia, J., concurring).

[18] ANTONIN SCALIA, A MATTER OF INTERPRETATION: FEDERAL COURTS AND THE LAW 40 (1997). The very "purpose of a constitution" is "antievolutionary." *Id.* at 44. In this book, Scalia repeated his statements from Antonin Scalia, *Common-Law Courts in a Civil-Law System: The Role of United States Federal Courts in Interpreting the Constitution and Laws*, THE TANNER LECTURES ON HUMAN VALUES, Princeton University, March 8 and 9, 1995, at 114, 118 [hereafter Scalia, *Common-Law Courts*].

[19] The Constitution mandated regular elections, provided for changes in the House of Representatives and the Electoral College as population changed, and mandated a decennial census to ensure their regular reapportionment. U.S. CONST. art. I, sec. 2, para. 3 (House and census); art. II, sec. 1, para. 2 (electoral college).

changes in the structure of government itself.[20] Centrally, it provided for the separation of powers and the possibility of checks and balances, but it could not and did not provide any instructions for the practical operation of those checks and balances. While separation of powers was a structural fact, the principle of checks and balances was something quite different, an abstract political aspiration. It was a hope that future generations would be able to tack among the levels and branches as best they could to maintain a salutary republican balance amid continuous and unpredictable developments. "It is impossible," the staunchly conservative Chief Justice William Howard Taft wrote more than a hundred years ago, "to avoid a twilight zone in the division of powers between the three branches which in their practical exercise constantly create controversy."[21] Equally important, the Constitution did not specify the meaning of many of its key terms and provisions, and instead employed general and abstract language that invited adaptive interpretations. Thus, the Founders did not make the slightest attempt to define and mandate changeless meanings. Finally, the Constitution did not specify how its republican principles and values were to be honored in new contexts and under altered conditions, nor—even more apparent—did it specify how those principles and values were to be interpreted when they came into conflict with one another, as they inevitably would and did.

Third, Scalia often relied on a "silence principle" mandating that, if the Constitution did not specifically mention a subject, then courts could not deal with it as a matter of constitutional law.[22] He argued, for example, that the Court should return the issue of abortion to the people "where the Constitution, by its silence on the subject, left it."[23] Scalia's close friend and co-author Bryan Garner explained the justice's silence principle

---

[20] E.g., Congress was given broad power to structure both the executive branch, U.S. CONST. art. II, sec. 2, para.2, and the federal judiciary, id. art. III, sec. 1 & sec. 2, para. 2, and also the power to admit new states to the Union, id., art. IV, sec. 3, para. 2, a cause of major changes in the operations of the federal structure that the Founders expressly anticipated. See EDWARD A. PURCELL, JR., ORIGINALISM, FEDERALISM, AND THE AMERICAN CONSTITUTIONAL ENTERPRISE: A HISTORICAL INQUIRY, ch. 7 (2007).

[21] William Howard Taft, The Boundaries Between the Executive, the Legislative and the Judicial Branches of the Government, 25 YALE L.J. 599, 600 (1916).

[22] E.g., Cruzan v. Missouri Department of Health, 497 U.S. 261, 292, 293 (1990) (Scalia, J., concurring); Romer v. Evans, 517 U.S. 620, 636 (1996) (Scalia, dissenting); Obergefell v. Hodges, 135 S. Ct. 2584, 2626, 2628 (2015) (Scalia, J., dissenting); NASA v. Nelson, 562 U.S. 134, 160, 162 (2011) (Scalia, J., concurring in the judgment). The Constitution was not perfect, he explained, and it did not remedy all possible evils. "In sum, it is simply untenable that there must be a judicial remedy for every constitutional violation." Webster v. Doe, 486 U.S. 592, 606, 613 (1988) (Scalia, J., dissenting). Accord SCALIA SPEAKS, 164–65; Heck v. Humphrey, 512 U.S. 477, 490 n.10 (1994) (Scalia, J.).

[23] Stenberg v. Carhart, 530 U.S. 914, 953, 956 (2000) (Scalia, J., dissenting).

clearly. "What's not in the Constitution simply isn't in the Constitution."[24] Yet Americans had long applied their Constitution to issues not explicitly addressed in its text, and Scalia himself recognized and accepted that interpretive practice in many areas where he found it useful. The Constitution failed to explicitly address flag burning, campaign finance, video games, electronic surveillance, thermal imagining devices, and the police use of helicopters to conduct overhead searches, for example, and it never mentioned executive privilege, a "unitary" executive, the sovereignty of the state and federal governments, "sole" executive agreements with foreign nations, an exclusive presidential power to recognize foreign nations, or the judicial lawmaking authority implied in the concept of "uniquely federal interests." Yet Scalia agreed that all those matters came within the Constitution's purview. Similarly, the Constitution did not provide that the Equal Protection Clause protected only against "intentional" discriminations, but he had no problem with the addition of that substantial limitation to the constitutional text.[25] The Constitution never specified a right to interstate travel, but he accepted that right as constitutionally protected.[26] Wholly contrary to his "principle of silence," he justified broad and nonoriginalist interpretations of the First, Fourth, Fifth, and Eleventh Amendments with his elastic and erratically applied "synecdoche" rationale.[27] Thus, the Constitution's "silence" was hardly determinative, and Scalia found constitutional "silence" decisive only on the issues he wished the Court to ignore.

Fourth, Scalia tried to deal with some interpretive questions by advancing a "narrowest meaning principle," a rule that words should be construed at the most specific level of meaning they had when adopted.[28] "Judicial activism," he charged, was an abuse that "in our federal system means giving an overly expansive meaning to the text of the Constitution." He rejected, for example, the idea that the Equal Protection Clause applied to women, though he acknowledged that "in the abstract the Equal Protection Clause could be given such a meaning."[29] There was, however, no originalist authority whatever

---

[24] BRYAN A. GARNER, NINO AND ME: MY UNUSUAL FRIENDSHIP WITH JUSTICE ANTONIN SCALIA 343 (2018).

[25] Crawford v. Marion County Election Board, 553 U.S. 181, 204, 207 (2008) (Scalia, J., concurring, citing *Washington v. Davis*, 426 U.S. 229 (1976) (White, J.)).

[26] Bray v. Alexandria Women's Health Clinic, 506 U.S. 263, 274, 276–77 (1993) (Scalia, J.).

[27] Antonin Scalia, *Common Law Courts*, 112. *Accord* SCALIA SPEAKS, 207 ("Of course, 'speech' and 'press' are stand-ins for the *expression of ideas*") (emphasis in original).

[28] Michael H. v. Gerald D., 491 U.S. 110, 127 n.6 (1989) (Scalia, J., announcing the judgment of the Court); James B. Beam Distilling Co. v. Georgia, 501 U.S. 529, 548, 549 (Scalia, J., concurring in the judgment).

[29] SCALIA SPEAKS, 282, 198.

for adopting that "narrowest meaning" principle, and the Court had long interpreted many constitutional terms at higher levels of generality, including interpretations that Scalia readily accepted involving such provisions as the Commerce Clause and the First, Second, and Fourth Amendments. He certainly did not apply any "narrowest meaning principle" to the Takings Clause of the Fifth Amendment, nor did he limit the meaning of "property" to the specific forms that existed in 1789 or 1868. Nor, even more obviously, did he limit the terms of Article II or the Second and Eleventh Amendments to their narrowest meaning. Like his other principles, his "narrowest meaning" principle was malleable and his use of it purposeful and selective.

Scalia also sought to reinforce his methodological claims about originalism with practical arguments. He argued, for example, that rejecting originalism meant that constitutional interpretation would be cast adrift and would be incapable of identifying correct and incorrect answers to constitutional questions. "If there are no right answers," he declared in *McDonald v. City of Chicago*, "there are no wrong answers either."[30] The claim was specious. While the American Constitution failed to dictate "correct" answers to certain perennial questions and to many more newly arising ones, its provisions and principles did nonetheless delimit the range of reasonable and persuasive answers that advocates acting in good faith could plausibly propose. Beyond issues that had long been settled by clear language, agreed interpretations, and accepted practices, it ruled out arguments and conclusions that would be unreasonable, inconsistent with the document's provisions and principles, or destructive to the nation's free republican constitutional order itself. Those valuable and constraining guidelines made many imaginable contentions and interpretations facially unwarranted, obviously unsound, or even patently ridiculous. While on fairly controverted questions the Constitution dictated no singularly "correct" answers, it did suggest a relatively constrained range of textually or structurally sound interpretations that eliminated as profoundly discordant and thus, in effect, "incorrect" a host of conceivable but wholly ungrounded ones.

Another practical argument Scalia advanced was based on the old saw that "[y]ou can't beat somebody with nobody."[31] Originalism's adversaries, he

---

[30] *McDonald*, 561 U.S. at 795 (Scalia, J., concurring).

[31] SCALIA SPEAKS, 196. Bork made a similar argument in Robert H. Bork, *Judicial Review and Democracy*, 3 ENCYCLOPEDIA OF THE AMERICAN CONSTITUTION, 1061, 1063 (Leonard W. Levy ed., 1986), and ROBERT H. BORK, THE TEMPTING OF AMERICA: THE POLITICAL SEDUCTION OF THE LAW 154–55 (1997).

argued, could not disregard its claims unless they came up with something better. "If originalism is to be supplanted, it must be supplanted with *something*," he asserted, but "there is no alternative to originalism but standardless judicial constitution-making."[32] There were two fundamental flaws in that claim. The first, as his own career demonstrated so vividly, was that originalism was not the objective standard he proclaimed but, rather, as elastic and manipulable as any that he condemned. In fact, theorists who rejected originalism had produced interpretative theories that were at least the equals of originalism and arguably more insightful, soundly based, intellectually rigorous, and empirically justified.[33]

The second flaw in his challenge was the fact that something else did exist, the de facto American constitutional tradition, a vibrant alternative that was far superior to his originalism. Contrary to his contention, that long-practiced and thriving, if admittedly manipulable and surely imperfect, constitutional practice had never been "standardless." American lawyers and judges had from the nation's beginning employed a variety of interpretative principles and methods—including but not limited to textual and historical analysis—that imposed varieties of constraints on judicial discretion and gave constitutional law a substantial degree of stability, continuity, and predictability.[34] Those standard techniques included reliance on philosophy, precedent, structure, prudence, economic efficiency, empirical sociological evidence, moral and ethical considerations, and estimates of the law's practical consequences. Those techniques were well-established products of the common-law tradition, generally accepted legal principles, and the ingrained

---

[32] SCALIA SPEAKS, 196 (emphasis in original), 197. Beyond originalism there was "no other criterion that is not infinitely manipulable." *Id.* at 221. "But if original meaning is not the criterion, what other criterion can there be that prevents judges from imposing their ideological preferences on society? Think about it. There is none." *Id.*, 212. *Accord* SCALIA, READING, 89.

[33] KARL N. LLEWELLYN, THE COMMON LAW TRADITION: DECIDING APPEALS (1960); ROBERT M. COVER, JUSTICE ACCUSED: ANTISLAVERY AND THE JUDICIAL PROCESS (1975); JOHN HART ELY, DEMOCRACY AND DISTRUST: A THEORY OF JUDICIAL REVIEW (1980); JESSE H. CHOPER, JUDICIAL REVIEW AND THE NATIONAL POLITICAL PROCESS: A FUNCTIONAL RECONSIDERATION OF THE ROLE OF THE SUPREME COURT (1980); RONALD DWORKIN, A MATTER OF PRINCIPLE (1985); HARRY H. WELLINGTON, INTERPRETING THE CONSTITUTION: THE SUPREME COURT AND THE PROCESS OF ADJUDICATION (1990); ARCHIBALD COX, THE COURT AND THE CONSTITUTION (1987); BRUCE ACKERMAN, WE THE PEOPLE: FOUNDATIONS (1991).

[34] *See, e.g.,* BENJAMIN N. CARDOZO, THE NATURE OF THE JUDICIAL PROCESS (1921) (identifying four methods of constitutional interpretation, including those using history and tradition); PHILIP BOBBITT, CONSTITUTIONAL INTERPRETATION (1991) (identifying six methods of constitutional interpretation, including those using history and text). Recent empirical evidence suggests that federal judges continue to use a variety of interpretive techniques and have not become "textualists." Abbe R. Gluck & Richard A. Posner, *Statutory Interpretation on the Bench: A Survey of Forty-Two Judges on the Federal Courts of Appeals*, 131 HARV. L. REV. 1298 (2018).

culture of the nation's legal profession.[35] Further, they were techniques that demanded rational arguments, factual foundations, and respect for the legitimate demands of both precedent and practicality. The justices on the Marshall Court, for example,

> drew upon a range of sources to justify their decisions: the text of the Constitution, the plain or ordinary meaning of words, common law definitions or principles, natural law, local practices and rules, principles of equity, and what they termed "general principles of republican government."[36]

The use of those varied judicial standards and methods in American constitutionalism, moreover, was further constrained by the assumptions and values embedded in the nation's political culture, its long-established commitment to ordered constitutional government, and ultimately its relatively stable, tolerant, inclusive, and pluralistic social order. Thus, as that long-established interpretative tradition enabled constitutional law to evolve over the centuries, it also channeled that evolution in relatively orderly, reasonable, and generally acceptable ways that sought to accommodate new conditions, concerns, and challenges. One can surely beat Scalia's intrinsically inadequate and vastly overhyped originalist "something" with that more inclusive, realistic, well-established, and culturally grounded "something else."[37] Indeed, for all its imperfections and shortcomings, that alternative "something else" was at least what it purported to be, not a false promise of authority and correctness. A silver standard is not a gold one, but it is far more valuable than one made of pyrite.

Scalia also defended his originalism with the direst of predictions. "Once the secret is out that the judges are evolving a new constitution rather than applying an old one," he contended, "the people will see to it that judges are

---

[35] Professional culture and its legal standards continued to channel Supreme Court decision-making, if less forcefully and consistently than it had, even in the hyperpolarized conditions of the early twenty-first century. *See* NEAL DEVINS & LAWRENCE BAUM, THE COMPANY THEY KEEP: HOW PARTISAN DIVISIONS CAME TO THE SUPREME COURT (2019).

[36] G. EDWARD WHITE, THE MARSHALL COURT AND CULTURAL CHANGE, 1815–35, at 114 (1988).

[37] Originalism's "failure fundamentally to reorient Supreme Court decision-making supports the view that American constitutional jurisprudence is best described empirically as an amalgam of plural modalities of argument that depend on competing conceptions of legal authority, which are never able wholly to displace one another." JOHNATHAN O'NEILL, ORIGINALISM IN AMERICAN LAW AND POLITICS: A CONSTITUTIONAL HISTORY 212 (2005). For some of the varieties in the nation's judicial tradition, *see, e.g.*, G. EDWARD WHITE, THE AMERICAN JUDICIAL TRADITION: PROFILES OF LEADING AMERICAN JUDGES (3d ed. 2007).

selected who will evolve it the way *they* want it to evolve." That would mean, in turn, that "the whole value of a constitution will have been destroyed."[38] Both his argument and his prediction were faulty.

His argument was faulty for two reasons. First, it was simply not a "secret" that judges had changed the interpretation and application of the Constitution over the decades. Indeed, that was precisely the charge that critics leveled against the Marshall Court in the nation's earliest years. Though many might bemoan the fact of changing interpretations or imagine a machine-like Constitution that "would go of itself,"[39] the nation's constitutional history had long made the facts of change readily apparent. It demonstrated that the Constitution had, in purpose as well as practice, created an institutionally dynamic and evolving form of government. Second, by portraying judges as "evolving a new constitution," rather than interpreting the "old" one in adaptive ways, he once again simply begged the question. How judges should interpret the Constitution, and what should and should not change in constitutional law, was quite simply the underlying interpretive problem of American constitutionalism itself. It established an enduring challenge, not a preemptive premise.

Equally, Scalia's prediction was faulty. First, it ignored the fact that the Constitution provided a great many values to the American people, including a flexible and sound governmental structure, time-honored republican principles, and fundamental social and political ideals. If people came to understand that judges shaped and sometimes changed constitutional law, that awareness would hardly cancel their embrace of those other values. Second, Scalia's argument failed to recognize that, if people came to truly understand the Constitution, they would also likely realize that its adaptability was a necessary and essential strength. Indeed, they would also likely recognize that it was designed to prevent them from making fundamental changes quickly or easily and to give them time for careful analyses and sober second thoughts. Finally, if people pressed for judicial nominees who shared their views, that process would simply represent the workings of the Constitution's own institutional structure and its principles of popular government. However problematic or tumultuous that process might become, it was at least based on a

---

[38] SCALIA SPEAKS, 200. Scalia argued much the same from the bench in *Planned Parenthood v. Casey*, 505 U.S. 833, 979, 999–1001 (1992) (Scalia, J., concurring in the judgment in part and dissenting in part).

[39] *See* MICHAEL KAMMEN, A MACHINE THAT WOULD GO OF ITSELF: THE CONSTITUTION IN AMERICAN CULTURE (1986).

THE METHODOLOGICAL FALLACY

true understanding of American constitutionalism. The Constitution, after all, recognized that the people were sovereign, and ultimately American constitutionalism depended on the judgment, acceptance, and continuing support of the people.[40]

Finally, Scalia defended his originalism by claiming that, at a minimum, it was better than any version of "living" constitutionalism because it offered a known and knowable norm. In contrast, he charged, all forms of nonoriginalism lacked uniform meanings and methods. The problems with this last defense were obvious. First, his premise—the fundamental claim that originalism provided a generally "knowable norm"—was demonstrably false, as Scalia's own career had demonstrated so clearly. Second, beyond their adoption of the same covering label, Scalia and other advocates of originalism were themselves unable to identify any uniform meaning and method to operationalize their interpretive claims.[41] Most obvious, Scalia himself had made his name as an advocate of "public meaning" originalism by attacking Robert Bork's "original intent" originalism.[42] Again, from one direction Raoul Berger disagreed with Scalia's emphasis on the supremacy of the text, arguing instead that the proven intent of the drafters should prevail over a text no matter how clear the text.[43] From an entirely different direction, Ronald Dworkin claimed an originalist foundation for his work based on its compatibility with "the framers' linguistic intentions" and declared that he would "never contradict" those intentions.[44] More generally, originalists

[40] See, e.g., BARRY FRIEDMAN, THE WILL OF THE PEOPLE: HOW PUBLIC OPINION HAS INFLUENCED THE SUPREME COURT AND SHAPED THE MEANING OF THE CONSTITUTION (2009).

[41] There has been an increasing number of diverse permutations of originalism. See, e.g., John Greil, Second-Best Originalism and Regulatory Takings, 41 HARV. J.L. & PUB. POL'Y 373 (2018); Stephen E. Sachs, Originalism as a Theory of Legal Change, 38 HARV. J.L. & PUB. POL'Y 817 (2015); Lawrence B. Solum, What Is Originalism? The Evolution of Contemporary Originalist Theory, in THE CHALLENGE OF ORIGINALISM: THEORIES OF CONSTITUTIONAL INTERPRETATION (Grant Huscroft & Bradley W. Miller eds., 2011); Douglas Kmiec, Natural Law Originalism—Or Why Justice Scalia (Almost) Gets It Right, 20 HARV. J.L. & PUB. POL'Y 627 (1997); Thomas B. Colby & Peter J. Smith, Living Originalism, 59 DUKE L.J. 239 (2009). For a relatively recent debate about originalist "methods" of interpretation, compare MICHAEL RAPPAPORT & JOHN O. MCGINNIS, ORIGINALISM AND THE GOOD CONSTITUTION (2013) (advocating an originalism guided by following the Founders' "original methods" of interpretation), with GIENAPP, SECOND CREATION (arguing that the Founders shared no consensus about "original methods" of constitutional interpretation).

[42] Similarly, defending his own version of originalism, Robert Bork disagreed with Scalia's interpretation of the First Amendment in the flag-burning case, Texas v. Johnson, 491 U.S. 397 (1989) (Brennan, J., joined by Scalia, J.). ROBERT H. BORK, THE TEMPTING OF AMERICA: THE POLITICAL SEDUCTION OF THE LAW 127–28 (1990).

[43] Raoul Berger, The Founders' View—According to Jefferson Powell, 67 TEX. L. REV. 1033, 1060–62 (1989); Raoul Berger, A Lawyer Lectures a Judge, 18 HARV. J.L. & PUB. POL'Y 851, 862–64 (1994).

[44] RONALD DWORKIN, FREEDOM'S LAW: THE MORAL READING OF THE AMERICAN CONSTITUTION 291 (1996).

who were political liberals found historical sources and developed legal arguments that supported conclusions substantially contrary to Scalia's.[45] Indeed, it was both illustrative and amusing that in her Senate confirmation hearing Justice Elena Kagan, a liberal Democratic appointee, could readily declare that "we are all originalists" in the middle of testimony outlining her version of a distinctly "living" constitutionalism.[46]

Most immediate and visible, Justice Clarence Thomas, the Court's other self-proclaimed originalist, split with Scalia on numerous occasions over the application of originalism. Unlike Thomas, Scalia recognized more commonly the claims of stare decisis and the complexity of the values and interests that had shaped the evolution of constitutional law.[47] Responding to questions about his more qualified and flexible version of originalism, moreover, Scalia replied not with a measured analytical response to explain and

---

[45] *E.g.,* JACK M. BALKIN, LIVING ORIGINALISM (2011); AKHIL REED AMAR, AMERICA'S CONSTITUTION: A BIOGRAPHY (2006); Jeffrey Rosen, *Constitution Avenue,* 243 THE NEW REPUBLIC 13, June 28, 2012; Andrew Sterritt, *New Originalist Interpretation of* Parents Involved, GEO. J.L. & PUB. POL'Y 433 (2017).

[46] *Hearings before the Committee on the Judiciary, United States Senate, One Hundred Eleventh Congress, Second Session on the Nomination of Elena Kagan to be an Associate Justice of the Supreme Court of the United States* (June 28–30 & July 1, 2010), 62. Kagan stated that the Founders were fully conscious that they were writing "a Constitution for the ages" and "knew all about change" and that "the world would change." They purposely incorporated many "broad principles" and "general" provisions that "were meant to be interpreted over time, to be applied to new situations and new factual contexts." *Id.* at 61–62.

[47] *See, e.g.,* Doe v. Reed, 561 U.S. 186, 228 (2010) (Scalia, J., concurring in the judgment; Thomas, J., dissenting disagreeing about the weight and relevance of originalist materials, at 228); Zelman v. Simmons-Harris, 536 U.S. 639 (2002) (Scalia, J., joining majority; Thomas, J., concurring separately on originalist grounds, at 676); Grable & Sons Metal Products, Inc. v. Darue Engineering & Manufacturing Co., 545 U.S. 308 (2005) (Scalia, J., joining majority; Thomas, J., concurring separately urging reconsideration of original meaning of statutory provision, at 320); Kelo v. City of New London, 545 U.S. 469 (2005) (Scalia, J., joining majority; Thomas, J., dissenting on originalist grounds, at 505); Haywood v. Drown, 556 U.S. 729 (2009) (Scalia, J., joining only part of the opinion of Thomas, J., but refusing to join other parts that presented extreme originalist states-rights views, at 742); *McDonald,* 561 U.S. 742 (Scalia, J., concurring on standard nonoriginalist incorporation grounds; Thomas, J., concurring on originalist Privileges or Immunities theory, at 791); United States v. Lopez, 514 U.S. 549 (1995) (Scalia, J., joining majority accepting post–New Deal Commerce Clause jurisprudence; Thomas, J., concurring on originalist grounds and urging the Court to reconsider post–New Deal jurisprudence, at 584); Gonzales v. Raich, 545 U.S. 1 (2005) (Scalia,J., joining majority; Thomas,J., dissenting on originalist grounds, at 57); Brown v. Entertainment Merchants Association, 564 U.S. 786 (2011) (Scalia, J., writing for the Court and invoking originalist reasoning; Thomas J., dissenting on narrower originalist grounds, at 821); National Federation of Independent Business v. Sibelius, 567 U.S. 519 (2012) (Scalia, J., dissenting, at 646; Thomas J., dissenting separately to advance narrower originalist interpretation of the Commerce Clause than Scalia advanced, at 707); Arizona v. The Inter Tribal Council of Arizona, Inc. 570 U.S. 1 (2012) (Scalia, J. writing for Court; Thomas, J., dissenting on statutory construction grounds informed by originalist interpretation of Constitution, at 22); Hamdi v. Rumsfeld, 542 U.S. 507 (2012) (Scalia, J., dissenting on originalist constitutional grounds, at 554; Thomas, J., dissenting on different constitutional grounds and reaching different conclusion, at 579). On Scalia and Thomas as originalists, *see, e.g.,* ERIC J. SEGALL, ORIGINALISM AS FAITH, ch. 7 (2018) [hereafter SEGALL, ORIGINALISM].

justify his differences with Thomas but rather with a conversation-ending barb: "I'm an originalist and a textualist, not a nut."[48]

Aside from their acceptance of a shared label, then, originalists did no better than "living" constitutionalists in producing a methodology that could identify and correctly apply an authoritative "knowable norm." There was "deep ambiguity in the meaning of originalism," explained law professor Lawrence B. Solum, a sympathetic commentator, for originalism took a wide variety of forms and produced substantial disagreements among its adherents. "The family of contemporary originalist constitutional theories contains substantial diversity," he concluded, "and there may be no single thesis upon which all self-described originalists agree."[49]

Thus, Scalia's originalism also failed to establish an accepted and authoritative model, and it failed equally to quash the burgeoning number of originalist theories, methodologies, and legal conclusions that began to sprout at the turn of the twenty-first century.[50] His own uses of originalist reasoning illustrated the ambiguities and elasticities in his particular variation as well as marking the places where his personal views and values held sway. Although originalism was a well-accepted technique of constitutional interpretation, lawyers and judges had long applied it in different ways to reach different results. When they sought to apply it to live constitutional controversies, they seldom reached generally accepted constitutional conclusions. As much as originalism was part of a long and continuous tradition of constitutional

[48] Nina Totenberg, *Justice Scalia, the Great Dissenter, Opens Up*, NATIONAL PUBLIC RADIO, Apr. 28, 2008, *available at* http://www.npr.org/templates/story/story.php?storyId=89986017 (last consulted July 21, 2019). *See* MURPHY, SCALIA, 411–12. For a supportive account of Thomas and his jurisprudence, *see* MYRON MAGNET, CLARENCE THOMAS AND THE LOST CONSTITUTION (2019).

[49] Lawrence B. Solum, *What Is Originalism? The Evolution of Contemporary Originalist Theory*, at 5, 41, *available at* http://scholarship.law.georgetown.edu/facpub/1353 (last consulted July 21, 2019). On "new" originalists and "new, new" originalists, *see* SEGALL, ORIGINALISM, chs. 5–6; on "fault lines" dividing contemporary originalists, *see* John O. McGinnis, *The Three Fault Lines of Contemporary Originalism* (May 30, 2019), *available at* https://www.lawliberty.org/2019/05/30/the-three-fault-lines-of-contemporary-originalism/ (last consulted July 22, 2019); on a persisting "schism among originalists," *see* Randy E. Barnett & Evan D. Bernick, *The Letter and the Spirit: A Unified Theory of Originalism*, GEO. L.J. 1, 13 (2018) [hereafter Barnett & Bernick, *Letter and Spirit*]; on the emergence of a proclaimed new third version of originalism, *see, e.g.*, William Baude, *Is Originalism Our Law?*, 115 COLUM. L. REV. 2349 (2015).

[50] *E.g.*, Steven G. Calabresi & Gary Lawson, *The Rule of Law as a Law of Law*, 90 NOTRE DAME L. REV. 483, 490–91 (2014) (two of Scalia's admirers disagree with him on the original understanding of the delegation doctrine); Jack M. Balkin, *Abortion and Original Meaning*, 24 CONST. COMMENT. 291 (2007) (originalism supports right to abortion); Barnett & Bernick, *Letter and Spirit*," 40 (*Heller* correctly decided on originalist grounds but dangerous "arms" can still be banned when they create "an unreasonable risk" and "even when properly used in self-defense"); Steven G. Calabresi & Hannah Begley, *Originalism and Same Sex Marriage*, Feb. 25, 2015, *available at* https://papers.ssrn.com/sol3/papers.cfm?abstract_id=2509443 (last consulted July 21, 2019) (originalism supports right to same-sex marriage.

argumentation, it was equally part of a long and continuous tradition of constitutional disagreement about the conclusions it warranted.

Spencer Roane and John Marshall, who participated together in the Virginia ratifying convention, illustrated that truth among the Founders themselves. In 1819 Marshall upheld federal power in *McCulloch v. Maryland*,[51] and Roane attacked his decision fiercely. Both claimed originalist justifications for their wholly contradictory positions. Marshall charged that Roane's views were based on "deep-rooted and vindictive hate," while Roane declared that anyone who agreed with Marshall's conclusions "must be a deplorable idiot."[52]

Scalia's jurisprudence and career highlighted the same animating truth that the impasse between Roane and Marshall exemplified, that neither originalism nor any other single "method" of constitutional interpretation could provide generally "correct"—much less just, wise, and enduring—answers to the perennial, shifting, and novel questions that the nation and courts continually faced. One principle reason for Scalia's long-term historical importance, then, is that—contrary to his repeated insistence—his originalist jurisprudence illustrated the "methodological fallacy," the persistent and understandable but unavoidably mistaken claim that some such method did exist. Ultimately, and quite unintentionally, Scalia illustrated a central characteristic of American constitutionalism: the fact that neither the constitutional text nor the writings of the Founders provide clear answers to either perennially disputed constitutional questions or novel controversies that historical change continually generates.

Thus, Scalia promoted two related claims that historical and jurisprudential evidence showed to be false. One was that originalism was an "objective" and "correct" method of constitutional interpretation, and the other was that he himself followed that method and applied it consistently.[53] He purported to find direction in "principles" that did not direct, heralded methods that were inadequate and manipulable, and applied those methods differently in different cases and on different issues. He claimed neutrality, objectivity, and

---

[51] McCulloch v. Maryland, 17 U.S. (4 Wheat.) 316 (1819).

[52] "A Friend of the Constitution" [John Marshall], Essay No. 1, at 155 in JOHN MARSHALL'S DEFENSE OF *MCCULLOCH V. MARYLAND* (Gerald Gunther ed., 1969); "Hampden" [Spencer Roane], Essay No. 1, at 110 in *id.*

[53] "[H]is doctrines were so flexible that he could reach a range of interpretations and still claim fidelity to his ostensibly neutral methodology." RICHARD L. HASEN, THE JUSTICE OF CONTRADICTIONS: ANTONIN SCALIA AND THE POLITICS OF DISRUPTION 174 (2018) [hereafter HASEN, JUSTICE OF CONTRADICTIONS].

constitutional fidelity, but the evidence demonstrated instead that his juris-prudence was commonly shaped in its specific applications not by textual and originalist sources but by his own personal goals and values.

This is not to contend, of course, that Scalia never applied his jurispruden-tial principles fairly and reasonably nor that he never followed those princi-ples to results that conflicted with his personal preferences. Sometimes he did both. Rather, it is to contend that it was in giving effect to his personal goals and values, not in applying his proclaimed principles and methods, that he remained most consistent.

More important, this is not to contend that Scalia was necessarily a con-scious hypocrite in his jurisprudence and judicial behavior. Rather, given what is known about his family background, his strict religious commitment, his staunch and rigid moral beliefs, his seemingly invincible self-assurance, and his determination to maintain the highest personal character,[54] it seems likely that he was so enveloped by his own intensely held views and values—that he believed so totally and passionately in the social, cultural, political, religious, and jurisprudential ideas and values that he so deeply cherished—that he was generally unable to recognize and realistically acknowledge the inconsistencies that marked his judicial performance.[55]

Indeed, beyond the characteristic pattern of ideological consistency and methodological inconsistency, and beyond its many glaring examples, Scalia on occasion simply gave away the intensely personal and parochial assumptions that infused much of his jurisprudence. It was only such deeply held personal views about race, for example, that led him to accept the inev-itable operation of racial prejudice in the operation of the legal system, even

---

[54] Scalia was deeply impressed by his father's "strict code of integrity," and his father taught him a fundamental lesson. "Brains are like muscles—you can hire them by the hour. The only thing that's not for sale is character." JOAN BISKUPIC, AMERICAN ORIGINAL: THE LIFE AND CONSTITUTION OF SUPREME COURT JUSTICE ANTONIN SCALIA 17 (2009) [hereafter BISKUPIC, AMERICAN ORIGINAL]. "Unless you increase, in equal measure with your knowledge, your judgment and character," Scalia told a high school graduating class that included one of his sons, "you will fail in the only thing that is really important, and from which all else follows." SCALIA SPEAKS, 332.

[55] One of Scalia's ex-clerks offered a more limited but somewhat similar opinion.

> I don't mean to intimate by any of this that the Justice was not a man of principle. I think he was. Nor do I mean to suggest that he was meaningfully worse along this dimension than many of his colleagues. I don't think that's true. What I think is that, as is true of many men and women of principle and of many other able and respectable jurists, Justice Scalia's instincts about what was right and what was wrong sometimes overwhelmed him and caused him to discard the principles that he applied honorably in many other contexts (including cases in which those principles commanded results he disfavored). And this happened, sometimes, when the stakes were very high.

Gil Seinfeld, *The Good, The Bad, and the Ugly: Reflections of a Counter-Clerk*, 114 MICH. L. REV.: FIRST IMPRESSIONS 111, 117–20 (2016).

in cases involving the imposition of the death penalty. The "unconscious operation of irrational sympathies and antipathies, including racial, upon jury decisions and (hence) prosecutorial decisions," he wrote in a capital case, "is real, acknowledged in the decisions of this court, and ineradicable."[56] Similarly, it was only such views that led him not merely to reject all racial affirmative action plans but, far more telling, to mock the very idea—accepted even by some of the other conservative justices who generally opposed affirmative action—that racial diversity in law school classrooms could, in fact, make social, political, and intellectual contributions to education, the legal profession, and the broader nation itself.[57] Equally, it was only such an intensely held personal commitment to Catholicism and Christianity that could inspire his obtuse disrespect for non-Christians when, over objections raised on behalf of Jews, he insisted in open court that it was "outrageous" not to accept the Latin cross as the proper symbol for all Americans who had died in the nation's wars.[58] Indeed, only such deeply held religious beliefs could lead him to indict the welfare state on the ground that it harmed Christians and their religious obligations. By taking upon itself "one of the corporal works of mercy," he declared, the welfare state "deprives individuals of an opportunity for sanctification and deprives the body of Christ of

[56] Scalia made the statement in a memo to the other justices during the Court's deliberations in *McClesky v. Kemp*, 481 U.S. 279 (1987) (Powell, J., joined by Scalia, J.), a case challenging the imposition of the death penalty in Georgia and presenting massive statistical evidence of its racially discriminatory nature. *See* Dennis D. Doran, *Far Right of the Mainstream: Racism, Rights and Remedies from the Perspective of Justice Antonin Scalia's McClesky Memorandum*, 45 MERCER L. REV. 1035, 1038 (1994).

[57] Grutter v. Bollinger, 539 U.S. 306, 346, 347–48 (2003) (Scalia, J., concurring in part and dissenting in part). In contrast, Justice O'Connor wrote for the majority and explicitly stated that the "educational benefits" of racial diversity were "substantial." It "promotes 'cross-racial understanding,'" undermines racial stereotypes and misconceptions, and makes classroom discussions "livelier, more spirited, and simply more enlightening and interesting." *Id.* at 329–30 (O'Connor, J.). Justice Kennedy, dissenting on the ground that the Court did not apply strict scrutiny, nonetheless declared that "I reiterate my approval of giving appropriate consideration to race in this one context." *Id.* at 387, 395. Revealingly, in arguing a different point and seeking to support his narrow view of standing, Scalia had previously accepted the idea that racial diversity had "important benefits." In *Lujan v. Defenders of Wildlife*, 504 U.S. 555, 578 (1992) he approved as sufficient the injury the Court had accepted in *Trafficante v. Metropolitan Life Insurance Co.*, 409 U.S. 205 (1972) (Douglas, J.). That injury was the "injury to existing tenants by exclusion of minority persons from the apartment complex" which caused the "loss of important benefits from interracial associations," *id.* at 209–10. Such an "injury" could not possibly have any "original" source but was the result of social change and legal transformation. On the harmful educational impact that lack of racial diversity has in law schools, *see, e.g.*, Walter R. Allen & Daniel Solorzano, *Affirmative Action, Educational Equity and Campus Racial Climate: A Case Study of the University of Michigan Law School*, 12 BERKELEY LA RAZA L.J. 237 (2001); Katherine Y. Barnes, *Is Affirmative Action Responsible for the Achievement Gap Between Black and White Law Students?*, 101 Nw. U. L. REV. 1759 (2007).

[58] Transcript of oral argument in *Salazar v. Buono*, No. 08-472 (Oct. 7, 2009), at 38–39 (remarks of Scalia, J.).

an occasion for the interchange of love among its members."[59] Thus, given Scalia's profound self-identification as a strictly objective judge who was neither "political" nor "result-oriented," it may have been psychologically and emotionally impossible for him to recognize most or all of the multitude of issues where his personal views led him to adopt inconsistent reasoning and support "result-oriented" conclusions.[60]

One suspects that, at most, he may have harbored inklings about those inconsistencies but found ways to push them to the periphery of his thinking or even beyond. When Jeffrey Rosen asked him at "a convivial dinner" about the problem his originalism had in justifying *Brown v. Board of Education*,[61] Scalia "replied, with a belly laugh, that no theory is perfect."[62] When asked at a law school lecture about opinions he wrote or joined that ignored the historical record when it pointed against the results he reached, he dodged the issue with a joking response: "What did Sarah Palin say? 'I'll get back to you on it.'"[63] Even at a Federalist Society event, he refused to answer a question about his puzzling concurring opinion in *Gonzales v. Raich* that defended a broadly expansive Commerce Clause.[64] "Oh, no," he protested. "Get another question."[65] And, as became widely known if not infamous, when repeatedly asked about his behavior in *Bush v. Gore*,[66] he had a standard and curt reply. "Get over it."[67] Scalia, it would seem, may simply have been unable to seriously question certain things, most centrally his own judicial behavior.[68]

---

[59] SCALIA SPEAKS, 338.

[60] "The worst thing you could say in the Scalia house," Scalia's wife Maureen once remarked, "was 'results oriented.'" EVAN THOMAS, FIRST: SANDRA DAY O'CONNOR 300 (2019). Talking with his clerks, for example, Scalia early on "began scoffing that O'Connor was a politician and not a judge." He "thought that she was not a rigorous legal thinker but rather felt her way to crowd-pleasing outcomes." *Id.* at 237.

[61] *Brown*, 347 U.S. 483 (1954) (Warren, C.J.).

[62] Jeffrey Rosen, *What Made Antonin Scalia Great*, THE ATLANTIC MONTHLY, Feb. 15, 2016, *available at* https://www.theatlantic.com/politics/archive/2016/02/what-made-antonin-scalia-great/462837/ (last consulted July 21, 2019).

[63] Elaine McArdle, *In Inaugural Vaughan Lecture, Scalia Defends the "Methodology of Originalism,"* HARVARD LAW TODAY, Oct. 3, 2009, *available at* https://today.law.harvard.edu/in-inaugural-vaughan-lecture-scalia-defends-the-methodology-of-originalism (last consulted July 21, 2019) [hereafter McArdle, *Inaugural Vaughan Lecture*].

[64] *Raich*, 545 U.S. at 33 (Scalia, J., concurring in the judgment).

[65] BISKUPIC, AMERICAN ORIGINAL, 9.

[66] Bush v. Gore, 531 U.S. 98 (2000) (per curiam). *See* chapter 8.

[67] HASEN, JUSTICE OF CONTRADICTIONS, 5.

[68] Scalia's defense of his decision to accompany Vice President Dick Cheney on a hunting trip when Cheney was at the same time a named litigant in a suit before the Court suggested the same conclusion. *See* MURPHY, SCALIA, 252–66, 298–304. Scalia seemed to dislike being asked questions in general. *See* JOHN GREENYA, GORSUCH: THE JUDGE WHO SPEAKS FOR HIMSELF 154 (2018).

Notwithstanding the many inconsistencies that marked his performance in *Bush v. Gore*, for example, he apparently continued to defend his actions in that case even when pressed sharply and persistently in private discussions. On one such occasion several years after the case was decided, he made a limited but ultimately inconsequential concession, acknowledging that his decision to join the per curiam opinion—but not his decision to join the concurrence or to terminate the recount—might have been "a mistake."[69] If so, he pleaded, the mistake was mitigated by "the severe time constraints, the pressure to come out with a near-unanimous opinion, and the fact that [the per curiam's equal protection theory] did not determine my vote in the case." For those reasons, he maintained, critics "should cut me some slack."[70] What was truly revealing about his ostensible concession, however, was that he gave not one millimeter on the decisive issue that went most directly to his judicial character: whether he behaved inconsistently and improperly when he joined the Court's per curiam opinion on the Equal Protection Clause. On that issue, he pleaded complete innocence. When he made his decision to accept the equal protection argument, he insisted, "I thought that ground correct."[71] If Scalia truly believed that statement, it suggested either a complete psychological inability—or a willfully steeled refusal—to seriously consider the glaring flaws in that ground or the more general inconsistencies and partisanship that marred his behavior in the case.[72]

In public, Scalia's ultimate inability or refusal to recognize his inconsistencies may have been exemplified most clearly in an appearance he made at the Harvard Law School after his opinion in *Heller* came down.[73] Addressing a large crowd on the "Methodology of Originalism," he faced some sharp questioning and responded defensively with a series of comments that went

---

[69] ALAN DERSHOWITZ, TAKING THE STAND: MY LIFE IN THE LAW 271 (2013) [hereafter DERSHOWITZ, TAKING THE STAND]. If Scalia was willing to admit a possible "mistake" in private, he was not willing to do so in public. In March 2012 he seemed to embrace the per curiam's equal protection rationale by claiming that *Bush v. Gore* was a 7–2 decision that "wasn't even close." Ian Millhiser, *Scalia Rewrites History, Claims 5–4* Bush v. Gore *decision "Wasn't Even Close," available at* https://thinkprogress.org/Scalia-rewrites-history-claims-5-4-bush-v-gore-decision-wasnt-even-close (last consulted July 21, 2019).

[70] DERSHOWITZ, TAKING THE STAND, 271.

[71] *Id.* at 271.

[72] To whatever extent he was unable to recognize the inconsistencies in his judicial behavior, there is evidence that on occasion he did acknowledge some kind of lapse in *Bush v. Gore*. The per curiam opinion he joined, he reportedly admitted, was "a piece of shit." CHARLES L. ZELDEN, BUSH V. GORE: EXPOSING THE HIDDEN CRISIS IN AMERICAN DEMOCRACY 237 (abridged & updated ed. 2010). Scalia's refusal to write his own opinion in the case also suggested that he was aware that he was violating his principles and allowing his personal desires to control. *See* chapter 8.

[73] District of Columbia v. Heller, 554 U.S. 570 (2008) (Scalia, J.).

far beyond the plausible or even barely credible. The Court, he declared, possessed "all the materials needed to determine the meaning of the Second Amendment at the time it was written." Because the briefing in the case was "nothing short of spectacular," there could be no method that "would be easier or more reliable than the originalist approach." As for the contention that the amendment was limited by its militia clause, it was "easy enough for the Court's originalists to show this was not so." Finally, in the words of the reporter who attended the meeting, he claimed that "the originalist methodology was able to establish an historical pedigree that led to an incontrovertible result."[74] If Scalia actually believed those statements, he could not have seriously examined either the full historical record in the case or his own thinking about it.[75]

Had Scalia been consistent in applying his jurisprudence, it would have been possible to contend that he was objective and neutral and that his originalist jurisprudence offered a sound judicial methodology. Given his pervasive and often systematic inconsistencies, however, those contentions seem beyond credibility. Rather, it seems far more likely that, consciously or not, he shaped his jurisprudence to justify the results he sought on the issues he cared about most passionately and that, when his jurisprudential principles failed to justify the many other results he desired, he was willing to modify, twist, distort, ignore, or simply abandon them. One need not highlight his most spectacular failures—cases such as *Boyle, Heller, Shelby County, Clinton v. Jones*, and *Bush v. Gore*—but only consider his decisions and opinions across his whole career to recognize both the pervasive inconsistencies in the reasoning he used and the patterned ideological consistencies in the results he achieved.

As a matter of methodology, then, the paramount flaw in Scalia's jurisprudence and judicial career lay in the claim that they were something that they were not. He once wrote that Congress did not "hide elephants in mouseholes,"[76] but in deploying the phrase "original public meaning" he hid a deeply felt personal ideology in a single label. The very fact that he was a major force in constitutional debates—and in the view of many one of the great justices in the Court's history—highlighted the importance of

---

[74] McArdle, *Inaugural Vaughan Lecture.* All of the quotations in this paragraph are statements attributed specifically to Scalia in the source cited except the last one, which is the author's statement summarizing the argument Scalia made.

[75] *See* chapter 7.

[76] Whitman v. American Trucking Associations, 531 U.S. 457, 468 (2001) (Scalia, J.).

his methodological failure. His jurisprudence and judicial career suggested convincingly that the very idea that such a particular and "correct" method existed was inconsistent with the fundamental nature and dynamic operations of American constitutionalism. Together, they provided a classic example of the methodological fallacy.[77]

---

[77] For a brief and elegant discussion of the relatively flexible and discursive nature of American constitutional reasoning, *see, e.g.,* H. JEFFERSON POWELL, CONSTITUTIONAL CONSCIENCE: THE MORAL DIMENSION OF JUDICIAL DECISION (2008).

11

The Fusion of Jurisprudence and Politics

While Scalia's interpretive methods failed in practice to accomplish what he promised, they nonetheless succeeded triumphantly in another realm. They helped forge a powerful union that linked him and his jurisprudence to the political goals and aspirations of certain segments of American society. His paeans to originalism, textualism, and traditionalism—and the substantive conclusions he attributed to them—appealed to large numbers of those who gathered together in the post-Reagan Republican Party: libertarians, business leaders, religious believers, gun advocates, market ideologues, disaffected whites, and traditional economic conservatives.[1]

Scalia became their constitutional voice, not merely defending their interests but affirming their most fundamental political views and moral values. Equally important, he proved for them that their views and values were also those of the Founders themselves and that they were written, one way or another, in the U.S. Constitution. His stance was fierce and his appeal exhilarating. Standing alone in *Morrison v. Olson*, defending the Reagan administration against the entire Court,[2] he may have evoked for some the heroic image of Howard Roark in Ayn Rand's novel *The Fountainhead*.[3] Scorning an oppressive and wrongheaded majority, he declared his unalterable personal commitment to his own principles and his own independence. Unlike all of the justices in the majority, he proclaimed, "I prefer to rely upon the judgment of the wise men who constructed our system, and of the people who approved it, and of two centuries of history that have shown it to be sound."[4]

---

[1] For the growing link between the Republican Party and originalism, *see, e.g.*, Ken I. Kersch, *The Talking Cure: How Constitutional Argument Drives Constitutional Development*, 94 BOSTON U. L. REV. 1083, 1095–1104 (2014); Robert Post & Reva Siegel, *Originalism as a Political Practice: The Right's Living Constitution*, 75 FORDHAM L. REV. 545 (2006).

[2] Seven justices were in the majority, and Justice Kennedy did not participate. Morrison v. Olson, 487 U.S. 654 (1988) (Rehnquist, C.J.).

[3] Rand's book attracted an audience on the hard-core right, and Justice Thomas even had his law clerks watch the movie version made in 1949. EVAN THOMAS, FIRST: SANDRA DAY O'CONNOR 274 (2019).

[4] *Morrison*, 487 U.S. at 734 (Scalia, J., dissenting).

Antonin Scalia and American Constitutionalism. Edward A. Purcell, Jr., Oxford University Press (2020).
© Edward A. Purcell, Jr.
DOI: 10.1093/oso/9780197508763.001.0001

For the groups that rallied to the post-Reagan Republican Party, Scalia confirmed their status as the Founders' true successors and blessed them with a sense of transcendent political and constitutional righteousness. Further, for some in those groups, he also confirmed their ethnic and religious authenticity as the Founders' true heirs. For those who wanted to believe in a romanticized past where everyone agreed on "traditional" values, loyally followed the Founders' clear commands, and equated being a true American with being white and Christian, Scalia's originalism proved compelling. Implicitly, and sometimes explicitly, it appealed to an imagined and highly comforting image of the past that many in those groups found particularly congenial and far preferable to the more recent social, political, and cultural changes that they had come to resent and reject. After all, the *Federalist* itself announced in its very second essay the underlying claim that Americans were not only "attached to the same principles of government" but were also "descended from the same ancestors" and professed "the same religion."[5]

Scalia's jurisprudence appealed to those groups for other reasons as well. It implicitly suggested that their adversaries were not only wrong but illegitimate. Those who rejected originalism and the Republican agenda, his admirers could readily believe, were neither committed nor loyal to the Constitution. They wanted only to twist it for their own selfish, elitist, and partisan ends. The apparently simple and straightforward principles of Scalia's jurisprudence, moreover, were easily packaged in punchy sound-bite terms suitable for ready political use. "It is necessary to judge according to the written law—period," he announced to one audience.[6] In terms of national politics, his ideas could readily be reduced to a message that perfectly tracked and seemed to provide a sophisticated jurisprudential foundation for the long-established anti–Warren Court Republican rhetoric that the courts should "interpret and not legislate."

Further, Scalia's jurisprudence—like the other variations of originalism that the Reagan administration inspired—served the goals of the Republican coalition in two other and broader ways. First, by transforming eighteenth-century ideas and attitudes into constitutional norms, originalism seemed well suited for undermining the legitimacy of modern legal developments that the coalition opposed—abortion rights, gay marriage, affirmative action,

---

[5] THE FEDERALIST PAPERS NO. 2, at 32 (Jay) (Clinton Rossiter ed., originally published in 1961, with Introduction and Notes by Charles R. Kessler, 2003) [hereafter FEDERALIST PAPERS].

[6] ANTONIN SCALIA, SCALIA SPEAKS: REFLECTIONS ON LAW, FAITH, AND LIFE WELL LIVED (Christopher J. Scalia & Edward Whelan eds., 2017), 245 [hereafter SCALIA SPEAKS].

labor unionization, elimination of the death penalty, expanded tort liability for corporations, rigid separation of church and state, institutional reform litigation, and federal antidiscrimination laws of all kinds.[7] Second, by focusing on eighteenth-century ideas and attitudes originalism also served to deflect attention from the pressing realities that marked modern America. In particular, it helped to deflect attention from the acute dangers of growing social and economic inequality and to obscure the fact that the law was increasingly being used to favor powerful private economic interests rather than ensuring equitable economic conditions for all Americans.[8]

Personally, Scalia was closely tied to major elements of the Republican coalition.[9] He served in both the Nixon and Ford administrations, worked with the right-wing and libertarian American Enterprise Institute, and helped found, strongly supported, and maintained close personal and professional connections with the staunchly conservative Federalist Society. Reagan appointed him to the federal bench and then raised him to the Supreme Court, and throughout his judicial career Scalia continued to maintain close personal friendships with Republican and conservative leaders, including Dick Cheney, Ted Olson, and many members and leading figures in the Federalist Society. Throughout his years on the bench, he actively courted the Federalist Society and encouraged its work, frequently participating in its events and building support for its nationwide expansion. In 2012 alone he traveled to speak at five separate Federalist Society events, and over the years the organization repaid his efforts handsomely by honoring him on a variety of occasions.[10] In addition, his two oldest sons worked at law firms that represented George W. Bush in *Bush v. Gore*, and one subsequently took a position with the Bush administration and later with the Trump administration.

---

[7] Edward A. Purcell, Jr., *The Courts, Federalism, and the Federal Constitution, 1920–2000*, in 3 THE CAMBRIDGE HISTORY OF LAW IN AMERICA: THE TWENTIETH CENTURY AND AFTER (1920–) 161–62 (Michael Grosberg & Christopher Tomlins eds. 2008).

[8] Edward A. Purcell, Jr., *Democracy, the Constitution, and Legal Positivism in America: Lessons from a Winding and Troubled History*, 66 FLA. L. REV. 1457, 1503–508 (2014).

[9] The material in the following paragraph is drawn from RICHARD L. HASEN, THE JUSTICE OF CONTRADICTIONS: ANTONIN SCALIA AND THE POLITICS OF DISRUPTION 13, 82, 86–113, 146–51 (2018) [hereafter HASEN, JUSTICE OF CONTRADICTIONS]; JOAN BISKUPIC, AMERICAN ORIGINAL: THE LIFE AND CONSTITUTION OF SUPREME COURT JUSTICE ANTONIN SCALIA 3–10, 40–41, 75–80, 158–60, 185–99, 248–49, 315–17 (2009) [hereafter BISKUPIC, AMERICAN ORIGINAL]; and BRUCE ALLEN MURPHY, SCALIA: A COURT OF ONE 42–44, 91–92, 190–97 229–32, 281–83, 294–95, 298–307, 451–57, 313–17, 482–85, 488–90 (2014) [hereafter MURPHY, SCALIA].

[10] NEAL DEVINS & LAWRENCE BAUM, THE COMPANY THEY KEEP: HOW PARTISAN DIVISIONS CAME TO THE SUPREME COURT 134 (2019).

Scalia's personal beliefs, moreover, tied him closely to the views and values that pervaded the post-Reagan Republican Party. As a particularly devout Roman Catholic who drove his family long distances to attend traditional Latin masses, he had the keenest sympathies for Christian religious beliefs. As a gun-owner and avid hunter, he nourished a passionate love of guns. He believed abortion and homosexual acts were immoral, embraced the principles of "free market" economics and linked them to Christianity, and regarded the death penalty as not only constitutional but desirable and effective. He dismissed "foreign" ideas and "foreign" law and showed little sympathy for immigrants and minority groups. Toward plaintiffs who sued private corporations he was callous if not overtly hostile, and he echoed Republican rhetoric by warning that "over most of the past century change has been moving from a *status quo* capitalism toward socialism."[11] His public statements and speeches rang out virtually every relevant political and social theme that the Republican Party sought to exploit. Late in his life he even seemed to cut himself off from individuals and sources he considered "liberal," leading one commentator in 2013 to note his "remarkable isolation from anyone who doesn't agree with him."[12]

More important, in spite of his inconsistencies in applying his originalist jurisprudence, he was generally reliable and consistent in reaching practical results that pleased his political supporters. On the conclusions built in to his premises, his jurisprudence led directly to the results his supporters approved. Addressing abortion, the death penalty, affirmative action, and both gun rights and gay rights, he delighted his followers. In limiting Congress, restricting the federal judiciary, and protecting executive power he pleased most if not all of them. Further, his decisions under the Constitution's religion clauses exerted an enormous appeal to much of the party's political base. He upheld government benefits to religious groups[13] and religious invocations at public ceremonies,[14] insisted that the Constitution

---

[11] SCALIA SPEAKS, 334 (emphasis in original).

[12] MURPHY, SCALIA, 492. "It's been a long time" since he attended a party with both liberals and conservatives, Scalia admitted. Jennifer Senior, *In Conversation: Antonin Scalia*, NEW YORK MAGAZINE, Oct. 6, 2013, *available at* http://nymag.com/nymag/features/antonin-scalia-2013-10/index5.html (last consulted Nov. 16, 2018) [hereafter Senior, *In Conversation*]. Scalia read *The Wall Street Journal* and the *Washington Times* regularly, canceled his subscription to the *Washington Post* ("so shrilly, *shrilly* liberal"), and did not read the *New York Times. Id.*, index1 (emphasis in original).

[13] *E.g.*, Mitchell v. Helms, 530 U.S. 793 (2000) (Scalia, J., joining plurality opinion by Thomas, J., upholding government aid to parochial schools for general religious instruction).

[14] *E.g.*, Lee v. Weisman, 505 U.S. 577, 631 (Scalia, J., dissenting, arguing that a prayer delivered at public school graduation was valid on "traditional" grounds and was not "coercive").

favored religion over irreligion,[15] and even defended a religiously inspired state statute that required the teaching of "creation science."[16] He managed to appeal to almost the entire Republican base—its religious wing as well as its libertarian, free-market, and traditional conservative wings—by linking Christianity closely to capitalism which, he argued, was "more *dependent* upon Christianity than socialism is."[17]

In practical terms Scalia was especially reliable in advancing the Republican agenda. Beyond working to expand rights involving guns and religion, he sought to sharply limit other rights raised by consumers, employees, tort claimants, environmental advocates, civil rights plaintiffs, criminal defendants, and those claiming to be victims of statutory and con-stitutional violations. In those efforts he was relatively successful because the other conservative justices were for the most part in agreement with his views. Their unity was hardly surprising because the Republican Party had been fully committed to those efforts since the Reagan administration and had worked assiduously to swamp the federal bench with judges who shared its anti-plaintiff and pro-corporate ideology.[18]

[15] The Founders "believed that the public virtues inculcated by religion are a public good." Lamb's Chapel v. Center Moriches Union Free School District, 508 U.S. 384, 397, 400 (1993) (Scalia, J., con-curring in the judgment). *Accord* Good News Club v. Milford Central School, 533 U.S. 98, 120 (2001) (Scalia, J., concurring); Locke v. Davey, 540 U.S. 712, 726 (Scalia, J., dissenting); Board of Education of Kiryas Joel Village School District v. Grumet, 512 U.S. 687, 732 (1994) (Scalia, J., dissenting); SCALIA SPEAKS, 322–24.

[16] Edwards v. Aguillar, 482 U.S. 578, 610 (1987) (Scalia, J., dissenting). Scalia's especially narrow in-terpretation of the Free Exercise Clause and his carefully designed interpretation of the Establishment Clause both favored majoritarian rule and, as a practical matter, implicitly favored Christian religions and values. HASEN, JUSTICE OF CONTRADICTIONS, 111–13: Erwin Chemerinsky, *The Jurisprudence of Justice Scalia: A Critical Appraisal*, 22 U. HAW. L. REV. 385, 386–89 (2000).

[17] SCALIA SPEAKS, 341 (emphasis in original). On the relation between the Republican Party, Christian religious groups, and support for the "free enterprise" system, *see, e.g.,* KEVIN M. KRUSE, ONE NATION UNDER GOD: HOW CORPORATE AMERICA INVENTED CHRISTIAN AMERICA (2015).

[18] The Republican Party became committed to anti-litigation rhetoric and policies, condemning litigation against business as largely "frivolous" and advancing various proposals for self-serving "tort reform." It regularly supported proposals designed to eliminate incentives and create disincentives for potential plaintiffs, and the conservative justices on the Rehnquist and Roberts Courts issued a long string of decisions implementing those ideas. *See, e.g.,* STEPHEN B. BURBANK & SEAN FARHANG, RIGHTS AND RETRENCHMENT: THE COUNTERREVOLUTION AGAINST FEDERAL LITIGATION, esp. chs. 2–4 (2017) [hereafter BURBANK & FARHANG, RIGHTS AND RETRENCHMENT]; WILLIAM HALTOM & MICHAEL MCCANN, DISTORTING THE LAW: POLITICS, MEDIA, AND THE LITIGATION CRISIS (2004); LEE EPSTEIN & JEFFREY A. SEGAL, ADVICE AND CONSENT: THE POLITICS OF JUDICIAL APPOINTMENTS (2005); NANCY SCHERER, SCORING POINTS: POLITICIANS, ACTIVISTS, AND THE LOWER FEDERAL COURT APPOINTMENT PROCESS (2005); Edward A. Purcell, Jr., *The Class Action Fairness Act in Perspective: The Old and the New in Federal Jurisdictional Reform*, 156 U. PA. L. REV. 1823, 1889–1904 (2008); Theodore Eisenberg, *U.S. Chamber of Commerce Liability Survey: Inaccurate, Unfair, and Bad for Business*, 6 J. EMPIRICAL LEGAL STUD. 969 (2009).

By one empirical yardstick the five conservatives (Scalia, Rehnquist, Thomas, Alito, and Kennedy) were the least supportive of private enforcement actions among the twenty-nine justices who most recently served on the Court, and by a second measure they were five of the seven most anti-private enforcement justices to sit on the Court in the past half century.[19] Their highly restrictive decisions on standing[20] and the Eleventh Amendment[21] served those goals, as did their decisions denying implied constitutional and statutory rights of action[22] and barring plaintiffs from the courts by forcing them to go to arbitration.[23] So, too, did their decision to void the right of action Congress established in the Violence Against Women Act,[24] their use of preemption to bar state law claims against pharmaceutical companies,[25] and their many rulings that raised obstacles in the path of claimants who brought suit under a variety of federal statutes, including the Privacy Act,[26] the Fair Labor Standards Act,[27] the Securities and Exchange Act of 1934,[28] the Civil Rights Act of 1964,[29] the Age Discrimination in Employment Act,[30] and Title IX of the Educational Amendments of 1972.[31] Across a range of cases their decisions grew increasingly favorable to business organizations and hostile

[19] BURBANK & FARHANG, RIGHTS AND RETRENCHMENT, 183, 173.
[20] E.g., Allen v. Wright, 468 U.S. 737 (1984) (O'Connor, J.); Lujan v. Defenders of Wildlife, 504 U.S. 555 (1992) (Scalia, J.); Arizona Christian School Tuition Organization v. Winn, 563 U.S. 125 (2011) (Kennedy, J.); Hein v. Freedom from Religion Foundation, Inc., 551 U.S. 587 (2007) (Alito, J.).
[21] E.g., Seminole Tribe of Florida v. Florida, 517 U.S. 44 (1996) (Rehnquist, C.J.); Alden v. Maine, 527 U.S. 706 (1999) (Kennedy, J.); Federal Maritime Commission v. South Carolina State Ports Authority, 535 U.S. 743 (2002) (Thomas, J.); Kimel v. Florida Board of Regents, 528 U.S. 62 (2000) (O'Connor, J.); Coleman v. Court of Appeals of Maryland, 566 U.S. 30 (2012) (Kennedy, J.).
[22] E.g., Texas Industries, Inc. v. Radcliff Materials, Inc., 451 U.S. 630 (1981) (Berger, C.J.); United States v. Stanley, 483 U.S. 669 (1987) (Scalia, J.); Schweiker v. Chilicky, 487 U.S. 412 (1988) (O'Connor, J.); Alexander v. Sandoval, 532 U.S. 275 (2001) (Scalia, J.); Correctional Services Corp. v. Malesko, 534 U.S. 61 (2001) (Rehnquist, C.J.); Stoneridge Investment Partners, LLC v. Scientific-Atlanta, Inc., 552 U.S. 148 (2008) (Kennedy, J.).
[23] E.g., American Express Co. v. Italian Colors Restaurant, 133 S. Ct. 2304 (2013) (Scalia, J.); Rent-a-Center, West, Inc. v. Jackson, 561 U.S. 63 (2010) (Scalia, J.); CompuCredit Corp. v. Greenwood, 565 U.S. 95 (2012) (Scalia, J.); Gilmer v. Interstate Johnson/Lane Corp., 500 U.S. 20 (1991) (White, J.); Shearson/American Express Inc. v. McMahon, 482 U.S. 220 (1987) (O'Connor, J.).
[24] United States v. Morrison, 529 U.S. 598, 627 (2000) (Rehnquist, C.J.).
[25] Mutual Pharmaceutical Co., Inc. v. Bartlett, 133 S. Ct. 2466 (3013) (Alito, J.); Pliva, Inc. v. Mensing, 564 U.S. 604 (2011) (Thomas, J.).
[26] Federal Aviation Administration v. Cooper, 566 U.S. 284 (2012) (Alito, J.).
[27] Christopher v. SmithKline Beecham Corp., 567 U.S. 142 (2012) (Alito, J.).
[28] Janus Capital Group, Inc. v. First Derivative Traders, 564 U.S. 135 (2011) (Thomas, J.); Morrison v. National Australian Bank, Ltd., 561 U.S. 247 (2010) (Scalia, J.); Central Bank of Denver, N.A. v. First Interstate Bank of Denver, N.A., 511 U.S. 164 (1994) (Kennedy, J.); Stoneridge Investment Partners, LLC v. Scientific-Atlantic, Inc., 552 U.S. 148 (2008) (Kennedy, J.).
[29] University of Texas Southwestern Medical Center v. Nassar, 570 U.S. 338 (2013) (Kennedy, J.); Vance v. Ball State University, 570 U.S. 421 (2013) (Alito, J.); Ledbetter v. Goodyear Tire & Rubber Co., Inc., 550 U.S. 618 (2007) (Alito, J.).
[30] Gross v. FBL Financial Services, Inc., 557 U.S. 167, 179–80 (2001) (Thomas, J.).
[31] Gebser v. Lago Vista Independent School District, 524 U.S. 274, 290–93 (1998) (O'Connor, J.).

to those who challenged their interests.[32] The Court had been "captured by the Chamber of Commerce," one scholar concluded in 2012, while another noted that in the 2012–2013 term the Court sided with the Chamber in fourteen of eighteen cases in which the organization filed an amicus brief.[33] In retirement, the ever courtly and polite Justice John Paul Stevens acknowledged the significance of Scalia's position rejecting implied constitutional causes of action. His assertions, Stevens wrote, "exposed a pro-defendant bias."[34]

To a large extent, Scalia was the point person driving those efforts. While teaching at the University of Chicago and editing the American Enterprise Institute's journal *Regulation* in the early 1980s he urged the abolition of "new tort theories" that affected interstate businesses,[35] and on the U.S. Court of Appeals for the District of Columbia his policy views had been quite clear. There, "he ruled against sixteen out of seventeen civil plaintiffs who claimed their constitutional rights had been violated" and proved "particularly adept at invoking procedural defenses to constitutional claims."[36] One of the early causes he joined, for example, was the corporate "tort reform" campaign to restrict federal statutes that offered attorneys' fees to prevailing parties. In the early 1980s he advocated legislation to curb the award of such fees. The courts had interpreted federal attorneys' fees statutes to favor plaintiffs but not defendants, he charged, and the law had become "an expanding wasteland of confusion."[37] Once on the Supreme Court, he joined the four other conservatives in limiting recoveries under the federal Civil Rights Attorneys' Fees Statute and added a separate concurrence to warn of the potential "inequity" and "evil" inherent in any broader rule.[38] One empirical study concluded that Scalia was among "the most anti-private enforcement justices

[32] The Court's pro-business orientation was especially noticeable after Chief Justice Roberts and Justice Alito joined the Court. Lee Epstein, William M. Landes, & Richard A. Posner, *How Business Fares in the Supreme Court*, 97 MINN. L. REV. 1431 (2013); ALAN B. MORRISON, SAVED BY THE SUPREME COURT: RESCUING CORPORATE AMERICA (2011); Jeffrey Rosen, *Supreme Court Inc.*, N.Y. TIMES MAGAZINE, Mar. 16, 2008.

[33] Paul D. Carrington, *Business Interests and the Long Arm in 2011*, 63 S.C. L. REV. 637 (2012); A.E. Dick Howard, *Ten Things the 2012–13 Term Tells Us About the Roberts Court*, 99 VA. L. REV. 48, 52–54 (2013).

[34] JOHN PAUL STEVENS, THE MAKING OF A JUSTICE 382 (2019).

[35] Antonin Scalia, *The Two Faces of Federalism*, 6 HARV. J.L. & PUB. POL'Y 19, 22 (1982).

[36] James G. Wilson, *Constraints of Power: The Constitutional Opinions of Judges Scalia, Bork, Posner, Easterbrook, and Winter*, 40 U. MIAMI L. REV. 1171, 1181 (1986).

[37] Unsigned [Antonin Scalia], *The Private Attorney General Industry: Doing Well by Doing Good*, REGULATION, May/June 1982, at 5–7 (quote at 6). "Such chaos often accompanies the initial attempt to abandon important and long-standing legal traditions." *Id.* at 6.

[38] Buckhannon Board and Care Home v. West Virginia Department of Health and Human Resources, 532 U.S. 598, 610, 618, 622 (2001) (Scalia, J., concurring). *Cf.* Farrar v. Hobby, 506 U.S. 103 (1992) (Thomas, J., joined by Scalia, J.).

to serve on the Supreme Court in a period spanning more than 50 years";[39] another found that he was the most conservative justice on the Court since 1953;[40] and a third found that he ranked as one of the most conservative justices to sit on the Court in the past three-quarters of a century.[41]

Scalia's efforts to deny injured and aggrieved parties access to the federal courts were strikingly apparent and relentless in two critically important areas. One was in civil rights cases where the Court persistently limited the reach and effectiveness of protective federal laws, and the other was in the broad field of federal litigation in general where the Court imposed new procedural burdens on plaintiffs that heavily advantaged defendants. For the most part the Court's other conservative justices joined him in both areas, and together they brought sweeping changes to the law that broadly handicapped individuals who sought to sue governments or private corporations.

In the first area, civil rights, Scalia made his political views clear as soon as he joined the Court,[42] but it was only after Anthony Kennedy took his seat and provided a fifth conservative vote in 1988 that the concerted ideological campaign took off. Then, beginning in the 1988–1989 term, a new five-justice conservative majority issued a string of restrictive decisions designed to limit federal civil rights and antidiscrimination laws.[43] Their decisions seemed so consistent in results and so driven by party ideology that the Democratic Congress rallied in opposition. In 1990 Democrats passed a relatively strong measure overturning some of the those recent decisions, but Republican President George H.W. Bush vetoed it, leading the next year to the passage and signing of a weaker compromise law.[44] With the new Civil Rights Act of 1991 in place, the conservative justices backed off a bit but nonetheless

---

[39] BURBANK & FARHANG, RIGHTS AND RETRENCHMENT, 34. *See id.* at 150–51.

[40] LEE EPSTEIN & JEFFREY A. SEGAL, ADVICE AND CONSENT: THE POLITICS OF JUDICIAL APPOINTMENTS 110 (2005).

[41] Lee Epstein, William M. Landes, & Richard A. Posner, *Revisiting the Ideological Rankings of Supreme Court Justices*, 44 J. LEGAL STUD. S295 (2015).

[42] *E.g.*, Newton v. Rumery, 480 U.S. 386 (1987) (Powell, J., joined by Scalia); Anderson v. Creighton, 483 U.S. 635 (1987) (Scalia, J.); United States v. Stanley, 483 U.S. 669 (1987) (Scalia, J.).

[43] *E.g.*, Lorance v. AT&T Technologies, Inc., 490 U.S. 900 (1989) (Scalia, J.); Martin v. Wilks, 490 U.S. 755 (1989) (Rehnquist, C.J., joined by Scalia, J.); Wards Cove Packing Co. v. Atonio, 490 U.S. 642 (1989) (White, J., joined by Scalia, J.); Jett v. Dallas Independent School District, 491 U.S. 701, 738 (1989) (Scalia, J., concurring in part and concurring in the judgment); Patterson v. McLean Credit Union, 491 U.S. 164 (1989) (Kennedy, J., joined by Scalia, J.).

[44] Kingsley R. Browne, *The Civil Rights Act of 1991: A "Quota Bill," a Codification of Griggs, a Partial Return to Ward's Cove, or All of the Above*, 43 CASE W. RES. L. REV. 287 (1993); Roger Clegg, *Introduction: A Brief Legislative History of the Civil Rights Act of 1991*, 54 LA. L. REV. 1459 (1994); Peter M. Leibold, Stephen A. Sola, & Reginald E. Jones, *Civil Rights Act of 1991: Race to the Finish— Civil Rights, Quotas, and Disparate Impact in 1991*, 45 RUTGERS L. REV. 1043 (1993).

continued their efforts to narrow the protections afforded by various federal civil rights laws.[45]

Sometimes, too, Scalia pressed for restrictions that were more extreme than even the other conservative justices were ready to accept.[46] Dissenting in *Crawford-El v. Britton*, joined only by Justice Thomas, he made the radical claim that the Court had been wrong in 1961 when it decided *Monroe v. Pape*, the cornerstone of modern civil rights litigation under Section 1983.[47] Overturning *Monroe* would severely limit Section 1983 as a viable remedy for those abused by the unlawful actions of local governmental units and state and local officials. Equally radical, he concurred alone in *Ricci v. DeStefano* to suggest that Title VII of the Civil Rights Act of 1964 was unconstitutional insofar as it allowed for liability on the basis of disparate impact. The "war between disparate impact and equal protection," he prophesied, "will be waged sooner or later."[48] Were the Court to strike down all "disparate impact" liability, it would make the enforcement of antidiscrimination laws exceptionally difficult and, in many or most instances, virtually impossible. Such a result did not concern Scalia, for he believed that the law often and properly denied remedies for injuries of many kinds. Indeed, even when fundamental rights were at issue, he readily insisted on the principle "that not all constitutional claims require a judicial remedy."[49]

To protect defendants from civil rights claims, Scalia also voted to strengthen the immunities that they could invoke to defeat actions under Section 1983. The text of that statute was silent as to immunities, an omission that readily suggested that Congress simply intended no immunities to apply. Writing on an analogous issue, Scalia acknowledged that congressional

---

[45] *E.g.*, Wilson v. Seiter, 501 U.S. 294 (1991) (Scalia, J.); Bray v. Alexandria Women's Health Clinic, 506 U.S. 263 (1993) (Scalia, J.); Heck v. Humphrey, 512 U.S. 477 (1994) (Scalia, J.); Lewis v. Casey, 518 U.S. 343 (1996) (Scalia, J.); Town of Castle Rock v. Gonzales, 545 U.S. 748 (2005) (Scalia, J.).

[46] In *Connick v. Thompson*, 563 U.S. 51 (Thomas, J.), for example, Scalia not only concurred in another 5–4 decision of the conservative justices denying a civil rights claim, but he also wrote separately, joined only by Justice Alito, to minimize the importance of constitutional wrongs that prosecutors' offices could make, dismissing them as mere insignificant "mistakes" and declaring that even "Large Numbers" of such transgressions would simply be insufficient to establish the office's liability. *Id.* at 72, 73.

[47] Crawford-El v. Britton, 523 U.S. 574, 611 (1998) (Scalia, J., dissenting, joined only by Thomas, J.). Monroe v. Pape, 365 U.S. 167 (1961) (Douglas, J.), ruled that "under color of law" was not limited to legally "authorized" actions by government officials but included any action, however unlawful, that was taken under a badge of authority.

[48] Ricci v. DiStefano, 557 U.S. 557, 594, 595–96 (2009) (Scalia, J., concurring).

[49] Webster v. Doe, 486 U.S. 592, 606, 614 (1988) (Scalia, J., dissenting). *See id.* at 612–13. *Accord* United States v. Windsor, 570 U.S. 744, 778, 781 (2013) (Scalia, J., dissenting); Arizona State Legislature v. Arizona Independent Redistricting Commission, 135 S. Ct. 2652, 2694 (2015) (Scalia, J., dissenting); Heck v. Humphrey, 512 U.S. 477, 490 n.10 (1994) (Scalia, J.).

silence readily supported that negative inference. "If one did not believe that state limitations periods applied of their own force," he acknowledged, "the most natural intention to impute to a Congress that enacted no limitations period would be that it wished none."[50] Whatever Congress may have intended in enacting Section 1983, however, the Court had applied common-law immunity doctrines to such actions long before Scalia took his seat, and on an issue that so well served his restrictive purposes he readily acceded to precedent.[51] In doing so he abandoned "the most natural intention to impute" to Congress as well as any pretense of adhering to the textualism that he so often claimed to honor.[52] For the most part he used those common-law immunity doctrines to support rulings that made it increasingly difficult for civil rights plaintiffs to prevail.[53]

To further discourage and defeat such plaintiffs, Scalia also tried to block them from asserting a number of specific claims. Although he abandoned originalism on some First Amendment issues, he nonetheless applied it strictly when it served to deny claims for which he had no sympathy. He readily rejected suits brought both by employees whom the government fired, demoted, or otherwise punished because of their political affiliations[54] and by those who were denied government contracts[55] or access to government funding programs[56] for political reasons.

---

[50] Agency Holding Corp. v. Malley-Duff & Associates, Inc., 483 U.S. 143, 157, 164 (1987) (Scalia, J., concurring in the judgment). *See also* Lampf, Pleva, Lipkind, Prupis & Petigrow v. Gilbertson, 501 U.S. 350, 364, 365 (1991) (Scalia, J., concurring in part and concurring in the judgment).

[51] "The doctrine of official immunity against damages actions under § 1983 is rooted in the assumption that that statute did not abolish those immunities traditionally available at common law." Richardson v. McKnight, 521 U.S. 399, 414 (1997) (Scalia, J., dissenting).

[52] Aware that he was engaging in "essentially legislative activity" in immunity cases, Scalia blamed the Warren Court for his actions. He argued that in deciding *Monroe v. Pape*, 365 U.S. 167 (1961), it had wrongly expanded the law. Consequently, he maintained, he was justified in supporting new restrictive rules that would limit the reach of that decision. *Crawford-El*, 523 U.S. at 611 (Scalia, J., dissenting). His rationale struck a triple blow, one against those who would criticize him for inconsistency, another against those who would bring actions under Section 1983, and a third against his regular target, the Warren Court.

[53] Scalia wrote for the Court in *Anderson v. Creighton*, 483 U.S. 635 (1987) (Scalia, J.), and joined restrictive majorities in, *e.g.*, *Van de Kamp v. Goldstein*, 555 U.S. 335 (2009) (Breyer, J.); *Saucier v. Katz*, 533 U.S. 194 (2001) (Kennedy, J.); and *Brosseau v. Haugen*, 543 U.S. 194 (2004) (per curiam). He urged further limiting qualifications in *Richardson v. McKnight*, 521 U.S. at 414 (Scalia, J., dissenting), and *Burns v. Reed*, 500 U.S. 478, 496 (1991) (Scalia, J., concurring in the judgment in part and dissenting in part).

[54] Rutan v. Republican Party of Illinois, 497 U.S. 62, 92 (1990) (Scalia, J., dissenting).

[55] O'Hare Truck Service v. City of Northlake, 518 U.S. 712, 726 (1996) (Scalia, J., dissenting). His opinion in the case appeared in *Board of County Commissioners, Wabaunsee County v. Umbehr*, 518 U.S. 668, 686 (1996).

[56] National Endowment for the Arts v. Finley, 524 U.S. 569, 590 (1998) (Scalia, J., concurring in the judgment).

Indeed, Scalia's use of First Amendment speech doctrine was especially revealing. Overwhelmingly, his decisions favored the rights of those who took conservative as opposed to liberal political positions. A statistical study of the Court's free speech decisions found that he was almost three times as likely to vote in favor of those who espoused conservative messages as he was to vote in favor of those espousing liberal ones.[57]

Scalia's ideological campaign was strikingly apparent in the area of voting rights. He not only joined the other conservative justices in restricting laws designed to safeguard voter rights but urged particularly narrow views of the protections the Constitution offered to those who sought to vote.[58] Concurring in the Court's judgment upholding an Indiana law requiring voters to present a government-issued photo ID, he declared that there was no valid legal objection to restrictions on voting merely because they had burdensome impacts on some identifiable groups of voters. He claimed that the Court's precedents meant that burdens on voting reached constitutional significance only if they impacted "voters generally." To make his implicit political point crystal clear, he declared specifically that the "Fourteenth Amendment does not regard neutral laws as invidious ones, even when their burdens purportedly fall disproportionately on a protected class."[59]

His argument seemed partisan on its face and designed to encourage more Republican-backed voter-suppression measures in other states. In addressing other constitutional rights, for example, he never suggested that a claimant could not prevail unless he or she showed that all other similar rights holders were equally burdened by the same restrictive law. Indeed, in the oral argument in the photo ID case he had seemed to acknowledge that the position he later took in his opinion was wrong when he noted that if "one half of one percent" of the voters found the photo ID requirement substantially burdensome, they would "have a cause of action to say you can't apply it to me."[60]

---

[57] Lee Epstein, Christopher M. Parker, & Jeffrey A. Segal, *Do Justices Defend the Speech They Hate?* (May 2, 2014), 4, *available at* http://epstein.wustl.edu/research/InGroupBias.pdf (last consulted July 24, 2019).

[58] *E.g.*, Shelby County v. Holder, 570 U.S. 1 (2013) (Roberts, C.J., joined by Scalia, J.); Northwest Austin Municipal Utility District No. One v. Holder, 557 U.S. 193 (2009) (Roberts, C.J., joined by Scalia, J.).

[59] Crawford v. Marion County Election Board, 553 U.S. 181, 204, 206 (2008) (Scalia, J., concurring in the judgment). "Scalia's opinion did not even address partisanship concerns, a sharp contrast to his focus on the issue of incumbency protection in the campaign finance cases." HASEN, JUSTICE OF CONTRADICTIONS, 131.

[60] Christopher S. Elmendorf & Edward B. Foley, *Gatekeeping v. Balancing in the Constitutional Law of Elections: Methodological Uncertainty on the High Court*, 17 WM. & MARY BILL RTS. J. 507,

Even more broadly, in *Vieth v. Jubilirer*, he sought to prevent the Court from interfering in any way with partisan gerrymanders, a manipulative device that Republicans were using effectively to strengthen their ability to control state legislatures and the House of Representatives. He acknowledged "the incompatibility of severe partisan gerrymanders with democratic principles" but pronounced that fact judicially irrelevant. He assumed that such gerrymanders could violate the Constitution but declared that even if they did the courts could still not interfere with them.[61] There was, he declared, no possible judicial remedy for such abuses.[62]

Underlying Scalia's attitude was a surprisingly open racial insensitivity. He ignored originalist historical evidence in condemning affirmative action,[63] dismissed extensive evidence of governmental responsibility for continuing racial discrimination and inequality in the twentieth century,[64] seemed to suggest that blacks were better suited for "slower-track" schools,[65] and scorned the Voting Rights Act of 1965 as a "perpetuation of racial entitlement."[66] Refusing even to acknowledge the substantive point involved, he mocked the idea that racial diversity in a law school's student body could

534 n.165 (2008) [hereafter Elmendorf & Foley, *Gatekeeping*]. Scalia's argument was "analogous to requiring a plaintiff-parishioner challenging a zoning ordinance expressly directed at churches to prove that the ordinance not only substantially burdens the plaintiff's exercise of religion (for example, by preventing his congregation from building a church on land that they own in the jurisdiction), but rather that the ordinance substantially interferes with the practice of religion generally throughout the jurisdiction (which it might not do if most major denominations already have houses of worship in the jurisdiction)." *Id.*

[61] Vieth v. Jubilirer, 541 U.S. 267, 292–93, 305–06 (quote at 292) (2004) (Scalia, J., announcing judgment of Court and delivering opinion for four-justice plurality). *See* HASEN, JUSTICE OF CONTRADICTIONS, 122–23.

[62] In *Rucho v. Common Cause*, 139 S. Ct. 2484 (2019) (Roberts, C.J.), over the dissent of the four Democratic justices, five Republican justices followed Scalia's lead and held that challenges to partisan gerrymanders presented "political questions" that were beyond the power of the courts to adjudicate.

[63] HASEN, JUSTICE OF CONTRADICTIONS, 58, 102, 105–07.

[64] *See, e.g.,* RICHARD ROTHSTEIN, THE COLOR OF LAW: A FORGOTTEN HISTORY OF HOW OUR GOVERNMENT SEGREGATED AMERICA (2017); IRA KATZNELSON, WHEN AFFIRMATIVE ACTION WAS WHITE: AN UNTOLD STORY OF RACIAL INEQUALITY IN TWENTIETH-CENTURY AMERICA (2005); KENNETH T. JACKSON, CRABGRASS FRONTIER: THE SUBURBANIZATION OF THE UNITED STATES (1985).

[65] Transcript of oral argument, Fisher v. University of Texas, No. 14-981 (Dec. 9, 2015), 67-68.

[66] Transcript of oral argument, Shelby County, Alabama v. Holder, No. 12-96 (Feb. 27, 2013), 47. Scalia's comments echoed the post-Reconstruction views of Justice Joseph Bradley who ruled the Civil Rights Act of 1875 unconstitutional and declared that "there must be some stage" when those who have "emerged from slavery" should "cease[] to be the special favorite of the laws" and be content with "the ordinary modes by which other men's right are protected." The Civil Rights Cases, 109 U.S. 3, 25 (1883) (Bradley, J.).

provide an "educational benefit."[67] Most overtly, he readily acknowledged and accepted what he regarded as an inevitable racial bias in the law.[68] Although he repeatedly declared that race should be irrelevant and that only individual merit should count,[69] he refused to recognize the significance of the fact that evaluations of individual merit not only required partially subjective judgments but also—and far more important—judgments that were easily and often made through racially biased lenses.[70] His views aligned closely with the views of some elements of the Republican coalition[71] and had the practical effect of privileging whites and disadvantaging blacks and other minorities.

In the second area where Scalia pressed to limit access to the courts, cases interpreting the procedural rules that controlled federal litigation generally, he joined the other conservatives in changing the Court's interpretations of several key provisions of the Federal Rules of Civil Procedure. The changes constricted the ability of plaintiffs to obtain relief in federal cases across the board, especially those in which government agencies or business organizations held the evidence necessary to plead and prove the claims at issue.[72] Together, the conservative justices tightened pleading requirements under

[67] Grutter v. Bollinger, 539 U.S. 306, 346, 347–48 (2003) (Scalia, J., concurring in part and dissenting in part).

[68] See Dennis D. Dorin, *Far Right of the Mainstream: Racism, Rights and Remedies from the Perspective of Justice Antonin Scalia's McCleskey Memorandum*, 45 MERCER L. REV. 1035, 1038 (1994). In rejecting the claim that Georgia applied the death penalty in a racially discriminatory manner, Scalia not only dismissed substantial empirical evidence that supported the claim but also informed the other justices that such racial disparities in the imposition of the death penalty, even if proven, would not trouble him.

[69] *E.g.*, Richmond v. J.A. Croson Co., 488 U.S. 469, 520, 527–28 (1989) (Scalia, J., concurring in the judgment); Antonin Scalia, *The Disease as Cure: "In order to get beyond racism, we must first take account of race,"* 1979 WASH. U. L.Q. 147 (1979).

[70] *See, e.g.*, Charles R. Lawrence III, *Two Views of the River: A Critique of the Liberal Defense of Affirmative Action*, 101 COLUM. L. REV. 928 (2001); Kristen Holmquist, Marjorie Shultz, Sheldon Zedeck, & David Openheimer, *Measuring Merit: The Shultz-Zedeck Research on Law School Admissions*, 63 J. LEGAL EDUC. 565 (2014); Aaron N. Taylor, *Reimagining Merit as Achievement*, 44 N.M. L. REV. 1 (2014).

[71] "The black freedom insurgency of the 1950s and 1960s dismantled the white supremacist southern Democratic Party, leading to a partisan realignment that saw the white South and much of the growing suburban fringe on the nation's cities vault toward the Republican party between the 1950s ad 1990s." ROBERT O. SELF, ALL IN THE FAMILY: THE REALIGNMENT OF AMERICAN DEMOCRACY SINCE THE 1960s, at 6 (2012).

[72] *E.g.*, Comcast Corp. v. Behrend, 569 U.S. 27 (2013 (Scalia, J.). *See, e.g.*, Edward A. Purcell, Jr., *From the Particular to the General: Three Federal Rules and the Jurisprudence of the Rehnquist and Roberts Courts*, 162 U. PA. L. REV. 1731, 1732–41 (2014) [hereafter Purcell, *From the Particular*]; Arthur R. Miller, *Simplified Pleading, Meaningful Days in Court, and Trials on the Merits: Reflections on the Deformation of Federal Procedure*, 88 N.Y.U. L. REV. 286 (2013); Judith Resnik, *Constricting Remedies: The Rehnquist Judiciary, Congress, and Federal Power*, 78 IND. L.J. 223 (2003); Stephen B. Burbank & Sean Farhang, *Litigation Reform: An Institutional Approach*, 162 U. PA. L REV. 1543 (2014).

Rule 8,[73] limited the availability of class actions under Rule 23,[74] made summary judgment easier for defendants under Rule 56,[75] and gave defendants added leverage to force low settlements on plaintiffs under Rule 68.[76]

Scalia's opinion in *Wal-Mart Stores, Inc. v. Dukes* was a particularly obvious example of his efforts to block court access.[77] There, he reversed two lower courts and denied class certification to a class of one and a half million women employees who brought gender-discrimination claims against Wal-Mart. To do so, he raised the requirements for class actions in the federal courts to demanding new heights and imposed "a decisive change in the meaning of Rule 23."[78]

His class action opinions made his social and economic sympathies clear. He privileged defendants by giving legal weight to the costs and burdens that class actions forced on them while dismissing the significance of the costs and burdens that foreclosing class actions forced on plaintiffs.[79] Absent the class action remedy, those costs and burdens would as a practical matter prevent literally millions of injured or aggrieved individuals from seeking judicial relief for their injuries. Indeed, he showed concern for protecting the monetary claims of individual class members only when such solicitude provided a useful argument against certifying a Rule 23(b)(2) "injunctive" class action and when the costs and burdens of actually pursuing those claims in separate individual suits would in practice preclude virtually all of them.[80]

Most apparent, like his actions in so many other areas, Scalia's efforts to restrict court access under the Federal Rules contradicted his fundamental methodological and jurisprudential principles. First, on their own terms the changes the conservatives made were inconsistent with originalism, textualism, and traditional understandings of the rules.[81] In their pathbreaking decisions the conservative justices changed the original meaning of the rules, reinterpreted their text in novel ways, and altered the long-established

---

[73] Bell Atlantic Corp. v. Twombly, 550 U.S. 544 (2007) (Souter, J., joined by Scalia, J.); Ashcroft v. Iqbal, 556 U.S. 662 (2009) (Kennedy, J., joined by Scalia, J.).

[74] Wal-Mart Stores, Inc. v. Dukes, 564 U.S. 338 (2011) (Scalia, J.); *Comcast*, 569 U.S. 27 (Scalia, J.).

[75] Celotex Corp. v. Catrett, 477 U.S. 317 (1986) (Rehnquist, J.); Scott v. Harris, 550 U.S. 372 (2007) (Scalia, J.).

[76] Burbank & Farhang, Rights and Retrenchment, 132–35.

[77] *Wal-Mart*, 564 U.S. 338 (2011) (Scalia, J.).

[78] Burbank & Farhang, Rights and Retrenchment, 142.

[79] *See* Amgen, Inc. v. Connecticut Retirement Plans & Trust Funds, 568 U.S. 455, 483, 485–86 (2013) (Scalia, J., dissenting); American Express Co. v. Italian Colors Restaurant, 570 U.S. 228, 234–38 (2013) (Scalia, J.); AT&T Mobility LLC v. Concepcion, 563 U.S. 333, 350 (2011) (Scalia, J.).

[80] *Wal-Mart*, 569 U.S. at 364 (Scalia, J.).

[81] Purcell, *From the Particular*, 1758–62.

meanings that the rule's drafters, the Congress, and the Court had all originally given them. As one class-action specialist serving on the Advisory
Committee on the Federal Rules declared, Scalia's opinion in *Wal-Mart*
"cannot be squared with the text, structure, or history" of Rule 23.[82]

Second, because the conservative justices made changes that were not based
on any alterations in the text of the rules themselves, their decisions flouted both
Scalia's oft-proclaimed respect for the legislative branch and the principle of
separation of powers. More specifically and egregiously, their decisions rejected
the Court's own prior and express commitment to abide by the rules as previously construed unless and until Congress changed them. Scalia had joined the
Court in repeatedly declaring that the Rules Enabling Act bound the justices
to follow the original meaning of the Federal Rules at the time when Congress
adopted and approved them.[83] Any change in the meaning of Rule 8, the Court
declared unanimously in 1993, "must be obtained by the process of amending
the Federal Rules, and not by judicial interpretation."[84] Six years later Scalia
and the Court again reaffirmed the same principle, this time addressing Rule
23. "The nub of our position is that we are bound to follow Rules 23 as we understood it upon its adoption," they declared. In any event, "we are not free to
alter it except through the process prescribed by Congress in the Rules Enabling
Act."[85] Scalia embraced that principle completely. He not only joined the Court's
opinion but also joined Rehnquist's separate concurrence stating explicitly that
"[u]nless and until the Federal Rules of Civil Procedure are revised, the Court's
opinion correctly states the existing law, and I join it."[86]

In the opening decade of the twenty-first century, however, Scalia turned
his back on those commitments and joined the other conservative justices in
contravening them. In doing so they bypassed Congress, ignored the principle of separation of powers, and abandoned the claims of originalism, textualism, and traditionalism. To achieve their policy goals, they made new
law reinterpreting Rules 8, 23, and 56 and barred untold numbers of injured
individuals from seeking lawful redress in the federal courts.[87]

---

[82] Robert H. Klonoff, *The Future of Class Actions: The Decline of Class Actions*, 90 Wash. U. L. Rev.
729, 776 (2013).

[83] 48 Stat. 1064, June 19, 1934, currently codified at 28 U.S.C. Sec. 2072.

[84] Leatherman v. Tarrant County Narcotics Intelligence & Coordination Unit, 507 U.S. 163,
168 (1993) (Rehnquist, C.J., joined by Scalia, J.). *See* Stephen B. Burbank, *Procedure, Politics, and
Power: The Role of Congress*, 79 Notre Dame L. Rev. 1677, 1681–89 (2004).

[85] Ortiz v. Fibreboard Corp., 527 U.S. 815, 861 (1999) (Souter, J., joined by Scalia, J.).

[86] *Ortiz*, 527 U.S. at 865 (Rehnquist, C.J., concurring, joined by Scalia, J.).

[87] *See, e.g.*, Burbank & Farhang, Rights and Retrenchment, ch. 4; Joe S. Cecil et al., Fed.
Judicial Ctr., Motions to Dismiss for Failure to State a Clam After *Iqbal*: Report to

Beyond his formal actions on the bench that advanced the Republican agenda, Scalia also worked steadily in other ways to secure and maintain a position of national leadership on the political right and to expand his influence and standing there. The conservative/libertarian movement that had gathered strength since the 1970s enjoyed a vibrant intellectual foundation, and as a man of ideas Scalia fit in smoothly and quickly took a leadership role.[88] Developing his jurisprudence in speeches and articles before he went on the bench, he continued afterward to refine them and, far more tellingly, to methodically promote them across the country. With his increased visibility as a member of the Supreme Court he became exceptionally active as a public speaker and published books and articles addressed to both professional and popular audiences. Seeking relentlessly to spread his ostensibly neutral and purportedly nonpolitical ideas about originalism, textualism, and traditionalism, he frequently appeared on radio and television to discuss them and tirelessly went on the road to sell them before literally hundreds of live audiences.[89] "He was doing at least a dozen major speeches a year," wrote Joan Biskupic. "Scalia is out there, figuratively and literally," she explained, and he was providing "an inspiring template for right-wing politicians and conservative lawyers and law students."[90] He assiduously sought to "develop followers," concluded another biographer,[91] while a third declared him "a leading preacher in the conservative revival."[92] In 2003 alone he was reimbursed by universities and bar groups for twenty-one separate speaking

THE JUDICIAL CONFERENCE ADVISORY COMMITTEE ON CIVIL RULES 9–11 (2011); Joe S. Cecil et al., *A Quarter-Century of Summary Judgment Practice in Six Federal District Courts*, 4 J. EMPIRICAL & LEGAL STUD. 861, 882–83 (2007); Jonah B. Gelbach, *Note, Locking the Doors to Discovery? Assessing the Effects of* Twombly *and* Iqbal *on Access to Discovery*, 121 YALE L.J. 2270, 2332 (2012); Kevin M. Clermont & Stewart J. Schwab, *Employment Discrimination Plaintiffs in Federal Court: From Bad to Worse?*, 3 HARV. L. & POL'Y REV. 103, 128 n.68 (2009); William H.J. Hubbard, *The Effects of* Twombly *and* Iqbal, 14 J. EMPIRICAL LEGAL STUD. 474 (2017).

[88] *See, e.g.*, JEFFERSON DECKER, THE OTHER RIGHTS REVOLUTION: CONSERVATIVE LAWYERS AND THE REMAKING OF AMERICAN GOVERNMENT (2016); AMANDA HOLLIS-BRUSKY, IDEAS WITH CONSEQUENCES: THE FEDERALIST SOCIETY AND THE CONSERVATIVE COUNTERREVOLUTION (2015) [hereafter HOLLIS-BRUSKY, IDEAS]; STEVEN M. TELES, THE RISE OF THE CONSERVATIVE LEGAL MOVEMENT: THE BATTLE FOR CONTROL OF THE LAW (2008).

[89] "Because of his voluminous off-the-bench speeches and appearances, Scalia opened the door for all manner of extrajudicial behavior by members of the Court. His widely reported and frequently controversial public remarks had changed the conventional perception of the justices from lofty judicial figures to partisan political actors." MURPHY, SCALIA, 306.

[90] BISKUPIC, AMERICAN ORIGINAL, 221.

[91] MURPHY, SCALIA, 163. *See id.* at 172, 222.

[92] RICHARD A. BRISBIN, JR., JUSTICE ANTONIN SCALIA AND THE CONSERVATIVE REVIVAL 1 (1997).

engagements.[93] He had, wrote Laurence Tribe and Joshua Matz, "evangelized originalism."[94]

Scalia was willing, for example, to employ the "block liberty" fallacy that libertarians and economic conservatives loved, treating the pivotal concept of liberty as if it had an unchanging and absolute meaning. Individual "liberty has been reduced" by Court decisions that eroded the rights of property, he declared, and "let us not pretend that that development has not been a *reduction* of individual liberty."[95] Striking was the absence of any consideration of the extent to which a reduction of some liberties in some areas for some people could increase other liberties in other areas for other people—employees, consumers, women, gays, political dissidents, racial and ethnic minorities, injured or aggrieved individuals, and all those who wanted a healthier and safer environment. Contrary to Scalia's contention, "liberty" was not a preexisting absolute, and restricting it in some ways and for some purposes was not a zero-sum game. Indeed, as political philosophers from Harrington and Locke to the present had all recognized, only by imposing restrictions on some liberties could republican society itself survive and prosper. Indeed, many years earlier then Solicitor General and future Supreme Court Justice Stanley Reed shrewdly pointed out the decisive social truth. "Claims of individual liberty may in reality be claims to domination over others."[96]

Appealing to his Republican base by deploying such "block liberty" rhetoric, moreover, Scalia ignored yet another genuinely shared originalist conviction that united the Founders: the unquestioned principle that constitutional liberty required reasonable limits on everyone's liberty so that all could enjoy the liberty that republican government sought to provide. "Individuals entering into society, must give up a share of liberty to preserve the rest," George Washington explained when he transmitted the newly drafted Constitution to the Confederation Congress.[97] "Without such restraint," Fisher Ames seconded in the Massachusetts ratifying convention, "there can be no liberty."[98] To rally his supporters, however, Scalia was

---

[93] JEFFREY TOOBIN, THE NINE: INSIDE THE SECRET WORLD OF THE SUPREME COURT 243 (2007).

[94] LAURENCE TRIBE & JOSHUA MATZ, UNCERTAIN JUSTICE: THE ROBERTS COURT AND THE CONSTITUTION 8 (2014) [hereafter TRIBE & MATZ, UNCERTAIN JUSTICE].

[95] SCALIA SPEAKS, 167 (emphasis in original). *Accord* Scalia, *Originalism*, 856.

[96] DANIEL R. ERNST, TOCQUEVILLE'S NIGHTMARE: THE ADMINISTRATIVE STATE EMERGES IN AMERICA, 1900–1940, at 141 (2014).

[97] George Washington letter transmitting the Constitution to Congress, Sept. 17, 1787, 2 THE RECORDS OF THE FEDERAL CONVENTION OF 1787 666 (Max Farrand ed., 1911).

[98] Fisher Ames, *Speech: Massachusetts Convention, 15 January 1788, in* FRIENDS OF THE CONSTITUTION: WRITINGS OF THE "OTHER" FEDERALISTS 1787–1788, at 198 (Colleen A. Sheehan &

willing to tout an entirely arbitrary concept of "liberty" that contradicted the thinking of the Founders but fit snugly with the antiregulatory rhetoric and policies underlying the Republican agenda.[99]

Even on the bench, Scalia spoke evocatively to the Republican base that listened far beyond the courtroom. Adopting the rhetoric of the religious right, he termed the campaign for gay rights a "culture war"[100] and denigrated "the so-called homosexual agenda."[101] When immigration became a hot-button national issue, he vigorously supported restrictive state efforts that went beyond national law and spoke sympathetically on behalf of his supporters who were hostile to immigration. American citizens, he declared, "feel themselves under siege by large numbers of illegal immigrants who invade their property, strain their social services, and even place their lives in jeopardy."[102] Dissenting from another Court decision, he identified with the most resentful parts of the Republican base when he agonized that "case by case, [the Court] is busy designing a Constitution for a country I do not recognize."[103] Similarly, he played to the right-wing gallery in the oral arguments on the Affordable Care Act by raising what Justice Ginsburg

---

Gary L. McDowell eds., 1998). *See* Edward A. Purcell, Jr., *What Changes in American Constitutional Law and What Does Not?*, 102 Iowa L. Rev. Online 64, 106–13 (2017).

[99] Scalia knew better and sometimes spoke differently. "Any system of government involves a balancing of individual freedom of action against community needs, and it seems to me quite foolish to assume that every further tilt in the direction of greater freedom of action is necessarily good." Scalia Speaks, 193.

[100] "[I]t is no business of the courts (as opposed to the political branches) to take sides in this culture war." Romer v. Evans, 517 U.S. 620, 636, 652 (1996) (Scalia, J., dissenting).

[101] "Today's opinion is the product of a Court, which is the product of a law-profession culture, that has largely signed on to the so-called homosexual agenda, by which I mean the agenda promoted by some homosexual activists directed at eliminating the moral opprobrium that has traditionally attached to homosexual conduct." Lawrence v. Texas, 539 U.S. 558, 586, 602 (2003) (Scalia, J., dissenting).

[102] Arizona v. United States, 567 U.S. 387, 416, 436 (2012) (Scalia, J., concurring in part and dissenting in part).

[103] Board of County Commissioners v. Umbehr, 518 U.S. 668, 686, 711 (1996) (Scalia, J., dissenting from the Court's holding that the First Amendment protected government contractors from retaliation for their political views). Subsequently, the trope became popular on the right. Robert Bork used it for a book title, *A Country I Do Not Recognize: The Legal Assault on American Values* (2005), while Laura Ingraham sounded it on Fox News. "[I]n some parts of the country, it does seem like the America that we know and love doesn't exist anymore," she complained. "Massive demographic changes have been foisted on the American people, and they're changes that none of us ever voted for and most of us don't like." Rachel Leah, *Laura Ingraham enforces racist stereotypes about people of color as the laments demographic changes*, Salon, Aug. 9, 2018, *available at* https://www.salon.com/2018/08/09/laura-ingraham-enforces-racist-stereotypes-about-people-of-color-as-she-laments-demographic-changes/ (last consulted July 25, 2019). For sociological analyses of disaffected whites in the South and Midwest that confirm the Republican appeal of this image, see Arlie Russell Hochschild, Strangers in Their Own Land (2016); J.D. Vance, Hillbilly Elegy: A Memoir of a Family and Culture in Crisis (2016).

bemoaned as the irrelevant "broccoli horrible."[104] That reference was to what one commentator called "the familiar taunting query of the right" that used "the invocation of broccoli as the sickening consequence of unrestrained big government."[105] In wielding the "broccoli horrible," Scalia responded to a particularly powerful political mobilization on the right and invoked the misleading image to further encourage it. "In the wake of Scalia's remarks at the oral argument," noted two scholars, "broccoli and the problem of limiting principles were all over the news."[106]

Scalia's dissents, moreover, sometimes sounded like the histrionics of a rabble rouser. The issue was "quite simply, whether the people, through their elected representatives, or rather this Court, shall control the outcome," he declared in one case, proclaiming grandiloquently that there was only one proper answer: "It shall be the people."[107] Outspoken on issues that aroused the Republican base, he warned during the oral argument in Heller that limiting gun ownership would endanger innocent families and prevent self defense "when you hear somebody crawling in you—your bedroom window."[108] Similarly, in a civil rights suit he opposed a remedial prisoner release order by warning about "the inevitable murders, robberies, and rapes" that the order would cause. Many of those to be released, he warned ominously in racially tinged language that would frighten and infuriate that base, "will undoubtedly be fine physical specimens who have developed intimidating muscles pumping iron in the prison gym."[109] Both his public speeches and his judicial opinions demonstrated that he saw his originalism as far more than a theory of jurisprudence. He saw it as an instrument of political polemics.[110]

[104] See Transcript of oral argument, Department of Health and Human Services v. Florida, No. 11-398 (Mar. 27, 2012), 13.

[105] Adam Gopnik, "The Broccoli Horrible": A Culinary-Legal Dissent, THE NEW YORKER, June 28, 2012, available at https://www.newyorker.com/news/news-desk/the-broccoli-horrible-a-culinary-legal-dissent (last consulted Aug. 5, 2019). In National Federation of Independent Business v. Sibelius, 567 U.S. 519 (2012), Chief Justice Roberts used the broccoli example (at 558), and a joint dissent by the four other conservatives—Scalia, Kennedy, Thomas, and Alito—also defended its use (at 660). Dissenting on another point, Justice Ginsburg mocked the reference as "the broccoli horrible." Id. at 615 and 617.

[106] Mark D. Rosen & Christopher W. Schmidt, Why Broccoli? Limiting Principles and Popular Constitutionalism in the Health Care Case, 61 U.C.L.A. L. REV. 66, 111 (2013). For the right's mobilization effort, see id. at 100–19.

[107] City of Boerne v. Flores, 521 U.S. 507, 537, 544 (1997) (Scalia, J., concurring in part).

[108] Transcript of Oral Argument, District of Columbia v. Heller, No. 07-290 (Mar. 18, 2008), 42.

[109] Brown v. Plata, 563 U.S. 493, 550, 561, 554 (2011) (Scalia, J., dissenting).

[110] Scalia claimed that he wrote his opinions for law students (Senior, In Conversation, index 7), which was surely true. His performances, however, were also intended for a much wider audience which he reached by public appearances, reports in the popular press, and the many professional acolytes and political admirers who spread his words in many forums.

In *United States v. Windsor*, a case involving gay marriage that outraged much of the Republican base, Scalia took the highly unusual step of dramatically urging a congressional confrontation with Democratic President Barack Obama. In *Windsor* the president had refused to defend the anti-gay Defense of Marriage Act, and a five-justice majority voided one of its central provisions. Dissenting angrily and passionately, Scalia charged that the president "did not faithfully implement Congress's statute" and exhorted the legislative branch to rebel against his infidelity. Although the Court could not properly act in the case because there were no truly adverse parties before it, he argued, the lack of a judicial remedy should not and did not limit the ability of Congress itself "to confront the president directly." The legislature, he exhorted, should force "a direct confrontation with the President" and deploy the "innumerable ways" the Constitution gave it "to compel executive action without a lawsuit." Not surprisingly, he justified his plea on originalist grounds. "Our system is *designed* for confrontation," he proclaimed. With demeaning turns of phrase he sneered at the president's "Executive contrivance" and urged Congress to "bring him to heel."[111] Seldom if ever has a justice launched from the Supreme Court bench such a partisan trumpet call to battle aimed at a sitting president of the United States.[112]

Scalia's judicial opinions commanded widespread attention, while his speeches, writings, interviews, and other public appearances and statements created a powerful and compelling popular image.[113] The barbed and often amusing nature of many of his public statements and the sheer nastiness that marked many of his judicial opinions made him a compelling public figure, while the political and social appeal of his personal views and judicial opinions made him the beloved judicial spokesman for the Republican coalition.

[111] United States v. Windsor, 570 U.S. at 791, 790, 787 (Scalia, J., dissenting) (emphases in original).

[112] Scalia issued another, if milder, charge against President Obama in *Arizona v. United States*, 567 U.S. 387, 416, 435–36 (2012) (Scalia, J., concurring in part and dissenting in part) ("Are the sovereign States at the mercy of the Federal Executive's refusal to enforce the Nation's immigration laws?" at 436). *See* TRIBE & MATZ, UNCERTAIN JUSTICE, 207–10.

[113] "Supreme Court clerks—liberal as well as conservative—were enthralled by him. 'There was a lot of Scalia envy in the building,' recalled the clerk of a liberal justice." EVAN THOMAS, FIRST: SANDRA DAY O'CONNOR 237 (2019). At a meeting of the Federalist Society, "young, conservative law students" recited the words from Scalia's dissent in *Morrison v. Olson* "as if it were Holy Scripture." Amanda Hollis-Brusky, *Here's Why Originalism Won't Be Buried with Scalia*, WASH. POST, Feb. 22, 2016, *available at* https://www.washingtonpost.com/news/monkey-cage/wp/2016/02/22/ (last consulted May 28, 2018).

As a result, Scalia became a true media celebrity, a new kind of popularly known and nationally prominent justice.[114] In part, his celebrity status was a function of social change. By the middle of the twentieth century the Supreme Court had become central to American life and politics in many areas, some of which directly and often profoundly touched millions of people in their daily lives. Further, modern media had created a celebrity culture that was constantly on the lookout for striking personalities who could command public attention. In that social context Scalia was a natural fit who offered the public stage an irresistible combination of personal qualities. He possessed legal brilliance and authority, a magnetic personality, theatrical instincts, a charming manner and quick wit, the poise of an experienced debater, self-assurance seemingly impervious to criticism, and a conviction of both intellectual outrage and moral righteousness. Perhaps above all, he harbored an unrelenting psychological drive to demand and hold the center ring.

As he increasingly insisted that originalism was easy and certain in application, he also seemed to court publicity with ever greater determination. He reveled in both his burgeoning fame and his highly controversial, though hardly dominant, position on the Court. Indeed, his failure to forge an originalist majority, write a larger proportion of the Court's major opinions, or fulfill his apparent hope of succeeding Rehnquist as chief justice may have stoked an intensifying desire to magnify his reputation and secure the recognition and influence he fervently believed that he deserved.[115]

---

[114] Scalia was not alone among the justices in reaching celebrity status. The Court's increasing limitation on its docket and its expanding number of law clerks apparently freed the justices to devote more of their time to public appearances. Barry Sullivan & Megan Canty, *Interruptions in Search of a Purpose: Oral Argument in the Supreme Court, October Terms 1958–60 and 2010–12*, 2015 UTAH L. REV. 1005, 1005–08 (2015). For a similar analysis of Scalia's efforts, *see* HASEN, JUSTICE OF CONTRADICTIONS, 76–82. On celebrity culture, *see generally, e.g.*, SUSAN J. DOUGLAS & ANDREA MCDONNELL, CELEBRITY: A HISTORY OF FAME (2019); SHARON MARCUS, THE DRAMA OF CELEBRITY (2019); KAREN STERNHEIMER, CELEBRITY CULTURE AND THE AMERICAN DREAM (2011); CHRIS ROJEK, CELEBRITY (2001); JOSHUA GAMSON, CLAIMS TO FAME: CELEBRITY IN CONTEMPORARY AMERICA (1994).

[115] "I don't care," Scalia sometimes said about his "legacy," but at other times he acknowledged that he did care. "When I'm dead and gone, I'll either be sublimely happy or terribly unhappy." Revealingly, when asked about any "heroic" opinions he wrote, he responded not to that question but to a different and unasked question, whether he worried that his fate might be like that of Justice George Sutherland, whom Scalia characterized as being "on the losing side of everything, an old fogey, [expressing] the old view." When asked whether that would actually be his fate, he replied by again declaring defensively, "I don't care." Immediately asked if he actually thought he might wind up like Sutherland, however, he volunteered that "I can see that happening." Senior, *In Conversation*, index 8.

In celebrity terms Scalia far surpassed the other conservative theorists and judges who had assaulted the Warren Court and who might have won popular acclaim and risen to celebrity heights. None, however, did. Not Raoul Berger or Robert Bork,[116] important intellectual figures who began modern originalism with their influential work in the early 1970s but who lacked both Scalia's personal qualities and his judicial authority. The same was true, however, of the other conservative justices who did possess that authority but lacked Scalia's commanding personality, ideological fervor, and psychological drive. Not Lewis Powell, who in many ways led the early conservative effort on the high bench to counter the rulings of the Warren Court. Not Warren Burger, who succeeded Earl Warren as chief justice and held the center chair for sixteen years. Not William Rehnquist, who pressed the assault on the Warren Court for thirty years and served as chief justice for almost two decades. And not Clarence Thomas, whose views were wholly compatible with the political values of the Republican coalition and who was a more consistent originalist than Scalia.[117]

But it was Scalia, not the others, who became the preeminent judicial spokesman for the Republican coalition and the vibrant judicial symbol of its values.[118] He fused the roles of theorist, apologist, polemicist, and public entertainer with the role of Supreme Court justice, and in the process became a national celebrity who was an ideological hero for the coalition's adherents. When one of his sons and one of his admirers collected his writings and published them posthumously, it was not surprising that they chose the pontifical title, *Scalia Speaks*.

One of Scalia's major achievements, then, was to make himself a political and cultural icon by merging a purportedly "objective" and "correct" originalist jurisprudence with the political and social values of a powerful and aggressive political coalition. In the last analysis, to most of his admirers—those in the public generally and even some in the

---

[116] Robert H. Bork, *Neutral Principles and Some First Amendment Problems*, 47 IND. L.J. 1 (1971); Raoul Berger, GOVERNMENT BY JUDICIARY: THE TRANSFORMATION OF THE FOURTEENTH AMENDMENT (1977). *See* JOHNATHAN O'NEILL, ORIGINALISM IN AMERICAN LAW AND POLITICS: A CONSTITUTIONAL HISTORY, chs. 4 & 5 (2005).

[117] Thomas was recognized among conservative lawyers as more consistently originalist than Scalia. *See, e.g.,* HOLLIS-BRUSKY, IDEAS, 54–57.

[118] "To the true believers in the movement, he is the heroic upholder of the conservative faith. The other justices, having reached the pinnacle of the legal profession, are heroic to those in that profession; Scalia is heroic in the larger and more committed world of political activists." Stephen A. Newman, *Political Advocacy on the Supreme Court: The Damaging Rhetoric of Antonin Scalia*, 51 N.Y.L. SCH. L. REV. 907, 924 (2006).

academy and on the bench—it made no significant difference that his judicial opinions were jurisprudentially inconsistent and methodologically erratic. Similarly, it made no significant difference that his public performances and personal statements often seemed to baldly contradict his judicial stance of objectivity, neutrality, restraint, and deference to Congress and the states. Finally, it made no difference that he now and then decided cases that were likely against his personal inclinations and contrary to the views of some or most of his admirers. Those were only occasional and relatively minor departures, for the most part unknown to the great bulk of those admirers. Most of the time—and always on the crucial and hot-button issues that were highly visible to the public and that mattered most to the Republican coalition—he was publicly and powerfully with them. He stood at the forefront of their lines, proclaiming their values and defending their policies. His consistent rhetoric and reliable behavior in the cases of paramount social and political importance were what truly counted with them. While Scalia failed to articulate and apply a convincing and soundly based jurisprudence, he succeeded in shaping and promoting a powerful and galvanizing constitutional rhetoric to serve their political interests.

For American constitutionalism, then, the second paramount reason for Scalia's historical significance lies in the fact that he stands as an exemplar of the close and sometimes—as in his case—intimate and carefully cultivated relationship that exists between constitutional jurisprudence and American politics and between abstract theory and personal values. The way he promoted his originalist jurisprudence, filled in its substantive content, and applied or ignored its principles in practice, helped unite and energize the diverse elements that formed the base of the post-Reagan Republican Party. It effectively advanced the varied political, social, and cultural interests of that base as well as the economic interests of its powerful corporate wing. Scalia gave that base a constitutional theory that validated its most fundamental beliefs and conferred on its adherents a profound sense of inherited authenticity, constitutional legitimacy, and political righteousness.

If the theoretical appeal of originalism arose from a wholly understandable if ultimately misconceived desire to find an objective method of constitutional interpretation, its practical appeal arose from an equally understandable and result-oriented recognition that it served the political goals of Scalia's base. As he declared forthrightly, the "questions that are the easiest for the originalist" were those involving "abortion, assisted suicide, sodomy, the death penalty."[119] In helping to forge that union between constitutional jurisprudence and practical politics, Scalia's career exemplified to an extreme and unusually obvious extent the merger of personal values and constitutional principles, the use of abstract theories to serve practical political ends, and the acclaim that those theories generated from those who approved the conclusions that the theories supposedly required.

[119] ANTONIN SCALIA & BRYAN A. GARNER, READING LAW: THE INTERPRETATION OF LEGAL TEXTS 402.

12

The Nature
of American Constitutionalism

The ultimate irony of Scalia's career is that his judicial performance disproved his own jurisprudential claims. It demonstrated that his decisions and opinions on the Court were often the result of neither a "correct" constitutional jurisprudence nor the consistent application of his own self-proclaimed interpretive methods. Rather, they flowed commonly from personal values and goals that overlapped for the most part with those of the post-Reagan Republican Party. In the forefront for both Scalia and the party was an infuriating image of the Warren Court and a fierce rejection of many of the social, political, and cultural changes that stemmed from the 1960s.[1] Responding to what he and many other conservatives considered malign forces, Scalia focused his career on designing and promoting a jurisprudence that would delegitimize the moral, political, and constitutional foundations that supported those forces.

It was ironic that Scalia based his jurisprudence on an appeal to a supposedly authoritative American past because, for his purposes, that past proved unreliable and dysfunctional. As much as it provided carefully selected pieces of evidence to support some of his claims, it also provided far more evidence that contradicted those claims. Above all, the cumulative evidence of the nation's history demonstrated what Scalia sought above all to deny. The founding era—and the text of the Constitution itself—revealed large and critical areas of ambiguity, incompleteness, uncertainty, avoidance, and disagreement, while the decades that followed demonstrated that social changes, economic developments, political conflicts, intellectual reorientations, and

---

[1] "Originalism was constitutional orthodoxy in the United States until, in historical terms, very recent times—the post–World War II era of the Warren Court." ANTONIN SCALIA, SCALIA SPEAKS: REFLECTIONS ON LAW, FAITH, AND LIFE WELL LIVED 189 (Christopher J. Scalia & Edward Whelan eds., 2017) [hereafter SCALIA SPEAKS]. *Accord id.* at 197, 203, 228–29, 266, 269. On the history of originalism in America, *see* ERIC J. SEGALL, ORIGINALISM AS FAITH (2018); JOHNATHAN O'NEILL, ORIGINALISM IN AMERICAN LAW AND POLITICS: A CONSTITUTIONAL HISTORY (2005).

Antonin Scalia and American Constitutionalism. Edward A. Purcell, Jr., Oxford University Press (2020).
© Edward A. Purcell, Jr.
DOI: 10.1093/oso/9780197508763.001.0001

institutional transformations drove complex processes of constitutional innovation and doctrinal evolution.[2]

Although Scalia rejected that view of the nation's past, American history nonetheless made those facts and processes all too apparent. The
Founders themselves were conflicted and uncertain about the meaning of
many and perhaps most of the provisions they wrote into the Constitution.
James Madison, the reputed "Father of the Constitution," changed his own
thinking about many issues before, during, and again after the Constitutional
Convention, as in one way or another did a good many of the others who
drafted and ratified it.[3] Subsequently, as external conditions and contexts
changed and increasingly exposed constitutional gaps and ambiguities,
Americans began what became their unavoidable and often stressful process of remolding the Constitution's operations and adapting its provisions
to resolve new disputes and meet new challenges.[4] As Scalia himself recognized, changing Court personnel was a principal institutional mechanism
that drove those processes at the highest and most formal jurisprudential
level.[5] Studies have repeatedly shown how the federal judiciary has generally

---

[2] Ironically, Scalia castigated the idea of a "living Constitution" for, among other things, turning
lawyers and law students from the study of history. SCALIA SPEAKS, 72. He pictured an either/or
relationship between history and the living Constitution when, in fact, they are intimately related.
Scalia was apparently unable to understand that relationship because he regarded the study of history as a method of establishing clear and static norms rather than as a method for truly understanding the nation's past and the contested and dynamic nature of its constitutional enterprise. As
Robert Gordon wrote, "calls to return to the world of the Founders are mostly attempts to escape
from history altogether—from controversy, contingency, development, the painful and shameful
elements of the past, and the troubling disturbances of modernity." ROBERT W. GORDON, TAMING
THE PAST: ESSAYS ON LAW IN HISTORY AND HISTORY IN LAW 364 (2017).

[3] See, e.g., LANCE BANNING, THE SACRED FIRE OF LIBERTY: JAMES MADISON AND THE FOUNDING
OF THE FEDERAL REPUBLIC 200-01, 374, 393 (1995); STANLEY ELKINS & ERIC MCKITRICK, THE AGE
OF FEDERALISM: THE EARLY AMERICAN REPUBLIC, 1788–1800, at 263–70 (1993) [hereafter ELKINS
& MCKITRICK, AGE OF FEDERALISM]; JACK N. RAKOVE, A POLITICIAN THINKING: THE CREATIVE
MIND OF JAMES MADISON (2017); Sveinn Johannesson, "Securing the State": James Madison, Federal
Emergency Powers, and the Rise of the Liberal State in Postrevolutionary America, 104 J. AM. HIST. 363
(2017). See generally, e.g., GORDON S. WOOD, THE CREATION OF THE AMERICAN REPUBLIC, 1776–
1787 (2d ed. 1998); GORDON S. WOOD, EMPIRE OF LIBERTY: A HISTORY OF THE EARLY REPUBLIC,
1789–1815 (2009); ELKINS & MCKITRICK, AGE OF FEDERALISM.

[4] Scalia himself began changing some of his views, and immediately after his death conservative
justices began to note that fact and use it in beginning to rethink issues of doctrine. He seemed to
be changing his mind, for example, on Chevron deference. See Daniel S. Brookins, Confusion in the
Circuit Courts: How the Circuit Courts Are Solving the Mead Puzzle By Avoiding It Altogether, 85 GEO.
WASH. L. REV. 1484, 1508 n.167 (2017).

[5] "Overrulings of precedent rarely occur without a change in the Court's personnel." South
Carolina v. Gathers, 490 U.S. 805, 823, 824 (1989) (Scalia, J., dissenting). Scalia was hardly the
only justice to recognize that same mechanism. See, e.g., Payne v. Tennessee, 501 U.S. 808. 844
(1991) (Marshall, J., dissenting); Michigan v. Long, 463 U.S. 1032, 1065, 1070–71 (1983) (Stevens,
J., dissenting). Scholars of varying political persuasions also agreed. See, e.g., BARRY CUSHMAN,
RETHINKING THE NEW DEAL COURT: THE STRUCTURE OF A CONSTITUTIONAL REVOLUTION 224–25

accommodated itself over time to dominant new political coalitions and adapted constitutional principles to serve their new goals and policies.[6]

Beyond formal doctrinal changes, moreover, American government itself also changed over the decades in organization and operation, in the interactions between the three federal branches, and in the working relationships that existed between the three branches and the steadily growing number of states that entered the Union.[7] From the nation's earliest days executive power gradually expanded and executive practices grew more important, developments that became increasingly noticeable in the latter half of the nineteenth century and accelerated rapidly during the twentieth and twenty-first centuries.[8] Similarly, in the early nineteenth century the Supreme Court charted pivotal and highly controversial new paths, and late in the century it began to extend federal judicial power to affect ever larger areas of American life, a process that continued into the twenty-first century.[9] So too with federal administrative agencies. Slowly growing since the nation's founding, those agencies expanded rapidly after 1887 when Congress began creating dozens of new administrative institutions and authorized many of them to exercise combined legislative, executive, and judicial powers in various subareas of law, a development that Scalia and many others viewed as establishing a new and "headless fourth branch" of government.[10]

(1998) [hereafter CUSHMAN, RETHINKING]; John Harrison, *Utopia's Law, Politics' Constitution*, 19 HARV. J.L. & PUB. POL'Y 917, 930 (1995).

[6] The classic study is Robert A. Dahl, *Decision-Making in a Democracy: The Supreme Court as a National Policy-Maker*, 6 J. PUB. L. 279 (1957). *See, e.g.*, KEITH E. WHITTINGTON, REPUGNANT LAWS: JUDICIAL REVIEW OF ACTS OF CONGRESS FROM THE FOUNDING TO THE PRESENT (2019) ("Rather than providing a sober second thought, the Court is more likely to act as yet another partisan participant in the policy-making process," *id.* at 312); KEITH E. WHITTINGTON, POLITICAL FOUNDATIONS OF JUDICIAL SUPREMACY: THE PRESIDENCY, THE SUPREME COURT, AND CONSTITUTIONAL LEADERSHIP IN U.S. HISTORY (2007); CUSHMAN, RETHINKING.

[7] The material in the following four paragraphs is drawn from EDWARD A. PURCELL, JR., ORIGINALISM, FEDERALISM, AND THE AMERICAN CONSTITUTIONAL ENTERPRISE: A HISTORICAL INQUIRY (2007), ch. 7 [hereafter PURCELL, ORIGINALISM] and numerous works cited therein.

[8] *See, e.g.*, STEPHEN SKOWRONEK, THE POLITICS PRESIDENTS MAKE: LEADERSHIP FROM JOHN ADAMS TO BILL CLINTON (1997); LOUIS FISHER, PRESIDENTIAL WAR POWER (1995); MICHAEL A. GENOVESE, THE POWER OF THE AMERICAN PRESIDENCY, 1789–2000 (2001).

[9] WILLIAM E. NELSON, THE FOURTEENTH AMENDMENT: FROM POLITICAL PRINCIPLE TO JUDICIAL DOCTRINE (1988); William M. Wiecek, *The Reconstruction of Federal Judicial Power, 1863–1875*, 13 AM. J. LEGAL HIST. 333 (1969); Edward A. Purcell, Jr., *Ex parte Young and the Transformation of the Federal Courts, 1890–1917*, 40 U. TOLEDO L. REV. 931 (2009).

[10] SCALIA SPEAKS, 374. *See id.* at 261–62. On the growth of administrative agencies and the ways they complicated American government and constitutional law, *see, e.g.*, JERRY L. MASHAW, CREATING THE ADMINISTRATIVE CONSTITUTION: THE LOST ONE HUNDRED YEARS OF AMERICAN ADMINISTRATIVE LAW (2012); DANIEL R. ERNST, TOCQUEVILLE'S NIGHTMARE: THE ADMINISTRATIVE STATE EMERGES IN AMERICA, 1900–1940 (2014); JOANNA L. GRISINGER, THE UNWIELDY AMERICAN STATE: ADMINISTRATIVE POLITICS SINCE THE NEW DEAL (2012); BRIAN

While those sweeping changes were altering the structure and operations of American government, Congress continued on paper as the most powerful branch. Its impact on the nation's course, however, began a slow and uneven decline, punctuated by periods of assertiveness and even of brief dominance.[11] Its division into two chambers, the quadrupling of the number of states in the Union, the resulting expansion in the membership of both houses, and the multiplying range of external pressures that fragmented the interests of their members combined to make Congress increasingly slow to take significant actions. Further, the expansion of executive and judicial power and the lure of divisive party loyalties often rendered it even less able or willing to assert itself. Sometimes those diverse forces combined to prevent it from acting at all. The fact that Congress—the branch that the Founders regarded as the Constitution's central and dominant institution[12]— increasingly lost or surrendered its intended leadership role reverberated through the levels and branches of government, gradually altering their distinctive operations and moving the governmental system ever further from the one that the Founders had envisioned. Gradually, more and more de facto power shifted to the executive, the judiciary, and the administrative agencies, shifts that brought substantial if usually incremental practical realignments in the relationships and lawmaking roles of all various levels, branches, and agencies of government.[13]

The states remained important sources of power, but the influence of individual states rose and fell while their collective influence periodically waxed and waned. As new states entered the Union the power of the older "original" states declined, while newer states began exerting their own distinctive and often conflicting demands. Moreover, the addition of new states and the development of new interests in older states gradually shifted the lines

BALOGH, A GOVERNMENT OUT OF SIGHT: THE MYSTERY OF NATIONAL AUTHORITY IN NINETEENTH-CENTURY AMERICA (2009).

[11] For an exploration of Congress's nonlegislative powers that could allow it a much greater role in American politics, *see* JOSH CHAFETZ, CONGRESS'S CONSTITUTION: LEGISLATIVE AUTHORITY AND THE SEPARATION OF POWERS (2017). *See generally Symposium: The Most Disparaged Branch: The Role of Congress in the Twenty-First Century*, 89 BOSTON U. L. REV. 331 (2009).

[12] *E.g.*, "In republican government the legislative authority necessarily predominates." THE FEDERALIST PAPERS NO. 49, at 312–13 (Madison) (Clinton Rossiter ed. Originally published in 1961, with Introduction and Notes by Charles R. Kessler, 2003) [hereafter FEDERALIST PAPERS].

[13] For a theoretical consideration of the way such institutional changes occur, *see, e.g.*, Arthur L. Stinchcombe, *The Sociology of Organization and the Theory of the Firm*, 3 PAC. SOC. REV. 75 (1960). For twentieth-century examples, *see, e.g.*, DAVID SCHOENBROD & ROSS SANDLER, DEMOCRACY BY DECREE: WHAT HAPPENS WHEN COURTS RUN GOVERNMENT (2003); DAVID SCHOENBROD, POWER WITHOUT RESPONSIBILITY: HOW CONGRESS ABUSES THE PEOPLE THROUGH DELEGATION (1993).

of sectional conflict and the different pressures that groups of states exerted on the national government.[14] Sometimes intrastate and interstate divisions reduced or negated state influence, while at other times broadly shared views about desirable policy goals at the state and local levels increased it. Similarly, the role and influence of the states waxed when the federal branches and agencies were divided or in conflict but waned when those authorities pursued mutually reinforcing policies.

Beyond those shifting relationships and evolving patterns of de facto authority, moreover, American law was changing in yet another way. By the latter half of the twentieth century both Congress and the Court were increasingly allowing private parties and institutions to control the scope, interpretation, and application of federal law. In such critical areas as civil rights, employment discrimination, and privacy law, a range of corporate officials, managers, consultants, and outside service and equipment vendors were shaping the law in ways that limited and sometimes distorted its basic purposes and goals.[15] In an even wider range of areas, the Court's severe restrictions on class actions and its vigorous promotion of adhesion contracts that imposed practical disadvantages on potential claimants[16] or required mandatory arbitration of federal claims further limited or even defeated the goals of the substantive law.[17] American constitutionalism was increasingly encouraging the outsourcing of both the content and application of national law to nongovernmental interpreters and enforcers.

In sum, while the formal skeletal structure of American government remained essentially the same on paper and in abstract contemplation,

---

[14] See, e.g., SVEN BECKERT, THE MONIED METROPOLIS: NEW YORK CITY AND THE CONSOLIDATION OF THE AMERICAN BOURGEOISIE, 1850–1896 (2003); RICHARD WHITE, THE REPUBLIC FOR WHICH IT STANDS: THE UNITED STATES DURING RECONSTRUCTION AND THE GILDED AGE, 1865–1896 (2017); Elliott West, Reconstructing Race, 34 WEST. HIST. Q. 6 (2003).

[15] LAUREN B. EDELMAN, WORKING LAW: COURTS, CORPORATIONS, AND SYMBOLIC CIVIL RIGHTS (2016); THOMAS O. McGARITY & WENDY WAGNER, BENDING SCIENCE: HOW SPECIAL INTERESTS CORRUPT PUBLIC HEALTH RESEARCH (2012); KENNETH A. BAMBERGER & DEIRDRE K. MULLIGAN, PRIVACY ON THE GROUND: DRIVING CORPORATE BEHAVIOR IN THE UNITED STATES (2015); THE SOCIAL CONSTRUCTION OF TECHNOLOGICAL SYSTEMS (Wiebe Bijker et al. eds., 1987); Ari Ezra Waldman, Designing Without Privacy, 55 HOUSTON L. REV. 659 (2018); Ari Ezra Waldman, Privacy Law's False Promise, 97 WASH. U. L. REV. 773 (2019).

[16] Judith Resnik, The Privatization of Process: Requiem for and Celebration of the Federal Rules of Civil Procedure at 75, 162 U. PA. L. REV. 1793 (2014); Judith Resnik, Contracting Civil Procedure, in LAW AND CLASS IN AMERICA: TRENDS SINCE THE COLD WAR 60 (Paul Carrington & Trina Jones eds., 2006); Edward A. Purcell, Jr., Geography as a Litigation Weapon: Consumers, Forum-Selection Clauses, and the Rehnquist Court, 40 U.C.L.A. L. REV. 423 (1992).

[17] See, e.g., AT&T Mobility LLC v. Concepcion, 563 U.S. 333 (2011) (Scalia, J.); Wal-Mart Stores, Inc. v. Dukes, 564 U.S. 338 (2011) (Scalia, J); American Express Co., Inc. v. Italian Colors, 570 U.S. 228 (2013) (Scalia, J.). See Stephen B. Burbank & Sean Farhang, Litigation Reform: An Institutional Approach, 162 U. PA. L. REV. 1543 (2014).

its varied components multiplied, changed internally, exercised different degrees of power, and restructured their relationships with one another and with the law itself. Indeed, not one of the three federal branches, the foundation stones of the constitutional system, remained the same in the early twenty-first century as it had been in 1789 or, for that matter, in 1865, 1920, or even 1980. They all changed profoundly in size, role, operation, internal complexity, scope of authority, and social and ideological orientation—multileveled changes that profoundly altered the nature and operations of the constitutional system.[18]

Those internal structural changes combined with the establishment of an enduring two-party system and massive changes in American society to continually reconfigure the dynamics of the nation's law, politics, and government. The two-party system was a dramatic innovation that contradicted the Founders' hopes about the way the government would function. It introduced organized and often dysfunctional competitions for power, periodic institutional transformations, and diverse partisan repercussions that rippled through the levels and branches of government.[19] The growth of cities, technological revolutions, transformations in the economy, expansions of interstate transportation and communications, growing religious and cultural diversity in the American people, the nation's changing role in international affairs, and the rise and disintegration of successive local, intrastate, and regional alliances and rivalries added ever more complex internal tensions, conflicting interests, and novel challenges. Together those developments made it clear that American constitutional government was an inherently complex, dynamic, and evolving institutional system that became increasingly so over the centuries, a system that the Constitution presided over only in part, and then only loosely, flexibly, and often indirectly.

Although, as Scalia believed, the nation's governmental structure was essential to achieve the Constitution's purposes, its dynamic and changing nature meant that its various institutional components not only underwent their own changes but also had to adapt to changes in the other levels and

---

[18] PURCELL, ORIGINALISM, ch. 7. Within the past few decades, for example, the Supreme Court has changed significantly, becoming increasingly polarized as it has been reshaped by sharply divided outside elites and more methodically staffed with rival ideological adherents by presidents from different parties. NEAL DEVINS & LAWRENCE BAUM, THE COMPANY THEY KEEP, HOW PARTISAN DIVISIONS CAME TO THE SUPREME COURT (2019) [hereafter DEVINS & BAUM, COMPANY].

[19] See, e.g., Daryl J. Levinson & Richard H. Pildes, *Separation of Parties, Not Powers*, 119 HARV. L. REV. 2311 (2006); David Fontana, *Government in Opposition*, 119 YALE L.J. 548 (2009); Curtis A. Bradley & Trevor W. Morrison, *Historical Gloss and the Separation of Powers*, 126 HARV. L. REV. 411 (2012).

branches in order to effectively serve their checking and balancing function. That process demonstrated, among other things, that there was a radical difference between the Constitution's two fundamental and commonly linked principles, "separation of powers" and "checks and balances." As the various separated institutions ordained by the former changed in organization and operation, the responses required by the latter had to be reconsidered and recalibrated. If the direct election of senators and the "nationalization" of Congress reduced the likelihood that the legislative branch would protect the states, for example, then the judicial branch had new reasons to move more fully into that role. Even more obvious, as presidential power expanded drastically, both the legislative and judicial branches had reasons to supervise executive actions ever more closely and rigorously. Whether or not the branches did reconsider and recalibrate their roles, however, and whether or not they actually "checked" the other branches, was a matter of political practice not principle, and the varying relationships that resulted over time were nothing that the Constitution itself could determine, direct, or even clearly guide.[20]

Scalia was surely right when he declared that one of the "most important roles" of the courts was "to preserve the checks and balances within our constitutional system,"[21] but he was profoundly wrong in believing that some kind of static originalism could possibly cope with the changes that were necessary to maintain those checks and balances in a complexly evolving governmental structure operating through new and often trying times. As an ongoing enterprise in popular and law-based government, American constitutionalism was not ultimately rooted in any purported and specific "original meaning"—nor could it be. It was a system that had to be maintained and operated flexibly and wisely. As Madison said in the Virginia ratifying convention, "no theoretical checks—no form of government can render us secure" unless "the people will have virtue and intelligence to select men of virtue and wisdom."[22]

In formulating the Constitution's "theoretical checks," however, Madison got at least two fundamental points wrong.[23] Although he recognized

---

[20] PURCELL, ORIGINALISM, 54–58.

[21] Antonin Scalia, *The Rule of Law as a Law of Rules*, 56 U. CHI. L. REV. 1175, 1180 (1989) [hereafter Scalia, *Rule of Law*].

[22] 3 THE DEBATES ON THE SEVERAL STATE CONVENTIONS ON THE ADOPTION OF THE FEDERAL CONSTITUTION AS RECOMMENDED BY THE GENERAL CONVENTION AT PHILADELPHIA IN 1787, at 536–37 (June 20, 1788) (Jonathan Elliot ed., 1910); Accord Federalist, No. 57, at 348 (Madison).

[23] Similarly, Madison was wrong about the predominance of the legislative branch in republics, at least as far as the United States was concerned. *See* text at nn.11–13 *supra*. He was also

the danger that diverse political forces could impede the operations of the Constitution's system of checks and balances,[24] he was mistaken in thinking that the principal danger to its operation would be an overreaching legislature and that "the weakness of the executive" would render it a less dangerous branch.[25] More important, he was equally wrong in thinking that by "giving to those who administered each department the necessary constitutional means" that would enable them "to resist encroachments of the others," the system would also give those officials the "personal motives" that would lead them to resist those encroachments. "The interest of the man," he argued, "must be connected with the constitutional rights of the place."[26] A wonderful idea, but one with a grave and inherent flaw. The fact was that the Constitution could not fully accomplish that goal because the interests and motives of individuals stemmed not only from the constitutional "place" they occupied but also—in varying ways and degrees in the different institutional "places" the Constitution established[27]—from extraneous social, political, cultural, economic, and ideological goals and commitments. Thus, the practice of the system of checks and balances was necessarily shifting, pragmatic, and highly political in its operations.[28] It was not a practice that worked automatically or consistently, and it was surely not one that was specified in the Constitution itself or that operated as the Founders had envisioned.

American constitutional government, with its distinctive rule of law, was a historically evolving, culturally rooted, value based, and institutionally channeled enterprise that remained in many ways open-ended and subject to periodic remolding. The Constitution offered no guarantees, and neither the Constitution itself nor any interpretive "method" provided an escape from that human and political reality. The polarization on the Supreme Court in the twenty-first century, for example, was due in large part to the drive of ideologically based social movements and the increasing polarization that divided the two national political parties and the opposing legal and political

wrong in arguing that the states would share united views about the powers of the national government and stand together when they thought that federal power was being abused. PURCELL, ORIGINALISM, 50–52.

[24] FEDERALIST PAPERS No. 49, at 312–13 (Madison); id. No. 50, at 316–17 (Madison).
[25] FEDERALIST PAPERS No. 49, at 312 (Madison); id. No. 51, at 320 (Madison); id., No. 48, at 307 (Madison); id. No. 73, at 441 (Hamilton).
[26] FEDERALIST PAPERS No. 51, at 319 (Madison).
[27] Even in the polarized times of the early twenty-first century, being a Supreme Court justice, as opposed to a member of Congress or the executive branch, seems to put serious constraints on partisan and ideological behavior. See, e.g., DEVINS & BAUM, COMPANY, 140–46, 151–52.
[28] PURCELL, ORIGINALISM, 57–58.

elites that influenced judicial selection and policy.[29] Those social and cultural developments increasingly determined the individuals who went on the Court, the views and values they brought with them, and consequently the directions in which they moved the law and helped to realign the system's operations.

Fortunately, a great many powerful constraints—legal, social, cultural, political, professional, and institutional—undergirded the operations of American government and channeled constitutional interpretation. Over the decades those forces provided substantial degrees of stability, reliability, continuity, and predictability. Because the fundamental jurisprudential problem of American constitutionalism lay in the fact that the Constitution was in large areas indeterminate, the nation's constitutional history was the history of Americans defining and redefining themselves over time.[30] Thus, American constitutionalism was a complex amalgam of historical practices sustained by many shared cultural beliefs, and the Constitution provided the structure for those practices, anchored foundational beliefs about the virtue of popular government, inspired the social and political values that Americans accepted as authoritative, and helped direct political action into channels that they recognized as acceptable. However, it did not—and certainly did not as an original matter—provide "correct" answers about how Americans should manage that structure and apply those values.

Scalia, then, promoted a profound misunderstanding of American constitutionalism. Most centrally, he advanced a flawed concept of constitutional "law" itself. "Today's decision on the basic issue of fragmentation of executive power is ungoverned by rule, and hence ungoverned by law," he insisted from the high bench.[31] His misunderstanding was basic. "Law" existed in a variety of forms and operated on a variety of levels, but the law of the Constitution was a special area, in many ways necessarily and radically different from the law that existed in other areas. Clear, known, and sometimes rigid rules were both possible and desirable in many areas of human life, from specific rules

---

[29] See, e.g., DOUG MCADAM & KARINA KLOOS, DEEPLY DIVIDED: RACIAL POLITICS AND SOCIAL MOVEMENTS IN POSTWAR AMERICA (2014); Neal Devins & Lawrence Baum, Split Definitive: How Party Polarization Turned the Supreme Court into a Partisan Court, 2016 SUP. CT. REV. 301.

[30] Most notable in formal terms were a series of constitutional amendments that moved American constitutionalism in the direction of requiring greater freedom, justice, and equality for all. U.S. CONST. amends. 13, 14, 15, 16, 17, 19, 23, 24, 26, and 27.

[31] Morrison v. Olson, 487 U.S. 654, 697, 733 (1988) (Scalia, J., dissenting). "Once we depart from the text of the Constitution, just where short of that do we stop?" he asked. Id. at 711. His conclusion was extreme. "This [decision] is not only not the government of laws that the Constitution established; it is not a government of laws at all." Id. at 712 (Scalia, J., dissenting).

setting automobile speed limits, defining criminal acts, and identifying property boundaries to more general rules establishing contractual rights, imposing tort liabilities, and providing government benefits. The Constitution, however, established a profoundly different kind of law, one that created a governmental structure and provided some specific rules but relied for the most part on generalized principles and provisions requiring wise interpretation and flexible adaptation. Scalia too often wrote and spoke as though virtually all of constitutional law—including the "law" of checks and balances—had, or at least should have, the same qualities as traffic law.

Equally, Scalia confused "law" with the idea of the "rule of law" which, he declared, required "a Law of Rules."[32] If "law" could often refer to relatively clear, known, and preexisting "rules" designed to govern specific areas of human conduct, the "rule of law" referred to something much broader and more fundamental.[33] It meant more than the mere enforcement of society's known and preexisting laws and properly promulgated rules, including those limiting the exercise of government power. It also meant that basic decisions about government actions and policies should be made by whatever institution the society accepted as authoritative, as long as those decisions were made in accordance with prescribed procedures and remained consistent with the society's fundamental norms. Thus, the "rule of law" included not only the good-faith enforcement of all of a society's ordinary "rules" and all of its "rules" about the limits of government power but also the properly made decisions of the society's authoritative institutions.[34] Further, in American constitutionalism the "rule of law" also meant that certain fundamental political and moral values should be honored and that an independent and authoritative judiciary should be available to enforce them. Although many and perhaps most Supreme Court decisions were not—and could not be— applications of the kind of preexisting "rules" that Scalia thought necessary for the "rule of law," they were nonetheless examples of the Constitution's own fundamental and essential, if surely malleable and fallible, "rule of law."

---

[32] Antonin Scalia, *The Rule of Law as the Law of Rules*, 56 U. CHI. L. REV. 1175 (1989).

[33] Even Albert Venn Dicey, the leading nineteenth-century English advocate of "the rule of law," changed his thinking later in his career and recognized the persistence and importance of flexible judge-made law. ROBERT STEVENS, LAW AND POLITICS: THE HOUSE OF LORDS AS A JUDICIAL BODY, 1800–1976 (1978), at 103–04.

[34] This general description of the "rule of Law" is somewhat similar to the "soft" positivism outlined in H.L.A. HART, THE CONCEPT OF LAW 250 (2d ed. 1997) (law as application of positive rules that can be construed in light of a society's moral and cultural norms). The description in the text is not based on jurisprudential theory, however, but on the historical practice of American constitutionalism.

Further, Scalia's jurisprudence drained American constitutionalism of its implicit moral foundation, however imprecise and contested. That foundation assumed the relevance of appeals to the moral ideal of justice and, increasingly after constitutional amendments, to the noble ideal of human equality.[35] In contrast, Scalia's originalism was an overtly positivist jurisprudence.[36] "It is necessary," he repeatedly insisted, "to judge according to the written law—period."[37] Seldom did Scalia speak of "justice," and when he did he insisted that trying to enforce any such moral ideal was foreign to his role as a judge.[38] Although Christian citizens had "a moral obligation toward the just state,"[39] judges themselves had no business consulting abstract moral ideas; they owed their obligation solely to the written positive law. Scalia insisted that he had learned nothing in law school or in legal practice that qualified him to rule on moral issues or to decide cases based on concepts of justice or fairness. Judges, he declared, "have no greater capacity than the rest of us to determine what is moral."[40] Indeed, he adopted an extreme procedural positivism, maintaining that persons sentenced to death after a proper trial who later came forward with proof of their actual innocence could, consistent with the Constitution, be lawfully executed.[41]

Although Scalia's constitutional thinking was flawed in those and other ways, his jurisprudence and career nevertheless remain particularly significant on another and quite different level, the way they illuminate the nature of American constitutionalism itself. First, his efforts to advance originalism

[35] See, e.g., EDWARD S. CORWIN, THE "HIGHER LAW" BACKGROUND OF AMERICAN CONSTITUTIONAL LAW (1955). See, e.g., MARY ANNE FRANKS, THE CULT OF THE CONSTITUTION (2019).

[36] See, e.g., SCALIA SPEAKS, 152–54; ANTONIN SCALIA, A MATTER OF INTERPRETATION: FEDERAL COURTS AND THE LAW 3–47 (1997); Sosa v. Alvarez-Machain, 542 U.S. 692, 739, 745 (2004) (Scalia, J., concurring in part and concurring in the judgment).

[37] SCALIA SPEAKS, 245. Scalia was a self-proclaimed positivist, and in standard jurisprudential terms he accepted the "hard" variety. In that view, law rested solely on authoritative and written sources of law and did not allow any role for moral and cultural values in applying it. It rejected "soft" positivism which allowed for the influence of such moral and cultural values. On the history of positivism in the United States, see, e.g., ANTHONY J. SEBOK, LEGAL POSITIVISM IN AMERICAN JURISPRUDENCE (1998); Edward A. Purcell, Jr., Democracy, The Constitution, and Legal Positivism in America: Lessons from a Winding and Troubled History, 66 FLA. L. REV. 1457 (2014).

[38] SCALIA SPEAKS, 248–49, 262–63, 267. E.g., Burnham v. Superior Court of California, 495 U.S. 604, 623 (1990) (Scalia, J.) (rejecting proposed test for personal jurisdiction as requiring "subjective assessment of what is fair and just").

[39] SCALIA SPEAKS, 141.

[40] SCALIA SPEAKS, 267. See id. at 248–49, 262–63, 267. "But abstract moralizing is a dangerous practice when it is reflected in the operating documents of a nation-state (or a federation of nation-states), which require the moralizing to be judicially enforced." SCALIA SPEAKS, 263 (emphasis in original).

[41] Herrera v. Collins, 506 U.S. 390, 427, 427–28 (1993) (Scalia, J., concurring).

and his agreement with the policy goals of the Republican Party demonstrated the classic jurisprudential pattern of American constitutionalism. Lawyers and legal advocates drew on the Constitution and the sources of American law to articulate interpretations that affirmed the supremacy of the Constitution while at the same time molding those interpretations to secure and advance their own views, values, ideas, and interests. Those who reached the Supreme Court were products of that same process and—though more tightly constrained by formal, professional, cultural, and institutional norms—tended consciously or unconsciously to do the same, considering themselves as properly following their own "conscientious and informed convictions."[42]

For Scalia, his own "conscientious and informed convictions" were particularly compelling, and he sought to enforce them with determination and vigor. While he believed that he was protecting democracy, enforcing the Constitution, constraining his personal preferences, denying his own moral views and values, and forcing the law into greater conformity with the thinking of the Founders, he was in fact—like some other major figures in American constitutional history—leading a campaign of constitutional politics. In his case it was a campaign that would not return the United States to the views and values of the founding generation but would move them toward the views and values of the post-Reagan Republican coalition.

Second, Scalia's jurisprudence and career illustrated the historical processes by which shifting branch and level affinities repeatedly reshaped the contours of constitutional law and politics.[43] From the nation's earliest days political adversaries defended the particular governmental institution or institutions that seemed most favorable to their respective causes. In the 1790s the Jeffersonian Republicans praised legislatures and attacked the executive, while Hamiltonian Federalists did the reverse, criticizing the former and defending the latter. After Jefferson became president he suppressed his suspicions of executive power and used it vigorously, while the out-of-power Hamiltonians suddenly began to denounce the terrible dangers they now saw in it. With many analogous shifts and reversals, subsequent political generations followed the same pattern, with rivals striving to shape constitutional thinking to favor the respective branch or level they controlled

---

[42] West Coast Hotel Co. v. Parrish, 300 U.S. 379, 400, 402 (Sutherland, J., dissenting).

[43] See, e.g., EDWARD A. PURCELL, JR., BRANDEIS AND THE PROGRESSIVE CONSTITUTION: ERIE, THE JUDICIAL POWER, AND THE POLITICS OF THE FEDERAL COURTS IN TWENTIETH-CENTURY AMERICA, ch. 1, 261–65, 285–95 (2000).

or that seemed most likely to foster their interests. In the twentieth century "conservatives" defended the federal courts until the New Deal by advancing constitutional theories that magnified judicial power vis-à-vis Congress and the executive. Their progressive adversaries naturally did the opposite. Then, with the Warren Court, political liberals switched branch allegiance and praised the vision of an enlightened and egalitarian judicial power, while their political adversaries suddenly became vigorous proponents of the legislative power that their conservative forebears had feared.

Scalia's jurisprudence simply tracked that well-established pattern. The Warren Court advanced bold new "liberal" rulings, so he countered by urging limits on the federal courts and proclaiming the lawmaking primacy of Congress. Congressional liberals sought to constrain the executive power under Nixon and Reagan, so he countered by advocating his theory of a powerful "unitary" executive. He was a particularly striking example of the traditional process of shifting level and branch affinities, moreover, because his efforts were so determined, shaped by his own political goals and values, and inventive in molding constitutional doctrine to serve his purposes.

Third, Scalia's judicial "conservatism" itself illustrated the inherently changing and dynamic nature of American constitutional law and politics. There had, after all, been many "conservatisms" in American history. The founding generation had embraced a Hamiltonian conservatism that stressed the importance of finance, manufacturing, and a strong central government, for example, while the middle decades of the nineteenth century gave rise to a "conservativism" that was pro-slavery, agriculturally focused, and hostile to ideas of a strong central government.

In the late nineteenth century judicial conservatism underwent another marked change. Between approximately 1890 and the First World War a new generation of conservatives abandoned the commitment of their mid-nineteenth-century forebears to decentralized federalism, suspicion of corporations, anxieties about monopolistic consolidation, and ideas about the severely limited reach of federal judicial power. In their place they embraced the emerging corporate and industrial economy and used judicial power to expand the reach of national law and the authority of the federal courts.[44] To protect private property, they broke with earlier conservative

---

[44] MORTON J. HORWITZ, THE TRANSFORMATION OF AMERICAN LAW, 1870–1960, esp. ch. 3 (1992); Edward A. Purcell, Jr., *Some Horwitzian Themes in the Law and History of the Federal Courts, in* TRANSFORMATIONS IN AMERICAN LEGAL HISTORY: LAW, IDEOLOGY, AND METHODS 271 (Daniel W. Hamilton & Alfred L. Brophy eds., 2010).

generations by interpreting the Fourteenth Amendment to incorporate the Fifth Amendment's Takings Clause and to create the doctrine of "liberty of contract." In addition, they enforced the principle of "dual federalism" and held to narrow interpretations of the Commerce Clause, the Equal Protection Clause, and the Bill of Rights.

Through the decades after 1910 succeeding conservative generations continued to shift in their ideas and assumptions as they faced new conditions and challenges. Early on they upheld more extensive federal regulatory efforts under the Commerce Clause and asserted a more activist judicial power by incorporating the First Amendment into the Fourteenth and extending the Due Process Clause to create certain new constitutional privacy rights. They remained suspicious of executive power and attacked it fiercely when Woodrow Wilson and Franklin Roosevelt exercised it, and in the 1930s they committed themselves to the strict regulation of firearms and a restrictive, militia-based interpretation of the Second Amendment. Then, after World War II they abandoned their predecessors' doctrines of "dual federalism" and "liberty of contract" and further broadened federal power under the Commerce Clause. In the 1960s they agreed to an expanded reach for the Equal Protection Clause, and Republican conservatives—unlike Southern Democratic ones—provided crucial support for the legislative and judicial achievements of the civil rights movement.

In their turn Scalia and his generation of late-twentieth-century judicial conservatives began implementing their own constitutional changes. They sought to limit many of the rights previously recognized under the Due Process and Equal Protections Clauses, diminish federal power under the Commerce Clause, restrict the role of the federal judiciary, limit or even prohibit government regulation of firearms under the Second Amendment, roll back legal protections for the civil rights of minorities, and provide greater protections for both private property and state sovereignty. Further, many of them—Scalia in the lead—sought to strengthen the executive branch by jettisoning earlier conservative suspicions about presidential power and advocating the theory of a largely unchecked "unitary executive."

A comparison of Scalia's views with those of the Court's leading conservative from the preceding, pre-Reagan generation illustrated the extent to which his distinctive judicial conservatism broke significantly from the conservatism of the immediate past. The second Justice John Marshall Harlan, appointed in 1955 by a Republican president before the party's post-1970s reincarnation, shared with Scalia many familiar conservative positions, including advocacy of both judicial restraint and deference to the states.[45] Like Scalia, Harlan was a powerful critic of the Warren Court, and he rejected many of its distinctive and innovative decisions, especially its rulings on criminal procedure and legislative redistricting.[46] He even dissented from the Court's decision to invalidate the poll tax on the quintessentially Scalian ground that "tradition" established a valid constitutional pedigree for the tax.[47] Recognizing him as one of his conservative predecessors, Scalia was happy to cite Harlan's earlier warning against the dangers of judicial law-making[48] and to quote his charge that the Warren Court was pushing an unwelcome and too "swift pace of constitutional change."[49]

Yet, Harlan's views and values also contradicted Scalia's in an eye-popping number of areas. In contrast to Scalia, Harlan urged an expansion of the grounds available to support standing,[50] voided school prayer as a violation of the Establishment Clause,[51] invoked substantive due process to justify new individual privacy rights,[52] agreed with efforts to broaden the reach of key federal civil rights laws,[53] joined in providing more expansive constitutional protections for blacks under the Fourteenth Amendment,[54] advocated

[45] Harlan died in 1971 while still on the bench. *See generally* TINSLEY E. YARBROUGH, JOHN MARSHALL HARLAN: GREAT DISSENTER OF THE WARREN COURT (1992).

[46] For criminal procedure, *see, e.g.*, Mapp v. Ohio, 367 U.S. 643, 672 (1961) (Harlan, J., dissenting); Escobedo v. Illinois, 378 U.S. 478, 492 (1964) (Harlan, J., dissenting); Miranda v. Arizona, 384 U.S. 436, 504 (1966) (Harlan, J., dissenting). For legislative redistricting, *see, e.g.*, Baker v. Carr, 369 U.S. 186, 330 (1962) (Harlan, J., dissenting); Reynolds v. Sims, 377 U.S. 533, 589 (1964) (Harlan, J., dissenting); Wesberry v. Sanders, 376 U.S. 1, 20 (1964) (Harlan, J., dissenting).

[47] Harper v. Virginia Board of Elections, 383 U.S. 663, 680 (1966) (Harlan, J., dissenting) ("Property qualifications and poll taxes have been a traditional part of our political structure," at 684).

[48] ANTONIN SCALIA & BRYAN A. GARNER, READING LAW: THE INTERPRETATION OF LEGAL TEXTS 4 (2014). Similarly, in his Senate confirmation hearings conservative Chief Justice Roberts twice cited Harlan as an example of balanced and thoughtful constitutional judging. Committee on the Judiciary, United States Senate, *Confirmation Hearing on the Nomination of John G. Roberts, Jr. to be Chief Justice of the United States*, 109th Cong., 1st Sess. (Sept. 12–15, 2005), 162, 259.

[49] Montgomery v. Louisiana, 136 S. Ct. 718, 737 (2016) (Scalia, J., dissenting) (citing Harlan's dissent in *Pickelsimer v. Wainwright*, 375 U.S. 2, 4 (1963)). Similarly, in opposing the application of the Fourteenth Amendment to areas beyond racial discrimination, Scalia cited Harlan twice in his dissent in *Tennessee v. Lane*, 541 U.S. 509, 554, 563, 564 (2004) (Scalia, J., dissenting, citing *Katzenbach v. Morgan*, 384 U.S. 641, 659 (1966) (Harlan, J., dissenting) and *Oregon v. Mitchell*, 400 U.S. 112, 152 (1970) (Harlan, J., concurring in part and dissenting in part).

[50] Poe v. Ullmann, 367 U.S. 497, 522 (1961) (Harlan, J., dissenting); Powell v. McCormack, 395 U.S. 486 (1969) (Harlan, J., joining Court opinion).

[51] Engel v. Vitale, 370 U.S. 421 (1962) (Harlan, J., joining Court opinion).

[52] Griswold v. Connecticut, 381 U.S. 479, 499 (1965) (Harlan, J., concurring in the judgment).

[53] Monroe v. Pape, 365 U.S. 167, 192 (1961) (Harlan, J., concurring); Griffin v. Breckenridge, 403 U.S. 88, 107 (1971) (Harlan, J., concurring).

[54] *E.g.*, N.A.A.C.P. v. Alabama, 357 U.S. 449 (1957) (Harlan, J.); Gomillion v. Lightfoot, 364 U.S. 339 (1960) (Harlan, J., joining Court opinion); Loving v. Virginia, 388 U.S. 1 (1967) (Harlan, J., joining Court opinion).

broad new principles that expanded the jurisdiction of the federal courts,[55] accepted the principle that the Fourth Amendment should be construed to protect a "reasonable expectation of privacy,"[56] and on narrow grounds seemed even to accept the incorporation of the Eighth Amendment.[57]

Two other positions Harlan affirmed captured the particularly wide gulf that divided him from Scalia. First, Harlan supported the Court's foundational decision in *Monroe v. Pape* drastically expanding the reach of Section 1983 of the federal civil rights laws and providing muscular new protection for a wide range of constitutional rights.[58] Unlike Scalia, moreover, he was moved in particular by the need to provide truly meaningful federal protection for rights that were of constitutional stature, in particular the right to vote and the right to attend a desegregated public school.[59] Second, Harlan accepted the power of the federal judiciary to imply private causes of action from both federal statutes and federal constitutional provisions, and he agreed with both of the Court's leading decisions exercising that power and creating such rights.[60] Scalia, in contrast, charged that *Monroe* was wrongly decided,[61] and he derided the two implied-right-of-action cases that Harlan supported as "relics" of the Warren Court that were wholly beyond the federal judicial power.[62]

The contrast between Scalia and Harlan spotlighted the changing nature of judicial "conservatism" and thereby provided a revealing example of the shifting nature of constitutional law and politics. It illustrated the fact that American constitutionalism was an evolving practice through which new generations of conservatives, like new generations of liberals, managed the nation's governmental enterprise and attempted through changing times to maintain according to their contrasting lights an orderly, democratic, and

[55] Textile Workers Union v. Lincoln Mills, 353 U.S. 448, 459 (1957) (Harlan, J., joining concurrence of Burton, J., urging an unprecedented and expansive federal "protective jurisdiction"); United Mine Workers v. Gibbs, 383 U.S. 715, 742 (1966) (Harlan, J., concurring in part of opinion giving federal courts broad "pendent jurisdiction").

[56] Katz v. United States, 389 U.S. 347, 360 (1967) (Harlan, J., concurring).

[57] Robinson v. California, 370 U.S. 660, 678 (1962) (Harlan, J., concurring in the judgment).

[58] Monroe v. Pape, 365 U.S. at 192 (Harlan, J., concurring).

[59] "There will be many cases in which the relief provided by the state to the victim of a use of state power which the state either did not or could not constitutionally authorize will be far less than what Congress may have thought would be fair reimbursement for deprivation of a constitutional right. I will venture only a few examples. There may be no damage remedy for the loss of voting rights or for the harm from psychological coercion leading to a confession. And what is the dollar value of the right to go to unsegregated schools?" Monroe v. Pape, 365 U.S. at 196 n.5 (Harlan, J., concurring).

[60] J.I. Case v. Borak, 377 U.S. 426 (1964) (Harlan, J., joining Court opinion); Bivens v. Six Unknown Agents, 403 U.S. 388, 398 (1971) (Harlan, J. concurring in the judgment).

[61] Crawford-El v. Britton, 523 U.S. 574, 611 (1998) (Scalia, J., dissenting).

[62] Thompson v. Thompson, 484 U.S. 174, 188 (1988) (Scalia, J., concurring in the judgment).

relatively just system of self-government.[63] Thus, juxtaposed to Harlan's jurisprudence, Scalia's originalism exemplified that process of ideological and interpretive evolution. As Harlan and a long line of earlier conservative justices
had done in their own times and contexts, Scalia developed his jurisprudence
in an effort to shape the Constitution to meet the values and goals he shared
with those in his own generation who called themselves conservatives.

Finally, Scalia's career also illustrated the uncertain, disputed, and
plastic nature of the most basic principles, provisions, and concepts of the
Constitution itself. In this regard, Scalia compares and contrasts in illuminating ways with another major figure in the Court's history, the Progressive
Justice Louis D. Brandeis. Aside from their self-assurance and intellectual
brilliance, the progressive Brandeis and the conservative Scalia were alike
in sharing many fundamental principles and convictions. Both praised the
values of democracy, defended the right of the people to govern themselves
through their legislatures, and urged respect for legislative power and deference to legislative judgments. Both urged judicial restraint, hailed the principle of separation of powers, and rejected the idea of substantive due process.
Both praised the values of federalism and sought to protect and enhance the
independence of the states. Both criticized the federal courts for their activism in bending the law to support the policy views of their judges, sought
to limit the lawmaking power of those courts, and worked to restrict their
jurisdiction in a variety of ways. Indeed, both used principles of separation
of powers to limit the federal courts. In particular, both emphasized the doctrine of standing as an effective doctrinal basis for limiting the federal courts
and agreed that the doctrine was rooted in Article III, Brandeis being the
first to clearly articulate that theory and Scalia enthusiastically adopting it.
Equally, too, both were ready to assert judicial power when necessary to advance the values they thought right, and both vigorously supported a highly
speech protective First Amendment. Brandeis could even invoke originalist
rhetoric when it served his purpose.[64]

---

[63] For a sample of the historical and institutional analyses of the Court's complex and changing
role in the nation's constitutional enterprise, *see, e.g.*, THE SUPREME COURT IN AMERICAN POLITICS:
NEW INSTITUTIONALIST INTERPRETATIONS (Howard Gillman & Cornell Clayton eds., 1999); THE
SUPREME COURT & AMERICAN POLITICAL DEVELOPMENT (Ronald Kahn & Ken I. Kersch eds., 2006);
SUPREME COURT DECISION-MAKING: NEW INSTITUTIONAL APPROACHES (Cornell W. Clayton &
Howard Gillman eds., 1999); THE CONSTITUTION AND AMERICAN POLITICAL DEVELOPMENT: AN
INSTITUTIONAL PERSPECTIVE (Peter F. Nardulli ed., 1992).

[64] *See, e.g.*, Myers v. United States, 272 U.S. 52, 240, 293–94 (1926) (Brandeis, J., dissenting);
Whitney v. California, 274 U.S. 357, 372, 375–77 (1927) (Brandeis, J., concurring).

Of course, they were also radically different in other ways. Brandeis's jurisprudence stressed facts and consequences, while Scalia's stressed text and formalities. Brandeis urged progressive adaptations, while Scalia stood on traditional practices. Brandeis was suspicious of executive power, while Scalia promoted it vigorously. Brandeis was an innovator in drawing on legislative history, while Scalia condemned its use across the board. Brandeis disliked corporations and believed in government regulation of the economy, while Scalia admired corporations and put his faith in the benevolence of the free market. Most fundamentally, Brandeis believed in a "living Constitution" that adapted to social changes, while Scalia condemned that concept as the root of all constitutional evil.

Thus, it was no surprise that the two construed their shared constitutional principles in quite different ways and invoked the exact same principles and relied on the exact same textual provisions to serve radically different purposes. Brandeis urged limitations on federal jurisdiction to assist injured and aggrieved individuals who did not want to be forced into the federal courts they struggled to avoid, while Scalia urged such limitations to keep such parties out of the federal courts they very much wanted to enter. Brandeis preached legislative primacy because he saw legislatures as sources of progressive reform measures, while Scalia preached legislative primacy because he saw legislatures as bastions of the conservative values he favored. Brandeis construed the Constitution and statutes to support efforts at all levels of government to regulate business and protect workers and consumers, while Scalia construed them to limit such efforts and protect business, property interests, and private economic power. Brandeis invoked the principles of separation of powers to limit executive power, while Scalia invoked those principles to protect and expand that power. Brandeis argued for a highly speech protective First Amendment to protect individuals and especially political dissidents, while Scalia did so to protect the rights of the corporations and wealthy political donors that Brandeis scorned.

Especially significant, too, Brandeis and Scalia were alike in one other critical way. To a highly unusual degree, they both associated themselves closely and actively with political movements of their day, developed constitutional methods that supported the goals of those movements, and emerged as judicial heroes to the movements' followers. Indeed, both became famous and particularly admired because they cultivated coteries of law clerks and law professors who praised their work and promoted their views to the legal profession and the general public. One might even suggest that they were also alike in being commonly paired with another distinctive justice, Holmes with Brandeis and Thomas with Scalia.

Those similarities and differences show that Brandeis and Scalia illustrated three major characteristics of American constitutionalism. One is that the Constitution's fundamental principles and the legal doctrines designed to implement those principles mean relatively little when abstracted from the context in which they are used and the purposes they are shaped to serve. That is especially true of doctrines of federalism and separation of powers whose meaning and significance depend for the most part on the politics and social conflicts of the day. A second characteristic is that general principles and doctrines, by themselves, seldom if ever actually determine the results that the justices reached in the difficult and controversial cases they decided. Rather, it was their personal goals and values that played key roles in shaping the particular meaning they gave to those principles and doctrines and that inspired the specific reasoning they used to justify the diverse results they reached. The third characteristic is that Americans tended to admire and praise them not for the abstract principles they proclaimed but for the way they gave particular meanings to those abstract principles and thereby justified the social and political results that their admirers favored.

The final overarching reason for Scalia's enduring historical significance, then, is the ironic fact that his career demonstrated the dynamic nature of American constitutionalism, the very "living" constitutionalism that he condemned so vigorously. He was a full participant in that national enterprise, standing in the grand tradition of American constitutional thinking by infusing his jurisprudence with assumptions, premises, and values that would ensure the results he sought in the areas that were most intensely important to him. His judicial thinking and career demonstrate the fact that the idea of "living" constitutionalism is not in the first instance or ultimately a "theory" of constitutional interpretation but a metaphorical characterization of the central and inherent reality of American constitutionalism itself. Scalia's "originalism" was but one more variation in the innumerable and often overlapping ways in which Americans have attempted to guide and channel the course of their "living" constitutionalism. He ranks among the nation's most heralded and influential justices even though he failed to recognize—indeed, insisted on denying—his true place in that tradition. Most fortunately for him, and unlike all but the barest handful of his judicial predecessors, he caught a powerful political and cultural wave that carried him to influential heights and transformed him into an iconic figure in American law and politics.

While on that broad historical level Scalia was in the mainstream of American constitutionalism, he was in other ways a distant and often discordant outlier. First and most fundamental, judged by his own announced standards—the jurisprudential methods and principles he continuously wielded to condemn others—he was pervasively inconsistent and self-contradictory. He regularly twisted, ignored, and abandoned his self-proclaimed methods and principles to reach the political, social, and ideological results he sought.

Second, whether consciously or unconsciously, he created and deployed his jurisprudence to obscure, hide, and deny the pivotal role that his own personal values played in his judicial decision-making. From the nation's earliest days to the present, the decision-making of the hundred-plus justices in the Court's history was unavoidably influenced to a greater or lesser extent by their own values. Not one, however, went to the extreme that Scalia did in attempting to obscure his personal goals and values by insisting that he rigorously followed an objective methodology and reached results that were pre-determined by textual and historical sources. Whatever one might think of Chief Justice Earl Warren's reasoning, for example, there was little doubt about what he thought valuable and important and little effort on his part to hide or deny those views.

Third, Scalia's public behavior frequently unmasked his formal jurisprudential stance of objectivity and neutrality. He was far more openly and overtly political than any of his predecessors. A good number of those predecessors had continued their political involvements in varying ways and degrees while on the Court, but none had pushed their political and partisan views into the public arena as freely, continuously, and emphatically as Scalia did. His countless writings, public speeches, and media appearances commonly lent support to the agenda of the political right, and together with his much heralded public work on behalf of the Federalist Society—the Republican Party's acknowledged judicial and administrative employment agency—they made his personal political and social allegiances vividly apparent. Scalia's public efforts tended to make the Court seem essentially a political body instead of the distinctive constitutional court it was, a unique structural creation whose unavoidable political role was channeled and restricted by legal, cultural, professional, and institutional limitations.

Finally, Scalia's judicial opinions assaulted the norms of judicial propriety that helped undergird the Court's legitimacy and authority. The nastiness he injected into many of his opinions—the frequent and unrestrained personal aspersions he hurled at the justices who disagreed with him—made the Court and its processes of constitutional interpretation seem petty, unserious, and even worthy of scorn. The most quotable and well-known statements in his opinions were barbs and insults. They detracted from the critical challenges the Court faced and denigrated the delicate and complex role it played in American constitutionalism.

"Originalism," in truth, is not necessarily a "conservative" ideology, not at least after the post–Civil War amendments repudiated the nation's "original sin" of race-based slavery and other subsequent amendments embedded egalitarian and democratizing principles in the Constitution.[65] If judges and theorists reject Scalia's crabbed and predesigned version of originalism, they can readily see quite different vistas and reach quite different conclusions. If originalism is identified with the aspirations of the Constitution's preamble and with the fundamental values and principles it enshrines, especially after its many egalitarian amendments, then originalism could lead to and justify conclusions far different from Scalia's. Indeed, in the minds of many it already has. True, the Constitution's goals and values are vague and imprecise; they readily spur disagreements about their meaning; and they often come into conflict with one another. Nonetheless, they do remain the true "guiding stars" of American constitutionalism, and they possess enough fundamentally clear and historically grounded meaning that Americans can test their application by asking and honestly answering—with knowledge, understanding, integrity, sensitivity, and as much wisdom as they can muster— specific questions about whether and to what extent all Americans are in actual fact being treated fairly, equally, and decently. Just as no interpretive method or theory can guarantee the nation's fate or the direction of the law's future development, the Constitution cannot guarantee that Americans will always exhibit and act on those qualities nor, most unfortunately, that even if they did so act, they would consequently agree on all or most things. Still, that approach would inspire a far different analytical approach to constitutional interpretation and lead to far different "originalist" results than would

---

[65] *See, e.g.,* JACK M. BALKIN, LIVING ORIGINALISM (2011); David A. Strauss, *Why Conservatives Shouldn't Be Originalists*, 31 HARV. J.L. & PUB. POL'Y 969 (2008).

the views and values that Scalia sought to advance with his own partisan and tightly time-bound jurisprudence.

Ultimately, then, Scalia serves as a classic example of the way that American constitutional thinking evolves and of the complex and varied ways the nation's constitutional system operates. The third and final reason for his enduring historical significance lies in the fact that he stands as a towering figure of irony. He was a justice whose judicial career disproved the grand claims of his own jurisprudence and who demonstrated, while striving insistently to deny it, the truly "living" nature of American constitutionalism.

Index

For the benefit of digital users, indexed terms that span two pages (e.g., 52–53) may, on occasion, appear on only one of those pages.